PRAYING FOR RAIN

JEROME WEIDMAN

Novels

The Harry Bogen Story
I Can Get It for You Wholesale
What's in It for Me?

The Benny Kramer Sequence
Fourth Street East
Last Respects
Tiffany Street

Others

I'll Never Go There Any More
The Lights Around the Shore
Too Early to Tell
The Price Is Right
The Hand of the Hunter
Give Me Your Love
The Third Angel
Your Daughter Iris
The Enemy Camp
Before You Go
The Sound of Bow Bells
Word of Mouth
Other People's Money
The Center of the Action
The Temple
A Family Fortune
Counselors-at-Law

Short Stories

The Horse That Could Whistle "Dixie"
The Captain's Tiger
A Dime a Throw
Nine Stories
My Father Sits in the Dark
Where the Sun Never Sets
The Death of Dickie Draper

Essays and Travel

Letter of Credit
Traveler's Cheque
Back Talk
A Somerset Maugham Sampler

Plays

Fiorello!
Tenderloin
I Can Get It for You Wholesale
Asterisk: A Comedy of Terrors
Ivory Tower (with James Yaffe)

Autobiography

Praying for Rain

PRAYING FOR RAIN

Jerome Weidman

1817

HARPER & ROW, PUBLISHERS, New York
Cambridge, Philadelphia, San Francisco, Washington,
London, Mexico City, São Paulo, Singapore, Sydney

FIRST EDITION

Designer: Charlotte Staub

Library of Congress Cataloging-in-Publication Data

Weidman, Jerome, 1913–
    Praying for rain.

    1. Weidman, Jerome, 1913– —Biography.
2. Authors, American—20th century—Biography.
I. Title.
PS3545.E449Z47   1986   818'.5209   [B]   86-45183
ISBN 0-06-015658-9

86 87 88 89 90 RRD 10 9 8 7 6 5 4 3 2 1

*This book is
for my granddaughter
Laura Elizabeth Weidman
and my brother-in-law
Dr. David Sinclair*

When you do not believe a story-teller he is done. When he succeeds he has forced you for a time to accept his view of the universe and has given you the pleasure of following out the pattern he has drawn on the surface of chaos. But he seeks to prove nothing. He paints a picture and sets it before you. You can take it or leave it.

W. Somerset Maugham

PRAYING FOR RAIN

This is a true story. However, with the exception of members of my family and certain prominent figures, I have changed names and identifying details of the people I describe.

one

Except for one brief passage, Dickens has always filled me with admiration. The exception consists of the twenty-seven words with which he opens *Copperfield:* "Whether I shall turn out to be the hero of my own life, or whether that station will be held by anybody else, these pages must show." The statement never fails to make me uneasy. Did the author intend it to be taken seriously? Or was he kidding? If, before he started to write his story, he had not yet settled on the identity of his hero, wouldn't it have been a matter of elementary fairness to the reader to wait until the author had made up his mind? Doesn't every novelist owe at least that much to his customers?

What was that, Mr. Dickens? Your readers are waiting for a clear answer.

For those readers who realize it may be a long wait, I feel as a member of the profession I should note that there are some of us—all right, sorry, there is at least one of us—who has never shared this particular Dickensian problem. I have never had the slightest doubt when I picked up my pencil—in later years my ballpoint—about the identity of any one of my heroes. On occasion, of course, it has seemed wise to disclaim all direct knowledge. For some reason known only to lawyers this dubious subterfuge always works. Or seems to. As anybody who has ever used it knows, however, it cannot carry its protective burden forever. Sooner or later the disclaimer wears thin. Even the author becomes aware of a loss of confidence in the shield behind which he has been hiding. He begins to grasp with reluctance that the time has come to face up. Not to his characters. The notion that, once set in motion, they live a demanding life of their own is a literary conceit invented by writers who are not quite sure of what they are doing. Like most literary conceits it is largely nonsense. A writer should be in control of his material. If he's not, he should wait until he is in control before he takes pen in hand, or he should look for gainful employment in some other field. I, for example, have never found it difficult to make any of my characters behave. Why should I? I have spent half a century honing the skills necessary to keep them in their place. No, it is not with my characters that I sense I am being driven to a showdown. On the contrary. It is to their creator that I feel I must at last face up. At the age of seventy-three he still gives me trouble.

The first sign that there might be a problem surfaced some time ago. Early in 1939 I decided to take a trip around the world. It was obvious that I would need a passport. There are people, I understand, who have this document prudently tucked away in their desk drawers, like an extra filler for their checkbooks, ready for instant use. I was not one of them. Not in 1939, anyway. Until then I spent every day of all the twenty-five years of my life within the boundaries of New York City. So, in 1939, I went to the post office for a passport application blank. It indicated that, in addition to filling in the answers to a number of questions, the applicant was required to supply the Passport Division of the Department of State with a birth certificate.

I took the subway down to the offices of the Board of Health on Pearl Street, asked a few questions in the corridors, and ended up in a large room to which, it soon became clear, a number of other citizens had come on similar errands. I took my place at the end of the line. By the time my turn came quite a few people had piled up behind me. From the other side of the counter a heavyset woman with thick glasses regarded me with annoyance. When faced with an irritated stranger I have always found it simpler to attribute his or her irritation to something with which I had not as yet had time to form any possible connection. The clock on the wall behind the scowling woman showed a few minutes before noon. I decided what was wrong with her was the signal she was getting from her stomach: it was time for lunch.

"Yes?" she said.

I placed the passport application blank on the counter between us.

"I would like a copy of my birth certificate, please."

She picked up the application blank and studied it for a few moments. Then she left the counter, crossed to a door at the far side of the room, and disappeared. A few minutes later, when she came back, it was obvious that her irritation had increased.

"You sure about this?" she said, tapping the application blank.

"Sure about what?" I said.

"This date April 4, 1913," she said. "This address 390 East Fourth Street."

"That's the date I was born, yes," I said. "And that's the address where I was born."

"I'm afraid you were not," she said.

Astonished, I said, "What do you mean?"

"There's no record," the woman said.

"No record of what?" I said.

"That you were born in this place," she said.

"That's ridiculous," I said, and then realized the statement was not helpful. I tried again. "There must be a record of everybody who gets born in this city."

"There should be and there usually is," she said. "But for you there just isn't. I'm sorry."

A sudden glimpse of the hitherto unsuspected implications made my gut contract.

"There's got to be a record," I said. "I was born. I mean here I am."

I was unaware of the panic in my voice until I saw the woman's reaction to it.

Suddenly very brisk, she said, "It's all right." She leaned around me and spoke to the people on the line. "We'll be closing up now for lunch. Back at one-thirty."

"But listen," I said.

"Not you," she said in a low, sharp voice. "You wait."

3

Leaning around me again she said, "That's all now until one-thirty. Everybody out, please."

With a good deal of grumbling the people behind me moved out of the room.

"Now let's see if we can work this out," the woman behind the counter said. "How do you know you were born at 390 East Fourth Street?"

"I lived there all my life," I said, then corrected myself. "Until 1930, I mean, when I graduated from high school and we moved to the Bronx. Until then, though, it was always 390 East Fourth Street." A happy thought struck me. "It's on all my school records."

"This name, too?" the woman said.

She tapped the passport application.

"My name, you mean?" I said.

"Yes, of course," she said. "You say it's on your school records along with the address 390 East Fourth Street?"

"Absolutely," I said.

"Were you born in a hospital?" the woman said. "Or at home?"

"At home," I said. "Three-ninety East Fourth Street. Dr. Slutzky once told me he had trouble getting me out."

The information seemed to be helpful.

"You know the doctor who delivered you?" the woman said quickly.

"All the time we lived on East Fourth Street he was our family doctor," I said. "Seventeen years."

"*S, l, u, t, z, k, y?*" the woman said, scribbling in the margin of the passport application.

"That's right," I said. "J. Morris Slutzky."

"Wait here," she said. "I'll be back in one minute."

She was back in eight. I timed it. The look of irritation on her face had moved over to make room for a trace of amusement plus an unmistakable touch of triumph. She was obviously proud of herself.

"The trouble with those old doctors and their home confinements," she said, shaking her head. "They didn't always listen carefully, and not many of them bothered about spelling."

4

She placed the application on the counter.

"You know who was born at 390 East Fourth Street on April 4, 1913?" she said.

"Sure," I said. "Me."

"No, you're a Weidman," the woman said. "Who was born at 390 East Fourth Street on April 4, 1913, was a Widdermuenzer."

She pushed another piece of paper across the counter. It was a photostat of a birth certificate. I compared it with the passport application. The name I had written on the passport application was certainly not the name to which her finger was pointing on the photostat.

"How does a thing like this happen?" I said.

"Ask your mother," the woman said.

When I did, an hour later in our Bronx kitchen, my mother disclaimed all knowledge. The disclaimer did not surprise me. My mother had never been very pindownable. The indiscriminate assumption of blame was not a trait by which she could be readily picked out of a crowd. The only thing for which I ever knew her to claim full responsibility was the sale of my first short story at the age of nineteen. She based her claim on the fact that she took the letter of acceptance out of our mailbox at noon, while I was downtown on my office boy job in the garment district, and she placed it on my bed where I found it when I came home late at night after my classes in the evening session of C.C.N.Y.

"How should I know what was happening in the Board of Health?" she said. "My job was to have a baby, and at 390 East Fourth Street I did my job. Nobody told me it was also my job at the same time to write the name of my baby on a birth certificate all the way downtown there on Pearl Street."

I could tell from her voice that she had moved the conversation beyond the boundaries within which I had been trying to keep it penned. Like most Hungarian girls, my mother was, in basic outline, a Gabor sister. It is not exactly stop-press news that by and large this is generally considered to be a rather pleasing outline and I must say that, in appearance, my mother has always pleased me. It is also, however, a misleading outline. It suggests fun and games. Nobody knew better than her son that there had been very little fun and games in the life of Annie Falkovitz Weidman. Keeping her family afloat had not been an easy business. The son who testifies without hesitation to the success of her efforts must, however, add a footnote: She never let her son forget that the efforts were made not only out of love but also as an investment. The day I brought home my first report card from P.S. 188 my role in my mother's scheme of existence was made unmistakably clear: I was her sweepstakes ticket. I took pride in the role, and I felt I was playing it as well as most sons, perhaps even a little better than many, until the day I broke the news to her about my plan to take a trip around the world.

"Why?" she said.

The question was, of course, not unexpected. I had given some thought to the answer, but without much success.

"I've never been anywhere" was the best I could come up with. "I've spent my whole life right here in New York," I said. "I think the time has come for me to take a look around at some other places."

"When I was your age," my mother said, "I ate herring and black bread for thirty-six days in the bottom of a ship to get from Antwerp to New York. Outside of New York there's nothing. Only a great big garbage pail they call Europe. If I didn't crawl across an ocean on my hands and knees to get here to New York my son would have been born where I was born. I escaped from Europe, and because I escaped my son also escaped. What kind of craziness is this that you want to go back there?"

I understood the terror she was unable to keep out of her voice. The trouble was I did not feel it. What I felt was something I knew I could not make her understand: the constriction that had been closing in on me since the publication of my first book. New York had become like a shirt in which I'd been caught in a downpour. It had shrunk so badly that it hurt.

"There are other places, not just Europe," I said. "Places you've never been either."

"No matter where you go all you'll see is what I saw when

6

I came here thirty years ago," she said. "You'll see that New York is the only place."

"Then you can be sure I'll come back."

I said it lightly, as a joke. She did not take it that way.

"Over there you can't be sure of anything," she said. "There's another war it says in all the papers it's starting any minute now. If you go you'll get caught the way I was caught by being born there. You'll never come back."

I got the picture. My plan was threatening the scheme of existence she had spent all of my lifetime putting together. I was placing her sweepstakes ticket in jeopardy.

"You're exaggerating," I said. "I feel I've got to take this trip. I'll be back before they have a chance to start a war."

For a long moment her eyes held mine. I had never known her to shed tears. Now, unexpectedly, I understood why. When she couldn't handle something from which other people found escape in tears, she went away. She stood up and left the kitchen. We never talked about it again until the day I came home from the Board of Health with the news about my birth certificate.

"I'm not saying it was your job to write my name correctly on my birth certificate," I said. "All I'm saying is I just found out somebody did the job wrong."

"So why don't you go tell it to the person who was paid to do it right?" my mother said.

"What name did you tell Dr. Slutzky to write down on my birth certificate?" I said.

"You'd better ask him," my mother said.

She had her fears, but she also had her pride. The discussion was over.

"All right," I said.

Today, of course, Dr. Slutzky would be retired. Or, if people talked about him today, that's the word they would probably use. In 1939, however, he was still living with his mother in the brownstone on East Seventh Street between Avenue C and Avenue D where he had been practicing medicine since sometime before the First World War. Perhaps in 1939 he was no longer practicing as actively as in 1913 when, in the tenements by which Dr. Slutzky's brownstone was surrounded, babies were still being born the way the infant Weidman or Wid-dermuenzer had been born. By 1939, however, home confinements were almost unheard of. Certainly by me. It was hospitals all the way. For that reason, perhaps, Dr. Slutzky himself opened his front door when I rang the bell. Before we moved to the Bronx, during all of my seventeen years in J. Morris Slutzky's neighborhood, his mother had always answered the bell for him. His greeting, however, had not changed.

"Where does it hurt?" he said.

My answer was the short, nervous laugh he had always considered an adequate reply from a frightened schoolboy with a pain. Following him down the hall, I took a look into the waiting room. It was empty. So was the cluttered room at the back of the house in which he used to peer down my throat across a tongue depressor and tap my chest with his stethoscope. From the tumbled condition of the knitted afghan on the brown leather couch behind Dr. Slutzky's desk it occurred to me that the doorbell had probably brought him out of a nap. He gestured to the chair beside the desk. Sitting down, I asked about his mother.

"She's all right, considering," he said. "But the stairs are too much for her. She stays on the second floor most of the time. You know how old she is?" I shook my head. "Ninety-two," Dr. Slutzky said. "And she still drinks ten cups of coffee a day. Not Sanka. Coffee. Ten cups a day. Can you beat it?"

I obviously couldn't, but that was not why I made no reply. I suddenly had a thought that had never before crossed my mind when dealing with older people. I was struck by the difference in our concerns. If Dr. Slutzky's mother was ninety-two, he was probably in his seventies. He and I were separated by half a century. My head was filled with ideas for stories and plans for books, and the excitement of an imminent long journey. I was suddenly wondering what sort of things filled Dr. Slutzky's head.

"You didn't come all the way down here to hear how many cups of coffee my mother drinks," he said. "What can I do for you?"

I told him. He listened as he always did, sitting up very

straight, as though he were in a saddle. The shoulders of his black broadcloth coat and the back of his desk chair were separated by at least two inches of light from the window. He peered at me through his gold-rimmed pince-nez with a look that had in it a touch of fierceness, as though he wanted me to know that if I omitted anything from my recital, the penalty would be swift and severe. In a slum neighborhood where men wore matching pants and jackets only on religious holidays, Dr. Slutzky appeared on the street always in one of the dark broadcloth suits that were tailored for him somewhere uptown. His vests were outlined with strips of white piping. His collars were stiff and high and rounded at the tips, the kind I grew accustomed years later to seeing in newspaper pictures of Herbert Hoover. A black silk ribbon dangled from his glasses. He never left the house without the two props that were his signature: his small black bag and the pearl gray fedora with the Dobbs label inside—once, when he wasn't looking, I peeked—that sat on his head as precisely as the turbans worn by Queen Mary. He had a small, trim mustache, a jutting chin, and the manner of a British statesman in the newsreels striding across Whitehall to a cabinet meeting. I have no idea how good a doctor he was. It had never occurred to me to ask or even wonder. I remembered clearly that, whenever I came into his back room, from the moment he fixed me with his fierce look I was immediately terrified into feeling better. As soon as I started telling him what I'd learned that morning about my birth certificate, I felt the problem was on its way to solution.

"Let me see that, please," he said when I finished.

I handed over the photostat I had brought uptown from the Board of Health. After studying the piece of paper for a few moments Dr. Slutzky came up with a question that surprised me.

"How do you take a trip around the world?" he said. I must have looked puzzled because he added, "I mean the arrangements. What do you have to do?"

I didn't know what other people did, so I told him what I had done. The plan was based on my one certainty: I wanted to go all the way around. I had no idea how long I would be gone, or how much time I would spend in any one place. I wanted to be free to move at will, but I did not want to be restricted by the fear that if I spent too much of my limited funds in one place, I would not be able to afford to go to another. Above all, I did not want to run out of money somewhere along the way and have to cable home for help. I wanted to make sure I would be able to get back to New York on my own. The man at Cook's on Fifth Avenue worked out a simple device. He sold me five steamship passages with open dates. One from New York to England. A second from France to India. A third from India to Singapore. A fourth from Singapore to Australia. And a fifth from Australia to San Francisco. Between these major points I would be on my own. When I decided to use one of those passages all I would have to do was make my way to the steamship company's nearest office, find out when a ship would be sailing on the next leg of my journey, book the passage for which I had already paid in New York, and then hang around Marseilles, Bombay, Singapore, or Sydney until the ship was ready to take on passengers.

"It sounds very simple," Dr. Slutzky said.

"I hope it works out that way," I said.

"Why shouldn't it?" Dr. Slutzky said.

"My mother is afraid before I get home I'll be caught by this war everybody is talking about," I said.

"What's there to be afraid of?" Dr. Slutzky said. "All these steamship companies are very reliable old firms. If a war should break out, I'm sure they'll give you a refund for any tickets you don't get a chance to use."

I gave him a closer look. I had never known him to make a joke. I decided he had not made one now.

"I don't think it's the refunds she's afraid of," I said. "What she's afraid of—"

"Is that you'll get killed," Dr. Slutzky said. "That's what they're all afraid of. My mother is ninety-two, and she drinks ten cups of coffee a day, not Sanka, real coffee, and she's afraid if I go to a movie without her, I'll get killed on the way."

There was no hint of complaint in his voice. He sounded precise, unhurried, a trifle dull, the way he had sounded all the years I'd known him. All at once, however, there were sounds in that cluttered back room I had never heard before. I didn't know what to say, so I said nothing.

"It's not that you'll get killed on a trip around the world or I'll get killed walking to Loew's Avenue B," Dr. Slutzky said. "That's not what they're afraid of. What they're afraid of is if you do get killed, who will bring up those ten cups of coffee every day to the second floor?"

He paused and looked thoughtfully at the photostat of my birth certificate. He seemed to be wondering how the scrap of paper had found its way into his hand.

"I was born in this house," Dr. Slutzky said. "My father was practicing medicine here on Seventh Street when Teddy Roosevelt was charging up San Juan Hill, and the only time in my life I put a foot out of New York City was one Sunday when my mother—" His voice stopped. The silence filled the room like an explosion. After a few moments he looked up from the photostat as though he was dragging his mind away from an unwelcome memory. "On this trip of yours," Dr. Slutzky said. "How would you like to take along a doctor to carry your bags?"

It would have been difficult to interpret this as anything but a joke, so I released a couple of bars of the short, nervous laugh that in the past had always served me in this room when I was a frightened schoolboy in pain.

"I'm afraid I couldn't afford it," I said.

"The doctor I have in mind would pay his own way," Dr. Slutzky said. "Just for the pleasure of your company."

"Unless I get a passport," I said, "I'm afraid I won't be able to go with or without company."

Dr. Slutzky touched the pince-nez on his nose to stop it from shivering.

"A passport?" he said. Then his mind seemed to come back into the room. "Oh, yes, your passport," he said. "What seems to be the trouble?"

"Before I can get a passport I have to produce a birth certificate," I said. "All my life I've believed my name is Jerome Weidman and I was born on April 4, 1913, at 390 East Fourth

Street. But down in the Board of Health this morning the only birth certificate they can find for April 4, 1913, at 390 East Fourth Street is for a Jerome Widdermuenzer."

Dr. Slutzky did something else I had never known him to do before. He chuckled.

"At least I got rid of the Jullyiss," he said.

"What?" I said.

"You know my full name?" Dr. Slutzky said.

"J. Morris Slutzky," I said.

"The *J*," he said. "What do you think it stands for?"

"Joseph?" I said.

"Jullyiss," he said.

"What does that mean?" I said.

"Julius," he said.

"Oh," I said.

In P.S. 188, where I first learned to cringe, Julius was a joke name, always good for a laugh.

"You like it?" Dr. Slutzky said.

"Would you like it if you had to live through P.S. 188 with that for your name?" I said.

"I lived through P.S. 188 fifty years before you did," Dr. Slutzky said. "I made up my mind if I could ever do anything about it, I would prevent anybody from going through what I had to go through."

A sliver of clarity penetrated the confusion into which I'd stepped a few hours earlier down on Pearl Street.

"The first thing you did was drop the name and keep the initial?" I said. "J. Morris Slutzky instead of Julius Morris Slutzky?"

"You're forgetting the Yiddish pronunciation," Dr. Slutzky said. "J. Morris Slutzky instead of Jullyiss Morris Slutzky. The years that followed I took every opportunity that came my way to do as much for a few other poor kids." He tapped the photostat. "Today, twenty-five years later, I learn for the first time that in at least one case I was successful."

"Then how did the Jerome get on that birth certificate for this Widdermuenzer?" I said.

"Your mother didn't trust me," Dr. Slutzky said.

"I always thought you were one of the few people she did trust," I said.

"Not on the subject of Jullyiss," Dr. Slutzky said. "When I delivered you I did what I did with every mother who was a patient of mine. I asked her what she wanted me to write on your birth certificate. She said Yeedle."

"She still calls me Yeedle," I said.

"A mother has a right to call her son anything," Dr. Slutzky said. "In this case, however, it's not a legal right. When she told me she wanted me to write down Yeedle I told her Yeedle is Yiddish, and in New York City birth certificates were written in English. She asked what was the English for Yeedle. Out of my long battle against Jullyiss, I had accumulated a few workable substitutes. I suggested Joseph, Jacob, Jesse, and Jerome. She didn't seem particularly impressed with any of them and told me to use my own judgment. On your birth certificate I put you down as Jerome because that's what I always wished my father had put down on my birth certificate."

"Then how did the Julius get on my P.S. 188 school records?" I said.

"I told you she didn't trust me," Dr. Slutzky said. "When the time came to register you in school she didn't send for me to help her. She did it herself, and she had them put down not the Jerome I suggested but the Jullyiss she liked."

"Which one of you was responsible for the Widdermuenzer?" I said.

"Contacts with the Board of Health in those days were verbal," Dr. Slutzky said. "I called in my births on the telephone. I did for you what I did for all my deliveries. I spelled out your name clearly and made the clerk read it back to me until I was sure she'd got it right."

"You couldn't have felt the clerk had got the last name right," I said. "It came out Widdermuenzer."

Dr. Slutzky shrugged.

"Who knows?" he said. "It's like arguing with the bank about a discrepancy on your monthly statement. They always have the last two words: human error. So why don't you look at it this way. Somewhere somebody named Widdermuenzer could be trying this very minute to get a passport. He can't help but be pleased to discover his name is actually Weidman."

I tried looking at it that way, but I couldn't concentrate on the effort. My basic problem remained.

"Never mind him," I said. "What about me? Am I Jerome Widdermuenzer or Jerome Weidman?"

"Why not let it go at being grateful for the discovery that you're not Jullyiss?" Dr. Slutzky said.

"The State Department won't let it go," I said. "They will insist on my telling them my legal name."

"All right," Dr. Slutzky said. He leaned across his desk, pulled over his pad of prescription blanks, and unscrewed the cap of his Waterman. "I'll write a note to the Board of Health," he said. "It's done all the time in cases like this. They always accept what the doctor writes and then issue a corrected birth certificate. All I have to do is describe the circumstances that caused the confusion and write the name by which the citizen in question wants to be known from now on."

The Waterman hovered over the prescription pad.

"Which one will it be?" Dr. Slutzky said. "Jullyiss Widdermuenzer or Jerome Weidman?"

two

For a startled moment I took Dr. Slutzky's question seriously. It was the sort of choice that belonged in an O. Henry story. In "Bagdad on the Subway" even Dr. Slutzky's neat little mustache and his elegant Dobbs fedora would have been the perfect disguise for the caliph who appears in the sleazy Bowery rooming house to the defeated, penniless, starving young man who has lost all hope and is about to turn on the gas.

"Stop! It's not all over yet! You still have one last chance! You can save yourself with a trolley ride! Here, I give you the fare. Take the uptown, or take the downtown. One leads to fame and fortune. The other leads to—oops, sorry, I'm not allowed to tell you what the other leads to. You must make the choice yourself. Which will it be?"

The moment vanished. I had no choice. It had been made for me long ago, as it is made for everybody, by circumstances beyond my control. My earliest recollections of the physical world in which I was embedded are dominated by the sounds and smells of the sea, by the life of a community nestled somewhere on the edge of salt water. I can still hear the groans in the night of mooring ropes straining with the rise and fall of the tide. The smell of brackish water, the noises of tugboat traffic, and the braying of a foghorn accompany me on my way to and from school. The winking of harbor lights and the rotating slash of a lighthouse beacon punctuate my dreams. For a while, perhaps struggling to assemble these shapeless sounds and smells and lights into a picture of home, I remember the feeling that my early years were lived on a barge.

Later, when I became aware that I had been born and raised on New York's Lower East Side, surrounded by decaying tenements and broken sidewalks, those early recollections still seemed completely appropriate. Our piece of East Fourth Street was not unlike a harbor town: the East River is not a river; it is a tidal estuary. Later the smells and sounds of my youth were recalled in places where the smells and sounds were as unmistakable as street signs: Folkestone, Puget Sound, Marseilles, Auckland.

In those early days we lived on the top floor of a tenement in a twelve-dollar-a-month railroad flat. From my bedroom I looked down on the river traffic: tugs and barges bringing from the north and west, via the Great Lakes and the Erie Canal, cargoes of lumber and coal to unload on the docks below my window. I slept and ate and played cheek by jowl with the people who lived and worked on those docks and barges. Before I knew that beyond Lewis Street—the last thoroughfare that ran parallel with the river—there was such a place as uptown, I knew the resinous smell of drying lumber, the sharp, breath-catching stink of freshly hosed coal, and my way around a deck and pilothouse. Before I saw the inside of a schoolroom or a synagogue, I accepted as part of my landscape the saloons that served the bargemen and the blacksmith who shod the horses that hauled the wagons loaded with coal and lumber to the builders and factories in the parts of the city about the existence of which I had not yet even heard.

After a while I became aware that what had given me the feeling that I had spent my earliest times on a barge was the fact that the members of my family seemed crowded together with me in the same sort of limited space in which I could see other people living on the structures moored to the docks immediately below me. Slowly I became aware that the people with whom I lived were different from the people on the barges. I began to pay attention to them. I grasped that one of them, my father, disappeared from our barge every morning, carrying something later identified as a lunch box, and returned every evening carrying something called the *Jewish Daily Forward* from which he read aloud to us at the supper table. My mother disappeared about the middle of the day carrying a folded black oilcloth shopping bag, and returned with the same bag bulging with fruit and vegetables purchased only two blocks west of Lewis Street on a wider thoroughfare lined with pushcarts, called Avenue C. My sister disappeared in the morning, came back at noon for lunch, and then disappeared again. I became aware of the word "school" before I knew to what it referred. By the time my brother came along I was six. When I became aware that he, too, was disappearing for a while every day, I was so busy with my own life that it didn't occur to me for years that he too, of course, was going to school.

By that time the vague shapes with which I had been living all my life had begun to take on identities that separated them one from the other. Because we were all a part of that seaside town, however, because we belonged to it totally, we had an identity not unlike the groups of total strangers who came to live down on the barges below us for a while, then cast off their moorings, sailed away, and were replaced by other groups.

The group to which I belonged never moved. In a peculiar way, even after almost seven decades of crowded living in other parts of the world, the group to which I belonged has never changed. For me, anyway. What we all added up to as a unit on East Fourth Street in the early years of this century, I still am. It doesn't matter whether I choose for my passport the name Jerome Weidman or Jullyiss Widdermuenzer. That time and that place, and the people with whom I lived at that time in that place, are like my fingerprints. They are the part of me that has never changed. I have a feeling—it grows stronger with the years—that it is the best part. Since then nothing has measured up. I am driven by a compulsion to discover why. To learn how a kid in knee pants named Jullyiss Widdermuenzer became a senior citizen who signs his books Jerome Weidman.

It is not a simple task. That small harbor town, my piece of East Fourth Street, has vanished. The tenement in which I was born—the home of which Robert Frost says that when you have to go there they have to take you in—was buried long ago under a slab of concrete called the East River Drive. Seeking a way to bring it back for examination, I feel like a cook who has been denied a friend's recipe for a wonderful dish. Praising her achievement outrageously the last time she served it, I have succeeded only in cajoling from her some of the leftovers for a later midnight snack. I have carried it home and here I am, spreading it out on my own kitchen table. Picking apart the ingredients, separating the different spices, pushing into small heaps the diced potatoes, the sliced carrots, the mashed turnips, the chunks of meat, all the things I have been able to identify with certainty. Going back doggedly for another session with the jumble that refuses to yield up its secrets. And failing once again to isolate the unidentifiable scraps in which the secret of the unique flavor is undoubtedly contained.

The difficulty surfaced, of course, in 1939 when I applied for a passport in connection with my planned trip around the world. It was the beginning of a lingering uneasiness. Half a century later it was clear that the uneasiness had grown into a major discomfort. Apparently I had not realized, when at nineteen I first saw my byline in print, that I had embarked on a double life. One of these lives obviously concerned itself with the events through which, like everybody else, I lived from day to day and over which I had very little control. The other was the life over which, because I had become a writer, I had total control. Looking back on that time, the cause of the discomfort comes clear: when I started doing it I did not think what I was doing was unusual. More accurately, I did not think about it at all. I just did it. Why I did it did not become plain to me until much later. In the meantime, without worrying or even thinking about why I was doing it, I stumbled along, solving problems on a hit-or-miss basis as they surfaced.

Occasionally, for example, when I had to go back to a published story to see if in it I had already used an actual incident or a real person, I made a puzzling discovery: I could not tell the real from the invented. In those days the puzzlement did not last long. My head was always so full of unwritten stories that it was easy to handle the threatened awkwardness of possibly writing a second time about something or somebody I had already used: I simply abandoned my plan for the new story and immersed myself in another that was pacing around impatiently in my head waiting its turn to be written.

As a result, even though I never lost the awareness that I was leading a double life, for half a century I have never had to question the propriety of what I was doing. Or even the wisdom. Today, however, I find myself unexpectedly confronted by an interrogator with a steely glint in his eye. "Of your two lives," I am being asked in a no-nonsense manner by an unidentified inner voice, "which is which? Or which was which?"

It is the sort of question that cannot be handled flippantly ("What was that, Mr. Dickens, please don't mumble, speak up, sir"). Nor can it be slipped into the "Out" tray initialed for the attention of someone named Widdermuenzer. This question is embarrassingly on target. As an irritatingly familiar voice asked just a few pages back, "Doesn't every novelist owe at least that much to his customers?"

The answer is yes, and this book is being written with the hope of settling that debt. In spite of Dr. Slutzky's help in 1939, in the author's mind today the confusion still remains. A glance at the list in the front of this volume indicates that the author has published thirty-eight books. All of them, especially the twenty-two novels, are in part at least—most of them totally—autobiographical. Yet in none does the author appear under his own name. In some he is called Benny Kramer. In others he is George Hurst, Sam Silver, Harry Bogen, Arthur Thacker, Peter Landor, Henry Cade, Vincent Slote, and on some occasions he is Margaret Gendron, or Julie Sarno, or Lily Chace with, as she insists on pointing out rather irritably, "a see not an ess."

Why, after half a century of—if not successful, at least industrious—efforts to bury his trail, does the author suddenly begin to feel the urge to exhume his true image? The answer is probably a part of the archaeologist's impulse to find the meaning of the present by digging up the past. It seems to me reasonable at my age to take a last look at, and perhaps add a few clarifying touches to, the picture of my own my native land. I am in its debt.

Because of it I never had any difficulty finding material to write about. It was always right there, waiting, whenever I wanted it, the way it is said Queen Victoria's chair always managed to be in the precisely correct place directly under the royal posterior no matter where or when without warning Her Majesty decided to sit down. What was always in place around me when I decided to sit down and write was not the British Empire, of course, but something about which I see now I have always felt equally possessive: the Lower East Side of New York. My belief that I was dealing with a private fief seems to have been total. For years it never occurred to me that, before I took pen in hand, somebody else might have had something to say about the place and its people.

Writing, as I remember my beginning efforts, was not something I undertook, like learning to roller-skate or conjugate verbs. Writing surfaced in my life the way walking and toilet training assumed their places among my accomplishments. One day I was crawling my way around the house in diapers, the next day I was walking toward the performance of my bodily functions the way other people did, getting to the appropriate place without assistance. The act of crossing a line from one skill to another left no mark on my memory.

As I grew older, and stories about the Lower East Side by other writers came my way, I remember being surprised by their existence and then reading them the way I first read *Vanity Fair*. As though I had found on the street a free ticket to a strange, exciting new country, a place about which I knew nothing but in which I was suddenly so absorbed that I could have been born there. It seemed odd, thinking about it later, to have read with the same feeling of fresh discovery novels like Mike Gold's *Jews Without Money* and Samuel Ornitz's *Haunch, Paunch and Jowl*, books that dealt with the same area and approximately the same period about which I was writing. I had no sense of envy, no feeling that I had encountered competitors. How could I? What they were doing was good, but they were not doing what I was doing, so there was no comparison. Except the obvious one, which instinct forbade me from making even to myself. Arrogance functions on the oxygen of its own modesty. The self-confidence that is a part of being young is sensibly flexible. These other writers had their merits, but I was *sui generis*. Some time later, when I was contributing short stories regularly to *The New Yorker*, I remember being shocked by something Wolcott Gibbs, my first editor on the magazine, said to me at lunch one day.

"We've got a scheduling problem with you," he said. "If we don't look sharp, and we run one of your stories in the same issue with a piece by Arthur Kober, that week the magazine looks like the *Menorah Journal*."

Without thinking too much about it—a tendency, I learned with regret as I grew older, that has colored every aspect of my life—I decided I was the first person who had ever written about the Lower East Side the way I wrote about it. The core of this conviction was that, unlike these other writers, all the years I was growing up I seemed to be unaware that I was doing it in a slum. I did not realize I was living in a poverty-stricken area where the inhabitants daily suffered the privations that, even as I lived with them, were being catalogued somewhere uptown by social workers putting together their doctoral theses. It was not until I was rubbing elbows at C.C.N.Y. with incipient social workers of my own age that I realized I had been the victim of a deprived boyhood. They told me.

Living as part of the sweaty traffic of New York's East River docks in the early years of this century was for me a time of excitement I did not even think about, much less understand. Then, in the Hamilton Fish Park Branch of the New York Public Library, I discovered Mark Twain, and everything came clear. Life for me on East Fourth Street when I was a boy was not unlike what life on the banks of the Mississippi had been for young Sam Clemens of Hannibal, Missouri. Guileless, untrained, and unselfconscious, I put the stories down on paper the way I had learned to walk. Years later, when I met Somerset Maugham, it occurred to me that the experience was hardly unique.

Dick Simon of Simon & Schuster, who was my first publisher, introduced me to Maugham at a small dinner party in Simon's house on West Eleventh Street soon after my fourth book was published. Dick mentioned my books, which Maugham had obviously not read, and my *New Yorker* stories, which it had never crossed my mind that any Englishman had ever read. Maugham surprised me.

"Ah, yes," he said, lifting his palms outward as though he

intended to slap a volleyball, "those wonderful *New Yorker* stories which always end—" the hands swayed delicately to the left—"when the hero goes away but—" the hands swayed to the right—"he doesn't really go away, does he?"

I didn't understand what he meant. In my mind I ran swiftly through some of my stories. Not one of them ended with a young man going away, much less with a young man going away but not going away. Years later, when Maugham and I had become friends, I reminded him of what he said at our first meeting and asked him what he had meant.

"I meant that I had contempt for the sort of short story *The New Yorker* favored," Maugham said. "Since then, however, I have changed my mind."

"Why?" I said.

"After years of turning me down," Maugham said, "I am pleased to tell you they have just bought one of my stories."

three

In 1975, while he was supposed to be hitting the books at Yale Law School, my younger son John wrote a play about Commodore Perry and the opening up of Japan. On his way to take the New York State bar exams he paused to leave the script with Harold Prince. The producer-director liked it and showed the script to Stephen Sondheim. The result was the first license to practice law in New York State ever issued to a member of the Weidman family, and the first Broadway production of *Pacific Overtures*.

The play won the New York Drama Critics Circle Award as the best musical of the 1975–76 season, and earned the fulsome—indeed, the just barely controlled—gratitude of the Japanese government. This was expressed in a letter to the authors extending an invitation to visit Japan as guests of the Japanese government. John accepted. The events prepared in his honor during a three-week tour of the islands were climaxed with a literary reception in the nation's capital. Among the guests on the receiving line appeared a University of Tokyo professor of American literature, a small, fragile old man with white hair, a wisp of beard, thick glasses, and an armful of books.

"This is for me a great honor, Mr. Weidman," he said to John. "I have been lecturing about your work at Tokyo University since the publication of your first novel in 1937."

"I think," said John, who has inherited a family gift for doing it quickly under stress, "I think you must mean my father."

The little old man adjusted his thick glasses, peered hard at the celebrated young visitor, then said, "Do you think your father would be distressed if, in his absence, you as his son inscribed his name on these books for me?"

John did not hesitate. Later, however, when he told me the story, I did. My first reaction was not pleasure. That came later, after I recovered from my initial surge of indignation. If the old man had been lecturing about my work at Tokyo University since 1937, why during the forty intervening years had I never received a penny in royalties from Japan?

Most writers I have known, on receiving the bit of flattering news my son John had brought from Tokyo, would have felt at least a small glow of pleasure before they exploded with fury at the news that they had been for so long victimized by a blatant act of copyright piracy. I think it is fair to say that the same sequence of reactions would have been mine if the incident had occurred before I became a writer. Becoming a writer was not only a surprise to me as well as to my family. Even now, after half a century, it seems an improbable thing to have happened to us.

My father was an immigrant from Austria who spent almost all his adult life bent over a sewing machine in a sweatshop on Allen Street. When he died, in his late eighties, he was considered by his peers to be one of the best pocket makers who ever carried an Amalgamated Clothing Workers of America union card. My mother was a farm girl born somewhere on the slopes of the Carpathian Mountains in Hungary. She came to this country a year after my father and was led, by a cousin who met her at Ellis Island, to a bench in a cigar factory not far from my father's sweatshop. A few months later they met at the home of one of the cousins. They were married soon after. When my mother died, also in her late eighties, she had been free for a long time from the daily struggle of assembling her family's meals, always with funds that were inadequate and, during the pocket maker's slack season, frequently nonexistent. Nevertheless, even in her later years of comparative affluence, she never lost completely the immigrant's never-ceasing worry about how to get the next meal on the family table. My father used to say of her with pride that his Annie could not only make a nickel go all the way to the grocery store unattended,

24

but it would also come back with the breakfast rolls and two cents change.

If I started to write the way I learned to walk, I learned to earn my share of the family groceries the way I started to walk: by following in the footsteps of the people with whom I lived. The members of my family, like the members of every family on East Fourth Street, were all gainfully employed not long after they were able to walk unattended to a place of employment. I started the way most kids on my block started: by selling newspapers in the street. I then moved on to a series of after-school jobs including soda jerk in a candy store and delivery boy for a man who rented tuxedoes. None of these jobs interfered with my schoolwork. I enjoyed them as a change from the classroom, and the sense of helping pay the family rent was satisfying.

During my last year in De Witt Clinton High School it became clear that after graduation I would not be able to go on to college. As valedictorian of my graduating class, I was eligible for three scholarships: Harvard, Cornell, and Long Island University. I was unable to accept any of them. These scholarships paid only tuition charges, nothing more. I did not doubt that I could earn my board and keep by working at the traditional college-student jobs: washing dishes and waiting on table. That sort of work, however, would not have solved the problem. I was almost seventeen, the age when, like all my East Fourth Street contemporaries, after-school jobs were no longer adequate. I was old enough to assume the responsibility for making a more serious contribution to the family exchequer. My problem was not choosing a college. My problem was—or would be on graduation—finding a job. My sister, who had graduated from Washington Irving High School two years earlier, had found one without difficulty. She was an expert stenographer. She suggested that I follow her example. During my senior year at De Witt Clinton, therefore, I spent all my free periods sitting in on a typing and shorthand class. By the time graduation day rolled around I could type sixty words a minute without errors, and take not-too-rapid but perfectly adequate dictation in Pitman shorthand.

25

The day after graduation I got out of bed early, bought a copy of the *New York Times*, and combed the want ads. I found one that looked promising. A firm of certified public accountants on Seventh Avenue "WANTED: office boy, stenographer, junior auditor. Only physically strong excellent typist with good head for figures need apply." When I got to the office of Monroe Geschwind & Company at 450 Seventh Avenue the ad began to look less promising. At least a hundred applicants were formed in a crude line that circled the firm's reception room and overflowed into the hall. They were all carrying folded-back copies of the *New York Times*. Without much confidence I took my place at the end of the line. Then I noticed that the line moved with surprising speed, and my confidence returned. On their way out the rejected applicants did not pause to chat. They looked sullen. When I reached Mr. Geschwind's private office I understood why. He was not a warm type. He was small and stooped. His lower lip was fixed by what appeared to be a birth defect in a permanent sneering scowl. His voice was rasping and unpleasant. He looked as though he had been kicked out of bed at the crucial moment in a complicated erotic dream.

"What do you write?" he said. "Pitman or Gregg?"

"Pitman," I said.

"Here," Mr. Geschwind said, shoving at me a pencil and steno notebook. "Take a letter."

He pushed me into a chair in front of a stenographer's desk in one corner of his large room and started to dictate. He did it as though he was discharging an unpleasant chore. He clearly expected no more from me than he had received from the long line of rejected applicants. I had no idea what his letter was about. The words had no meaning to me. I concentrated, as I had been taught at De Witt Clinton, on the sounds Mr. Geschwind was making. When he finished he took a sheet of paper from the desk drawer and pointed to the typewriter.

"Type," he said.

I rolled the sheet of paper into the machine and went to work. When I finished Mr. Geschwind said, "Can't you go any faster than that?"

"Yes, sir," I said.

"What's stopping you?" he said.

"I didn't want to make any mistakes," I said.

Mr. Geschwind studied the piece of paper I had typed. I held my breath. I did not know what I had typed, but I knew I had done it without any strikeovers.

"Take another letter," Mr. Geschwind said. "This time type as fast as you can go, and let me worry about the mistakes."

When I finished Mr. Geschwind leaned across my shoulder and, before I could touch it, yanked the sheet from the typewriter. He did it so fiercely that the platen came alive with a whining hum. Mr. Geschwind scanned the page hastily as though, while he read, his body was moving forward in a trot, like an inspector from Con Edison reading a meter.

"You know how many mistakes you made?" he said.

"No, sir," I said.

I had been afraid to look.

"How much do you know about auditing?" Mr. Geschwind said.

I sensed from the change in his voice that I had made some sort of impression. Good or bad I couldn't tell. I decided to hedge my bets. I placed myself squarely on the side of honesty as the best policy.

"Nothing," I said.

"Then how come you answered the ad?" Mr. Geschwind said.

"The ad put office boy and stenographer first, junior auditor last," I said, talking fast. "It doesn't take much brains to be an office boy, and I know from my teacher in school I'm a good stenographer. Besides, the ad didn't say wanted good auditor, it just said good head for figures, and I always got good marks in math."

It was a long speech. I got it out without stopping for breath. I was afraid if I slowed down he might snarl me out of the office in the direction taken by the other applicants.

"How good?" Mr. Geschwind said.

I drew the deep breath I felt I'd earned.

"I was valedictorian of my graduating class," I said.

"What school?" he said.

"De Witt Clinton," I said.

Mr. Geschwind straightened up, placed a hand on his heart, as though getting into position to recite the Pledge of Allegiance, and joyously sang:

> *"De Witt C, l, i, n, t, o, n, BOOM!*
> *Clinton, oh Clinton, ever to thee,*
> *Fairest of high schools,*
> *Give her three times three, oh fellows—"*

I came in smoothly with:

> *"Long may we cherish thee,*
> *Faithful we'll be—"*

Our voices slid into the rousing finish:

> *"Clin—ton, oh Clin—ton,*
> *For you and me!"*

In one of the great clichés of the period: P.S. I got the job.

This was no small achievement in the summer of 1930, eight months after the Wall Street Crash, six months before the first apple vendors appeared on the streets of midtown Manhattan. I was unaware, however, of the dimensions of my triumph. Like the boy from Hannibal, Missouri, adjusting to the California of Bret Harte's day, the boy from East Fourth Street was totally absorbed in the excitement of adjusting to the Broadway of Jimmy Walker's day. The garment district, in which most of the clients of Monroe Geschwind & Company functioned, was so close to Times Square that the two areas overlapped.

Daily I moved in and out of both, performing my duties as the Monroe Geschwind & Company office boy, Mr. Geschwind's private secretary, and one of the junior auditors of his large staff who was sent out on assignment when an extra body was needed on a fast audit. Almost none of the Geschwind audits was unhurried. They all arrived in a rush. Most of them were commissioned by creditors' committees who desperately sought the answer to a question from which the human race has not been free since money was invented: Should they sell a defaulting debtor's assets under the hammer and divide the proceeds among themselves? Or would they be wiser to call in the bankruptcy court to do it for them? The latter course meant that from every dollar realized by liquidating the debtor's assets, the fees plus expenses of the Receiver in Bankruptcy would have to be deducted before the helpless creditors could put their hands on what, if anything, was left. It was a nerve-wracking business to be in.

In the beginning I did not realize this. I was too absorbed in growing accustomed to a totally new way of life. Soon, however, I began to notice how much of my time as the Geschwind office boy was spent on fetching bicarbonate of soda and aspirin for the staff. My next observation in this area was that none of these medications was consumed by Mr. Geschwind. He was a tight-faced little man, with sucked-in cheeks and eyes set in a look of permanent distrust. He reminded me of a firecracker impatiently waiting to be ignited. Yet he rested peacefully in the center of his domain, which stretched throughout the garment and theatre districts, like a spider taking a break from his endless weaving. He sat at his large desk in his large office, a view of the Palisades on his left, the Paramount clock on his right, smoking fifteen-cent Garcia y Vega cigars and reading Dickens. It did not occur to me for some time that what I assumed was a passion for the creator of Mr. Micawber was actually an indiscriminate addiction to the printed word.

Mr. Geschwind's feeling for print was not unlike that of the drunkard for his bottle. Underneath a reasonably placid exterior lived a man in terror of being separated from his anodyne. He kept a set of Dickens in his office the way an alcoholic might keep a case of Scotch in his bedroom closet: an anchor to windward against running dry in the middle of the night. Between bouts with Dickens Mr. Geschwind read periodicals. Or, rather, he subscribed to periodicals. He received weekly and monthly copies of every magazine I'd ever heard of, as well as many that were completely new to me. It was one of my duties as the firm's office boy to keep his private quarters looking neat. His office, the largest room in the suite, was used regularly for creditors' committee meetings. When a meeting was scheduled it was my job to set up rows of bridge chairs in the space between Mr. Geschwind's large desk and the library table against the back wall on which the periodicals that never stopped arriving waited to be read.

Very few of them ever made it. They arrived more rapidly than Mr. Geschwind could read them. In those days magazines came through the mails rolled up in brown paper like lengths of salami of varying thickness. I tried to keep them stacked on the library table in such a way that they would not slide to the floor every time the door was slammed. This was not easy. Some were skinny, some fat, some long, others short. Arranging them in a neat pile was not unlike trying to make a reasonably solid structure by racking together a mixture of pencils, lengths of copper tubing, scraps of uncooked spaghetti, baseball bats, and peppermint sticks. Even before a slammed door set the accumulation rolling off the table it was in constant slithering motion.

"Wouldn't it help keep these things in better shape," I said to Mr. Geschwind one day, speaking cautiously, "if you let me remove the wrappers and arrange the magazines in flat piles by their names and dates?"

"For a De Witt Clinton man," Mr. Geschwind said, "you took a long time coming up with that idea."

His attitude toward praise was similar to his attitude toward salaries. Mr. Geschwind believed in keeping down the overhead. I started opening the periodicals when they arrived and stacking them flat on the library table. This kept them from slithering and rolling but raised a new problem. Wrapped in their brown casings, they had been an anonymous pile of unidentified material that required no attention except being picked up from the floor and replaced on the table when they rolled off. Naked and exposed, however, they became a crowd of gaudy complainers. Some of them—the stack of Kelly-green *American Mercurys*, for example—seemed positively shrill in their soundless clamor for attention.

"They're driving me nuts," Mr. Geschwind said one day when he came back from a 21-A examination in the office of a Referee in Bankruptcy on John Street, lighted a fresh Garcia y Vega, and settled down at his deck with *Bleak House*. "From now on let's just keep the current issue of every one of these things and throw out the rest."

At that time throwing out an unread magazine seemed to me as blasphemous as tossing into the garbage pail a borrowed book instead of returning it to the public library. I could not drop the surplus magazines into the wastebasket, so I started taking the back issues home. In this way, on the long subway rides to and from the Bronx—where we had moved soon after I graduated from De Witt Clinton and the family income was increased by my salary from Mr. Geschwind—I discovered things like "A Clean Well-Lighted Place" in *Scribner's*, "A Rose for Emily" in the *American Mercury*, Thomas Beer in the *Saturday Evening Post*, and a mimeographed ten-page publication called *American Headlight*.

On the last page of *American Headlight* I found a small box: "If this is your first experience with *American Headlight*, and you would like to see our two previous issues, send 60¢ for one or a dollar for both to the following address." Two more issues of *American Headlight* seemed too many, and a dollar in those days was too much for almost anything, so the next day I took sixty cents in stamps from the office postage box, filled in my name and address on the coupon, and put both in an envelope addressed as indicated on the last page of *American Headlight*.

To say that a week later I received a letter unlike any I had ever seen before is a statement of the simple truth. The simple truth, however, gives no hint of the width of the gap between this letter and my previous experience with the mails. Most of this experience had been gained down on East Fourth Street. In the Bronx many things were different, but not the mails. In 1930, in the Bronx as well as on the Lower East Side of Manhattan, surprises rarely arrived via the post office. An envelope on which the name and address were typewritten could be counted on to contain a bill from Con Edison, or what was known as a lawyer letter: a communication from some member of the New York bar, usually with an office down on East Broadway, informing the recipient that he was behind in his rent and, unless he paid up at once, the next communication he could count on receiving was an eviction notice, known in the local vernacular as a *moof tzettle*. Handwritten envelopes, in my experience, contained family gossip from Aunt Elsie in Albany or Uncle Isaac in New Haven. The gossip from the non–New York segments of the Weidman clan was rarely of a pulse-racing nature. Also, while I had seen any number of typewritten envelopes, and as Mr. Monroe Geschwind's private secretary I typed many of them daily, I had never received one personally. Certainly not with anything like the eight ink-scrawled words jammed into the envelope's lower-left-hand corner: PERSONAL, IMPORTANT TO BE OPENED ONLY BY ADDRESSEE!!!!! The letter, typed and then corrected with additions scrawled in black ink, was on an oddly shaped piece of paper that looked as though it had been torn from a roll of the stuff our butcher down on East Fourth Street used to keep on his counter for wrapping meat.

Hotel Woodstock
45 West 35 Street
NYC 7/11/30

Dear Mr. Weidman:

Please have herewith my belated word for it that I'm pretty ashamed not to have sent you that copy you sent me 60¢ for I received okay, yet! They're inaccessible in a place (hardly any more available—even at $100 apiece!!!—at bindery—& haven't had time to sleep, so much work, consequently haven't had half-day or so 'twould consume to dig that mag out & fulfill obligations to you and couple other fellers—the cash we get in like you sent it in is so almost non-existent that I've had to 'tend to "terribly" late mss. & what-not—also to keeping my family alive, grub and roof over our heads first—'fore the damn little, non-pay-for-themselves magazines at all).

This letter is to say that I really will dig it out & send you what you've paid for soon. Also to tell you please, *please*—since I'm being asked (immediate job) to write three (3) articles defending young (I presume y're not Methuselah—sp.?) writers (so) send me some of yr stories at once pronto instanter—also account of just what & where & everything you've published, *dates* "& everythin' "—(help me in this all you can & I'll perhaps be in some position to make *some* amends for my dilatoriness & seeming intended rotten dishonesties to you).

Well, anyway, I'm taking this few minutes to get better acquainted with you—to beg yr attention to these matters

promptly (however late circumstances pile-it-up-on-me to be)—
&—in real determination that your PROPERTY (THAT copy
will soon follow!)

Yours (I intend it!) really appreciatively (your getting into
the big magazines means nothing to me—I "turn down" the
reputation-guys more quickly than anyone else—Dubuque
paper says of us "not big names but big writing"—but in
notion that YOU may be an exception, that YOU—despite
MERCURY & what-not!!!—may really be worthy of our
poverty-mimmag, non-pay-ANYBODY-inc.-editor-publisher-
who-works-the-hell-out-of-himself-over-the-damn-things—may
really be able to "write"): (I like your letter):—

I dispatch this, now, to you hastily (please act promptly
upon it—wil you—& can you forgive me—again)—(I think YOU
can: there seems a fine spirit-understanding in *yr* letter)—

I remain, once more "Yours sincerely—
[Signed] Lindsay C. Trimingham
(L. C. T.)

[Handwritten]

P.S. "Medallion" is ("also!!!") "sometimes a good magazine
to appear in. "Congrats) (so far!!!)   (L. C. T.)

P.S.2. I enclose covers of our mags to give you immediate
idea of theme sorts (stories) gutzy ones to send me.   (L. C. T.)

It was obvious even after the first reading—and I gave the
piece of butcher's paper several goings over before I allowed
myself to arrive at any definite conclusions—that Mr. Trimingham had confused me with somebody else. Who? The letter addressed to me had been intended, I guessed, for a man
who was apparently a writer and, even more apparently, in the
course of the letter that had brought on Mr. Trimingham's puzzling reply, had made the mistake of bragging about the sale of
a story, perhaps more than one story, to what Mr. Trimingham
called the big magazines. As a result of his success the unknown writer had entered the ranks of the "reputation guys," a
group Mr. Trimingham wanted to make it clear he took pride
in turning down "more quickly than anyone else." I wanted
very much to believe that Mr. Trimingham was telling the truth
about his pride, but somehow I couldn't. If he was telling the
truth about his pride, he was leaving out some other and prob-

ably more important truths of which it was possible he was unaware. As a result I was glad the letter had not been meant for me, because in the confusion I was certain of only one emotion: I felt sorry for Mr. Trimingham without being sure what there was to be sorry about.

The only thing I did feel sure about was that the only similarity between me and Mr. Trimingham's unknown correspondent was that we had both sent him sixty cents in stamps for copies of *American Headlight* and Mr. Trimingham felt guilty about not having sent the magazines to us. This made it my turn to feel guilty, because the sixty cents I had sent along had come not out of my pocket but out of Mr. Geschwind's office stamp box. On top of that, until Mr. Trimingham's letter arrived, I had completely forgotten I'd sent for the magazine. For a few minutes I thought of writing to Mr. Trimingham and explaining the mistake, even suggesting that he forget the sixty cents in stamps and not bother sending the copy of *American Headlight*. Some instinct, however, told me I would be wiser to let well enough alone. Maybe the best thing that could have happened was precisely what did happen: Mr. Trimingham had got his wires crossed. Not—it seemed reasonable to assume from a study of his letter—for the first time. I decided to forget about the whole thing.

About a week later, it was Sunday night, I was home alone, studying for an exam I was scheduled to take the following night in my C.C.N.Y. Economics II class. About nine o'clock the doorbell rang. I came down the hall from my room and opened the door. A short, fat, rumpled man blinked up at me.

"Mr. Weidman?"

"Yes?" I said.

"Jerome Weidman?"

"Yes?" I said.

"L. C. T.," the man said, sticking out his hand. "Glad to catch up with you at last."

"Who?" I said, taking his hand.

It didn't seem to have any bones.

"Lindsay C. Trimingham," he said.

Like a small, sharp shove I remembered the puzzling L. C. T.

scrawled in parentheses under the signature at the bottom of the letter about the undelivered copy of *American Headlight*. On the heels of the initials the entire letter came at me in a rush. Oy, I thought.

"Oh," I said.

"Here it is," Mr. Trimingham said, holding out a battered clasp envelope that had obviously seen at least as much service as his frayed sports coat. "I may be late, but sooner or later L. C. T. always delivers."

"Well, thanks," I said.

We stared at each other. I didn't know what to do, but I didn't know I didn't know. I was too confused on too many levels to hunt for a handle out of the confusion. Nobody had ever called on me at home before. Not in the Bronx, anyway. On East Fourth Street my friends came and went all the time, the way I did at their homes. They knocked on the door, or I knocked on theirs, and if I was home, they came in. If I was not home, they told my mother to tell me they'd been there. I left the same messages with their mothers. It had gone on for years. In the Bronx, however, nothing had been going on for any length of time, much less years. We had moved into the Tiffany Street apartment less than a month after I graduated from De Witt Clinton and landed the job with Monroe Geschwind. The Bronx was still so strange to me that among my confused first thoughts on being confronted with Mr. Trimingham was a feeling of astonishment that he should have been able to find me in what was still for me terra incognita. I had no friends in the Bronx. Not yet.

"Aren't you going to ask me in?"

I came out of the fog and realized the hoarse, shaky voice had emerged from Mr. Trimingham.

"My mother and father aren't home," I said.

"You live with your father and mother?"

Astonished is probably not the precise word for the way L. C. T. sounded, but I've never been able to describe anything accurately until I've seen or heard it more than once, or had a chance to work it over in my mind. I had certainly never before heard anybody sound the way Mr. Trimingham sounded when he asked—no, he didn't ask; it was not a question; it was more like a choked scream—if I lived with my father and mother. My face grew hot, but I stood my ground.

"Yes, I do," I said. "But they're not home right now."

"Do they allow you to receive visitors?" Mr. Trimingham said.

I found my handle, as in the past I always had, and as I grew older I made sure I always did, when I stumbled into an embarrassing situation.

"Yes, they do," I said. "But they insist I do it in my own room."

I didn't know where that came from. I just made it up to fit the situation, and I knew I'd done the right thing. Mr. Trimingham laughed.

"Okay," he said. "Lead the way."

I led him to the back of the apartment. My room looked out on a small yard, crisscrossed by clotheslines, that had an ugly but tough little tree poking its way up out of the middle of the cracked cement. The furnishings of the room could be described as not lavish, but not by me. I am trying to set down a true record. The furnishings of the room had come from a secondhand furniture store on Intervale Avenue. The best that could be said for them is that they were paid for by me out of my salary from Monroe Geschwind & Company. A badly scarred but serviceable secretary's desk, six-fifty. A four-dollar bookcase, which I had repainted. A golden oak swivel chair with two staves missing from the fan back, which the secondhand dealer had thrown in for free when I agreed to pay ten dollars for the couch. At night the couch opened up into my bed. Before going out for the evening my mother had neatly turned down the covers. She was a good housekeeper. Even in the way she handled secondhand furniture, it showed,

"This be all right?" I said, pointing to the swivel chair.

Mr. Trimingham looked startled, as though I had indicated a trapdoor in the floor. Then, as he pushed his glasses up on his nose, his face cleared, and I realized that much of Mr. Trimingham's strange appearance was probably due to his eyesight. Like the rest of Mr. Trimingham, it was apparently not in very good shape.

"Of course," he said.

He eased himself into the chair as though his body was a sack of perishable vegetables that bruised easily. He lowered himself with caution. I wondered if he suspected that perhaps he had been trapped in a practical joke and he had to consider the possibility that the chair might have no bottom. When his pants touched wood he blew out his breath, leaned back, and looked around the room slowly. I found myself doing the same, as though I had never seen it before and it suddenly seemed important to try and see my surroundings the way Mr. Trimingham was seeing them. I'm not sure that I did, because I wasn't sure he could see anything through his pinched-together eyelids, but I was suddenly seeing the room in a new way, and I wondered if maybe I had left out something important when I furnished it. Up to now it had seemed just right. Now I was uneasy.

"Take a look," he said.

I obviously did not respond quickly enough because he leaned across the narrow space that separated the desk from the turned-down bed and tapped the clasp envelope he had given me.

"Sure," I said.

As I pulled out the copy of *American Headlight* for which Mr. Geschwind's stamp box had paid, Mr. Trimingham made a small warning noise in his throat, not unlike a gearbox being shifted, and he set his voice in motion. Turning the pages of the mimeographed publication, I tried to listen to the voice of their editor, but I couldn't seem to keep the two separate in my mind. Mr. Trimingham talked as he wrote, in short, choppy phrases that seemed to have trouble making their point because they had to keep fighting off other phrases that insisted on shoving their way in rudely from all sides. What emerged slowly, probably because the endless repetitions began to give strength to a central complaint, was a catalogue of disasters. They crowded one on top of another, adding up to a picture of a life that was hopelessly unendurable but which this fat, middle-aged, asthmatic, desperate man managed somehow to endure, and damned proud of it he was, too.

He had brought the copy of *American Headlight* in person because he could not afford the postage to mail it, even though,

I remembered guiltily, postage was all I had sent in payment. "I've been kicked out of every college in the country," I heard him say in a moment of clarity surrounded by a confused mixture of clinical details about the hopeless condition of a blind wife, a retarded daughter, and the backbreaking work he had recently undertaken "in the wheat fields because that's where you find out what life is all about," and it came clear that he believed that's what *American Headlight* was all about.

"Best title in the country," he said, tapping the mimeographed pages on my lap, and the proud statement was shoved aside at once by an uneasy mumble, half truculence, half whine, that nobody understood what he was trying to do. A sudden drive into some hidden recess of the shapeless tweed coat produced a fistful of clippings. They proved to be ecstatic reviews of a novel by an author I'd never heard of, but Mr. Trimingham obviously had.

"I made the son of a bitch," he said in a small eruption of fury to which his general physical condition seemed ill suited. "And what thanks do I get?"

The question was apparently rhetorical because there was no room for an answer between it and a sudden denunciation of the *New Republic*.

"They go ahead and do an article on the Little Magazine Movement in this country, and they run a list of all of them, not just the best ones, every single Goddamn little magazine in the whole Goddamn country, and they don't even include me! Me, the guy who invented the whole Goddamn thing!"

For a terrified moment I was afraid he was going to cry, and then I realized that was exactly what he was doing. The blubbery body shook with sobs that came tearing out of him like adhesive tape being ripped in great lashing strips from a bandaged wound. I stood up.

"Is there anything I can do?"

"Yes!" he said savagely. "Send me manuscripts, your best stuff, gutsy, meaty, send me life!"

I knew the only fair thing to do was tell him he'd made a mistake, he was confusing me with somebody else, a writer who had sent him sixty cents in postage for a copy of *American*

Headlight. It was the only thing to do, and I knew it, and I knew I couldn't do it. I had a feeling the truth about the foolish misunderstanding would be a blow that, coming on top of his other troubles, might destroy him.

"I'm sorry," I said, "I don't have anything right now." The implication that sometime later I might have something I would send to him came to me only after I heard my words, which sounded so preposterous in my own ears that I stumbled on quickly with "Is there anything I can do right now?"

He fell back in the swivel chair as though some sort of scaffolding that was sustaining him had been kicked away without warning.

"Yes," he mumbled in a whisper. "Get me a drink, for God's sake."

I went out to the kitchen and turned on the tap in the sink. I let the water run until I felt it was cool enough for drinking, then filled a glass and brought it back to my room. Mr. Trimingham looked a little better. Anyway, he had stopped crying.

"Sorry," he said. "It's just that every once in a while the whole thing gets too—too—"

His voice stopped. He stared at the glass I was holding out to him. Then he looked up at me. Today, of course, I know what was going through his mind. I've known for half a century. In 1930, however, on Tiffany Street in the Bronx, all I knew from the look on his face was that in some cruel way I had failed him. I did not know how, but I knew I felt awful. Scraping desperately through my mind for a clue to what I had done wrong, it occurred to me that he was the first visitor to my home for whose entertainment I was personally responsible. Mr. Trimingham had not come to see my mother and father. He had come to see me. I was his host. It was a new role for me. Not knowing what to do about it, I fell back on wondering what my mother and father would have done, and I found the answer.

I turned and hurried down the hall to the living room. There, on the sideboard, my mother kept the cut-glass decanter she had carried to America all the way from Hungary. Along with two huge featherbeds, the decanter made up the dowry with which my unknown grandmother had provided her young daughter when she set out for a country from which the mother knew her child would never return. She didn't, and the daughter had done with the decanter and the featherbeds what her mother had intended. She brought them to the home of the man she married.

Every year after they became husband and wife my father made his family's Passover wine with blue Concord grapes he bought from the pushcarts on Avenue C and, later in the Bronx, from the fruit market on Intervale Avenue. After Passover the decanter was always kept full of my father's wine, ready to serve to visitors. I had seen it done many times, and now I had a visitor of my own.

I grabbed the decanter and hurried back with it to my room. Mr. Trimingham was holding the glass of water. Without a word I took it from him, stepped into the bathroom, and poured the water down the drain. I came back into my room, returned the glass to Mr. Trimingham, and took the stopper out of the decanter.

"My father makes this himself," I said. "Say when."

Perhaps the editor of *American Headlight* did not hear me. At any rate he paid no attention to what I said. He watched in a sort of grim trance as I poured. I stopped only when I had to: the tumbler was full. Mr. Trimingham raised it to his lips the way I had always pictured Roland doing it in the great moment when he sounded the horn at Roncesvalles. The noises Mr. Trimingham produced were less romantic. He sounded the way I did when on a hot day I chugged an iced Coke from the bottle. When the glass was empty he wiped his mouth with the back of his free hand. With the other he held out the empty glass. Neither of us spoke while I refilled it. Mr. Trimingham took a long pull at his second fix, then paused and looked slowly around my room. He did it as though before leaving he wanted to make sure he had memorized the position of every object by which he was surrounded.

Watching him, I suddenly understood the nature of the pleasure that comes with the role of host. My disorganized, exhausted, defeated visitor had, for the moment, come to some sort of terms with his demons. In a way not quite clear to me I had apparently had something to do with it. It occurred to me that what kept him going was the unexpected appearance at regular intervals of small islands of sanity not unlike the one we had both just stumbled into. At any rate he no longer looked as though he was searching desperately for a window ledge to climb out on. He seemed to be giving his full attention to the quest for an answer to a puzzle that he felt should be visible from the appearance of my room. For some troubling reason, however, it kept eluding him. His glance moved from the clean top of the old desk, to the carefully shelved books in the battered but freshly painted bookcase, and finally came to rest on the neatly turned-down bed.

"Funny," Mr. Trimingham said, his voice full of wonder. "You don't look like a writer."

four

Mr. Trimingham's remark troubled me. I did not realize this until the next day when, unexpectedly, I found the words of the *American Headlight* editor elbowing their way into my annoyed thoughts about Mr. Geschwind's passion for tongue-on-rye sandwiches.

"Get me a Lou G. Siegel Special," my boss said to me at noon. "And see if this time you can get that dumb bastard at the counter to make it right."

It was not a surprising order. Mr. Geschwind issued it at least three or four times every week. Even his unpleasant tone was not unusual. When it came to issuing orders Mr. Geschwind had only one speed on his gearbox: what was known at De Witt Clinton High School as "F.S.A.S." or "Full Speed Ahead, Stupid!"

Ordinarily I would have complied without giving it any thought. It had not, however, been an ordinary day. Mr. Trimingham's visit had preempted my study time the night before. As a result I woke up feeling inadequately prepared for the exam in Economics II that I was scheduled to take that evening at C.C.N.Y. I planned to catch up—as I usually did with my schoolwork—on the subway ride to the office. I was too curious, however, about the magazine Mr. Trimingham had left with me. On the subway that morning, therefore, instead of Economics II, I read *American Headlight*.

According to that day's office assignment chart I was directed to join the squad that had been falling behind on a rush audit for the Irving Trust Company. During such an assignment it was not unusual for a Geschwind staff member to sneak away for an hour or so to tend to some private matter: a date with one of his own secret clients, known as a "subway account"; a shopping expedition with a spouse; an assignation with a girl friend; a dentist's appointment. Without attracting the attention of the senior in charge of the Irving Trust audit, I was sure I could, therefore, while on the job, slip in a small refresher course in Economics II before I was due to sit for the exam that night. When I got to the office, however, I learned that Mr. Geschwind had switched my signals.

"You're coming downtown with me," he said.

Downtown meant the Federal Court House on Foley Square. Here the Honorable George Z. Medalie, then the federal prosecutor for the Southern District of New York, faced what was in those financial hard times a recurring task: to recover if possible for disgruntled creditors assets their debtors had allegedly siphoned illegally out of their businesses during the last desperate days before they were thrown into bankruptcy. The cornerstone of Mr. Medalie's case was always the rush audit performed by Monroe Geschwind & Company for the Referee in Bankruptcy. For the presentation of this crucial evidence to the jury the federal prosecutor usually called on Mr. Geschwind in person: my boss was a skilled and persuasive witness. As I was not the first to discover, however, he was also a lazy son of a bitch. In those early days of the Great Depression the computer had not yet, of course, been invented. Bookkeeping records were less sophisticated, meaning they were bulky and heavy. The average accounts-receivable ledger, for example, looked not unlike a paving block and frequently weighed somewhat more. To make sure his testimony was not marred by weariness, Mr. Geschwind avoided the subway. He always had himself carried from his Seventh Avenue office to Foley Square by expense-account taxi, and he was always accompanied by an assistant who carried the paving blocks.

For the assistant this particular morning was distinguished by two irritations: there were more paving blocks than usual, and Mr. Geschwind was particularly proud of the plan he had worked out for presenting his testimony. Before he was called to the stand to deliver it, therefore, he insisted on feeding me in gleeful whispers a preview of the plan's fine points. After he took the stand he kept catching my eye to make sure with a series of broad winks that I understood the skill with which he was helping Mr. Medalie weave the noose around the neck of the poor son of a bitch who had been thrown into bankruptcy. My role as Mr. Geschwind's claque made it impossible for me, while in the courtroom, even to open my textbook for the brief Economics II refresher that I felt was important to get me through that evening's C.C.N.Y. exam. My last remaining hope was to work in a bit of concentrated study in the Automat during my lunch hour. The hope vanished when Mr. Geschwind and I got back to the office from Foley Square. Having disposed of the paving blocks in the storage room, I was on my way out to lunch. Mr. Geschwind stopped me. As he fired up a fresh Garcia y Vega and settled back with *Great Expectations*, he ordered me to fetch a Lou G. Siegel Special for his lunch.

A Lou G. Siegel Special was a tongue on rye assembled in Mr. Siegel's delicatessen on Thirty-eighth Street just west of Seventh Avenue. What made it special was more than the price. In the language of the garment center, a Lou G. Siegel tongue on rye retailed for eighty-five cents. In addition, however, the Lou G. Siegel Special, if used properly, could serve as a significant status symbol. Most of Mr. Siegel's customers consumed their tongue sandwiches on Mr. Siegel's premises. None of these, however, was a mover and shaker. They were all hewers of wood and drawers of water who earned first-rate money in second-string jobs and could afford to spend eighty-five cents on a gourmet lunch. To get more out of it than gustatory pleasure, however, to enjoy the kudos of belonging to an inner circle, the consumer of a Lou G. Siegel Special had to be in a position to order an underling to go to the source and bring it back to his desk. Lou G. Siegel did not deliver.

"And for Christ's sake," Mr. Geschwind always added as I left his presence on the double, "see if this time you can remember to tell the asshole who makes it to cut away all that lungy stuff."

That lungy stuff, Mr. Geschwind had explained to me the

first time he gave me the order, was at least half, frequently more, of the truly edible area of every slice of tongue that even a high-class purveyor of delicatessen like Lou G. Siegel tried to fob off on the ignorant customer.

"There ought to be a law against serving that part of the tongue on an eighty-five-cent sandwich," Mr. Geschwind said. "It turns my stomach just to look at it. All I want to see on that rye bread is what I'm paying for, nice clean slices of the front of the tongue. Tell the bastards that's what I want, and see that you get it even if they charge extra."

"They" was a barrel of a man with a belly like a side of beef wrapped in a white apron. His eye had the untamed dedicated look that not too many years later I began to see staring out at me from newspaper photographs of Adolf Hitler. I learned very quickly that, at the slicing counter in Lou G. Siegel's delicatessen, this mound of suet believed he filled his post the way Babe Ruth filled his flannel knickers when he stepped up to the plate. At this point in the relationship between the man with the knife and the office boy at the other side of the counter it was obvious that the man with the knife saw himself precisely as the Sultan of Swat saw himself when he faced the pitcher's mound. Both men were *sui generis:* artists whose performances could be imitated but never duplicated. The product I came to fetch for my boss was in the hands of the only man in the whole wide world capable of delivering it properly. If you didn't like the way he took his cut at the tongue on the board, you could do what the jerk in the bleachers could do if he didn't like the way the Babe took his cut at the old apple.

The man at the other side of the cutting board was not, however, my boss. In my then scheme of existence the feelings of the slicing artist were irrelevant. What carried weight with me was the order of Mr. Monroe Geschwind. I never failed to instruct the man with the knife firmly to cut away all that lungy stuff. I never failed to feel as though I had addressed the winds of heaven. The man with the knife proceeded to make the sandwich for Monroe Geschwind as he made it for every other Lou G. Siegel customer. He made it, he wrapped it in wax paper, he slapped it down on the counter in front of me, and I refused to pick it up. I repeated my instructions about cutting away all that lungy stuff, adding that, for getting the sandwich the way I wanted it, I would pay extra. The man with the knife always gave me a glare of enraged disbelief and sent his imperious glance across my head at the next customer. I never budged. I couldn't. My job was at stake. My stomach tangled in a knot of shame, my eyes avoiding the glances and irritated comments of customers backed up behind me, I stood my ground. I repeated my offer to pay extra. The artist behind the counter refused to acknowledge my existence.

"Next!" he bellowed across my head.

I stood firm. Soon the disruption of the smooth flow of sandwiches across the cutting board brought Mr. Siegel or a member of his family from some other part of the restaurant to see what was wrong. Doggedly I repeated my request and my offer to pay extra. It always took some time but I always succeeded in getting if not exactly, it seemed to me at least an adequate approximation of, what Mr. Geschwind wanted. Never, however, did it prove to be more than an approximation. A certain amount of that lungy stuff always remained in the sandwich I placed on Mr. Geschwind's desk. He always ate it, but never without making it clear what he thought of a De Witt Clinton man who was incapable of bringing back from a delicatessen store a tongue sandwich which fit the palate of a civilized citizen who was willing to pay for an exact fit.

It was humiliating, but I forced my mind not to linger too long in that area. When I didn't, I found myself edging up too closely on the precise definition of a phrase I was beginning to learn it was wiser not to examine: swallowing my pride. In 1930, six months after the stock market Crash, I knew without checking statistics that I was not unique. To hold on to their jobs in those days a lot of people were doing what I was doing. The trick was to do it and then pretend you hadn't. Until that particular morning I didn't begin to suspect that perhaps I had become too skillful at working the trick. What brought on this suspicion, I suddenly understood, was the voice of Mr. Lindsay C. Trimingham, heard but not quite listened to the night before. All at once I could hear him again, and this time I was listening.

"You know," the voice full of wonder was saying, "you don't look like a writer."

I saw no reason why I should. My mind went back to the morning after I graduated from De Witt Clinton High School, the moment in Mr. Geschwind's office when he told me the job was mine. It was obviously a moment of triumph. I had just succeeded where a hundred or more other applicants had failed. Unfortunately it was also—although I did not realize it at the time of impact—a moment of shock. Until that moment in Mr. Geschwind's office my life had been built around a central area: school. For eleven of my sixteen years I had functioned in that area to the sound of a very special music: applause.

On the day my mother took her five-year-old son around the corner and enrolled me in the kindergarten class at P.S. 188, Annie Falkovitz Weidman's offspring demonstrated a skill with finger paints that caused Miss Fenwich to release clucking noises of surprised approval and urge the other kids in the class to gather round this new star who had without fanfare surfaced in their midst. It was the beginning of an approach to organized education that was, I came to understand later, far from admirable but at the time was for me irresistible. I never cracked a book, but I always stood at the head of my class. There were, of course, inevitable moments of retribution.

In third grade, when we were beginning to tangle seriously with spelling, we used a textbook that consisted of brightly colored pages on which numbered artifacts from different areas of human activity were pictured in a group. Underneath every picture the word identifying the numbered object was spelled out. A picture of a kitchen, for example, would show a stove, a plate, a knife, a fork, a spoon, a ladle, and so on. A regular homework assignment was to study one of these pages, memorize the spelling of every object in the picture, and be ready, when called upon the next day in class, to spell aloud one or more or all the words in the picture. The flaw in my approach to the educational process was demonstrated the morning after the homework assignment consisted of a page that pictured a group of carpenter's tools: a hammer, a nail, a screwdriver, a screw, a saw, etc. I did not, of course, do my homework that night because I never did my homework on any night. The next morning, when I was called upon to recite, I did what I had always done before: I drew the spelling of the word out of my head, where all words were stored automatically by my ear as I heard them. I heard them, of course, not only on the street but also at home. What I heard at home was a mixture of English, Yiddish, and Hungarian. On that morning in class the word I was called upon to spell was "screw." Out of my head came the phonetic spelling of this word as I had heard it all my life: *s, c, r, o, o, l*. The class fell apart. Miss Schenck was not amused.

Neither was Mr. Hirsch, who, in my second year at J.H.S. 64, was our German-language teacher. The day after our homework assignment had been to memorize and come to class prepared to recite the days of the week in German, I rose to respond the way I had been responding since my German studies under Mr. Hirsch began: by speaking Yiddish with my notion of a faintly British accent. The names for the first six days of the week sound in Yiddish almost exactly as they do in German because their spelling is very similar. The similarity vanishes with the word "Saturday." Even when pronounced with an authentic Etonian accent, the Yiddish word *shobbis* bears not the remotest resemblance to the German word *Sonnabend*. Mr. Hirsch, a man with a caustic nature and a cutting wit, made the most of the opportunity I had provided. However, neither my grade nor my confidence in myself as a student suffered. My classmates applauded what I see now they must have considered a rather outsize display of *chutzbah*.

Their admiration was never more visible than on the night I won the Lower Manhattan segment of a city-wide oratorical contest on the Constitution sponsored by the *New York Times*. This section of the contest was played out on a May evening in the auditorium of Washington Irving High School on University Place. There was not then, and there is not now, any form of public transportation between East Fourth Street and University Place. It was a long walk. I did not consider it unusual, however, that my entire J.H.S. 64 class, plus the members of Boy Scout Troop 224, of which I was senior patrol leader, and my sister and her Yipsel—Y.P.S.L. for Young People's Socialist League—friends, accompanied me on what proved to be a parade of cheering fans. Nor did I consider it unusual that I won. In the area where I had spent all of my young life I had grown accustomed to admiration. On the walk back to East Fourth Street from my triumph on University Place, I recall moving without the help of my leg muscles. I floated along in a pleasant daze, accompanied by an excited procession not unlike the athlete in Housman's poem whose admirers "chaired him through the market place." I don't believe I was arrogant or conceited. I do believe I felt I was receiving no more than my due. This feeling reached what seemed to me a perfectly natural climax on graduation day at De Witt Clinton when I delivered the valedictory address to my graduating class. The speech, which I had composed myself, closed with a section from Richard Hovey's poem:

> *You to the left, and I to the right,*
> *For the ways of men must sever,*
> *And it well may be for a day or a night,*
> *And it well may be forever,*
> *But whether we meet or whether we part,*
> *For the end is past our knowing,*
> *Here's two frank hearts and the open sky,*
> *On the way we all are going.*

I did not realize when I wrote the speech, not even when I delivered it, that we were going in directions so dramatically different. A few of my East Fourth Street classmates went on to college, most of them found jobs, but to my knowledge all of them continued to live where we had spent our first seventeen years together: in that little seaside village on the banks of the East River. The hero they had chaired through the market place, however, was moved by his family up to the Bronx. It was not unlike moving young Sam Clemens from Hannibal, Missouri, to the Great Barrier Reef. I did not for years again set eyes on any of these early friends. By the time I did, as we started to run into each other in midtown Manhattan, I had adjusted to the long separation. In those first days with Monroe Geschwind & Company, however, I was still in what I know now was a state of shock.

The people with whom I worked on the Geschwind staff were not unfriendly. On the contrary. They could not have been more friendly. Neither, however, could they help being what they were: my superiors. I felt isolated and suspended, like a prisoner sentenced to solitary confinement without being told why he had been separated from his fellows or how long he would be incarcerated. At odd moments during the day, carrying Mr. Geschwind's tongue on rye down Seventh Avenue to the office, or setting out the chairs for a creditors' committee meeting, I would suddenly become aware that my forehead was wet with sweat, that for the past few minutes I had been not on the street or in an office on Seventh Avenue but back on the platform at De Witt Clinton on graduation day, trying to relive that last moment of glory. I knew, of course, it was stupid. The knowledge did not stop my mind from making the return journey over and over again.

Years later, when I looked back on this time, I marveled at the fact that nobody—neither Mr. Geschwind, nor the people with whom I worked in his office, not even the members of my own family at home—noticed anything wrong. From the vantage point of the present I can see what at that time I had been able only to feel: the slow, steady, downward pull from a state of confusion, fear, and resentment, toward an accelerating state of hopeless indifference out of which, before long, it might have become impossible to climb back to anything resembling normalcy. It still puzzles me that nobody noticed. From this distance I can only conclude that some instinct of self-preservation had, without my knowledge, thrown up around my inner turmoil a polished protective carapace. It must have reflected to the outside world the reassuring image that the world wanted to see: an eager, bright, industrious youngster working hard at his job and—after I enrolled in the evening session of C.C.N.Y.—at his studies in a pattern that, for the brainy and virtuous, was so widely considered to be the inevitable road to success and happiness.

It seemed to me the only way to hold on to my sanity was to go about my daily tasks as though I, too, believed my success was inevitable, even though the evidence of my own eyes in those 1930 days on the streets of New York indicated with brutal clarity just the opposite. As an employee of Monroe Geschwind & Company, the very nature of my daily tasks made the idea of success a mockery. Almost all my daily tasks involved other people's disasters, helping with the rush bankruptcy audits for Monroe Geschwind's most lucrative client: the Irving Trust Company.

I remember the day on which the audit with which I was helping involved one of the larger Seventh Avenue dress-manufacturing companies which had gone down the tube very rapidly. So rapidly that the people at the creditors' committee meeting, for which a week earlier I had arranged the chairs in Mr. Geschwind's private office, kept telling each other in dazed voices, "It happened without warning!" This was, of course, nonsense. One thing I learned in Mr. Geschwind's line of work was that no business enterprise goes into bankruptcy without warning. The danger signals become apparent long before the disaster occurs. The trouble always proves to be the same: the people who should have read the warnings were otherwise engaged or, for reasons of their own, preferred not to read them. In all cases the tracking down of these disregarded warnings was the core of the Monroe Geschwind & Company rush audit. The staff worked smoothly, as a team, each junior member performing the role to which the senior member assigned him. My role, which as an auditor was minor, in one respect was major. It was my job to keep a steady flow of cardboard coffee containers moving from the nearest drugstore to the auditing staff.

Late in the afternoon of that day an odd thing happened. As I was making my way around the bankrupt's premises, distributing my latest delivery of coffee containers, I became aware of two girls at a desk in a corner of what had been the models' dressing room. One girl was a Monroe Geschwind employee, the other an assistant bookkeeper for the bankrupt firm. They were engaged in a process known as reconciling the defunct company's final bank statement. Not a difficult chore but one that requires concentration. What attracted my attention to those girls was that, while it was obvious they were deeply engrossed, on getting closer to them with my containers of coffee it became more obvious that what they were engrossed by was not the rush audit. They were caught up in something one girl was telling the other. A certain amount of skillful hovering on my part revealed that the assistant bookkeeper was recounting for the girl from the Geschwind staff an incident involving the kid brother of a friend: a bright, cheerful youngster with an excellent school record who, the day before, had tried to commit suicide.

I found myself becoming excited by a combination of three curious facts. One, I knew how that boy felt. Two, the girl who was talking seemed totally unaware that the shocking incident was actually more funny than tragic. And, three, she did not seem to grasp that the other girl was not giving the recital her undivided attention.

The most interesting aspect of the experience, however, was that I was not puzzled by my excitement. It seemed perfectly natural because it flowed from a sudden knowledge—where the knowledge came from I could not say, and at the moment I did not care—that I could fix what was wrong with that girl's performance. I knew—in whatever physical or mental recesses my deepest convictions take root I was all at once absolutely certain—that I could take this tragic, yet attractive because it was well formed, incident and make it seem so attractive that the girl who was not really listening would snap to immediate and total attention.

I did not know then what I was to learn later through tedious experience: the incident struck me as well formed because it was that great rarity, a casually overheard fragment that had a beginning, a middle, and an end. In short, it was not an incident at all. It was a story.

I carried this excitement, my first in months, out into the factory of the bankrupt firm where the cutting tables, now abandoned by their former employees, had been converted into makeshift desks for the Geschwind auditing staff. Feeling as though I was gulping a spoonful of medicine Dr. Slutzky had prescribed as a cure for my depression, I sat down at the end of a long table that had been assigned to me and bent over what I hoped the senior in charge would think was my share of the

audit. Actually I had forgotten all about the audit. I was thinking of the story I had just heard the girl in the models' room
tell the girl with whom she was supposed to be reconciling the
bank statement. Working in Pitman shorthand, so that nobody
coming through the factory area would have any reason to suspect I was engaged in anything but the audit, I managed—
perhaps because most of the words I used were not mine but
the girl's—to set the incident down on paper in less than an
hour.

The remainder of the day was a curious, not unpleasant,
agony. I could set down the story under the eyes of the senior
in charge of the audit, but I could not really see what I had
done until I had access to a typewriter and transcribed my Pitman squiggles into words. From the premises of the bankrupt,
when the rest of the Geschwind staff went home, I went downtown to C.C.N.Y. and, managing to control my inner excitement, took my Economics II exam. After the exam I returned
to the Geschwind office on Seventh Avenue. I was annoyed,
but not surprised, to discover that two staff members were still
at their desks. People who had jobs in 1930 suffered from a
tendency to put in more hours than they were paid for, in the
hope that, as the Depression deepened and staffs were cut, their
devotion to duty would be remembered and help move them
lower on the inevitable list of those to be fired. This fear, with
which like everybody else in that office I had for so long lived,
vanished as soon as the two staff members left for the night and
I settled down at the typewriter. When the transcription was
finished I held in my hand what, after more than half a century, still seems to me, an admittedly prejudiced commentator,
one of the more satisfying things the human animal can produce: a finished story.

I was so satisfied that I almost resented considering the
question that at once presented itself: What was I going to do
with it? The thought of sending the story to Mr. Lindsay C.
Trimingham entered my mind, but did not stay long. In fact it
fled in desperate haste. The solution was supplied, somewhat
surprisingly, by Mr. Geschwind. It occurred to me years later
that, in addition to being a compulsive reader, he might just

conceivably also have been a perceptive critic. "Here, you can throw this out," he told me irritably one afternoon as he handed over the copy of *Look Homeward, Angel* he had sent me to Macy's to buy for him the day before because he had read a glowing reference to it in one of the innumerable magazines to which he subscribed as industriously as other men subscribe to profanity. "Throw it out?" I said. "You mean you don't like this book?" Mr. Geschwind made a short, sharp gesture of annoyance that scattered Garcia y Vega ash in his office boy's face as he said, "For Christ's sake, I was writing compositions in that kind of cockamamie English for Miss Garrigues when I was a freshman at De Witt Clinton." What, I asked myself with contempt dripping from every unspoken word, what could you expect from a Philistine who felt my talents were worth not the twelve dollars a week for which I had asked but the eleven he decided were adequate.

Quite a lot, I discovered twenty minutes later as I shuffled through the unread magazines that were stacked like cordwood on the table in his office. All were so forbiddingly impressive in one way or another that I could not see any of them as the proper frame for my four-page—beautifully typed but still merely four-page—manuscript.

I was about to give up when, near the bottom of one pile, I found something that looked promising. It was clearly not a magazine and yet, even though it was even more clearly a four-page newspaper, it did not look like any newspaper I had ever seen. Half the front page, I discovered with interest, was devoted to two short stories, both almost exactly the same length as the one I had just written. I carried it back to my desk, copied the address under the masthead onto an envelope, helped myself to the proper postage from the office stamp box, and dropped the envelope down the mail chute. On the subway ride home I made a calculation: allowing one day for the envelope to reach the publication's office at 55 Fifth Avenue, one day for the manuscript to be read, and one day for the reply to reach me, the entire transaction should take three days.

I was wrong. Two days later, in my Bronx mailbox, I found a note that ended with the typewritten words: "The Editors."

Above this appeared a single sentence: "We like your short story and are accepting it for publication in the *American Spectator.*" Aside from my miscalculation about the length of time that would elapse before I heard from the magazine, I saw nothing at all unusual about the entire transaction. I was seventeen.

I was also free from the shackling depression that had been crippling me for months. All kinds of new emotions were tumbling around inside me. One was a feeling I did not quite understand. I worked on it without success all the way downtown in the subway and for most of the morning. Toward noon I had it. I looked up the *American Spectator* in the phone book, called the number, and asked the girl who answered if her employers paid for the contributions to their publication. They certainly did, she said, and wanted to know why I had asked. I told her. She urged me to hold on for a few moments while she looked something up. When she came back on the phone she uttered nine words that changed my life as suddenly and irrevocably as the eruption of Krakatoa changed the geography of the Sunda Strait.

"Your check for ten dollars will be mailed today."

The new emotion I carried with me out of the phone booth was one that I am convinced was not unlike the emotion with which Alfred Dreyfus stepped out of his Devil's Island cell when word came that the hideous farce was over at last. Wrapped in my new and exhilarating sense of freedom, I did not walk into Mr. Geschwind's office, punch him in the nose and stalk out. Even in 1930 a check for ten dollars was not the wealth of the Indies.

It was, however, something infinitely more important, something I sensed on that extraordinary day that writers, painters, sculptors, creative people of every kind must have been discovering for more years than I could imagine, namely, that the artist is the only truly free man. With his imagination and his hands—in my case with the help of a pencil and a pad of paper—he breaks the gyves that bind his less fortunate brethren to the treadmill of dreary breadwinning. He is not, of course, free from the necessity to earn that bread. It is the manner of the earning, however, that sets him apart. Perhaps only a desperate teenager would grasp this at once, in a blinding moment of discovery, like Saul on the road to Tarsus. I grasped it so clearly that, even though as I left the phone booth I was still blinded, I nonetheless saw clearly that, while others less fortunate would have to continue to do the bidding of those in authority who could withhold or limit the amount of their daily bread, I would not. I had just joined a select company. My days of running tailor-made tongue sandwiches from Lou G. Siegel's delicatessen to Monroe Geschwind's desk were over. Or at least numbered.

So was my bout of euphoria. While I was still in its grip I decided to celebrate the happy change in my life by running one of Lou G. Siegel's Specials not to the desk of Monroe Geschwind, but to the palate of one of the newly anointed: Annie Falkovitz Weidman's son Yeedle. The decision carried me as far as the front door of Mr. Siegel's delicatessen. Here I paused to check the contents of my pockets the way I had learned to do on East Fourth Street before I entered any store. I made a sobering discovery. I did not have on my person the eighty-five cents for which a Lou G. Siegel Special retailed. I came back into the world of reality.

I walked over to Sixth Avenue and, from a sidewalk vendor, bought my usual lunch: a Gabila's potato knish. Munching my nickel delicacy, I worked my way down slowly from my *American Spectator* high into a hard look at the facts. What had happened had brought me out of my depression, and for that I would be foolish not to be grateful. On it, however, I could not hope to build a career. I had been trained to believe that could be achieved only by learning a skill for which there would be a demand in the market place. It was the only way to achieve, as Mr. Musaius used to say to us in P.S. 188 on East Fourth Street, a nice steady flow of Yankee bean soup coming in daily over the windowsill. That did not mean the *American Spectator* experience should be disregarded. It deserved to be noted. Even though common sense told me I would have to continue my night classes at C.C.N.Y. as well as my job with Mr. Geschwind, it was worth being aware and grateful for the fact that because of the *American Spectator* experience the friends who had once chaired me through the market place, then disappeared, had been replaced by something even more satisfying: a friendship that depended solely on me: my work.

Years later I learned from Dick Simon of Simon & Schuster that it could be a dangerous friendship. Dick had been meeting with Edna Ferber—who at that time was apparently unhappy with her current publisher—about joining the Simon & Schuster list. In the course of their talks the fact that she had never married entered—or perhaps blundered its way—into the conversation. Dick told me Miss Ferber gave him a smile and said, "My writing has been the only husband I have ever needed, and my books the only children I've ever wanted."

Fortunately, at seventeen in 1930, this thought had never yet crossed my mind. What did cross my mind was the risk involved in my surprising achievement. It was wonderfully heartwarming to know that by selling a story to the *American Spectator* for ten dollars I had joined a select company of free spirits. The hard facts of life as I was then living it, however, warned me that this wonderfully heartwarming achievement would have to be kept secret. In my heart I might feel I had a foot in the door that opened on the world of Dickens and Thackeray. In my head I knew that the moment Mr. Geschwind learned about this triumph my career in his office would be over. What kept our relationship in balance was our shared provenance: De Witt Clinton High School. Knowing his passion for reading, I knew also that nothing would upset that balance more quickly than the appearance of my name in print. My place in Mr. Geschwind's scheme of things was firmly established: fetcher of his Lou G. Siegel Specials. Breaking into print would be for Mr. Geschwind the equivalent of a servant forgetting his place. Monroe Geschwind would not, of course, be the first to note that his office boy had won a foot in the door that opened on the world of Dickens and Thackeray. He would, however, be the first to see to it that, as a result of this triumph, his office boy was out on his ass. I needed the secret warmth of my achievement, but at that moment in my life I needed something else even more: the eleven dollars in the envelope Mr. Geschwind handed me every Saturday. I was not yet capable of stating it for myself in words, but I had not the slightest difficulty feeling I had learned one of the great lessons of my life: secret pleasures are the best.

I returned to my duties with Monroe Geschwind and my studies at C.C.N.Y. with renewed determination. I kept the *American Spectator* episode firmly locked away in a corner of my mind, like a secret bank deposit to which I could turn if the flow of Yankee bean soup ever gave signs of drying up. A week later, while I was supposed to be listening to Professor Jarshauer in my Economics II class, I found myself peppering my notebook page with the Pitman squiggles of another story.

I was a little shocked to find myself departing so quickly from my resolution to stick to my studies, but I was not displeased. It occurred to me that perhaps I had been too hasty with my resolution. Or wrong in assuming that by adopting it I had excluded the possibility of any other form of activity. So many members of my class slept through Professor Jarshauer's lectures, what was wrong with one member using the time to do something more enjoyable? Even in those days I had already learned that the rhetorical question was my favorite form of inquiry: I could always come up with a satisfactory answer. I finished the story before Professor Jarshauer finished his lecture.

That night, after running it through the typewriter, I sent off the manuscript to the brand-new friends at 55 Fifth Avenue who, even though we had never met, I felt I had been neglecting. I did this every day for a week, toward the end of which I began to be troubled by the fact that "The Editors," who had been so prompt with their reply to my first offering, had been silent for seven—no, eight, then nine, finally ten!—full days.

On the twelfth day I decided I was unable to continue living with the suspense. As well as with the five additional manuscripts I had accumulated but decided not to send until I had some news of what was happening to the seven I had already, since my initial triumph, submitted. I decided to write and ask what was happening. Having reached the decision, I did not quite know how to act on it. How did one address a letter to a publication the editors of which, according to their masthead and stationery, were George Jean Nathan, Ernest Boyd, Theodore Dreiser, Sherwood Anderson, James Branch Cabell, and Eugene O'Neill?

To single out one might be considered a slight by the others. "Gentlemen" or even "Dear Sirs" seemed cold and unfriendly from a man they had, less than a fortnight before, plucked from the galleys. While I was struggling with the problem, my second letter from the *American Spectator* arrived. It began, a trifle coldly I naturally thought, "Dear Sir." It ended with those by now familiar two typed words, "The Editors." They seemed to me, however, because of the paragraph above them, as warm as flowing lava.

> We like all seven of your stories, and to prove it we are buying three, but we must point out that we are a four-page, once-a-month publication. If we ran everything you sent us, there would be very little room, in fact none, for other material, and since we started the *American Spectator* more or less as a forum for our own ideas, this would not only vitiate our original intent but it would also make us resentful of you, and we like your work too much to allow that to happen. We are taking the liberty, therefore, of turning over the four stories we cannot use to the editors of other magazines with whom we are friendly and in whose literary judgment we have sufficient confidence to make us feel that they will buy these stories. If they don't, do not be angry with us. Also, since we will be running your stories several months apart, and we now own four, we hope you won't mind our suggesting that you don't send us any more stories for at least two years.

I did mind but, for a couple of reasons, I followed the suggestion of "The Editors." First, by the time the two years were behind me, the four stories my distinguished but to me unknown friends at the *American Spectator* had sent on to their friends had been sold, along with several others, and, second, sadly, the *American Spectator* was no longer in business.

I use the word "business" advisedly. It underscores a point I feel—as a former president of the Authors' League of America, Inc.—should be made.

Some time after the *American Spectator* experience, when I

had become a regular contributor to *The New Yorker*, I gave Wolcott Gibbs an account of my meeting with Lindsay C. Trimingham and how, inadvertently, the encounter had led to my first appearance in print. Gibbs took a thoughtful sip from his glass and surprised me with a small essay.

"There is abroad in the land a lamentable tendency to confuse failure with quality," he said. "The notion that because nobody will buy it, it must be great, is as foolish as the belief that a rookie who can't find the plate is obviously major league material. I'm sure the history of publishing is full of stories about great manuscripts that editors were too stupid to buy. I'm equally sure the word 'full' is an outrageous exaggeration. Human beings make mistakes, and editors are human beings. It's been my experience that, by and large, material that merits publication manages somehow to get published. The boys in the ivory towers are probably doing worthwhile work, but I think it's worthwhile only to them, the way an aspirin is worthwhile to a man with a headache. It isn't really art. It's therapy. For the man in the ivory tower, I mean. It's foolish, even inhuman, to be against that kind of therapy, but it's equally foolish, and to me even more inhuman, to try to foist the treatment on the healthy. What the man up there in the ivory tower produces is worthwhile only when it has value to the man down in the street. When that happens, I take off my hat to him up there, and while I may think he's a little foolish to live in such an odd place when he could afford to come down and enjoy the fun of the rest of the human race, it's a matter of *de gustibus*, and I respect his right to choose his own digs. I ask in return that he respect my right to insist that, if you'll bear with the pun, clarity is all. Comprehensibility is more important than euphony, although if you can achieve both you are doing a better job. Obfuscation, I have found, is the refuge of the second-rater, and life is too short to waste time on second-raters. Always write as well as you can, without ever forgetting how important it is to keep trying to write better than you can, but never forget that writing is a form of communication, probably the noblest ever invented by the human animal, and for God's sake don't ever stop battling us to pay you higher prices for what you write."

I never did, even though I was then too young to under-stand all of what he said. Years later, when he was dead, I suddenly grasped, from another man's words, what he had meant.

I had attended the opening night of a play that moved me deeply. So deeply that, when a week later I read in my morning paper that the play had closed, I wrote a note to the playwright—who was a total stranger, but whose work I had known for years—telling him not only what I thought of his play but also of a public that could turn its back on so worthy a piece of work. His reply was for me as great a revelation as that moment in the phone booth in 1930 when I learned I was a free man.

"Thank you for your very nice note," Archibald MacLeish wrote. "I'm glad you liked my play. So did I. Unfortunately, it is not enough for just the two of us to like it."

It has never been enough for me. More often than not, however, I have had to pretend that it was.

five

In 1940, immediately after the Dunkirk evacuation, a cartoon by David Low appeared on the front page of the London *Evening Standard*. It showed a British Tommy, knee-deep in bomb wreckage, shaking his fist defiantly at a sky darkened by the Luftwaffe, over the caption: "Very well, then—alone!"

He could have taken the 1930 words out of my mouth in the Bronx when I emerged from my post-high-school-graduation depression. I could feel the refreshing inner breeze of a new leaf turning. I didn't exactly spit on my hands, hitch up my pants, and tighten my belt, but I did force myself to articulate a decision: there was only one thing to do with my years from zero to seventeen: write them off. I would have to start life all over again, on my own, from the beginning. As a symbol of this new determination I took the ten-dollar check from the *American Spectator* to the Dry Dock Savings Bank, across the street from the Monroe Geschwind office on Thirty-fourth Street, and opened an account. The satisfaction was immediate but short-lived. I was aware that I could not share the satisfaction with my family. In fact I knew I had to keep the bank account a secret from my mother. The problem was money.

My mother knew that money came from her husband, and she knew that what he did to earn it was no less productive than what the husbands of most of her neighbors did, but not nearly so productive as what was done by some other husbands. At any rate, so she had been given to understand, or had heard, or had been told, or thought she had been told. How my mother grasped that there were other husbands who earned more money than her husband earned was never clear to me. Nor, I suspect, even to her. All I know on this point is that the knowledge did not come to my mother from anything she had read. My mother couldn't read.

Until I was old enough to understand that particular aspect of her problem, and I began my fumbling attempts to correct it, my mother was illiterate. Totally. Not only in English. She was illiterate in her native Hungarian as well. This, plus a pride so deeply rooted that it was almost a crippling physical ailment, stood not only between my efforts to teach her how to read and write: it stood also between her life as the peasant she had left behind in Europe and the life into which she emerged when as a young girl she stepped out of her steerage passage at Ellis Island into a new world. She was totally unprepared for it. The obvious form of preparation—which almost all her immigrant neighbors embraced, namely, night school—was denied her by pride. To be seen going to school was a public confession of a humiliation my mother could not tolerate: the admission of ignorance. How she handled herself until I came along with my English lessons, I can only guess. My guess is she did too well. The conclusions she worked out for herself during those crucial formative years could never be unlearned. Till the day of her death she was never free from the crippling, ineradicable terror of poverty.

Even though for a long time I did not understand this, I sensed her humiliation, the humiliation she was able to conceal successfully from the rest of the world. It made me angry. I hated to see her cower, even if nobody else could see it. I wanted to do something to wipe away her shame. As a schoolboy I soon realized I was powerless to do anything. Then, as I began to become aware of the strength that comes with the exercise of the imagination, I slowly grasped that there was no limit to what a writer can do. All he has to do is want to do it. If my mother was unhappy, why could I not create happiness for her? How? By changing the world, of course. The world that had made her unhappy. I was certain I could do it. All I had to do was choose the right moment. I embarked on a secret vigil, waiting for my opening. I never doubted that it would come.

It did, in 1971, when I began to publish a trilogy about a boy from East Fourth Street named, after the young hero, "The Benny Kramer Sequence." Benny, like his creator, does not understand his mother, but he loves her. And Benny, who, like his creator, will one day become a writer, has no qualms about portraying her as a woman so fiercely dedicated to her family that in order to augment her husband's meager earnings, she begins to draw on hitherto unsuspected talents. In the second volume of the trilogy, called *Last Respects*, Benny's mother appears as a bootlegger. In the third volume, *Tiffany Street*, she not only moves her family from the slums of East Fourth Street to the then attractive suburbia of the Bronx. She also becomes the organizer and local entrepreneur of a cottage industry in which her neighboring Bronx housewives work for her in the manufacture of what were then known as jazz bows: preknotted bow ties that fastened around the male neck with a strip of elastic.

The facts in both books are basically true, but only basically. During the Prohibition years many women on the Lower East Side earned an occasional dollar by delivering, through a Bowery distributor for whom they did the legwork, the liquor needed for weddings, bar mitzvahs, and other local celebrations. Four blocks north of our tenement, on Eighth Street, a jazz bow manufacturer, operating out of a cellar under a tenement, fed out to any woman who came to pick them up bundles of machine-cut jazz bows for finishing by hand in their own kitchens. My mother tried both. She worked hard at delivering the bottles and sewing the bow ties, but her earnings were pitifully small. As a bootlegger she was hampered by her terror of the police. As a piecework maker of jazz bows she was defeated by an almost total lack of skill with needle and thread. Her pride prevented her from acknowledging her fear of the police as well as her inadequacy as a seamstress.

Benny Kramer corrected all that. He portrayed his mother not as she was but as he wanted her to be. He stripped away her terror of the police and made her, in *Last Respects*, a fearless and courageous bootlegger. She played her fictional role with so much verve that her son the creator, carried away by the fun she was having, threw in a passionate love affair between his mother and a dashing young Irish rumrunner from Chicago. I was so pleased with the change in her that I forgot it was all a fabrication. For the final volume of the trilogy, *Tiffany Street*, Benny Kramer retained all the qualities for which we both loved her—not the least of which was, of course, that she loved us—and we added something about which she was totally ignorant but in which, because of her lifelong terror of poverty, Benny and I could see her in our fantasies reveling: we made her the Hetty Green of the South Bronx. In the eyes of Annie Falkovitz's son the storyteller, she turned in a Tony Award performance. She may not have known it, but it was the only truly happy period of her life.

In this book, where I am trying to tell the truth about her, I see that all I accomplished with my inventions was a further blurring of what had never been a clear picture to begin with. I can imagine her laughing with delight at the roles in which I cast her, but not for long, and in the end with bitter sadness. Her demons had placed her at their mercy by presenting her at birth with the most brutal of all gifts: an incorruptibly pure vision of herself. No storyteller, not even her son, could alter the picture she was doomed for all time to see clearly in her own inner mirror. I suspect that her legacy for which I should be most grateful is that she was apparently incapable of passing on to her son the ability to see her as she could see herself.

From my earliest recollections of her when I was an infant, to the very end at near-ninety in the Peretz Memorial Hospital on Queens Boulevard, she always gave me the impression of a former prisoner who—for reasons that had never been explained to her—had been seized without warrant and thrust into darkness, and then, after she was released, had spent the rest of her long life trying to believe the light into which she had emerged was better than the darkness that had almost destroyed her. I don't think the lifelong attempt to believe ever succeeded. The wherewithal for belief had been denied at birth. In spite of my belated clumsy efforts to provide her with the tools, she never got the hang of their use. To the very end she remained an ex-con who thought it was probably better to go straight but in her heart she did not believe it.

Sitting at her side when she was dying, I held her hand the

way a man in total darkness lost in a tunnel will hold on to his flashlight long after the batteries have gone dead. I was still wondering, as I had been wondering all my life, where I had gone wrong in my efforts to help her, when I heard her mumble something. I leaned closer. I did not understand the sounds. They may not have been words. The small whimpering noises were one last puzzle released by a life that for me had always been a series of puzzles. There was in the incomprehensible, perhaps inhuman, sounds neither fear nor despair. Not even surprise or outrage. Only angry relief. The meaningless fear she had been condemned to bear so long was over at last.

I was reminded of those moments long ago when, late at night in our Bronx kitchen, she would drop her pencil and push herself away from the table and the lesson that had not gone well, and she would say angrily in Yiddish, "Not tonight. Maybe next time." I knew she knew it would not be better next time. If she came back to the table to make another effort, it would not be because she felt she still had a chance to get what had been denied her when the getting was possible. If she came back to the table, it would be because she did not want me, her sweepstakes ticket, to be infected by her discouragement. At the time I did not understand that. I finally did, in that last moment in the Peretz Memorial Hospital, and the moment of comprehension was worse than the half century of troubled puzzlement. She had been afraid not of her own darkness, which she hated. She had been afraid that my failure to open the window for her might discourage me from the effort to open it for myself.

Perhaps I shared some of her fears. I must have been afraid that if I told her about the check from the *American Spectator*, and what it had done to my thinking, I would become vulnerable to the same disease of shapeless terror that had crippled her. Like so many people who have never tasted success, she believed that to achieve it you had to discipline yourself relentlessly until tunnel vision becomes your only window on life.

I had become an accountant by accident. I agreed to go on to law school because she wanted me to. Telling her about the check from the *American Spectator* and how I felt about it would have added a new terror to the load she had always carried: the fear that I would be deflected from her great dream. So I did not tell her, and my silence made it possible for me to scheme and act out the pretense of the next four years. The pretense that by attending New York University Law School at night, I was moving toward the achievement she wanted and, because she wanted it, my father also wanted. What she wanted—with the single-mindedness Miss Havisham poured into wanting Estella to despise men—was a son practicing at the New York bar.

He never made it. I tried. Anyway, I tried to convince her I was trying, but my heart was not in it. At the time, however, the deception seemed to be working. The publication of my first story in the *American Spectator* attracted no attention. None discernible or audible in the Bronx or on Seventh Avenue. That was a matter of relief to me. Feeling certain that, if he learned I had broken into print, Mr. Geschwind would fire me, I was aware that, if I lost my job, I would have to tell my mother why. I told myself I was perfectly happy with the arrangement. After all, secret pleasures were the best, weren't they? On the day the issue of the *American Spectator* containing my story appeared on the stands, the arrangement was put to the test. That night I brought a copy to C.C.N.Y. and showed it to the girl who sat next to me in Economics II.

"Seen this?" I said casually.

Not much of a speech, but I'd worked on it for hours. I didn't want her to think I was pushing. My story was on the front page. My name under the title was, of course, in somewhat smaller type than the banner at the top of the page, but that was customary, was it not, with all publications? To anybody who knew me, however, certainly to somebody who sat next to me three nights a week in a classroom, it seemed to me the name should have done for this girl what it did for me: the letters of my name seemed to be winking on and off that front page of the *American Spectator* like the words on the huge electric sign that never stopped moving around the top of the New York Times Building as it spelled out the day's headlines high above Times Square.

"What is it?" the girl said.

"A new magazine," I said, dropping it on the writing arm of her chair.

Like a feather duster sweeping a piece of bric-a-brac, her glance skipped along the list of distinguished editors whose names, immediately below the title, spread across the entire top of the front page like a proudly unfurled pennant. My heart jumped when her glance swept down the page, then jumped again when she reached the bottom. Her eyes had crossed my name without pause. She opened the pages, gave the middle section two slashing glances, one left, the other right, and completed her inspection by slapping the pages together for a fast look at the back.

"Looks interesting," she said.

"Would you like to borrow it?" I said.

The copy I offered her had come in the morning mail. On my lunch hour I had combed the garment center for extra copies. There were no copies of the *American Spectator* in the garment center. Then I remembered Brentano's and I hurried across to Fifth Avenue. Brentano's had it, all right. There were four copies in the rack. I bought all four.

"Between my job during the day and my classes at night I don't get much chance for outside reading," the girl said, handing back my unread first appearance in print. "Thanks just the same."

During the next few days my suspicion that nobody had time for outside reading became a certainty. Finally, my confused feelings about this indifference led to recklessness. I worked a copy of the *American Spectator* into my mother's late-night English lesson. Using the front page as my model, I copied off our family name in large block letters on a pad.

"This is your name," I said to my mother as with my pencil I tapped off each of the seven letters, one by one, first on the newspaper page and then on my pad. "W, e, i, d, m, a, n. Now, here, you do it."

She took the pencil, wet the tip on her tongue, and started.

"W," she said and laboriously lettered. "E," she said and lettered. "I," she said and stopped. She scowled at the *American Spectator*, then looked up. "This is our name?" she said.

68

"That's right," I said, and with my pencil I again tapped each of the seven letters in the name printed under the title of my story, "*W, e, i, d, m, a, n.*"

My mother scowled at the printed page for several moments. Then, holding her pencil the way a child on a beach holds the shovel of a sand pail, she tapped the six letters that preceded our family name.

"And this?" she said. "What is it, this?"

"My first name," I said.

"Yeedle?" she said.

"This is an English-language newspaper," I said. "Jerome."

"So together it's your whole name there in the paper?" she said.

"That's right," I said.

"How did it get there?" my mother said.

I told her. She listened with a frown.

"You wrote this thing?" my mother said finally. "This story you wrote? And you sent it to them? The people they own this paper?"

"Yes," I said.

"Why?" my mother said.

"I hoped they would buy it," I said.

I chose the second verb with care. Her face reflected a moment of confusion.

"That means money?" she said.

The ruse had worked.

"Yes," I said.

"How much?" she said.

"Ten dollars," I said.

Her eyelids went into action. They always did when she was thinking something through. They moved up and down slowly, as though marking the progress of her thoughts, one into the other, building toward a conclusion or sum, like the clicking of an abacus.

"It took long to write?" she said finally.

"About an hour," I said.

A glance of pleasure darted across her face. It happened so rarely that, until it did happen, I kept forgetting how beautiful she was.

69

"Mr. Geschwind he pays you eleven dollars for a whole week," my mother said with a small girl's chuckle of delight. "For only one hour you paid yourself ten?"

"I didn't," I said. "This magazine paid me."

"But you did the writing that they paid you for," she said.

"That's right," I said.

"What did you do with the money?" my mother said.

I hesitated. I could feel the whole fabric of my deception trembling in the balance, but I could not resist adding to her pleasure.

"I put it in the bank," I said. "For law school expenses."

The look on her face became a grin of happiness. My heart skipped a beat. I could see what had happened. My worry that she might think my secret writing would deflect me from my studies had in her mind been converted—by a moment of storyteller's inspiration—into a reinforcement of what she believed was my determination to become what she wanted me to be: a lawyer.

"You could maybe write more stories?" my mother said.

"I already have," I said.

"You already wrote another story?" she said.

"Three more," I said.

Her eyebrows, going up, phrased the question she was afraid to ask. I had no fears about how to answer it. When a story is going well, I had learned, the ending is inevitable. All the storyteller has to do is wait for it to show up. The story I was putting together was going so well that, when the ending slid smoothly into place, it brought along in a sort of carefully wrapped CARE package the precise words in which it insisted on being phrased.

"When the time comes for your next winter coat never mind looking for something that doesn't show the dirt," I said. "I want you to pick out something just because it looks nice."

"Things like that they're for people with money," my mother said.

"For your next winter coat," said her son the storyteller, "the money is already in the bank."

six

Happily, when the time came for her next winter coat, the reality of how to pay for it had managed to catch up with the storyteller's invention. The money actually was in the bank. So was the money for my law school tuition. I was still finishing my undergraduate work in the night session at C.C.N.Y. but I had already applied for entrance to N.Y.U. Law School. By comparison with present-day tuition charges the cost in those days was very low: ten dollars a point. For someone who earned eleven dollars a week, however, this was a large sum. Without the money from my few short story sales I would not have dared to file my entrance application. Knowing her coat and the impending law school fees could not have come out of my eleven-dollar salary from Mr. Geschwind provided my mother with another source of worry.

"It's hard?" she said one night across the kitchen table. "To study in college at night and at the same time to write stories?"

"Not if you don't do both at the same time," I said.

Her eyes crinkled.

"So late at night when you come home and you think in the bedroom I'm thinking you're in the kitchen studying," she said, "you're not studying?"

"Not always," I said.

"But you study enough?" she said.

"Enough to be first in my class," I said.

This was not true, but she had no way of knowing that, so the crinkles became a smile.

"So the writing is just for extra money?" she said.

"From Mr. Geschwind's money you can't buy a winter coat with a fur collar," I said.

Her eyes held mine for a long moment.

"Enough sleep you're getting?" she said.

"When I need more," I said, "I won't take it from the studying."

She looked down at her hands, as though her attention had suddenly been caught by a wrinkle, and she smoothed it away from her knuckles.

"I know you've been worrying because you think I've been worrying," she said. "In the beginning, yes, I was worrying, but only a little. You're my son. Both of us know how to do more than one thing at one time. I'm not going to worry any more."

I was tempted to share her confidence. I was aware that the money for her winter coat had made its way into the bank because the *American Spectator*, if it had no readers in the Bronx, had loyal followers elsewhere.

Two of these, I learned, were the editors of *Story*, a magazine that had been started in Vienna by Whit Burnett and Martha Foley, a couple of American writers who were interested in expanding the development of the short story as an art form. In 1933 their interest had attracted publishing interest in New York. As a result the magazine shifted its headquarters so that, as one hopeful contributor assumed, writers based in the Bronx could offer their work at domestic rather than foreign postage rates. The assumption proved to be not totally incorrect.

I sent my first contribution to *Story* the week my third contribution to the *American Spectator* appeared on the newsstands. A month later *Story* returned my story. The rejection slip arrived in the same mail that brought a letter from New York University advising me that I had been accepted as a student in the Law School's evening session. Because I never told my mother about my rejection slips, the mail for her that day consisted only of the N.Y.U. letter. It made her very happy. It meant to her that the gap between her single-minded ambition, and my achievement of it for her, was now officially narrowed to four years: the time it took to complete the course for a bachelor of laws degree at New York University Law School in the evening session. I did not share her happiness. She'd had time to learn how to handle the waiting game. I was still too young for that particular skill. I managed, however, to conceal my disappointment.

As a member of a Socialist family on Tammany-dominated East Fourth Street, I had learned early the advantage of being secretive about failure. The tendency to diminish the pain by seeking solace in talking about it did not work for me. I caught on early to the fact that, when you sought that kind of comfort, even when you got it you could not avoid getting something else along with it: an enlargement of the circle of witnesses to your humiliation. I learned the wisdom, in moments of disaster, of limiting the audience to one, namely, me. I was never sure about handling others. Except, of course, in a story, where I was the one who did all the handling. For a long time I kept my rejections as secret as Mata Hari kept the names of her employers. Then, one day after I had been contributing stories to *The New Yorker* for a couple of years, John O'Hara changed all that for me.

I started reading *The New Yorker* the year it started publication, before I entered high school. Long before I ever thought of contributing to it, O'Hara was already one of the handful of unique talents who had surfaced in its pages. By the time I started writing for the magazine he was the undisputed king of the publication's fiction hill. His work astonished me. So did his reputation as a curmudgeon because, when I met him, he did not live up to it. O'Hara treated me like a new kid on the block who had not yet crossed him. I made it a point to keep it that way. This was easy enough because, while we both lived in New York, I did my living in the Bronx, at N.Y.U. Law School, and in the office of Monroe Geschwind & Company. O'Hara preferred "21" and the Stork Club. When our paths crossed it was usually at a cocktail party in the home of a *New Yorker* editor or in the magazine's offices. The encounters were always brief and, at least for me, always pleasant. I'm never quite sure I'm right when I think people like me, but I'm never wrong when I think they don't. I never felt O'Hara disliked me.

One day when I ran into him as I came out of the elevator

from a visit to the *New Yorker* office on West Forty-third Street, he stopped me with a sharp look.

"They been giving you the business upstairs?" he said.

I knew what he meant. Any *New Yorker* fiction writer would have known what he meant. It was *New Yorker* policy at that time not to discuss editorial changes with an author until the story the magazine had purchased had been set in type. After the author's editor had worked on the galleys they were sent to the author for approval and action. Reactions to this practice were varied among the *New Yorker* writers I came to know. These reactions ran all the way from docile acceptance to outraged fury. The needle on the face of the meter that monitored my reaction tended to hover somewhere in the middle. O'Hara's tendency to shatter the meter by sending the needle on its roaring way to the top of the measuring device provided the raw material for some of the magazine's juiciest gossip. The day our paths crossed in the 25 West 43rd lobby and he asked if "they" had been giving me the business upstairs, the answer was yes and no.

During the years that I wrote for the magazine I had four editors: Wolcott Gibbs, Katharine White, William Maxwell, and, finally, Gus Lobrano. I had no trouble with any of them. I did have quite a lot of trouble with myself. My reaction to editorial suggestions was not unlike my reaction to my own manuscripts. Writing in longhand, I never knew what to think of a piece of work until I ran it through the typewriter. When I did, I was always impressed by the improvement. Even when the typescript contained not a single change from the handwritten original I was still impressed by the improvement. Common sense told me that this made no sense, common or otherwise. I had to force myself to go over the typescript with care to find things that could be eliminated or done better. After I sold my earliest stories to the *American Spectator*, *Story*, and the *American Mercury* I never had a chance to inspect them again until I saw them in the magazines. It never occurred to me to compare my file carbon copy of the story with what appeared on the newsstand. I assumed they were identical. I had not yet learned that editors did more than buy stories. I had no idea that they might want changes. This was due to my ignorance about how printed material was transferred from typescript to something you could buy on a newsstand. I had never heard of galleys. When I encountered them, in the form of my first set from *The New Yorker*, I was shocked. The handwritten markings and marginal queries that surrounded the narrow column of type running down the center of the long white sheets threw me back to my school days. I looked nervously at the upper-right-hand corner of the top galley the way I used to look at the upper-right-hand corner of the compositions Miss Garrigues handed back to us after a test in De Witt Clinton: hunting for the numbered grade she had awarded the paper. Once I got over the shock, I felt about the change from my typescript to the printer's galleys the way I used to feel about the change from my handwritten copy to the typescript. The mere physical change was such an obvious improvement that, automatically, I was on the side of the printer. Having made this adjustment, the next was inevitable: I found myself on the side of the editor. He or she was trying to improve my performance. How could I refuse to accept the help?

In the beginning I didn't try very hard. Later, when I did, all I accomplished was to set in motion a second round of editorial suggestions, more tartly phrased, more firmly documented, more quickly accepted. The day I met John O'Hara in the lobby I had gone through one of the final phases in a *New Yorker* writer-editor disagreement: the face-to-face encounter. The suggestion I had rejected twice by mail from my Bronx workroom was so clearly an improvement when explained patiently by an editor in his or her Forty-third Street office that my only desire was to leave the editorial presence as quickly as possible while I was still able to do so standing upright rather than crawling on my knees. I thought I had made it safely, carrying with me some shred of face-saving honor, until O'Hara stopped me in the lobby with his "They been giving you the business upstairs?"

I realized at once that, while I had made my escape while still on my feet, and I had not crawled from the editorial presence on my knees, on my face were writ large all the telltale details of my humiliating surrender. I tried for a deprecating smirk.

"Oh, you know how it is," I said.

O'Hara put his arm through mine.

"Let's have a cup of coffee."

He led me out to Forty-third Street and into a coffee shop down the block. I went along, fully intending to reveal nothing, determined to keep it light, planning to pass it off as a joke. Ten minutes after we sat down facing each other across the coffee cups, I realized not a single joke had crossed my lips. I had poured out in loathsome detail the whole humiliating experience. My face grew hot. I stopped babbling.

"Sorry," I said. "I didn't mean to bore you."

The cold eyes in the flat, pale, movie-handsome gangster's face flicked angrily. It was the sort of face I had come to know on East Fourth Street. It was a predominantly Jewish neighborhood, but there was an enclave of *goyim* on the southeast corner where Fourth Street crossed Lewis Street before plunging onto the dock that jutted into the river. These gentiles centered around a saloon that catered to the seamen who worked on the river barges. Among them there were always on view a few representatives of that group my father called *leidigeiers*, meaning young men who carried no loads: they traveled light. They did not seem to have jobs, yet they dressed well, and obviously had money in their pockets. The other *goyim* moved in and out of the saloon, downing their shots of rye, gulping their beer chasers, and hurrying back to their work on the barges. The *leidigeiers*, however, lounged around the corner lamppost, making jokes, laughing it up, smoking endless cigarettes, whistling at passing girls, and managing to create in their immediate vicinity an atmosphere of menace. Most Jewish kids on the block avoided them, and so did I, but in a curious way, because they were so different from everybody else on the block, I found them attractive, the way years later I found O'Hara attractive. On East Fourth Street he would have been identified—by my father, anyway—as a *leidigeier*. On Forty-third Street I sensed a significant refinement: he was a *leidigeier* who had gone straight.

"Bore me?" he said. "What the hell do you think I'm doing down here at this hour of the morning? I have to go upstairs and do a repeat performance for the West Coast of what they just put you through."

I tried to keep my astonishment from showing. Learning that the king of the hill was subjected to the same indignities that were visited on me lifted my spirits. Here was a man whose work I admired. If, to make it as good as it was when I read it, he had to go through what I went through, perhaps by going through it more cheerfully I could bring my own work nearer to his level.

"What the hell are you laughing at?" he said.

I told him.

"If that makes you feel good, here's something that should make your day," O'Hara said. "I'm not going up there to have an argument about some misplaced commas. I have to go up there and tell this ugly broad if she rejects this story she wrote me about yesterday she's written me her last letter on that fucking magazine's stationery."

The word "reject" went off in my head like a gong. It came as so great a surprise that I shied away from believing O'Hara could be talking about himself. In the shying-away process I found myself thrown back to the day the mail that brought my mother the good news that I had been accepted by N.Y.U. Law School had also contained a letter I didn't tell her about: Whit Burnett's rejection of the first story I sent to *Story* magazine. It was O'Hara's turn to laugh. He did not do it well. Partly, I think, because his fear of dentists was so great that he rarely had his teeth cleaned or repaired. As a result his upper teeth were an unsightly mess. He tried to keep them concealed, so that in conversation he frequently looked like a ventriloquist at work, but he was not always successful. He did laugh occasionally, and this was one of those occasions, but in the sound there was no mirth.

"I know what's going through your mind," he said. "Yeah, well, it's true, I get them back. Everybody does. In my early days on the magazine I was writing pretty nearly a piece a day. They couldn't use them all, and I knew that, but I knew something they didn't know, and on a day like this I think it might make you feel better if you know it, too."

"What's that?" I said.

"Once a writer has finished a story to his own satisfaction,"

John O'Hara said, "there's only one thing he can do to improve it, and that's tell the editor to go fuck himself."

I've never done that. Not because I was never tempted. There have been times when it seemed the only appropriate comment to make. The trouble is that it can be made only at the moment when a writer knows that, if he does not make the comment, the editor will probably end up buying his story, or he would not have been summoned to a face-to-face encounter in the first place. This was not the situation on the morning when I learned Whit Burnett had turned me down for *Story* magazine. On that morning I had nobody to talk to. I had to keep the rejection to myself. It proved to be one of those mornings on which I learned the wisdom, in moments of disaster, of limiting the audience to one, namely, me. I had a few bad hours but I kept my trap shut.

Later in the day, carrying a Lou G. Siegel Special back to the office for Mr. Geschwind's lunch, I passed a newsstand. The bright green cover of the new issue of the *American Mercury* caught my eye. I stopped to look and, as always when I saw my name in print, my heart did a little jig. This time it did a bigger jig. This was the first time I'd seen my name in print on the cover of a magazine. I had not forgotten, of course, that I'd sold the story to the *American Mercury*. What I had forgotten was that I had not been told when it would appear in print. I bought a copy at once and read my story on the street as I walked along carrying Mr. Geschwind's Lou G. Siegel Special. By the time I reached the office I had forgotten all about the wound the *Story* rejection slip had inflicted that morning. I was astonished to discover a few days later that the editors of *Story*, however, had not. It took a few minutes, after I opened their letter, to understand what they were talking about.

> Dear Mr. Weidman: I have just read your story in the current *Mercury*. I like it very much. It reminded me that I've also liked a couple of your things in the *American Spectator*, and when I mentioned this to my wife, she reminded me that she had liked a story you showed us a few weeks ago. Neither of us can remember the title, but we do remember that it was about a boy who worries because his immigrant father spends

long hours sitting up late in the dark staring at nothing. Anyway, if you haven't disposed of the story elsewhere, we'd like to take another look at it, if we may. Yours, Whit Burnett.

Here, I was pleased to discover, was an experience that conventional wisdom insisted was nonexistent: there was something new under the sun. Not because an editor had underscored what years later Wolcott Gibbs had stated was fact, namely, that all human beings make mistakes, and that editors—if we accept their humanity—are bound to make some even as you and I. No, it wasn't that. What made this experience new was that Mr. Burnett—who I had assumed was capable of doing only one thing for me: buy my story—had managed to do something else for me, something that conceivably was more important than making a contribution toward the cost of my mother's next winter coat. Inadvertently Mr. Burnett had provided me with a title. His description of the story he wanted to see again was so much better than the title I had put on it that, in my sudden excitement, I was convinced all I had to do was substitute his description for my title, and the story would be snapped up by the next editor who saw it. That was all I did, and that was exactly what happened.

I took the story out of my desk, threw away the top sheet, and typed a new one: "My Father Sits in the Dark, by Jerome Weidman." The first editor who saw it was, of course, Whit Burnett. Or perhaps the day my story made its second visit to the *Story* office it was his wife's turn to open the mail, so that the first editor who saw "My Father Sits in the Dark" may have been Martha Foley. Anyway, they bought the story. Not long after it appeared in their magazine, "My Father Sits in the Dark" was chosen for inclusion in the *O. Henry Memorial Award Prize Stories* of 1935. The book was edited by Harry Hansen, literary editor of the New York *World-Telegram*.

It was the seventeenth appearance of this annual anthology, but it was the first time I had heard of its existence. It was not, however, until I held in my hand the free copy sent to me by the publishers, Doubleday, Doran & Company, Inc., that I realized appearing in the volume also meant being entered in a contest. For inclusion in the book the nineteen stories were selected by Mr. Hansen. For awarding the contest prizes the judges were Tess Slesinger, Clifton Fadiman, and Joseph Henry Jackson. I was so impressed by seeing my story bound between the covers of a book that the next morning, leafing through the pages over and over again on the subway, I did not realize until the train pulled into Times Square that I had been entered in a contest in which I had won nothing. Even now, half a century later, I have to take the book down from the shelf, and refresh my recollection by reading the introduction, to be able to record that the $300 first prize went to Kay Boyle, the $200 second prize to Dorothy Thomas, and a special $100 prize for the best short short went to Josephine Johnson.

I require no mnemonic aids to recall the surprising result of my appearance in the O. Henry volume that helped ease the disappointment of not ending up in the winner's circle. A few days after the book was published I received a letter on a piece of the most exotic-looking stationery I had ever taken out of our Bronx mailbox. The paper was thick and cream-colored, with dark brown type that rose from the paper like Braille markings. The sheet, which was cut clean at the top, trailed away at the bottom into a sort of fuzzy lace that could have been woven from the lint that gathers in the corner of a coat pocket. The message contained in this letter had been tapped out through a chocolate-colored typewriter ribbon.

> Dear Mr. Weidman: I read your story "My Father Sits in the Dark" in the new O. Henry Memorial Award volume and I liked it very much. I represent Fannie Hurst, Hugh Walpole, Viña Delmar, Vachel Lindsay, Carl Van Vechten, William Dean Howells, Paul Gallico, Booth Tarkington, Warwick Deeping, Octavus Roy Cohen, Rudyard Kipling, Christopher Morley, Elinor Glyn, Joseph Hergesheimer, and W. Somerset Maugham, among others. You have the sort of talent with which I have always been very successful. If you are not otherwise represented I would like to offer you my services. Sincerely, Jacques Chambrun.

I had, of course, heard about literary agents. The way I had heard about stockbrokers, corporation lawyers, and plastic surgeons. I believed in their existence the way I believed—because my teachers in school insisted it was hard fact—that the earth was round even though the evidence of my own eyes indicated clearly it was as flat as the pavements of East Fourth Street. Nobody I had ever known personally on East Fourth Street or in the Bronx had used the services of a stockbroker or a corporation lawyer or a plastic surgeon, but I did not doubt the existence of people who did. The proof was in the newspapers I read in which their doings on Broadway and in Washington and Hollywood and the capitals of the world were chronicled daily. Just as the language of the newspapers was one I read every day but never spoke, so the lives of the rich and famous were a part of my daily life even though I never clapped eyes on any of them. So it was with literary agents. I accepted the fact that people like Hugh Walpole and Fannie Hurst dealt with them regularly, the way I dealt with the corner grocer, but it never occurred to me that their services could be a part of my life. I had never met a literary agent. This is hardly surprising. At that time, aside from Lindsay C. Trimingham, I had never met a writer or an editor. The few stories I had managed to sell had gone to market and ultimately come home with checks the way it seemed to me only proper they should for a writer who lived in the Bronx: through the mails, after a series of rejections that I accepted as a necessary prerequisite to achieving a sale.

Mr. Chambrun's letter, therefore, had for me something of the quality of a winning lottery ticket. In one way it was an expected, even commonplace event. After all, every lottery had to come up with a winning ticket, and people won them all the time, as the newspapers indicated regularly. This winner, however, was not a picture in a newspaper. This winner was me. I found this fact so startling that I did not know how to accept it. Not immediately, anyway. The clients listed by Mr. Chambrun were not unlike the glamorous guests at a state function listed by Walter Winchell in his column. The list was so overpoweringly impressive that it struck me the word "impressive" was inaccurate. "Astonishing"? Closer, perhaps, but not exactly on the nose either. Digging more seriously into the debris of memory I was struck by the thought that Mr. Chambrun's list of clients seemed to me unbelievable. Yes, that was it. "Unbelievable" was the word, but I remember trying to fight it off. I didn't want to wake up, so to speak, and find it had been only a dream. Wake up, however, I did. My head was suddenly full of the mounting excitement that surely must be the common experience of all lottery winners. The slow awakening to the fact that, yes, it was true. Mr. Chambrun's letter was unmistakably addressed to me. I chewed on the excitement as slowly as I could, trying to make it last, like a Hershey bar.

Then I went to my desk, pulled out all my story files, and crammed them into my briefcase along with the textbooks I used at N.Y.U. Law School. It made for a heavy load, but not nearly so heavy as some of the loads I carried regularly for Mr. Geschwind when he went down to the Federal Court House on Foley Square. On my lunch hour I scarcely felt the weight as I carried the briefcase across town to Mr. Chambrun's office at 745 Fifth Avenue. It consisted of two rooms plus a reception area in which, when I came in, a girl was typing at a secretary's desk. I showed her the letter I had taken from my Bronx mailbox a few hours earlier.

"Let me see if Mr. Chambrun is in," she said.

I wondered how, in an office that small, she could have any doubts. She disappeared with my briefcase into one of the two rooms behind her. A few minutes later she reappeared with my law school textbooks. In my excitement I had forgotten to remove them from the briefcase.

"Mr. Chambrun says he won't be needing these," she said.

Taking the textbooks, I said, "What else did he say?"

"He'll call you when he finishes reading your material," the girl said.

I could see a complication. A couple of moments of swift thought, and I had it solved.

"During the day there's nobody to answer my phone at home, and on the job I'm in and out of the office all day," I said. This was not true but, until I knew whether Mr. Chambrun's news would be good or bad, it seemed a good idea to keep my mother out of it. "It would be better if Mr. Chambrun got in touch with me by mail," I said. "If that's all right?"

"I'm sure it will be," the girl said.

I ticked off the succeeding hours the way, years later, when my wife and I were waiting for the birth of our first child, I ticked off the days on my desk calendar. With every passing month the number of days in each month seemed to increase. Toward the end I was perfectly willing to believe the ninth month, in which I had already ticked off what seemed to me a couple of seasons, would never end. It did, of course, and so did my wait for Mr. Chambrun's letter. On checking back on my calendar for this period I find that the actual elapsed time between the day I left my stories with Mr. Chambrun's secretary and the day I received his letter was eight days. Mr. Chambrun wrote: "Dear Mr. Weidman: I am happy to report that I have sold your story 'Chutzbah' to *The New Yorker* for $125.00. The check, less my ten per cent commission, is enclosed. Sincerely, Jacques Chambrun."

I stared at the check for a long time. It would be easy enough to describe my feelings. I have never forgotten them. They all seem too ignoble, however, especially for a man determined to set down a truly true account. I will, therefore, record only one reaction. Before I knew I was involved in an arithmetical calculation I had worked out an interesting fact: the money I had been paid for this first sale to *The New Yorker* came to five dollars short of the total I had received from the sale of my five previous stories to the *American Spectator*, the *American Mercury*, and *Story*. The check from *The New Yorker* went into the bank and that night, after I came home from law school, I went back to my desk. Before I could finish the new story I had another letter from Mr. Chambrun: "Dear Mr. Weidman: I am happy to report the sale of your story 'My Aunt from Twelfth Street' to *The New Yorker*. The check, less commission, is enclosed. Sincerely, Jacques Chambrun."

I had just managed to get this second check into the bank when I received a third letter from Mr. Chambrun: "Dear Mr. Weidman: I am happy to report the sale of your story 'The Kinnehorrah' to *The New Yorker*. The check, less commission, is enclosed. Sincerely, Jacques Chambrun."

A couple of years later, when I was back in New York after

a trip around the world, I ran into Harold Ross—the founder and editor of *The New Yorker*—at a cocktail party in the home of Mr. and Mrs. E. B. White. Mrs. White had succeeded Wolcott Gibbs as my editor at *The New Yorker*, and I had just sold them a story based on an incident in which I had participated on the P. & O. ship that carried me from Marseilles to Bombay. I had met Ross three or four times, always in the office, and I always found the meetings uncomfortable. I had gathered early from the queries on my galleys that my editor was not the only one who asked difficult questions. The most difficult, indeed the only unanswerable ones, always seemed to be added by Ross, who apparently read everything that went into the magazine. Even though I had not yet seen galleys on my new story, he obviously had read it. Anyway, he had a few comments to make. One of them was: "You're the guy who sold us your first three stories in one week?"

"That's right," I said.

"You could do me a favor by telling that to O'Hara," Ross said. "He's always bitching if he sends in a new piece too soon after we've taken one, we always send the new one back."

"He could be right," I said.

Ross had the kind of hair that stands up straight, like a porcupine pelt. It looked as though each hair was set in his scalp so tightly that they were forced to huddle together, as though for warmth, and there was no room for them to bend over. When he moved his head sharply, however, they swayed. They swayed now.

"What does that mean?" he said.

"I wrote those stories over a period of a year," I said. "You turned down all three of them three times each, before you finally bought all of them three days apart."

He gave me a hard look.

"What happened?" Ross said.

"I got an agent," I said.

I thought he would laugh. He didn't.

"I don't believe that," he said.

His voice matched his look. My face grew hot.

"I can prove it," I said.

"How?" Ross said.

"I've got files," I said.

"Bring them to the office tomorrow," Ross said and walked away.

I was upset by his reaction. If I'd suspected he might be angry, I never would have told him. I was not, however, worried about proving what I'd said. I kept good files. I'd learned how in the office of Monroe Geschwind & Company. My files consisted of a manila folder for each story. The folders for "Chutzbah," "My Aunt from Twelfth Street," and "The Kinnehorrah" contained, in the batches of rejection slips attached to their carbon copies, three rejection slips each from *The New Yorker*, as well as from the other magazines that had turned them down before *The New Yorker* finally relented in the small deluge of three acceptances in one week.

"What made you keep sending them back to us?" Ross said in his office the next day after he examined the files.

"I felt you were making a mistake by sending them back to me," I said.

"I didn't," Ross said. "It was the mice."

"The what?" I said.

"Let's go to lunch," Ross said.

He took me to "21" and explained about the mice. It was the office code word for a group of Ivy League youngsters who wanted publishing experience and, to get it, were willing to do for *The New Yorker* what I, who wanted to eat, had been willing to do for Monroe Geschwind. The equivalent of running Lou G. Siegel Specials in the office of Monroe Geschwind was, in the office of *The New Yorker*, opening envelopes containing unsolicited manuscripts that came in from unknown authors or, in the trade phrase, over the transom. Just as Mr. Geschwind was strict with his instructions about cutting away all that lungy stuff from the tongue that went into his sandwich, equally strict were the instructions from Harold Ross to the mice about how to handle the unsolicited manuscripts that came in over the transom.

"We couldn't afford to have our regular editors, people like Gibbs and Mrs. White, waste their time with stuff like that,"

Ross explained. "We also didn't want people to think we disregarded this material. So we had these kids open every envelope, clip a printed rejection slip on whatever was in it, shove it back into the return envelope that usually accompanied these unsolicited things, and throw the envelope into the outgoing mail sack. That way we were covered, more or less, anyway, and we saved the valuable time of our editors for reading what came in from agents. The theory was that anything from an agent had gone through at least one professional vetting by a guy who put out hard cash for office rent and a secretary and a telephone. I can tell from the way you're giving me the hairy eyeball that you think that was cruel and barbarous treatment to the unknown geniuses out there with talent. From where I sit, however, I have to work on the theory that if he's got enough brains to get himself an agent, he'll get discovered sooner or later. That's what you did, and it worked out okay, didn't it?"

It worked out better than okay, although neither Harold Ross nor I planned it that way. Just about the time we were having lunch at "21" on Fifty-second Street, somewhere a few blocks further downtown in their offices on Madison Avenue, the people who ran Doubleday, Doran & Company, Inc. were setting in motion a plan that would change the course of a number of lives. One of these proved to be mine. It was the spring of 1934 and the Doubleday plan was for a novel contest. It was to be open only to those authors who had published one or more stories in *Story* magazine.

I suppose that, kicking around in the churning mass of unformed odds and ends, fuzzy ideas and fragmentary plots, half-baked notions and almost but not quite meticulously crafted stories, the untidy grab bag of junk and near junk that probably most young people—certainly all young writers—call their minds, I must have had a hope, shapeless of course, that someday I would write a novel. I had never given it more attention than I'd given to some of my other shapeless plans, such as getting around someday to beating Gertrude Ederle's freestyle time from the sceptered isle to Cap Gris-Nez, or discovering some confused morning that it was Betty Grable who was nudging me awake. While my plans for swimming the English Channel and making out with Betty Grable remained what they always had been, namely, the wishful thinking of an inventive but not very well organized mind, all at once the hope that I would write a novel came to the surface of the mess churning around in my head with all the force of a direct order.

The Doubleday contest was limited to authors who had been published by *Story*. Since the magazine ran about ten stories per bimonthly issue, and there had been only two or three years of such issues, the number of contestants was limited to about a hundred, perhaps two hundred at most. By a happy accident I was one of them. That night my last class at N.Y.U. Law School seemed interminable. I couldn't wait to get home to the Bronx and start writing. The closing date for the contest was November 1, 1934. That gave me about six months. Not much time for a dreamer whose idea of a novel he wished he had written was *Vanity Fair*. More than enough, however, for a writer who had learned to get his work done between running sandwiches for Monroe Geschwind and digesting cases in Williston's *Contract Law* at N.Y.U. Law School. By comparison with these two taskmasters the judges of this novel contest would be a pleasure to work for: Martha Foley of *Story* magazine; Lewis Gannett, book critic of the New York *Herald Tribune;* and Harry Maule representing Doubleday. Aside from what, by comparison with Monroe Geschwind and *Williston on Contracts*, struck me as a benevolent squad of cheerleaders, there was the prize. The award for the best novel submitted was to be $1,000 over and above royalties. Looking at what Lindbergh—just a few years earlier and even fewer years older—had been forced to do to pick up Raymond Orteig's $25,000 prize money, I swept all thoughts of difficulties out of my mind and set to work.

On what? On the story that, as soon as I decided to write a novel, rose to the surface of my mind as fully formed as a crossword puzzle when you open the morning paper. It's all there, ready and waiting. All you have to do is fill in the blank spaces. I learned early, before I realized a lesson was being hammered home, that advance planning is as necessary to the construction of a story as it is to the building of a house. It was not until some time later, when I was struggling to get beyond the lesson to the problems of implementing it, that I learned the dangers of too much planning. I was reminded of my experience with those how-to books on sex that we used to pass around in plain brown wrappers at Junior High School 64. Chapter 1, "The Male Sex Organ." Chapter 2, "The Female Sex Organ." Chapter 3, "The Human Reproductive Process." I never got to Chapter 4. By the time I reached the end of Chapter 3, I knew the next step was to forget the book and move on to the really tough part of the job: find a girl.

The same, I discovered, is true with writing a story. Planning is necessary, but a lifetime of planning will get you no further than the beautifully printed crossword puzzle in the morning paper. The time has come to forget the plan and pick up the pencil. It is not until I pick up the pencil that, I discovered, the creative process goes to work. Once the writer learns this, he must cling to what he has learned the way Troilus tried to cling to Cressida. By the time he has fashioned the shape of the crossword puzzle, he is ready to turn over to his subconscious the task of coming up with the letters to fill in the blank spaces. If he truly has faith, if he has come to terms with his subconscious and is not afraid to trust it completely, it will never let him down because the subconscious never runs dry. It is like the automobile battery that recharges itself as the car is driven. It is a stream that stocks itself for endless fishing. The subconscious spends its owner's time sucking up the life around him, storing it and cross-indexing it for convenient access when needed. That is why so many knotty plot points are solved while the writer thinks he is merely knitting up the ravelled sleave of care.

At N.Y.U. Law School we had a brilliant but boring professor who was known to his students as Ex-Lax because "he works while you sleep." The school hours of an evening-session student begin after he has put in a long, hard day on a job that provides him with the money to pay his tuition. As a result, when he opens his textbooks he not infrequently finds it difficult not to close his eyes. Evening-session students frequently wear sunglasses: they do a lot of surreptitious sleeping in class. So do writers. I don't recall that, merely because of dozing off, anybody in my class ever flunked a course. I do recall that, if only because I had learned to trust my subconscious, I solved many a story problem while catching up on my allotted forty winks while Professor Alison Reppy was droning on about common law pleading.

When I sat down to write the novel I intended to enter in the Doubleday-*Story* contest, the completely formed crossword puzzle came sliding up to the surface of my mind and clicked into place, ready and waiting for me to pick up my pencil. This particular puzzle had been taking shape, without my knowledge, of course, during my time in the C.C.N.Y. evening sessions while I was preparing to enter N.Y.U. Law School. In those days the requirements for entering law school were two: the price of the tuition, plus half the credits necessary for a B.S. or B.A. degree. In other words, the equivalent of having completed the freshman and sophomore years at an accredited liberal arts college. C.C.N.Y. was accredited, all right, but it had no endowments. It depended for its funds on the New York City budget. During the Depression the city budget was not very dependable. Not, at any rate, to young people who could get their education only in free classes that were available in the evening, after their breadwinning day's work was done.

Most of these young people came from the slums. Their only chance for escape from poverty was an education. They worked for a college degree the way an entrepreneur works for financial backing. It was the slum kid's capital. As the Depression forced deeper cuts in the city's educational budget, the evening sessions of the city colleges were the hardest hit. The number of teachers available to provide the necessary courses kept growing smaller. Acquiring the equivalent of the two years of a liberal arts degree necessary for entering law school had been for a long time, in the evening sessions, a three-year stint. By the time I started on the road so many others had taken before me, the Depression had stretched that stint to four years. Soon I began to see, as others did, that if the city budgets continued to be cut, only a fortunate few would be able to make it in five or even six years. The registration sessions, which had always been hectic, because they were run on a first-come, first-served basis, grew unpleasant. In my time at C.C.N.Y. I saw these registration sessions of the city college night schools become, literally, a bloody war. Like many wars this one remained unreported. The public seemed unaware of the situation. I never saw it mentioned in the newspapers. Everybody involved in those C.C.N.Y. evening sessions, however, was aware of the ugly struggle.

When I sat down to write the novel I planned to submit to the Doubleday-*Story* contest, my subject was ready and waiting. My outline called for a book of thirty-one chapters. I wrote them in thirty-one sessions late at night after I got home from my N.Y.U. classes, seated at the kitchen table in our Bronx apartment, working on the yellow foolscap pads provided without his knowledge by Mr. Monroe Geschwind, while munching away at the array of leftovers set out for me by my mother before she went to bed. The title, like the story itself when I began writing, was waiting for me when I finished: *Ten O'clock Scholar*.

What Nelson Doubleday called it is anybody's guess. Mine, I suspect, would be a better guess than most. I am, after all, privy to certain inside facts unknown to outside guessers. They are part of a sequence of events that began with my taking the *Ten O'clock Scholar* manuscript down to my agent's office. Up to this moment all my business with Jacques Chambrun had been conducted by mail. We had never even spoken on the telephone. This was our first face-to-face encounter.

"You look younger than I thought," he said.

I had just turned twenty, but it had not crossed my mind that he had been doing any thinking about me. By selling my stories he had made some money for me and, therefore, some for himself, but not very much. Not enough, certainly, for him to be preoccupied with the question of my age.

"So do you," I said.

This was a lie, of course, because I had formed no mental picture of him in advance. If anything, now that I was thinking of him, I thought he should have looked like the Marquis de Lafayette. I mean like the picture of Lafayette in my De Witt Clinton High School textbook on American history. After all,

Lafayette had been French. Mr. Chambrun, however, did not look like Lafayette. Not because he did not wear a powdered wig. Mr. Chambrun did not look like Lafayette because he was a dead ringer for Mussolini's son-in-law Count Ciano, who looked like Mr. Imbesi the shoemaker down on East Fourth Street. All these thoughts about who looked like who were confusing. I record them here because Jacques Chambrun was, I soon learned, a confusing man. Opinions about him in the literary world were on occasion varied but never restrained.

Max Wilkinson, a young fiction editor on *Collier's* magazine, said to me, "The son of a bitch isn't even a Frenchman. He's a renegade Argentinian. Stay away from the bastard." I saw no reason to take this advice. Jacques Chambrun was helping me overcome my terrors about embarking on the financial uncertainties of a career as a freelance writer. He was selling my stories. No other agent had offered to do so. The conversation with Max Wilkinson took place, in fact, shortly after Chambrun had sold Wilkinson my first *Collier's* story and the editor took me to lunch. Then as now the literary world traveled like Napoleon's armies: on its stomach. I have on occasion wondered how an editor would continue to function if the institution known as taking a writer to lunch was abolished. The editor could, of course, take himself to lunch, but that would be not unlike a Catholic priest taking his own confession. Rome would not go for it and, given the choice, neither would I, because I am grateful for the practice.

Without it I would have wasted far too much time learning how to bridge the gap between consuming the blintzes my mother set before me at our kitchen table in the Bronx and the ritual ingestion of the expensive delicacies served in the small cathedrals of midtown Manhattan that service the literary faithful in the Mecca of the Western world. I learned how to pretend, while wearing a small knowledgeable frown as I studied the menus that looked not unlike a press release by the Congress of Vienna, that I understood what I was reading. My J.H.S. 64 French was no help in sorting out the mysteriously named dishes which—when what I ordered, for example, proved to be a couple of fried eggs spoiled only slightly by a sauce the color of spit-out tobacco juice—I discovered somewhat incredulously were setting my host back slightly more than I had paid for my last pair of shoes. It is not a difficult game to learn, but it is important to bear in mind that it is no more than a game, and it is essential to learn it because, like tennis, it is a game ruled by snobbery. A good tennis player does not play with a duffer, and the duffer who does not learn that lesson will suffer in other areas where his career, for example, makes it necessary for him to deal with these better players. In not dissimilar fashion a publisher, much of whose life is built around the ostentatiously knowledgeable consumption of cheese, wine, and Upmann Specials, will not be inclined, in the distribution of royalty percentages, to equate the writer who knows his way around the Escoffier terrain with the ink-stained wretch who, when it is set before him for the first time, will take a swig at the contents of his finger bowl.

Fortunately, I enjoy being taken to lunch, and I am grateful to Max Wilkinson and his colleagues for introducing me to the ritual. Not only did they, with unfailing courtesy and at no expense to the recipient of their attention, help to sandpaper down the rougher of my edges in this area. They helped me to develop a feeling of confidence in dealing with the movers and shakers who were underwriting the cost of the lessons with which they were unconsciously providing me. These, in addition to the pleasures provided by food and drink, usually carried with them dividends in the way of useful information. At my first lunch with Max Wilkinson, for example, he spent most of our time together telling me stories about Jacques Chambrun's treachery. I made it clear that Chambrun had never stolen a penny from me.

"He will," said Wilkinson, and went on with another example of Chambrun's perfidy. Not too many years later Wilkinson got involved in a divorce and, not surprisingly, found he needed money. In the hope of augmenting his income he shifted from buying short stories to writing them. I never saw one in print, which may be a comment on his talent, but it could just as easily have been a comment on his knowledge of character. As his agent Max Wilkinson chose Jacques Chambrun.

Years later, long after Chambrun and I had parted company, I told Somerset Maugham about that first letter I received from Chambrun in which, to support his claim that he was a good agent, he listed some of his distinguished clients.

"Your name was among them," I said.

"It still is," Maugham said.

This surprised me. I pointed out the obvious: he was one of the most successful writers in the world. Any one of the many distinguished and completely trustworthy literary agents in the business would have been delighted to represent him. Why did Maugham remain with a man who had never bothered to deny widely circulated statements that he was a crook?

"Crookedness, if you are not a victim of it, can be a virtue," Maugham said. "I like Chambrun not because of his morals but because he lives beyond his means. As a result he is always hopelessly in debt, and to stay afloat financially he must work many times harder to earn a dollar for his clients than his rivals are willing to work for theirs."

This did not strike me as the raw material for an aphorism that might make it into a new edition of *Poor Richard's Almanac*. Maugham, however, had made more money in his day than Poor Richard had made in his, so I dropped the subject. It was raised again by Bernice Baumgarten of the Brandt & Brandt literary agency who, by that time, were my agents. Bernice and I were meeting in her office about a business matter, when her secretary came in with the afternoon paper. The *Journal-American* headline read, "Serge Rubinstein Murdered in His Fifth Ave. Mansion." Rubinstein was one of those mysterious characters who show up regularly in New York and spend a few years living in Broadway columns, where they are identified as financiers. Nobody seemed to know what Serge Rubinstein was a financier about, or perhaps I was once told but have forgotten. What I remember is his chief claim to fame. Rubinstein was notorious for spending large sums on electronically bugging the beds of his many mistresses all over Manhattan in his endless efforts to learn the identity of the men with whom they were cheating on him. Bernice Baumgarten and I looked at the headline announcing his murder, and she asked her secretary why she had brought it to our attention. The secretary pointed to a paragraph in the story she had circled in red. It said a police search of Rubinstein's papers revealed that his last deal seemed to have been a contract for his memoirs that he had signed with a New York publisher only a few days before the murder. The contract, the story said, had been negotiated by the well-known literary agent Jacques Chambrun. Bernice looked up from the *Journal-American* and uttered five words that strike me as the perfect epitaph for the man who helped me overcome my nervousness about abandoning the peace of mind of life as a salaried employee. She said, "There will be no estate."

There wasn't, but nobody knew that on the summer day in 1934 when I brought the *Ten O'clock Scholar* manuscript to Jacques Chambrun. I explained about the Doubleday-*Story* contest and told him *Ten O'clock Scholar* was my entry. Chambrun seemed surprised.

"That contest was announced only a few weeks ago," he said. "Were you working on this novel at the time?"

"No," I said.

"You started after the announcement was made?" Chambrun said.

"Yes," I said.

He flipped to the last page and looked at the number in the upper-right-hand corner.

"You're a fast worker," Chambrun said.

"I wanted to be the first," I said.

"As long as you get the manuscript in before the deadline," Chambrun said, "in a contest it is sometimes better to be the last submission that comes in."

I hadn't thought of that.

"You think we should hold up sending in my entry until it's closer to the November first deadline?" I said.

"I think we should decide whether it would be better for you to send in the manuscript yourself or let me as your agent submit it for you," Chambrun said.

"What's the difference?" I said.

"People who run novel contests, especially first-novel contests, are understandably anxious to discover new and profitable talent," Chambrun said. "They also look forward eagerly to the discovery that they are dealing with a certain amount of business innocence. There's nothing wrong with letting them feel they're getting it, especially if it works in the contestant's favor. It's important, however, to make sure the agent comes into the picture when the time arrives to draw the contract."

The statement sounded not unlike the kind of talk I had been hearing at the creditors' committee meetings in Mr. Geschwind's office for which I arranged the chairs, and in the testimony he gave in the Federal Court House for which I helped him carry the paving blocks to Foley Square. I suddenly became aware of a warning tremor in my stomach. I had run head on into one of the problems of leading a double life. Mr. Geschwind's office where I arranged chairs was commerce. My Bronx room where I wrote stories was art. All at once I could see Mr. Lindsay Trimingham's ravaged face, and I could hear his exhausted voice, and I could see his shaking hands clutched around a tumbler of my father's sacramental wine, and the tremor in my stomach identified itself. I had been granted a glimpse of one artist's future. It was accompanied by an involuntary shiver. My mother would have said somebody had just walked across my grave.

"What would you advise?" I said.

"First let me read your manuscript," Mr. Chambrun said. "I'll call you tomorrow."

One of the publications to which Mr. Geschwind subscribed was *Vanity Fair*. A regular feature of the magazine was a page called "Impossible Interviews." On it two famous people from entirely different walks of life, with diametrically opposed opinions and attitudes toward all of the world's knowledge and experience, faced each other every month without spoken words, only those brilliantly implied by the artist's devastating drawings of both people. I could see Mr. Chambrun facing my mother on the phone. For *Vanity Fair*, perhaps. For my present situation, no.

"Let me call you," I said. "What would be a good time?"

Mr. Chambrun looked at his desk calendar.

"I'll be here all morning until twelve-thirty," he said. "Then

95

I have a lunch date, but I'll be back here at, say, two-thirty or three."

The next day, at noon, on my way to Lou G. Siegel's for Mr. Geschwind's Special, I stopped in a phone booth and called Jacques Chambrun.

"I like your novel," he said. "In view of the subject matter and your treatment of it, I think a touch of innocence would work well for us with a group of contest judges. My advice would be to send the manuscript along on your own, as though you do not have an agent. I can do it for you right from here in my office and keep my name off the parcel. If you win, I'll come in to supervise the contract. If you lose, we can have a talk about where to send the manuscript next."

Jacques Chambrun and I never had that talk. A few weeks later, before the winner of the contest was announced, I received a letter from a man whose stationery indicated he was a member of the editorial staff of Doubleday, Doran & Company, Inc.

"Dear Mr. Weidman: Your novel did not I regret to say win the contest but it impressed me and Burton Rascoe. We feel it should have won. Contest or no contest, however, we would like to publish your book here at Doubleday. Could you meet us for lunch next Thursday at 12:30 in the Murray Hill Hotel? Sincerely, Ken McCormick."

I called Chambrun, read the letter to him, and asked his advice.

"Keep your lunch date, say nothing definite about anything including my relationship to you as your agent, and call me back," he said. "Do you know where the Murray Hill Hotel is?"

The question did not strike me as odd until later, when it caused me to think that perhaps Jacques Chambrun understood writers better than Max Wilkinson understood agents. All Chambrun knew about me was that I lived in the Bronx, I had a job somewhere in the garment center, and my short stories dealt with life on the docks of the Lower East Side during the early years of the twentieth century. Why should I know the location of the Murray Hill Hotel?

"No, I don't," I said. "I'll look it up in the phone book."

"It's on the northwest corner of Fortieth Street and Park Avenue," Jacques Chambrun said. "If you enter from the Park Avenue side, the bar will be on your right and the dining room straight ahead. Mr. McCormick will probably be waiting for you in the open space just outside the dining room. If he isn't, ask the headwaiter for his table."

I was an American and Mr. Chambrun, legitimate Frenchman or renegade Argentinian, was a foreigner. He obviously understood, however, that to a young man late of the Lower East Side and now living in the Bronx, the midtown Manhattan area in between might be terrain just as foreign as it had once been to him.

"Thanks," I said. I was sorry I'd been told all those stories about Chambrun's thievery. I was beginning to like him. "Do you know Mr. McCormick?" I said. "And who is Burton Rascoe?"

"Rascoe used to be a book reviewer somewhere out west," Chambrun said. "Chicago, I think, although I'm not sure, and then he was on the New York *Herald Tribune* for a while, but I do know he was quite an important figure in his field. Last year he was appointed editor-in-chief at Doubleday. I've had no business dealings with him, but Nelson Doubleday must think highly of him. I understand his salary is fifty thousand dollars a year. I met Ken McCormick once at a cocktail party, and we've corresponded on several things, so I can say he's very nice and quite bright. He used to run the Doubleday bookshop in Philadelphia. I feel quite sure this is his first editorial job. It's not a top spot, and I can't believe it pays very well, but his enthusiasm for your novel is more important to us than his salary. If his enthusiasm proves well placed, by helping you get your novel published he may be helping himself toward one day getting Mr. Rascoe's job. Do you drink?"

If it were not for that Sunday-night encounter with Lindsay C. Trimingham, I might have been puzzled by Mr. Chambrun's question. As it was I knew what to say.

"Not during the day," I said. "Why?"

"Rascoe and McCormick probably will have something, but

at this first meeting I would suggest you don't," Chambrun said. "It would be more helpful to both of us if you came away with a clear and complete account of everything that happens."

The account I gave him could not have been more clear, but it was not complete because the circumstances took me by surprise. Ken McCormick was waiting exactly where Mr. Chambrun had said he would be, and he seemed, as Chambrun had described, very nice and quite bright. I guessed him to be a few years older than I, but not many, and I had no trouble finding a slot to slide him into. My mother would have called him "one of those clean-cut uptown *goyim*," which I learned later, as I began to sort things out uptown, meant what Mr. McCormick's peers probably would have meant by a WASP. Mr. McCormick was wearing a dark brown tweed suit of which my father the pocket maker would have approved. It was the sort of thing he liked: "conservative but also a little snappy." Mr. Geschwind, on the other hand, would have considered it an example of "that Brooks Brothers shit these Yale boys who think they're credit men feel safe in." To me Mr. McCormick could have been a teller in the National City branch on the street floor of 450 Seventh Avenue, or any one of my younger instructors at N.Y.U. Law School.

"Burton will probably be a little late," he said. "He's driving in from Westport. Why don't we sit down?"

The waiter led us to a table, McCormick told him we'd be three, and asked, "What will you drink?"

"Nothing, thanks," I said.

Even though I was very tense, I managed to say it smoothly enough. My training with Max Wilkinson and other magazine editors was paying off.

"Ah, well," Mr. McCormick said, and he frowned for a moment. "Some sherry for me, please," he said to the waiter, who nodded and went away. Mr. McCormick hesitated, as though running through his mind several ways to start the conversational ball rolling and then, obviously finding one that pleased him, his face broke into a dazzling smile. "You know," he said, "you're a surprise to me."

"In what way?" I said.

98

"I expected a much older man," Mr. McCormick said. I could have said the same, but I wasn't sure that spreading my age around would be good or bad at this moment, so I decided to avoid the subject by pretending he had said nothing. This seemed to upset him, so he rushed in with, "I mean it's such a damned mature book."

He said a lot more, all of it pleasant, but none of it very sharply defined. So that while I gathered he wanted me to know he thought highly of me and my novel, he also wanted me to be aware his opinion was not the one that counted, except perhaps as a sort of warm-up for the imminent appearance of the opinion that did. It arrived in the form of a small, thin, angry-looking man walking rapidly toward us across the restaurant. He was carrying a fat briefcase and the wings of his trench coat flapped as though they were sails with which he was trying to catch a breeze.

"Sorry to be late," he said. "It's that damned traffic. Gahd!"

He didn't look sorry at all. From the sharp, hard examination he gave me I had the feeling he was trying to decide whether I was worth joining at table. The decision apparently went in the affirmative, but it seemed to take him by surprise. He sat down suddenly, hitting the chair the way I've hit the water when somebody pushed me without warning into a swimming pool, and I saw that the sharp, hard glance had shifted from me to Mr. McCormick's glass.

"What's that?" the newcomer said.

"Sherry," Mr. McCormick said.

"Gahd!" the newcomer said. "Waiter!"

The word went out across the restaurant like a batted fungo sailing for the fence. I almost expected the waiter to take off in an effort to snag it before it went out of the ball park, but he stood his ground. His ground was perhaps eighteen inches to the left of the newcomer's ear.

"Yes, Mr. Rascoe?" he said quietly.

"Oh, there you are," Mr. Rascoe said. "Gahd, that damned traffic. Bring me a dry martini and a large order of snails. If you haven't got them, send out for them. I want snails."

"We have them, Mr. Rascoe," the waiter said.

"Good," Mr. Rascoe said. "Make that martini a double, and bring it the same way."

"Sir?" the waiter said.

"On the double," Mr. Rascoe said.

"Yes, sir," the waiter said and went away.

"Burton, this is Jerome Weidman," Ken McCormick said.

"I should hope so," Burton Rascoe said. "If it was anybody else after that damned traffic, I'd get up and leave." He shoved his hand across the table as though he was pushing his way through a swing door. "It's a great pleasure to meet you," he said as our hands met. I was pleasantly surprised. His grip was not at all like his fuss. It was clean and hard, like his glance. "I hope Ken told you how we feel about your book."

"He did," I said.

"Good," Mr. Rascoe said, but apparently it was not good enough. For him, anyway, because he proceeded to tell me on his own, and it made for some very pleasant listening. Not only because what he said was complimentary to me, but because the way he said it made for pleasant listening even after my name disappeared from the sentence. Mr. Rascoe's speech was like his handshake, stuck full of sharp images that were not only decorative but also provided glimpses of the image maker's personality. At one point he was saying something about my style, and I had a moment of shock. It had not occurred to me that I had a style. I just wrote. I wondered nervously what he meant. A few moments of that particular kind of nervousness and I decided I'd better stop wondering and get back to listening before I became confused about the way I did what I had been doing without self-conscious analysis for almost four years. When I resurfaced into Mr. Rascoe's monologue he was winding up a short verbal essay on style in general, and was just mentioning a young poet he admired. "For my money," Mr. Rascoe said, "that young man has written some of the finest sonnets ever set down in the English language by anybody, and that does not exclude the shorter work of Mr. William Shakespeare." The entertainment had an extra dimension. It made you feel you belonged to the enlightened circles for which the performer usually entertained.

Ken McCormick was obviously accustomed to these circles,

but I was not, so I kept my mouth shut and listened. What I heard among other things was a discourse on the recuperative powers of snails on the human body, especially if ingested as the first meal of the day after what Mr. Rascoe called "a short night." I watched with fascination as he ate his way through a mound of what I had never before known is a widely consumed human comestible but, of course, I had never before seen a human being eat them. Doing it, Mr. Rascoe provided more entertainment for his audience than some jugglers I had in my time paid to see at the Old Jeff on Fourteenth Street. Mr. Rascoe ordered a second helping while Ken McCormick and I worked our way through eggs Benedict, a dish I had only recently seen eaten in public. It was set before me because, when Mr. McCormick ordered his, I employed one of the gambits I had picked up in my earlier Max Wilkinson skirmishes: I gave up the pretense of studying the menu and said, "I'll have the same."

Somewhere between the turns in Mr. Rascoe's variety bill, which Mr. McCormick kept in motion like a skilled director hidden in a prompter's box, the reason for our meeting was thoroughly explored. I can't remember now just how it was done but I came away with two things. First, the feeling that without Mr. McCormick's deft behind-the-scenes management, so to speak, nothing about me and my novel would have been mentioned; and, two, a clear summing up of the status of *Ten O'clock Scholar* at Doubleday, Doran & Company, Inc.

"They both like the book and they want to publish it," I reported to Jacques Chambrun from a phone booth on Seventh Avenue later that afternoon.

"But?" he said.

"But?" I said. "What do you mean 'but'?"

"But they're not going to publish it is what I mean," Jacques Chambrun said.

"I didn't say that," I said.

"They said it, though, didn't they?" Chambrun said.

"How do you know?" I said.

"If they did not say something like that, I think you would not have started your report by saying Mr. McCormick and Mr. Rascoe want to publish your novel," Chambrun said. "I think you would have started your report by saying they plan to publish your novel. What's the problem?"

"Nelson Doubleday," I said. "He owns the company."

"I am aware of Mr. Doubleday's relationship to Doubleday, Doran & Company, Inc.," Jacques Chambrun said. "Why is he trouble in your case?"

"He says the house of Doubleday has never published a book with words in it like the ones I use in *Ten O'clock Scholar*, and he's not going to start now."

"So they're turning the book down?" Chambrun said.

"Oh, no," I said. "It's nothing like that."

"Mr. Weidman," Chambrun said, "I would like to point out that in his relationship to an author's book the publisher has only two alternatives. He can accept it or he can reject it. What is Doubleday doing with yours?"

"Neither," I said.

"Meaning what?" Jacques Chambrun said.

"Mr. Rascoe and Mr. McCormick feel they can change Mr. Doubleday's mind," I said.

"How?" Jacques Chambrun said.

"By putting up a fight for the book," I said.

Pause. A rather long one.

"Mr. Chambrun?"

"Yes, I'm on," he said. "I was just thinking."

"About what?" I said.

"What Mr. McCormick and Mr. Rascoe have in the way of ammunition for such a fight," Chambrun said.

"Mr. McCormick admits he has very little," I said. "Mr. Rascoe, however, has his job."

Pause. Very short.

"His fifty-thousand-dollar-a-year job?" Chambrun said.

Very dry.

"His seventy-five-thousand-dollar-a-year job," I said.

"He's got a raise?" Chambrun said.

Even drier.

"Not yet, but his contract comes up for renewal next month," I said. "If it is renewed, his salary goes to seventy-five thousand dollars a year."

"And unless Nelson Doubleday agrees to publish *Ten O'clock Scholar* Burton Rascoe will refuse to renew his seventy-five-thousand-dollar-a-year contract?"

"As of now," I said.

"What happens after as of now?" Chambrun said.

"I don't know, but Ken has promised to call me in a few days and let me know," I said.

"You call him Ken?" Chambrun said.

"He asked me to," I said.

Pause. Not long, not short. Sort of in between.

"Did my name come into the discussion?" Chambrun said.

"No, I followed your instructions on that," I said. "Neither Ken nor Mr. Rascoe knows that I have an agent."

"Good," Jacques Chambrun said. "Let's keep it that way until you hear from Ken."

I heard a week later. Ken McCormick sent me a note. It consisted of one sentence. "Could you meet me for lunch next Tuesday at 12:30 at the Richelieu."

I called Jacques Chambrun and read the note to him.

"Do you know where the Richelieu is?" he said.

"No," I said.

"It's an old Stanford White mansion that was a speakeasy during Prohibition," Chambrun said. "Now it's an expense-account clip joint on Thirty-eighth Street just off Madison, across the street from the J. P. Morgan Library. May I make a suggestion?"

"Of course," I said.

"Let's not change our tactics," Chambrun said. "Let Ken do all the talking, you continue to keep my name out of it, and then report to me as soon as you can get to a phone."

On Tuesday, after my lunch with Ken McCormick, I said to Jacques Chambrun from a phone booth, "It's sort of funny."

"In what way?" Chambrun said.

"Ken reported that they lost the fight with Nelson Doubleday," I said.

" 'They' means Burton Rascoe too?" Chambrun said.

"Both of them," I said.

"I haven't heard any gossip in the trade that he's quit his

fifty-thousand-dollar-a-year job which next month will be paying him seventy-five thousand," Jacques Chambrun said.

It occurred to me that, while the jury may still have been out on two points—whether Jacques Chambrun was a bona fide Frenchman or a renegade Argentinian, and whether he was an honest agent or a crook—on one point I did not need the services of a jury for enlightenment. All I had to do was recall my father's observations about the young men on East Fourth Street he used to call *leidigeiers*. Although these vaguely menacing characters did not seem to have any visible means of support, they were able to consume in public large quantities of East Fourth Street's most popular delicacy, the charlotte russe: a small ring of sponge cake encased in a white cardboard container, topped by whipped cream, and surmounted by a red maraschino cherry. Because of their dedication to this concoction these *leidigeiers* were also known on the block as charlotte-russe-niks. As soon as I set eyes on Jacques Chambrun I knew that underneath the accent lurked a Gallic version of an old-fashioned, garden-variety, East Fourth Street charlotte-russe-nik.

"Ken said that was a sort of exaggeration on Mr. Rascoe's part," I said. "Just to prove to me how strongly he felt about my book."

"Ken must have said something more," Chambrun said.

"He said he was so mad at Nelson Doubleday's stupidity, and so was Mr. Rascoe, that they want to talk about the book to some of their friends in other publishing houses around town."

"What's stopping them?" Chambrun said.

"They want my permission," I said.

"Why?" Chambrun said.

"Because what it would amount to, Ken said, it would mean they'd be sort of acting as my agents, if you know what I mean."

"But you already have an agent," Chambrun said. "You are talking to him right now."

"I know," I said.

"What did Ken say to that?" Chambrun said.

"I didn't tell him," I said.

"Why not?" Chambrun said.

"You told me not to change our tactics," I said. "You told me to keep your name out of it."

Pause.

"Mr. Chambrun?"

"Yes, I'm here," he said. "As of now, then, neither Ken McCormick nor Burton Rascoe knows you have an agent?"

"That's right," I said.

Another pause. It grew longer. I did nothing to interfere with its growth. The ball, as John Kieran was fond of saying in his *New York Times* sports column, was in the other man's court.

"If you have no objection," Chambrun said finally, "I think it would be a good idea for us not to change our tactics at this stage."

"You want me to say yes to them?" I said. "They should go ahead and show *Ten O'clock Scholar* to their friends in other publishing houses?"

"Unless you have other thoughts?" Chambrun said.

I had many, but I still did not feel sure of myself with any of these uptown people. Not completely, anyway. I kept running into things with them that would not have surprised me on East Fourth Street or Seventh Avenue. To have accepted them in places like the Murray Hill Hotel and the Richelieu, however, from people who ate snails and published books, would have diminished the very special feelings I had achieved unexpectedly when I received that letter from "The Editors" of the *American Spectator* and, sitting in the subway on the way to work, I had leafed through the copy of the O. Henry Memorial Award stories that had been sent to me free by the publisher because my story "My Father Sits in the Dark" appeared in it. To have acknowledged to myself that I was upset by those thoughts about these uptown people would have smudged the brightness of those moments from a completely new world that I would never have touched without them. I decided to give them the benefit of the doubt and stick with the brightness. I didn't know where it was leading, but I felt strongly it would be better than East Fourth Street or the Bronx.

"I have only one thought," I said. "I want to get my book published."

"This may be the way to do it," Chambrun said. "With a fifty-thousand-dollar-a-year Doubleday editor trying to sell a book to a rival publisher the chances are your book won't be over-looked."

It wasn't. Ken McCormick made that plain at our third lunch. This one took place in Childs. I never asked, but I suspect this lunch did not find its way onto Mr. McCormick's Doubleday expense account. He ordered pancakes. I said I'd have the same. While I ate them he told me of a sad discovery he and Burton Rascoe had made.

"Everybody to whom we showed the manuscript agreed with our judgment, they all said it was wonderful, but nobody was sufficiently interested to take it on."

Ken had a marvelous smile, but it was not nearly so marvelous as his look of grief. When Ken was sad the expression on his face looked as though it had been borrowed from the illustrations of Cervantes's knight of the doleful countenance. As he continued I could feel my heart struggling with the desire to ache for him, but I forced it to behave because I wanted to pay close attention to what he said.

Ken McCormick said, "What Burton and I apparently overlooked was that all these people to whom we showed the manuscript, the more enthusiastic we were, the more suspicious they seemed to become. They didn't say so to me and Burton, of course, but it got back to us that they all called each other up and said if it's such a great novel, why doesn't Doubleday publish it?"

Since this was precisely the question that had been churning around in my head for some time, I thought it would have been rude to ask it now. I finished Ken's pancakes, thanked him for everything he and Mr. Rascoe had tried to do for me, and asked him to return the manuscript. When it arrived in the Bronx I stuffed it into my briefcase and carried it down to Chambrun's office.

"I'll see what I can do," he said. "But I think selling *Ten O'clock Scholar* is going to be difficult. Your friends at Doubleday must have shown it to all the better houses. I'll do the best I can, but I have a feeling I'll just be following in their footsteps. Maybe it would be better if we just put this one aside for a while, and wait until you have something else?"

"That's what I've been thinking," I said, and pulled another manuscript from my briefcase. "Here's a new one you might have a look at."

Surprise was not an expression that made frequent appearances on Jacques Chambrun's face. When it did, as it did now, it was a little unsettling. Like opening a valentine and discovering it was from Jack the Ripper.

"When did you write this?" he said.

"While Ken McCormick and Burton Rascoe were showing *Ten O'clock Scholar* to their friends in other publishing houses," I said. "I'll be interested to hear what you think."

Jacques Chambrun's thoughts were not encouraging.

"The new book seems to be a sequel to *Ten O'clock Scholar*," he said to me the next day.

"That's right," I said. "*Ten O'clock Scholar* deals with my hero when he is a student in the evening session at C.C.N.Y. This new book deals with him later in his career, when he's a shipping clerk in the garment center."

"After the reception the first Harry Bogen manuscript has just received," Jacques Chambrun said, "I wonder if it's wise to circulate to the publishers a second book about the same character so soon."

I had a moment of indecision. No, not indecision. I had a moment of cowardice. A couple of months earlier—before my lunch with Ken McCormick and Burton Rascoe at the Murray Hill—I would have suppressed my true feelings and acquiesced at once in Chambrun's suggestion. It was not, however, a couple of months earlier. It was a couple of months later. I had been moving up with reluctance on a slowly emerging revelation: the man who had told me how to enter the Murray Hill Hotel from the correct side, and how to find the Richelieu, may very well have taught me all that, in the end, any agent can teach a writer. He couldn't teach you how to feel about your work. Only the person out of whose feelings the work has managed to get down on paper could teach you that.

"Stop listening," an inner voice was suddenly hissing in my ear. "His job is to sell it. Let him do his job."

"I planned the Harry Bogen story as a trilogy," I said to

Jacques Chambrun, trying hard in an attempt at firmness to forget the moment of cowardice. "I'm already at work on a third volume, so I feel we might as well send the second one to market. If you don't feel you can do that, maybe I should get somebody else to try it for me?"

Chambrun's glance held mine for a long moment. I was pretty sure that if he couldn't read in my eyes that I was bluffing, he certainly should have been able to hear it from the pounding of my heart. I was, however, sure of something else. If I was right, and underneath the bona fide Frenchman or the renegade Argentinian there lurked an old-fashioned, garden-variety East Fourth Street charlotte-russe-nik, he would recognize in his cocky young client at least his match and, in this situation, at any rate, conceivably his master. As the client who could pick up his marbles and go find a more congenial game elsewhere, I had the whip hand.

"Very well," Jacques Chambrun said with a smile. "I'll see what I can do."

This proved to be not much. After the sixth rejection, a copy of which he sent me as he had sent me the first five, I typed a short note.

"Dear Mr. Chambrun: Thanks for sending along the rejection letters. Please do not send me any more communications about this manuscript until you feel it has been seen by every possible market. Reading these rejection letters seems to get in the way of my work on volume three of the Harry Bogen saga."

Two days later Chambrun was on the phone.

"I just had a call from Richard L. Simon's secretary," he said. "That's Richard L. Simon of Simon and Schuster. She told me she had a telegram from her boss in Florida. He's there with the Artists and Writers Club. On the train going down he read your story in this week's *New Yorker*. As soon as he got off the train he wired her saying he'd never read anything by you before, in fact he's never heard of you, but he liked the story. He told her to call *The New Yorker*, find out if you have an agent, and ask if you have a novel-length manuscript."

"You know I have," I managed to say calmly to Jacques Chambrun. "Send Mr. Simon the second Harry Bogen novel."

"I did," Chambrun said. "They turned it down last week. I didn't tell you about it because you instructed me not to send any more rejection letters."

I tried to re-create the situation in the Simon & Schuster office, using as my model the only office I knew: Monroe Geschwind & Company. Inside my head I put Mr. Geschwind on a train to Florida. I sat him down in a club car and gave him a copy of the current *New Yorker*, and I didn't have to go any further. I was sure I knew what had happened.

"Mr. Weidman?"

"Yes, I'm on," I said into the phone. "The fact that Simon and Schuster turned the book down last week doesn't matter."

"Why not?" Chambrun said.

"Richard L. Simon didn't turn it down," I said.

"What difference does that make?" Chambrun said. "A rejection is a rejection."

"Not necessarily," I said. "Simon and Schuster must have the same office setup that Doubleday and all publishers have. They have to or they couldn't function. Unsolicited manuscripts go to the editorial department, not to the head of the firm. Who signed the Simon and Schuster rejection letter?"

"Hold it a moment, please," Chambrun said. When he came back on the phone he said, "Quincy Howe, editor-in-chief."

"Here's what you should do," I said. "Don't say anything to anybody about the rejection last week, and don't mention Quincy Howe's name. Just send the manuscript back marked for the personal attention of Mr. Simon's secretary, and we'll see what happens."

What happened was so overwhelming, and it came so fast, that I never had time to examine any of it in detail while it was happening. All I could do was feel, and what I felt did not feel right. It was not like that moment, after I sold my first story to the *American Spectator*, when I came out of the telephone booth in a pleasant daze, with the conviction that my life had changed as suddenly and irrevocably as the eruption of Krakatoa changed the geography of the Sunda Strait. It wasn't like that at all.

What happened after Jacques Chambrun sent the manuscript of the second Harry Bogen novel to Simon & Schuster marked for the personal attention of Mr. Simon's secretary was what happened when Aladdin rubbed the lamp and Arthur drew the sword from the stone. The world I had known all my life started to fall away from me and I could feel myself falling into a totally new one. All at once what I had for so long lived with as a secret dream was being handed to—no, hurled at—me in such great big shattering chunks that there was no time for coming out of phone booths in a pleasant daze. Everything was happening too fast. I felt not pleasure but fear. The kids I grew up with, Mr. Geschwind and his staff, my workroom in the Bronx, girls I'd come to know at C.C.N.Y. and N.Y.U. Law School, even the members of my own family, all seemed to be receding, leaving me among strangers. Worst of all, my ambivalence about stepping out into the world stopped being an ambivalence. It became a hard fact into which I was kicked before I could think, or protest, or do any more stalling. I couldn't turn back the clock. I could no longer pretend to myself I was trying to make up my mind. It had been made up for me. Whether I liked it or not, the days of working toward a nice steady flow of Yankee bean soup with a comfortable pension at the end of the road, all that was behind me. I was no longer a law student who did a little writing on the side to pick up some pocket money. I was a professional. Out in the market place. Responsible for supporting myself and my dependents. I was a freelance writer, for Christ's sake. And I was scared stiff. That small unidentified inner voice stepped in, pulled me up short, and took over.

"Stop thinking," it said. "Don't do anything. Just ride along with it until the dust settles, and then you can pause for more careful examination."

"How do I know I'll be able to pause?" I said.

"You're a writer, aren't you?"

"But this isn't a story," I said.

"How do you know?"

I hadn't thought of that.

"Stop thinking," the voice said. "You can worry about the story in it later. Right now, while you're in the middle of it, before you lose some of the details, just jot down what's happening."

What was happening was what would have happened in the office of Monroe Geschwind & Company if they had been in the business of publishing books instead of auditing them. The Simon & Schuster editorial department never knew the manuscript had made a second appearance in their office. It went directly from Jacques Chambrun to the desk of Richard L. Simon's secretary, a girl named Lee Wright. She read the manuscript, liked it, and held it for Mr. Simon's return from Florida. When he came back Mr. Simon read the manuscript. He liked it, bought it, and published it.

The book was a success. Hemingway said I was the American Balzac. "Don't let them get you down, kid," he wrote me in the Bronx. "Because I think you can write just a little better than anybody else that's around." Rebecca West said I was "a brilliant novelist, a true satirist, and a deadly wit." Almost everybody—except Ring Lardner, of course—said I was the new Ring Lardner. Mr. Geschwind said good-bye. On the long-distance phone from New Haven my Aunt Sadie said to my mother, "I hear Jerome has written an anti-Semitic book called *I Can Get It for You Wholesale.*"

"I haven't had a chance to read it yet," said my mother who, of course, could not read English or any other language. "But if it's good enough for Simon and Schuster, it's good enough for me."

seven

The success of *I Can Get It for You Wholesale* took me by surprise. It looked good, but it felt wrong. Until the morning of May 5, 1937, when the novel was published, my yardstick for the feel of success was the hour after I had my first editorial conference in the office of *The New Yorker*.

I'd had a note from Wolcott Gibbs asking me to come in for a talk about some corrections he felt should be made in "Chutz-bah," the first story the magazine bought from me. "Some corrections" proved to be a surprisingly long list. The first item on the list was the title of the story. Gibbs was not sure about whether he had ever heard the word spoken aloud, but he was certain the top sheet of my manuscript was the only place he had ever seen the word on paper. He asked how it was pronounced. I pronounced it for him. He tried it.

"No, not with a *p*," I said. "The word is *chutzbah*. With a *b* as in boy."

"Are you sure?" Gibbs said.

"Positive," I said.

"The copy department feels it should be spelled with a *p*," Gibbs said.

"They're wrong," I said.

"Hmm," Gibbs said. For a moment or two his pencil circled indecisively over the top galley. "In that case," he said finally, "I take it you don't want the title changed?"

"No," I said.

The pencil did some more fussing in the air, as though it had a life of its own and he was having difficulty keeping it from coming down to mark the paper.

"What makes you so certain you're right about the pronunciation?" Gibbs said.

"I first heard the word from my mother," I said. "That's the way she pronounces it."

He gave me a long, hard look.

"All right," he said finally, and made a note at the top of the first galley. "Now let's see what else we have here."

It was my first contact with the editorial we. We went through the rest of the list without too much trouble. Most of the questions struck me as sensible, the kind Miss Garrigues, my English teacher at De Witt Clinton, would have asked. There was no reason why Wolcott Gibbs should have known any more than she did about East Fourth Street.

"Well, that does it," Gibbs said when we finished. "The only thing left we have to cope with then is the title. The copy department gets a bit sticky about these things. Is there any chance you might change your mind?"

"No," I said.

"Why not?" Gibbs said.

"My mother would disapprove," I said.

He gave me another sharp look, then grinned and put out his hand.

"Nice meeting you," Gibbs said as we shook. "Come in again soon."

In order to understand how I felt when I walked out of his office it helps me to remember that I began to read *The New Yorker* in 1925, the year it started publication. I was twelve. Two years later, when I entered De Witt Clinton High School, I discovered that to every one of us in Miss Ellen M. Garrigues's English class the magazine had already assumed a relationship not unlike that of James Boswell to Dr. Johnson. There is a word for it: reverence. The feeling and the word moved side by side with me when I walked out of Wolcott Gibbs's office carrying the manila clasp envelope containing the galleys of my first *New Yorker* story.

I had stolen the time for the conference from the hours that, for the eleven dollars a week he paid me, I owed Mr. Geschwind. As soon as the conference was over I should have hurried back to his office on Seventh Avenue before he suspected the theft, but I was in no condition to face anybody. I was in the grip of a need to be alone. I walked from the *New Yorker* office on Forty-third Street to Bryant Park on Forty-second Street and sat down on a bench facing the back of the New York Public Library. That's all I did. I just sat there, my hands resting in my lap on the envelope containing the galleys. I watched the people crossing through the park and I listened to my thumping heart settle slowly back to a normal beat. I wondered how the passersby would react if I called out.

"Hey, you guys, you know what I've got here? A set of galleys from *The New Yorker*. That's right, *The New Yorker*. Galleys. Yeah, mine. A story I wrote. They bought it. They're going to publish it. That's right, *The New Yorker*. You don't believe me? Here, look."

I didn't call out, of course. That would have spoiled it. Without thinking about it I knew the intensity of the pleasure was caused by the fact that it was so intensely private. Nobody else was involved. Just the two of us, me and it. This incredible thing that had happened to me, the owner of the face I scraped with a razor every morning. This thing that set me apart from all these people crossing Bryant Park, from all my classmates in Miss Garrigues's English class, from Mr. Geschwind and all the members of his staff, and I was the only one who knew it had happened to me. For the moment I wanted to keep it that way. Because I had already learned how much better it was at this moment than it would be when the inevitable sharing time came rolling around.

My trouble with the publication of *I Can Get It for You Wholesale* was that when it came along it did not bring with it a Bryant Park bench. There was no time or place to pause for a slow soak-up of private pleasure. It was not unlike the detonation of a land mine in a modest backyard vegetable garden. I had been strolling among the radishes and tomatoes, quietly pleased with the way my plants were flourishing. A few short stories sold at pleasantly spaced intervals, a certain amount of praise from a few editors, a sense of slowly growing confidence in myself. Carefully concealed, of course. Not so much out of modesty as a secret dread about tempting fate. I grew up believing that if something good happened to you—topping your class in an exam, for example—it was all right to feel delighted, even gleeful, but it was important to pretend outwardly that it had happened to somebody else. If you blew your own horn, if you showed off in even the smallest way, you were calling to yourself the attention of The Man Up There who, it seemed to me, was in the business of maintaining a sharp lookout for people who were asking to have themselves taught a lesson. As each of my small triumphs occurred I allowed myself a short private celebration. In public, however, which meant even to the members of my own family, I gave it what was known at De Witt Clinton as the S.K.A.S. or Shit Kickers Aw Shucks treatment.

I Can Get It for You Wholesale was a totally different experience. It was not a short story that, along with other stories by other writers, appeared in a thing called a magazine sold on newsstands. *I Can Get It for You Wholesale* was a book. The contents were written by one person. The book was sold not on newsstands in the subway or kiosks on street corners. It was sold in special places built and maintained solely for its distribution: bookstores. It could not, like a short story, be shielded from public scrutiny by being jammed in a magazine along with other stories. *I Can Get It for You Wholesale*, being a book, was singled out for individual attention by people hired to do so: reviewers, sometimes called critics. They treated the appearance of a book the way plays were treated when they appeared on a stage: in a special section of a newspaper or a magazine reserved for the appearance of such comment. It was rare for an issue of a magazine to be reviewed in the press, even more rare for a particular story in a magazine to be singled out for special comment from the other stories with which it appeared in a magazine. The short-story writer was, therefore, more or less immune from public comment until he assembled some of his stories in a collection and published them as a book.

I had been reading book reviews almost as long as I had been reading books. If I had given the matter any thought, I am sure I would have been aware that a favorable review was a matter of pleasure to the author of the book, and an unfavorable review was a matter of pain. The pleasure as well as the pain, however, had never been very real to me. Any more than the blows Jack Dempsey gave and took in the course of a bout were real to me. When he won I shared his pleasure because I was one of his fans, and when he lost, which as I recall he almost never did, I'm sure I would have shared his pain—because I was more than a fan: he was one of my heroes—but even then the emotions were secondhand. The publication of *I Can Get It for You Wholesale* was my first contact with these emotions at first hand.

The reviews, it seemed to me, were all good. Anyway, I now think they were. I cannot recall a bad one. More accurately, probably, time has edited the bad ones out of my memory. So that all I remember is an outpouring of favorable comment, concentrated in the brief period before and after publication. The comments came so fast that there was no time to treat each one separately, the way I had grown accustomed to treating the praise of editors when they bought one of my short stories: with a private inner pause for thorough absorption. There was nothing private about the reviews of *I Can Get It for You Wholesale*. It was a public onslaught. There were no inner glows. I was caught in a bonfire. There was no way to stand aside modestly to avoid the attention of The Man Up There. I was thrust forward to take the heat. Common sense told me taking it was part of success. If it had been in my power to do so, I knew I wouldn't have avoided a moment of it. I also knew I was being singed. I could feel the blisters coming up. I wanted to turn and run. I didn't know how to do that, however, so I stood there and grinned happily as I felt myself shrivel inwardly.

Part of the intensity of the heat, I learned later, was an accident. At that time Simon & Schuster was already famous in publishing circles for the large amounts of advertising space it purchased in the pages of the *New York Times*. As a result, by committing themselves in advance to buying a certain amount of lineage per annum, they were able to obtain from the *Times* substantially reduced rates per line. Just before *I Can Get It for You Wholesale* was published, Dick Simon discovered that the

Essandess list for the balance of the year was smaller than his firm had anticipated when they signed their last contract with the *Times*. Unless they used up the space for which they had contracted, they would lose the privilege of the lower rates the *Times* had quoted. Dick Simon decided on a gamble. Instead of spreading out the paid-for space on all the books he thought they would be publishing when he signed the *New York Times* contract, he shot the works on the only book Simon & Schuster then had ready for publication: *I Can Get It for You Wholesale*.

On May 5, 1937, the official publication date, even a non–book reader of the *New York Times*, thumbing his way to the sports section or the stock market quotations, was probably jolted to a pause on the book page. A single ad, running from the top to the bottom, dominated the page. For the next few weeks the ad dominated not only other pages, in the Sunday *Book Review* as well as the daily *Times*, but my every waking moment. The first such moment, of course, came on publication date, when I came into the office and found Mr. Geschwind waiting for me. He was holding a five-dollar bill.

"Get over to Macy's," he said, shoving the bill at me. "Get me this book."

He pointed to a copy of the *New York Times*. It was folded back to the book page. The Simon & Schuster ad for *I Can Get It for You Wholesale* leaped out at me like Charlie Paddock breasting the tape. The ad consisted of a picture of the book jacket. The jacket consisted of twelve words splashed in large letters across the page: "*I Can Get It for You Wholesale*, A Novel by Jerome Weidman." I could not believe Mr. Geschwind had not noticed my name on the jacket of the book he was sending me out to buy. I waited for him to say something more.

"Get the lead out," he said. "I'm in a hurry."

The Seventh Avenue entrance to Macy's is directly across the street from the Nelson Tower, the building in which Monroe Geschwind & Company had its office. The half mile of Seventh Avenue that runs from Times Square to Penn Station is probably the most congested piece of jammed traffic in the world. The huge trucks loaded with dresses rarely manage to move faster than a crawl. Nobody waits for traffic lights. On that morning I certainly didn't. I headed out into the wide street in a leaping life-threatening zigzag. The Macy's book department was on the ground floor, separated from Seventh Avenue by the men's haberdashery department. Pushing my way through the crowd, long before I made it out of the shirts and neckties, I could see up ahead at the top of a pyramid of books a copy of *I Can Get It for You Wholesale*. When I did break through into the book department I found myself on the edge of the shoppers gathered around the *I Can Get It for You Wholesale* display. I made no effort to move faster. I allowed myself to be carried closer to the display by easing my way around customers who were coming away from the table with their purchases. Not until I paid for my copy with Mr. Geschwind's five-dollar bill did I realize my book was retailing for two dollars.

Before I managed to break out of the crowd into a cleared space where I could pause to examine my purchase, my mind had leaped up to the Bronx, where, in the drawer of the desk in my bedroom, my Simon & Schuster contract rested. Inside my head I flipped the pages until I came to the clause marked "Royalties." It called for a straight 10 percent royalty based on the book's retail price. By sending me out to buy a copy of *I Can Get It for You Wholesale* Mr. Geschwind had earned for me twenty cents in royalties. In a small way—as though a solid platform on which we had both been standing for a long time had during the night settled significantly into the ground—I felt our relationship had suffered an abrupt change.

"Don't just stand there," Mr. Geschwind said irritably when I delivered the book and the three dollars in change from his five-dollar bill. "They're waiting for you on the Cantor-Greenspan audit. Get over there and stay with it until—" He looked at his wristwatch. "Meet me back here at twelve sharp. Don't be late. It's important."

Cantor-Greenspan was not a bankruptcy audit. The Cantor-Greenspan Company was one of Mr. Geschwind's regular clients, a fabrics house whose books and records the Geschwind staff audited every month. I had been going to the Cantor-Greenspan premises with other Geschwind employees ever since Mr. Geschwind had hired me. I knew the staff. They knew me.

Yet today they acted as though they did not. Nobody paid any attention to me. I reported to the senior in charge. He assigned me to the accounts-receivable ledger. I took my place at the appropriate desk and went to work. Nobody spoke to me, not even about the audit. I wondered if it was possible that none of these people had seen that morning's book page in the *New York Times*. Knowing my colleagues on the Geschwind staff pretty well by now, I decided it was not only possible but also probable. It occurred to me that, without being aware of it, they were providing me with that bench in Bryant Park for which only a few hours earlier I had been yearning. Now, instead of yearning, I was burning. Could it be they were jealous? Were they deliberately snubbing me? Well, two could play at the same game. I snubbed back. At a quarter to twelve I stood up and went across to the senior in charge of the audit. He saw me coming. He glanced at his watch.

"Mr. Geschwind told me he wants you back in the office at twelve sharp," he said. "You better take off."

When I got to the Geschwind office the switchboard operator told me Mr. Geschwind was not in.

"He left word you should meet him at Pat Caruso," she said.

Pat Caruso was a custom tailor on Thirty-ninth Street. He had a large clientele among garment-center salesmen and people who functioned in the area known as around Broadway. Pat Caruso made Mr. Geschwind's clothes. Up to that time I'd had only two experiences with clothing stores. First, the cramped shops on Stanton Street to which my father used to take me when I was a boy for the annual purchase of my "good" suit. I wore it to synagogue during the high holidays and, after that, for all ceremonial occasions during the rest of the year. My second experience was with Howard's, the chain store. In its Herald Square shop, soon after I went to work for Mr. Geschwind, I bought the first suit for which I paid with money I had earned myself. My father understood my desire to make the purchase on my own. He could not, however, resist giving me a piece of advice.

"A suit you have to wear a long time after you walk out of

the store," he said. "So don't buy only with the eyes. Buy also with the head. Make sure you pick something that's conservative, but also a little snappy."

I had never been inside an establishment like Pat Caruso's. It was not congested, like Stanton Street. It was not vast, like Howard's. It was intimate. The window display consisted of a bolt of tweed cloth artfully spread across a velvet trestle. The lighting inside was subdued, the atmosphere hushed. There was, when I walked in, only one customer. He stood on a small, slightly raised platform, like a statue on a plinth in the park. He was attended by two men. One was elderly, with a look of expensive weariness. He reminded me of an actor playing a member of Balkan royalty in a movie about political intrigue during the period that preceded my father's broom service behind Franz Josef's cavalry. The other and much younger man could have been his equerry. The older man had a tape measure around his neck. He held a piece of marking chalk between thumb and forefinger as though it was the pen with which he was about to sign a treaty that had been long in the making. The equerry wore an alpaca coat. Both lapels were stuck with pins the way a baked ham in the Hormel ads is stuck with cloves. He held a pad and pencil as though they were the inkwell into which his chief was about to dip his quill pen. The man on the plinth was Mr. Geschwind.

"Just in time," he said, stepping down. "Your turn."

"For what?" I said.

"To replace that Howard's twenty-two-fifty-with-two-pair-of-pants number you've been wearing since you came to work for me."

I had managed for some time to live with Mr. Geschwind's tone of voice. Today I felt the huge ad on the book page of the *New York Times* had provided me with a platform of my own to stand on.

"It's the best I could afford," I said.

"What I can't afford anymore is to have you go around looking like you went to the High School of Commerce," Mr. Geschwind said. He turned to the member of Balkan royalty with the poised marking chalk and jerked his thumb in my direction. "Take his measurements."

120

I sensed something more in the air than the customary flailing about of Mr. Geschwind's uncontrolled irritability. I stepped up on the plinth. After the measurements were completed we spent some time flipping the pages of swatch books. Aware of my father's invisible glance peering across my shoulder I chose something conservative but also a little snappy. Mr. Geschwind grunted but did not object. Neither did he speak as he led me from the subdued Middle European elegance of Pat Caruso to the low-key British crispness of Whitehouse & Hardy on the street floor of the Metropolitan Opera House at the corner of Fortieth Street and Broadway. The cordovan wing tips of which he approved were priced at exactly the same figure as the Howard's-with-two-pair-of-pants number: $22.50. The shoes I was wearing had come, a long time ago, from Thom McAn: $4.00.

"Throw them away," Mr. Geschwind said to the clerk. "He'll wear the new ones."

"Mr. Geschwind," I said, "I haven't got the money to pay for these."

"You will have," he said. "Now get back to the office and wait for me."

He came in twenty minutes after I did. He was carrying a paper bag. He led me into his private office and closed the door.

"You sit here."

He pointed to the chair beside his desk. I sat down. Out of his desk drawer Mr. Geschwind pulled the copy of *I Can Get It for You Wholesale* he had sent me across the street to Macy's to buy for him when I showed up in the office that morning. He set the book in front of me and plucked one of the two fountain pens from the onyx base on his desk.

"Here," he said. "While I unpack this stuff you make like an author."

I had never before autographed a book. I did not find this first effort easy. Mr. Geschwind's conduct since early morning had been unsettling. While I tried to think of something appropriate to write on the flyleaf of my book, I watched him take his seat behind the desk. He ripped open the paper bag and pulled out two Lou G. Siegel Specials.

"You've been shlepping these things for my lunch for a long

time," Mr. Geschwind said, pushing a tongue on rye across the desk toward me. "I figure for this ceremony the time is ripe for me to shlep one for you."

"What ceremony?" I said.

"I'm changing the guard," Mr. Geschwind said. "I spent the morning reading your book. It's a sockdologer." He raised half his Lou G. Siegel Special as though it was a glass of champagne. "Here's to all the good things you've got waiting for you up ahead." He took a huge bite. Around the mouthful of tongue on rye from which I hoped all that lungy stuff had been cut away, Mr. Geschwind said, "You're fired."

"Thanks," I said, even though I felt not thankful but a little scared. The nice steady flow of Mr. Musaius's Yankee bean soup had just stopped coming in over my windowsill. The pen I'd been holding suspended over the copy of *I Can Get It for You Wholesale* came down to the flyleaf. I wrote, "With every best wish to Monroe Geschwind, my first boss."

I pushed the book across the desk. Mr. Geschwind studied the flyleaf, then reached for the second pen in the onyx base. After my word "boss" he wrote two of his own: "and last." He pushed the book back across the desk. "Initial the inserted clause," he said. "To make it legal."

I did. Mr. Geschwind pulled the book back, studied the inscription, then nodded.

"The next time you come through that door," he said, "I expect you to bring me a piece of paper."

"I'm afraid that won't be very soon," I said. "My royalties are twenty cents a copy. At that rate, piling up the cost of a pair of Whitehouse and Hardy shoes and a Pat Caruso suit will take a little time."

"I wasn't talking about a check," Mr. Geschwind said. "The shoes and the suit are your graduation presents from M.G.U."

"From what?" I said.

"Monroe Geschwind University," he said. "The next time you come through that door I expect you to be carrying a photostat suitable for framing. The Pulitzer or the Nobel, whichever they hit you with first."

"I'll do my best," I said.

"One Clinton man never asks more than that from another Clinton man when they go out on the field to beat the ass off Commerce," Mr. Geschwind said. "Ready?"

"Ready," I said.

"See the little Commerce boys, Commerce boys, Commerce boys," my first boss chanted. *"See the little Commerce boys coming to play."*

"Football with Clinton," I sang, *"Oh, football with Clinton,"* and our voices rose together in the rousing climax: *"Oh, see the little Commerce boys coming to play!"*

eight

My mother did not need a bench in Bryant Park to help her adjust to the success of *I Can Get It for You Wholesale*. Her satisfactions were simple and immediate.

"No more sardine cans with kerosene," she said.

On East Fourth Street the four feet of every bed we owned had to be kept standing constantly in sardine cans filled with kerosene. It was the only way to keep the bedbugs from making it up from the cracks in the decaying wooden floors to our mattresses.

"And no more we need a policeman to stand over the *braytil*," my mother added grimly.

Braytil is the Yiddish word for a wooden board. On East Fourth Street it meant a toilet seat because they were all made of wood. *Braytils* were part of the yardstick by which tenement accommodations were measured and rents determined. There were three categories. The bottom of the list was occupied by tenements with "toilets in the yard." All tenants in such buildings had to come downstairs to use a common latrine in the backyard. The top of the list was the tenement with "toilets inside." Every apartment in the building had its own private facility. Sitting squarely in the middle of the list, and by far the most common, were the tenements with "toilets in the hall." My mother was fiercely proud of the fact that we never lived with toilets in the yard. And she never complained about not living in a building with toilets inside. She knew we couldn't afford it. She was never completely happy, however, with our accommodations at 390 East Fourth Street: a tenement with "toilets in the hall."

We lived on the third floor, one of six families that shared a common latrine. It was centrally located, out in the hall, facing the stairwell. The problem was, of course, cleanliness. My mother, like all our neighbors on the third floor, was a good housekeeper. So were most women in the neighborhood. They had to be to survive in the decaying structures we called home, where nothing new was ever installed, nothing broken was ever repaired, and nothing that ceased to function was ever replaced. Every mother on the third floor of our building took her turn at sweeping the floor and scrubbing the *braytil* of the common latrine. Every child knew the rules for using the facility and the punishment for breaking them. For boys, of course, the most important rule was always but always to lift the *braytil* before use. The rule was strictly observed. Until I was in second grade, when, unexpectedly, there was a flurry of *braytil* wettings in our building that shattered the peace of the third floor. Every mother, including mine, denied that a son of hers could be the culprit. The *braytil* continued to be inundated daily. The denials grew more heated. A meeting was called in Mrs. Licht-blau's apartment. Notes were compared. The time of day when the violations seemed to be occurring was narrowed down and pinpointed: the period when all the kids in the building came racing home from school for lunch. The housewives of the third floor, my mother included, mounted a secret vigil. On the first day of the surveillance the culprit was caught wet-handed by his own mother in the presence of her neighbors.

"He has a weak bladder," the humiliated Mrs. Pflug said of her seven-year-old Velvil. "By the time he comes running from the school and he climbs up the stairs and he falls into the toilet, he hasn't even got time to close the door, so how can he wait to pick up the *braytil*?"

For my mother the success of *I Can Get It for You Wholesale* meant, among other things, the end of *braytil* policing. The Weidman family's days with toilets in the hall were over. Our building on Tiffany Street in the Bronx was a "toilets inside" structure. My mother liked Tiffany Street.

"It's like a park," she said. "But you don't have to walk to it. It's right there outside your window."

There were trees on both sides of the street.

"But the people," she said, and hesitated. "About the people, I don't know."

I did. It was a street out of Sinclair Lewis. Small apartment houses painted white and yellow surrounded by foliage. Almost no traffic. Women strolling with baby carriages. A sense of small-town quiet. A feel of surrounding emptiness. There were eight tenants in our building and all of them worked downtown and came home to Tiffany Street at night to sleep. There was no time to get to know them. On East Fourth Street in our tenement there had been forty-eight large families. With none of them had my mother been involved in any sort of relationship. She was a brooding loner. On East Fourth Street, however, there had been the river traffic. If you lived on a river, you didn't need friends. There was no river traffic on Tiffany Street. No blacksmith clanging away with his hammer and striking sparks from a white-hot horseshoe. No pushcart market, surrounded by people yammering in Yiddish and Italian. No horse-drawn wagons carrying heavy loads of coal and lumber to that mysterious place known as uptown. There was no feel on Tiffany Street, as there had been on East Fourth Street, of being crowded onto a small island surrounded by a great, complicated, exciting, busy metropolis. It did not occur to me until years later that, for someone who remained at home all day, as my mother did, Tiffany Street could not have been a very exciting place.

It was different for my father. For him it meant two hour-and-a-half subway rides every day, to and from his shop on Allen Street, but he didn't seem to mind that. It seemed to add to the pleasure he obviously took in the quiet, almost rural atmosphere of his new home. I remembered one of his few complaints about my mother. Once, when I was very small, and my kid brother was still a baby, my father took the whole family on a Sunday picnic from East Fourth Street to Prospect Park in Brooklyn. We were loaded down with large bags of food and bundles of blankets to spread on the grass. After a long walk to the subway on Delancey Street, the ride to Brooklyn, and then the long walk to Prospect Park, we were all tired but full of anticipation. We made our way from the entrance gates to a pleasant winding path that led through a cool wooded area and opened onto a deserted grassy knoll shaded by huge trees. After the long hot walk it felt cool and pleasant. My father was pleased and started setting down the bundles of blankets.

"No, no, not here," my mother said. "Let's keep walking until we get to a nice place."

"What could be nicer than this?" my father said.

"It's no good," my mother said. "Let's keep walking."

We kept walking until even my sister, who is not a complainer, said she was too tired to continue walking.

"We'll find a place," my mother said. "Come on."

We went on.

"Annie, for God sakes, what kind of place are you looking for?" my father said.

"A place where there's people," my mother said.

Years later I understood my father's quiet pleasure, after the long subway ride home, in his evenings on Tiffany Street. My sister was almost never home in the evening. She had acquired a new group of friends based on the girls in the office where she worked, and the young men in her evening-session classes at C.C.N.Y. She was popular and I grasped that, for social reasons, she preferred the Tiffany Street address to 390 East Fourth Street. My kid brother's preferences were not taken into consideration by the Board of Education. He was assigned, not to De Witt Clinton, but to James Monroe High School in the Bronx. Soon he, too, was socially involved with his classmates. Of his many C.C.N.Y. contemporaries who used to move in and out of our house a little later, I remember only one: Irving Howe. Years after, when he had achieved eminence, we talked about those days. I asked him what had attracted him to our house.

"Girls," Irving Howe said. "It was a great place to meet girls."

I stared at him in astonishment. I am six years older than my kid brother. Not until that talk with Irving Howe did I realize what a six-year gap can mean when you are young. I could not remember any of the girls with whom Irving Howe and my kid brother had spent time in our house. The reason, I think, is that when I was six years older than my kid brother at the time he was still a schoolboy, I was no longer a young man strolling among the radishes and tomatoes of my modest backyard vegetable garden, quietly pleased with the way my plants were flourishing. I was the author of *I Can Get It for You Wholesale.*

I did not feel different. In fact, because the publication of the book had caused Mr. Geschwind to cut me off from what I had always leaned on, namely, a weekly salary, I clung to other things that nobody knew about and I did not advertise. I still did not have a checking account. I still deposited the checks from the sale of my short stories, and later my royalty checks from Simon & Schuster, in the Dry Dock Savings Bank of West Thirty-fourth Street. Every Friday I took the subway downtown from the Bronx and withdrew enough cash for my mother's weekly allowance and the pocket money to underwrite my social life for the next seven days. Every second week I crossed the street from the Dry Dock Savings Bank to the Nelson Tower for a haircut in the lobby barbershop I had been using since I graduated from De Witt Clinton and went to work for Mr. Geschwind. The extent to which becoming a published author had changed my relationship to the rest of the world did not come clear until one day in 1938, when I received a telephone call from Richard L. Simon a few months after the publication of *What's in It for Me?*

What's in It for Me? is the sequel to *I Can Get It for You Wholesale,* which concluded the Harry Bogen trilogy I had begun with *Ten O'clock Scholar,* although nobody but Jacques Chambrun and I were aware of the existence of the *Ten O'clock Scholar* manuscript. After the publication of *I Can Get It for You Wholesale* I asked him if we should bring the *Ten O'clock Scholar* manuscript to Mr. Simon's attention.

"No," Chambrun said. "That would be moving backward. You've had a brilliant start, thanks to Mr. Simon's backing, and I'm sure he wants to see you move forward. I would suggest you finish the third volume. We'll show it to Mr. Simon. Depending on his reaction, we can then decide what to do about *Ten O'clock Scholar.*"

Mr. Simon's reaction to *What's in It for Me?* was not unlike his reaction to *I Can Get It for You Wholesale*. So were the reactions of the critics and the book-buying public. *Time* took its favorite thoroughfare—the high road—and stated, "*What's in It for Me?* will rejoice readers. Author Weidman gives his hero a moral shellacking which only an idiot would miss." John Chamberlain, after itemizing his reasons for calling the book "pure joy," went on to express his opinion of the man who had delivered this moral shellacking: "Mr. Weidman should be knighted for his courage." After the excitement of the publication of my second novel settled down, I again raised with Chambrun the subject of bringing *Ten O'clock Scholar* to the attention of Richard L. Simon. Chambrun urged against it.

"We may run into a peculiar situation," he said. "Once, when Bernard Shaw was called upon for a curtain speech after his most spectacular success, and a single catcall cut through the enthusiastic applause of the opening night audience, Shaw said from the stage to the heckler in the gallery, 'I agree with you, sir, but who are we two to stand up against so many?' "

"You mean you think Mr. Simon won't like *Ten O'clock Scholar?*" I said.

"I mean it is possible that Mr. Simon will be disappointed," Jacques Chambrun said. "He met Harry Bogen at the peak of his powers as a son of a bitch in the garment center, and the shock of the meeting fired Mr. Simon's enthusiasm for the book. Mr. Simon's second meeting with Harry Bogen in *What's in It for Me?* provided not only the shock of recognition but the satisfaction of seeing a villain caught and defeated, for which Mr. Chamberlain suggested you be knighted, and from which Mr. Simon drew the satisfaction not only of watching Harry Bogen get a moral shellacking but the even greater pleasure, since Mr. Simon is in the book business, of doing it as the publisher of another best seller by his brilliant new author. To bring him now, at the triumphant end of the Harry Bogen saga, the beginning of the story that he never even knew existed could very well be a letdown. The best way to treat sleeping dogs is to let them lie. I suggest we both forget the *Ten O'clock Scholar* manuscript and you go on with the new book you've been telling me about. Sometime in the future, when the initial excitement of Harry Bogen has turned to what I predict will be nostalgia for his great moments, we might revive Mr. Simon's interest in Harry by bringing *Ten O'clock Scholar* out of mothballs."

The advice seemed sound, especially since I was working along happily on a new novel, and I put *Ten O'clock Scholar* to rest in my dead file. Years later the success of *I Can Get It for You Wholesale* as a Broadway musical brought about the nostalgic interest in Harry Bogen's beginnings that Jacques Chambrun had predicted. Unfortunately, by that time both Chambrun and Richard L. Simon were dead. Both, however, were still very alive in 1938 on the day Mr. Simon called me in the Bronx with the news that a man from the West Coast had just arrived in town and wanted very much to meet me.

"About what?" I said.

"I think it would be best if he told you himself," Mr. Simon said.

I asked no further questions. I left my workroom, walked over to the subway, and caught the next train downtown. Even late in the morning, when the rush-hour crowd had cleared out of the subway, the trip from the 180th Street–Bronx Park South station to Grand Central was a fifty-five-minute ride. Add to this the walk from Grand Central to the Simon & Schuster office at 386 Fourth Avenue—not yet known then as Park Avenue South—throw in the time spent in whatever the meeting is about, then add the return trip to the Bronx, and the most creative part of the writer's working day has been effectively wiped out. To embark on such a time waster without nailing down a sensible reason for doing so would certainly strike me, if I were not a participant in the enterprise, as a comment on Mr. Simon's personality or his victim's powers of resistance. It would be difficult to come up with a better analysis of the situation.

Dick Simon was a charmer and, from the moment we met, I was charmed by him. I think we liked each other because we were so totally different on almost every level and, at the same time, we were both fascinated by the details of each other's existence on those different levels.

Richard Leo Simon was a second-generation American Jew

from a German family that had its roots in Berlin. I was a first-generation American Jew with vaguely defined ties on my mother's side to a Hungarian dairy farm and, on my father's side, to a family coaching inn on one of the tributary roads that fed the main highway between Vienna and Budapest. Simon's forebears moved comfortably in the world of Arthur Schnitzler. Mine moved uneasily in the world of Sholem Aleichem. We were both, however, born and bred New Yorkers. Simon spent his youth in a brownstone on West Eighty-seventh Street, between Columbus and Amsterdam avenues, in the days when the area was one of New York's "better" neighborhoods. His father was a highly successful importer of exotic feathers for women's hats. It was a musical family on whose piano, Dick Simon once told me, George Gershwin played an early, unfinished version of the *Rhapsody in Blue*. The reader who has come thus far knows where I spent my youth in the days when the area was one of New York's slum neighborhoods. My mother never owned a hat with a feather, and music to my father the pocket maker and his son the storyteller meant the chant of the cantor in the synagogue on the sabbath.

Not long after Dick Simon and I met and it became clear, at least to me, that we had become good friends, I made an effort to figure out why. I came to a surprising conclusion about which I was never completely sure, so I never mentioned it to anybody, certainly not to Dick Simon. I think there is enough truth in my conclusion to make it worth setting down.

When I met Dick Simon he had just come through a deep analysis. During all the years I knew him he had a continuing dependence relationship with his analyst, to whom he turned in moments of stress. For all his intelligence, his talent, his good looks, his charm, the qualities he had in abundance that brought him the great success as a publisher he deserved and cherished, there was a great empty space in the middle of Dick Simon's life. He was intensely aware of it. He never stopped trying to identify the nature of this emptiness or his efforts to fill it. When he met me, a younger man from every conceivable other side of the railroad tracks, his world was full of men he admired and envied, men who had made it from my side to his side of the railroad tracks, the rags-to-riches successes in the arts and business and politics around whom had grown up the legend of the Grand Street Boys. I think Dick Simon felt that if he had been born on East Fourth Street to a couple of penniless, illiterate immigrants, he would have had whatever it was that belonged in this empty space in the middle of his life with which these friends of his had been born. As I said, I was never sure of this theory, and I am far from certain of it now, but if there is any truth in my feeling that this is what he believed, I am glad the subject never came up between us.

This may seem a circuitous way to explain why, when on that day in 1938 Dick Simon called me in the Bronx and asked me to come to his office to meet a man from the West Coast who wanted to meet me, I went at once. It would have been simpler, of course, to say I went because I was under Dick Simon's spell. Simpler and perhaps more accurate. The call had certainly come from a man I had grown to like and trust and coming into whose presence was for me always a pleasure. The pleasure did not last very long on that day in 1938 when I came into his office and found him with the man from the West Coast who wanted to see me.

"This is Nate Spindgold," Dick said from behind his desk.

Mr. Spindgold rose from his chair, came forward to meet me, and held out his hand. The gleam of his fingernails indicated that they had just been manicured. This guess was backed up by a strong, expensive barbershop smell that accompanied Mr. Spindgold across the room like an invisible cape. Our hands met, and I sensed trouble up ahead. Dick Simon had said on the phone the visitor from the West Coast was anxious to meet me. The visitor's handshake, in which all the shaking was done by me, made it clear that what had brought Mr. Spindgold across the continent was not an uncontrollable eagerness to present me with a sack of gold.

"Jerry, why don't you sit here," Dick Simon said, touching the back of the chair to the right of his desk. I sat down. Mr. Spindgold returned to the chair on the left, and I could almost feel the sudden tension in the room. It reminded me of the first moments when I came into Mrs. White's office at *The New Yorker* for a face-to-face encounter about corrections she wanted on a story: the politeness was not unlike that of a couple of boxers who had just entered the ring and were dipping their toes in the resin box.

"Mr. Spindgold is a vice president of Columbia Pictures," Dick Simon said. "Nate, why don't you tell Jerry what you told me?"

It did not take long. Almost as soon as Mr. Spindgold started talking I understood why Dick preferred not to tell it to me himself. What I did not understand were my own feelings. I had never before met a Hollywood executive. I felt at once, however, not only that I had known Mr. Spindgold for a long time, I also felt I knew everything there was to know about him. Talking to me, he could have been Monroe Geschwind, in his office at 450 Seventh Avenue, addressing a creditors' committee. There was that same use of complicated words, which everybody reads daily in the newspapers but nobody ever uses in ordinary conversation, to transmit unpleasant facts in what was hoped would be received as a palatable manner. The two men looked somewhat alike. Overweight in a faintly repulsive rather than jovial way. Hung with clothes not as a protection from the elements but as badges of station in life. Like Mr. Geschwind, the man from the West Coast seemed to be studded with jewelry, including what could have been two sets of massive gold cuff links, and his shirt was cut from the cloth much favored by successful Seventh Avenue dress salesmen: white on white. If he had been wrapped in an apron, Mr. Spindgold, like Monroe Geschwind, could have been mistaken for the man who put together the hot tongue specials behind the slicing counter in Lou G. Siegel's delicatessen. As soon as this image crossed my mind, the reason for the confusion about my feelings came clear. From his appearance and manner I expected Mr. Spindgold to be antagonistic, to refuse to cut away all that lungy stuff even if he was paid extra for doing it. Instead, Mr. Spindgold seemed eager to make me think well of him.

"I'm sure," he said when he finished, "you understand how we feel."

133

By "we" he meant the small group of Hollywood studio executives for whom he was acting as spokesman. What had brought them together, even though they were rivals in the movie business, was a common concern for the mounting threat that Hitler's rise to power in Germany was posing to Jews all over the world, including America. They had banded together, these important men of the movie industry, to see what they, in their own small way, could do to fight the acceleration of anti-Semitism in this country. They had made an agenda, and they had sent Mr. Spindgold to New York to see what he could do about the first items on it. These were three books, all published by Simon & Schuster, that these Hollywood executives felt should be withdrawn from publication. The first was a book about the Leica camera, written by Richard L. Simon, called *Miniature Photography: From One Amateur to Another*. Mr. Spindgold and his colleagues felt this book, by promoting the sale of Leica cameras, increased Germany's dollar credits in this country. The other two books Mr. Spindgold and his colleagues had decided should be suppressed were my best-selling novels *I Can Get It for You Wholesale* and its sequel, *What's in It for Me?*

"Jerry, what do you think?" Dick Simon said.

I had forgotten he was in the room. I had been concentrating on Mr. Spindgold and the way his voice, throbbing with sincerity, caused the veins on his naked skull to pulse up and down like the bubbles of a pancake just poured on the griddle. I turned to Dick. He looked troubled. Dick Simon had an open, intelligent, guileless face. When he looked troubled it was a painful thing to see. It made the viewer want to help him. But how? In my confusion I fell back on the device I had used all my life in moments of stress. I pretended I was writing a story. I saw myself in it. Facing Mr. Spindgold. He had stated his case. His scene was over. The next scene was mine. I drew a deep breath and stepped into it.

"Could you tell me exactly, Mr. Spindgold, which parts of my books you consider anti-Semitic?" I said. "Be specific, please."

Mr. Spindgold leaned—no, fell—back in his chair. He looked shocked, as though he could not believe I had failed to be overwhelmed by his persuasive eloquence. He felt nervously for his cuff links, as though they were talismans from which in moments of uncertainty he sought reassurance. This took a few moments because he seemed to be wearing so many and he wanted to be certain that none was slighted in this ritual of seeking help. Finally he cleared his throat.

"I'm very sorry," Mr. Spindgold said coldly. "I'm a very busy man. I don't have time to read books, and I didn't read yours, but I've been told as much as I have to know about them by my colleagues."

For several moments after his voice stopped I could not speak. Then memory came in with a sharp nudge. It pointed me toward John O'Hara. Into my mind came his advice about how to deal with editors but, in the heat of his exaggeration, I could now see a larger truth, as one usually can in the work of all really good writers. There were people beyond civilized intercourse. It was stupid to try to deal with them except in their own terms. With an inner nod of thanks to the king of my particular hill for the use of his words, I said to Mr. Nate Spindgold, "Go fuck yourself," and I walked out of Dick Simon's office.

When I got home to the Bronx my mother told me Mr. Simon had called. He wanted me to call him back. It was important. I called him back.

"Congratulations," he said. "I wish I'd had the guts to say it myself."

Now he tells me, I thought.

"Never mind what I said," I said. "What are you going to do?"

"Nothing," Dick said. "We couldn't withdraw your books even if we wanted to. We have a contract with you. We honor our contracts."

"What about your photography book?" I said.

"Oh, well, that's different," Dick said. "It's not a work of art like a novel. It's just a how-to book, and he's got a point about increasing Germany's dollar credits in this country by the sale of Leicas."

"You mean you're going to pull your book out of the stores?" I said.

"I don't see how I can refuse," Dick Simon said.

135

A couple of hours later we both found out. Jacques Chambrun called me in the late afternoon.

"Have you seen the *World-Telegram?*" he said.

"No," I said. "Why?"

"You're on the front page," Chambrun said.

He read me a headline and the boxed story under it. Simon & Schuster, the story reported, under pressure from a group of Hollywood executives to stamp out anti-Semitism in this country, had agreed to withdraw three of its best-selling publications from the bookstores.

"The *World-Telegram* has that all wrong," I said.

"How do you know?" Chambrun said.

I told him about my meeting in Dick Simon's office, and our phone talk that followed.

"Do you believe him?" Jacques Chambrun said.

Astonished, I said, "Believe who?"

"Mr. Simon," Chambrun said.

"I just told you," I said, trying to conceal my irritation with this slur on my friend's integrity. "Mr. Simon told me only a few minutes ago he is withdrawing his photography book from the stores, but he is not touching my books."

"Then the *World-Telegram* has just called him a liar," Jacques Chambrun said.

"What does the *World-Telegram* know about it?" I said.

"Something you as my client, and I as your agent, had better find out," Chambrun said.

"How are you going to do that?" I said.

"I'm going to call Mr. Simon and read him a clause from the contracts he signed with you through me on both those books," Jacques Chambrun said.

"Mr. Simon knows about the contracts," I said. "He told me on the phone a few minutes ago it's because of those contracts that he couldn't withdraw my books from the stores even if he wanted to."

"Why didn't he tell that to the *World-Telegram?*" Chambrun said.

"Will you forget the *World-Telegram?*" I said. "I trust Mr. Simon."

"I think perhaps you would be well advised to be a trifle

more reluctant before you place your faith in the word of a publisher," Chambrun said.

"I don't know why you're making such a big thing about my faith in the word of Mr. Simon," I said.

"The copy of the *World-Telegram* I'm holding in my hand must have gone to press while you and Mr. Spindgold were meeting in Mr. Simon's office," Jacques Chambrun said. "How did they get the story before your friend Mr. Simon arranged for you to hear about it?"

"I just told you," I said. "I don't know."

"Don't you think you should ask Mr. Simon?" Chambrun said.

"You're my agent," I said. "You ask him."

As soon as I slammed down the receiver I knew I had made a mistake. The phone rang again. It was a reporter from the New York *Post*.

"Have you seen this story about you on the front page of the *World-Telegram?*" he said.

"No, but it was just read to me," I said. "What can I do for you?"

"You can give me a statement," the reporter said.

"A what?" I said.

"A statement," the reporter said. "How you feel about these Hollywood big shots accusing you of anti-Semitism, your publisher agreeing with them, and he yanks your books off the market."

"He doesn't," I said.

"He doesn't what?" the reporter said.

"My publisher doesn't agree with them. He refused to do what these Hollywood big shots asked him to do. He has not yanked my books off the market. All you have to do is walk into any bookstore in town and ask for a copy of *I Can Get It for You Wholesale* and *What's in It for Me?* and you'll get them."

Pause, then: "What about Mr. Simon's book on photography?"

"I don't know about Mr. Simon's book about photography," I said. "All I know is about my books. Mr. Simon assured me—"

My voice stopped. I had made another mistake. A bad one.

"Okay, Mr. Weidman," the reporter said, and I could tell

from the change in tone that he knew I had made a mistake. "Thanks a lot."

"What are you going to do?" I said.

"What the hell can we do?" the reporter said. "If you won't make a statement about this *World-Telegram* story, we'll just have to run it the way they ran it."

"In the *Post?*" I said.

"That's the paper whose nickel I'm using to make this call," the reporter said.

"But the story is not true," I said. "I've just told you it's not true. How can you run a story that you know is not true?"

"If it's not true, then we won't be doing anything worse than the *World-Telegram* did," the reporter said. "We can't let ourselves be scooped by the competition. We'll run a retraction in a later edition."

They did. So did the *World-Telegram.* The retractions ran in the back of the papers, somewhere between the real estate and the want ads. Among the people who did not see the retractions was Hendrik Willem Van Loon, known in the trade as Simon & Schuster's meal ticket. The enormously successful author of *The Story of Mankind* called Dick Simon and told him that if the newspaper stories about the suppression of my books were true, he, Van Loon, a lifelong foe of censorship, would take steps at once to find himself another publisher. Dick Simon assured him the stories were untrue and told Van Loon he could call me for confirmation. Van Loon called me. I confirmed Dick's statement. That night, on his regular WQXR radio broadcast, Van Loon denounced all publishers who would succumb to the pressures of semiliterate movie mogul Philistines and deprive the public of books that had been hailed by the critics as works of art. Dick called me. He was very upset. He wanted to know what I had said to Van Loon. I told him.

"Then why did Van Loon make that broadcast?" Dick said.

The anger in his voice was not difficult to interpret.

"Why don't you ask him?" I said.

My voice, which I tried to control but couldn't, matched his.

"I can't," Dick said. "It would look as though I'm calling him a liar. Would you do me a favor and call him for me?"

The cynical features of Jacques Chambrun came out of the storyteller's subconscious to glare a warning.

"I've already called him for you," I said. "What can I tell Van Loon today that I didn't tell him yesterday?"

Pause.

"I suppose you're right," Dick Simon said.

I don't think he slammed down the receiver, but he hung up without another word, and I felt as though he had slammed down the receiver. It was clear that, in some way I did not understand, he believed I had let him down. The next call, which was from Burton Rascoe, did not help matters. Rascoe was no longer editor-in-chief at Doubleday. He had moved on to *Newsweek*, for which he wrote a weekly column called "Book-week." The sharp, nervous voice came stabbing at me out of the telephone.

"What's all this about Simon and Schuster suppressing your books?" Rascoe said.

I told him what I had told Jacques Chambrun and the New York *Post* reporter and Hendrik Willem Van Loon.

"The whole thing is a misunderstanding," I said. "Nobody seems to know where the *World-Telegram* got the story, but I do know, and this is easy enough to confirm, that Simon and Schuster have not suppressed my books."

Rascoe's reply was the bark of a prosecuting attorney.

"Why are you holding Dick Simon's coat?" he said.

"I don't understand what you mean," I said.

"Instead of pulling his chestnuts out of the fire," Burton Rascoe said, "you should be sore as hell because of what he got you into."

"It's a mix-up," I said again. "No damage has been done, so I see no point—"

"Let me help you see the point," Rascoe snapped. "You say the first you knew about all this was when you walked into Simon's office and you were confronted by this Spindgold character?"

"That's right," I said.

"Don't you see that for the shabby trick it was?" Burton Rascoe said. "How dare Dick Simon call on you the writer to make the decision that he as the publisher should have made?"

"I didn't think of it that way," I said.

"As a writer it's your duty to think of it that way," Rascoe said. "It's your duty to all your fellow writers to tell this loathsome fascist son of a bitch from the Coast to drop dead."

I thought John O'Hara's words were more to the point.

"I'm sorry," I said. "If there's anything I can do—"

"You can read my next 'Bookweek' column," Burton Rascoe said, and there was no doubt about how he ended the conversation. The slammed receiver made me jump. I stared at the telephone for a few moments until I began to sense uneasily that it would be unwise to wait for the appearance of Mr. Rascoe's next "Bookweek" column. I called Dick Simon and reported. When I finished he said, "I think it's important for us to see him in person as soon as possible. I'd like you to come with me."

"Where?" I said.

"A meeting with Rascoe," Dick said.

"If you want me, of course I will," I said.

"Stand by," Dick said. "I'll call you back."

When he did he told me Rascoe had agreed to meet us in his apartment on West Seventy-ninth Street. An hour later I met Dick on the sidewalk in front of the apartment house. We went in together. We were admitted by Mrs. Rascoe, who, after identifying herself, led us into a large living room and left us with her husband. I had not seen Rascoe since the day he ate two orders of snails at the Murray Hill Hotel while he and Ken McCormick told me how much they liked the manuscript of *Ten O'clock Scholar*. Except for his clothes Rascoe had not changed. This time he was wearing a pair of black pants with satin stripes down the sides, apparently part of a tuxedo, a white sweat shirt, and black patent-leather pumps. He didn't exactly push us into chairs, but his manner made it plain that if we did not take the ones to which he gestured, we could remain standing. Rascoe himself did not sit down. He paced as he talked, pausing to snatch salted almonds, jelly beans, licorice bits, chocolate creams, and other delicacies from small silver bowls scattered on end tables all over the room like pit stops on the path of a long-distance automobile racer.

"This is my next week's column," he said, scooping up a

sheet of paper from an end table with one hand and a fistful of jelly beans with the other. He popped a few jelly beans into his mouth and, as he chewed and paced, he read aloud: " '*Mein Kampf* Elbows Its Way into the Inner Sanctum.' "

The seven hundred or so words marched along crisply, discharging colorful metaphors and wisecracks mixed with classical references, providing what seemed an entertaining but puzzling fireworks display until Rascoe had drawn a parallel between what Dick Simon had done to the cause of free expression by allowing Mr. Nate Spindgold to enter his office, and what the French General Staff had done to Alfred Dreyfus by packing him off to Devil's Island. By unavoidable implication the comparison made the point that, just as the act of the French General Staff had led to Emile Zola's *J'Accuse*, the act of Richard L. Simon had led to Burton Rascoe's "Bookweek" column. It was heady stuff. I looked at Dick. He was lighting a cigarette. He had a trick, when in deep thought, of turning his hand as though the wrist was a swivel so that he could stare directly into the burning end of the cigarette between his fingers.

"You know, Burton," he said finally, "I never knew you were that passionate about freedom of expression."

A licorice bit paused on its way to Rascoe's mouth.

"As a publisher," he said, "I should think you'd share that passion."

"I do," Dick Simon said. "In fact, I'd like to help you. That's why I brought something along I'm sure you'll find interesting."

From his breast pocket he pulled a small batch of folded galleys and held them out. On his way from the salted almonds to the chocolate creams Burton Rascoe scooped the galleys from Dick's hand.

"What's this?" Rascoe said.

"A story we're about to publish," Dick Simon said. "It's called *Address Unknown* by Kressmann Taylor. Review copies haven't gone out yet. Aside from our staff you're the first person who's seen it."

"What's this got to do with the subject of the column I just read to you?" Rascoe said.

"I think you'll find it a better subject for an anti-Nazi col-

141

umn than Nate Spindgold," Dick Simon said, pushing himself up out of the chair.

He was right about the Kressmann Taylor story being a better anti-Nazi subject than Nate Spindgold. Unfortunately, not being a writer, Dick Simon had apparently missed a point that struck me at once in the situation as crucial: Burton Rascoe was in love with the column he had written. Even when filtered through munched gumdrops and salted almonds the pleasure he took in his composition was obvious. Dick Simon may have believed he was providing Rascoe with the material for a substitute column. I knew instinctively, from the way Rascoe had read his work aloud, that for him there could be no substitute. I was right, but only in part.

Address Unknown was a gimmick story. It dealt with a German who had risen in the Gestapo ranks to a point where, following orders, he was forced to destroy the family a boyhood friend had left behind in Germany when he emigrated to America. The friend in America did not realize what had happened. All he knew was that the letters he wrote to his family in Germany started coming back marked "Address Unknown." When he learned the truth about their death and his old friend's complicity in their murder, he embarked on a campaign of revenge. He started writing letters from America to his old friend in Germany, the Gestapo official, describing a totally nonexistent relationship he had invented for them. The letters drew a picture of a couple of plotters, this Gestapo officer and his old friend, now posing in America as an anti-Nazi writing to a fellow anti-Nazi who was working underground in Germany to bring down the Hitler regime. The early letters from America contained only casual references to the anti-Nazi feelings allegedly shared by the correspondents. The early replies from Germany were nervous warnings to the American friend to refrain from writing letters containing such statements because all mail from America was censored and placed the recipient in jeopardy. The American correspondent increased the incriminatory content of his letters. The German's replies became frantic pleas for his old friend in America to desist. The final letter from the American to his Nazi friend in Germany comes back to America marked "Address Unknown."

I don't know how Burton Rascoe would have handled the Kressmann Taylor story if it had come to him in the ordinary way, one small book among many in the steady stream of books that crosses a reviewer's desk. I see no reason to suppose he would have treated it differently from the way most reviewers treated it: as a moving account of an ingenious act of revenge by an innocent victim against a despicable perpetrator who deserved what he got. To Burton Rascoe, however, *Address Unknown* was not just another publication in the stream of books that crossed his reviewing desk. It was a piece of ammunition brought to him by a man Rascoe was preparing to denounce with the hope that Rascoe would be so impressed with the piece of ammunition that he would abandon his attack on Richard L. Simon for aiding and abetting Nate Spindgold in his attempt at censorship. Anybody who heard the admiration in Rascoe's voice as he read the attack aloud would have known that asking him to abandon it was not unlike asking Roy Rogers to abandon his horse Trigger. On the other hand Burton Rascoe was a journalist, with a column of type to fill every seven days, and he had been offered a scoop over his book reviewing colleagues. The man who had been paid $50,000 a year by Nelson Doubleday for editorial advice had no difficulty combining the best of the two attractions he had been offered.

Keeping his original title—"*Mein Kampf* Elbows Its Way into the Inner Sanctum"—Burton Rascoe rewrote his "Bookweek" column to denounce a reactionary publisher who took his orders about censorship from a Hollywood fascist, and then went on to publish with pride a gruesome anti-Semitic story about a savage American Jew who destroys a schoolboy friend in Germany by loading his letters with conspiratorial inventions the German censors take literally.

Neither Dick Simon nor I ever mentioned the failure of his attempt to defuse Burton Rascoe's attack, nor did we ever talk about the Nate Spindgold affair. Dick seemed just as content as I was to pretend the incident had never taken place. No amount of pretending, however, could change the fact that it had stained our friendship, or that others were unwilling to join us in the pretense that the Nate Spindgold incident had not happened. A year later, when I came back from Australia on the last leg of my trip around the world, I stopped off in Hollywood for a few days to see friends. One night I had dinner with John O'Hara and his wife, Belle.

"There's been a lot of talk that your trip was Dick Simon's payoff for withdrawing your books from the stores," John said. "Is it true?"

"What are you doing for lunch tomorrow?" I said.

"I'll be at the studio," he said.

"How about Belle?" I said.

"Is that an invitation?" she said.

"It is," I said.

I took her to the Brown Derby and, after lunch, I asked her to take me to the best bookstore in town. She did, and I asked the clerk if they had copies of *I Can Get It for You Wholesale*, *What's in It for Me?*, and *The Horse That Could Whistle "Dixie,"* my first book of short stories, which had been published by Simon & Schuster while I was in India. The clerk produced copies of all three. I bought them and inscribed them to Belle and John. She thanked me and laughed.

"None of this will do you any good if he's made up his mind the books actually were withdrawn," Belle said. "You know John."

I soon discovered I knew a great many other people who believed as John O'Hara did. There was no way to convince them of the truth. After a while I stopped trying. So did Dick Simon. I did not want to believe our friendship had been permanently damaged. There was one moment during the war when I thought perhaps it had not. It came at the time when Marshall Field made his offer to buy Simon & Schuster, Inc. Some members of Dick's family were in favor of the sale, others were not. Dick invited me to lunch and asked my advice. I had heard enough about the subject from mutual friends to know I was not equipped to come up with anything that could be described as advice.

"What would you like to know?" I said.

"Should I sell or shouldn't I?" Dick said.

I begged the question by reminding him of an incident that took place shortly after we met. I had gone out to Westport with him for dinner with his family and I spent the night. The next morning I walked with Dick from Grand Central to his office to pick up some papers. As we came into the reception room Dick Simon made a funny little sound in his throat. When we got to his office he made it again. It sounded like a suppressed giggle.

"What are you laughing at?" I said.

"Me," he said. "Every time I open the front door and step into that reception room I feel like a kid who doesn't believe something he knows is true. This place, this business, that reception room, all of it, it's mine, we did it, we built it from the ground up, just me and Max, nobody else, just the two of us. Silly for a grown man to feel like that, isn't it?"

Not to me, it wasn't. I understood exactly how he felt. That's why, years later, I brought it up. I saw at once that I'd made a mistake. I shouldn't have reminded him of that incident at a time when he was trying to make up his mind about selling Simon & Schuster to Marshall Field. He looked shocked, as though I had said something obscene. Perhaps I had. I never saw him again. It was probably just as well. I liked him because he brought out the best in me, but I now know something he could never have known: he also brought out the worst. As a result I've never been completely sure about my feelings for this man I still remember with so much affection. For a final verdict, therefore, I borrow from Winston Churchill's summation of a contemporary for whom his relationship was not unlike mine to Richard L. Simon.

"He did not stoop," Churchill wrote. "He did not conquer."

nine

It is not true that Golda Meir said, "If Hitler is still alive, I hope he is on the road somewhere trying out a musical show." I know quite a few people, however, who could have said it. I am one of them. The special horror of being on the road with a musical show was unexpectedly crystallized for me one day in the spring of 1962. I was in Boston working on the out-of-town tryout of my adaptation for the musical stage of my novel *I Can Get It for You Wholesale.*

It had been a long day: rehearsals, a ragged performance, a midnight conference, a grinding headache. At two-thirty in the morning, when I got back to the hotel, I found a message slip under my door: "Call Mr. Andrew Turnbull."

I did not know anybody named Andrew Turnbull, the telephone number he had left rang no bells, and I was dog-tired. Nevertheless my heart leaped up. For the first time since the company had arrived in Boston a week ago, I had received a message from somebody, whoever he was, not connected with the show. It was as though the Man in the Iron Mask had found a note that had been slipped under his cell door while he was asleep: a sign from a remote place about the existence of which, in a week of total absorption in an agonizing task, I had completely forgotten: the outside world. The discovery was exhilarating. It proved there was life beyond the confines of the Shubert Theatre and the Ritz-Carlton Hotel. Somebody who had nothing to do with the road tryout of *I Can Get It for You Wholesale* had remembered my existence. I held the proof in my hand. A trifle giddy with excitement I carried the message slip to the phone and called Mr. Turnbull's number. It rang for a long time. I was about to hang up when a sleepy voice came on the wire.

"Hello?"

"Mr. Turnbull?"

"Yes, what—?"

"I just got back to my hotel and found your message."

"Who is this?"

I told him.

"Who?"

I told him again.

"Oh!"

It was only a syllable, but it could have been uttered by Stanley when at long last he stumbled onto Livingstone.

"Forgive me," Mr. Turnbull said. "I was asleep."

"Sorry to wake you up," I said.

"Not at all," Mr. Turnbull said. "I'm very eager to talk with you."

"About what?" I said.

"Scott Fitzgerald," Mr. Turnbull said.

"Fine," I said. It would be a welcome change from talking about the showstopper in Act II that we had not yet found. "Come on over," I said.

"Now?" Mr. Turnbull said.

"Why not?"

"It's ten minutes to three in the morning."

I looked at my watch. So it was.

"How about breakfast here at the hotel?" I said.

"When?"

"Eight o'clock okay?"

"Isn't that a little early?" Mr. Turnbull said.

"Not for me," I said. "I've got a meeting at the Shubert at nine."

"Eight o'clock where?" Mr. Turnbull said.

"Come to my room," I said.

Five hours later, when I let him in, I had a moment of surprise. At three o'clock in the morning on the telephone Mr. Turnbull had sounded like a doctor trained to be soothingly

147

polite with an excited patient who woke him in the middle of the night. Coming into my room for breakfast, he looked like a Harvard undergraduate keeping an early date with his tutor. He wore a far from new but good heather-colored tweed jacket, a button-down oxford shirt open at the throat, and, between the two, a tan crew-neck cashmere sweater. Mr. Turnbull was quite a departure from the student types with whom I had spent the days of my nonage at C.C.N.Y. and N.Y.U. Law School. He was tall, slender, handsome, and sharp-eyed. His manner was relaxed, even shy, but I had the feeling that when he looked at something, he saw it in depth. He reminded me of pictures I had seen of the man he had come to talk to me about.

"What can I tell you about Scott Fitzgerald?" I said.

"I'm writing a biography of him," Mr. Turnbull said. "I've been talking to as many of his friends as I can find."

"How did you get to me?" I said.

"When I called you in New York yesterday your wife said you were up here with a show and it was all right to call you at the hotel, which made it simple for me. I live in Cambridge."

"That's not what I meant," I said. "How did you get the idea Fitzgerald and I were friends?"

"Weren't you?" Mr. Turnbull said.

"I never laid eyes on him in my life," I said.

"That's funny," Mr. Turnbull said, his gentle manner indicating that that's all it was, but his John O'Hara eyes made it plain he thought the other man in the room was lying.

"What's funny about it?" I said.

"Several of his friends mentioned you as someone I should talk to," Mr. Turnbull said.

Now it was my turn to think the other man in the room was lying.

"Did Fitzgerald's friends say why?" I said.

Mr. Turnbull stared at me in silence for a few moments. His eyes, I noticed, did not blink. It was as though, while examining a specimen under a microscope, he had noticed something so extraordinary that he did not want to risk losing it by the flick of an eyelid. I thought perhaps he had not heard my question, but I was wrong. With slow, deliberate movements he pulled a sheet of paper from his breast pocket and unfolded it carefully.

"I've been given access to all Fitzgerald's papers at Princeton," he said. "Here's one that may explain the confusion. It's a letter written by Fitzgerald from Hollywood in 1939, when he was out there working for the movies. The man he was writing this letter to was an old Princeton classmate named John Biggs, Jr. They roomed together in the fall of 1917 and co-edited the *Tiger*. Biggs went on to become a federal judge and ended up as Fitzgerald's literary executor. For years they corresponded pretty regularly. At longish intervals Fitzgerald used to write Biggs gossipy letters, family things, stuff about his work, catching his friend up on things that had been happening to Fitzgerald since he wrote last, including books he'd been reading and his opinions about new writers. In this letter, after a lot of other literary stuff, he gets around to you. I've marked the passage on this photocopy."

I took the sheet of paper from Mr. Turnbull and read, "As for Americans there's only one—Jerome Weidman, whose two books *(I Can Get It for You Wholesale* and its sequel *What's in It for Me?)* have been withdrawn as too perspicacious about the faults of his own race. He's a grand writer, tho—only 25 and worth fifty of this Steinbeck, who is a cheap blatant imitator of D. H. Lawrence. A book-club return of the public to its own vomit."*

I looked up. Mr. Turnbull was watching me closely, his calm, even apologetic manner underscoring what I suddenly realized was the barely controlled fury in his eyes. It occurred to me that he may have already used the material from this letter in the book on which he was working, and my comments might conflict with whatever use he had made of it. Knowing my own feelings about editorial changes, it was not difficult to imagine Mr. Turnbull's.

"I admire Fitzgerald's work enormously, and I'm delighted to learn he thought well of mine," I said, putting out each word

*Andrew Turnbull, ed., *The Letters of F. Scott Fitzgerald* (New York: Scribner's, 1963), 581.

149

in front of me as though I were picking my way through a minefield. "But I'm afraid he got it all wrong."

"Got what all wrong?" Mr. Turnbull said.

His tone was that of a hanging judge who wants no trace of emotion to color the rendition of his customary verdict.

"The so-called withdrawal of my books from the bookstores," I said. "It didn't happen that way."

"How did it happen?" Mr. Turnbull said.

I went to the phone, ordered up breakfast, and told him. When I finished he said something that surprised me.

"I hope it didn't affect your friendship with Dick Simon."

After all those years I had thought myself capable of describing the unhappy event with complete dispassion. Apparently not. Mr. Turnbull had obviously read something in my voice.

"I hope so, too," I said. "But I'm not sure."

It was because in 1939, two years after the publication of *I Can Get It for You Wholesale*, I was not sure about a great many things that I decided to get out of New York for a while.

ten

"If you don't let a man die," my father once told me, "he won't let you live."

I don't remember what caused him to say it, but I do remember thinking it was a surprisingly harsh comment from a gentle person, and it stuck in my mind. Years later, when I told him how my mother felt about my planned trip around the world, my father added what I don't think he intended as a clarifying footnote, but that's the way it struck me.

"If you don't go while you can, you'll never stop thinking about what you could have done when you had the chance," he said. "That kind of thinking could spoil the rest of your life."

I don't doubt that my father knew what he was talking about. He had learned a lot about disappointment. He was the youngest of seven sons. They had all been born in a small town called Woloshonowa located in either Austria or Poland, depending on where at the time the official border was located: it shifted regularly with the ebb and flow of the region's erratic politics. My father and his six brothers were raised from infancy to help their father with the operation of Woloshonowa's only claim to distinction: a coaching inn on one of the tributary roads that fed the main highway from Vienna to Budapest. Shortly after my father came home from his three years of military service Emperor Franz Josef announced that, because of the troubled international situation, all the young men of my father's class would be called up at once for a second three-year term of military service.

"Three years with a broom behind Franz Josef's cavalry horses was not a picnic, but everybody did it, so I also did it," my father said. "Six years was too much, so I said no."

He said it to himself, of course. It would have been dangerous to tell anybody about his decision. It was more sensible, if and when his absence was discovered, that none of the members of his family should have any information about him that would have to be concealed from the authorities who came to look for him. Wearing the work clothes in which he had spent the day with his brothers working in the fields that surrounded the inn, my father slipped away in the middle of the night without a word of farewell or a groschen in his pockets. When he landed at Ellis Island he was carrying, tied in a knotted handkerchief, twelve dollars' worth of the assorted currencies of the countries through which he had passed on his way from Woloshonowa to Amsterdam. It had taken him two years to work and walk his way from the threat of another three years behind Franz Josef's cavalry horses to the Dutch ship that carried him to New York. Years later, when I told him I was, in effect, going back for a look at the continent from which he had escaped, my father's reaction was different from my mother's denunciation of what she considered an irrational and, in view of the threatening international situation, conceivably a suicidal move.

"You shouldn't have told her," my father said. "The way when I left Woloshonowa I didn't tell my father."

He spoke quietly, through the gentle smile that was his shy way of indicating he didn't want me to take his words literally. He never criticized my mother.

"You know I couldn't do that," I said. "Her feelings would have been hurt and, besides, there are arrangements to be made."

Among these was the bank account I had to open in their names in the Bronx Federal on Vyse Avenue so that they would be able to draw, while I was away, the weekly allowance I had been giving them in person.

"I was making a joke," my father said. "Just the same it would have been better if you told only me."

"Why?" I said.

"Your mother is disappointed in America," my father said.

152

I had, of course, known this for a long time. What surprised me was the implication that he did not share her disappointment. My father's first job on American soil had been as an oyster shucker. It was one of the skills he had picked up on the many jobs at which he had worked during his long trek across Europe to Ellis Island. The other immigrants, with whom he found his way to a congested, evil-smelling rooming house on East Fourth Street, had all been met at the dock by waiting relatives who led them at once to jobs in the Allen Street sweatshops. Not my father. Joseph Tadeus Isaac Weidman was met by nobody, so he had nobody to lead him.

On his first morning in the Golden Land he did what he had always done in Europe. He awoke at first light. He tiptoed out of the rooming house into the street and started walking in the direction of the rising sun. Everything he saw interested him, mainly because much of what he saw was not unlike what he had seen on the streets of Istanbul and Marseilles. Perhaps an hour after he left East Fourth Street he stopped to watch a man unload baskets of oysters from a horse-drawn wagon. My father had earned many a meal in Marseilles by unloading oysters. The man asked my father to lend a hand. He did so gladly. When the wagon was unloaded the man asked my father to join him at breakfast in what proved to be the service kitchen of Fleischmann's Hotel on Lower Broadway. Conversation did not languish. In those days everybody in New York talked Yiddish. Or so it seemed to my father. Indeed, so it seemed to his son until I was almost five years old and my mother enrolled me in the kindergarten class at P.S. 188.

Until then Yiddish was the only language I knew. I still speak it in a manner that used to excite ridicule from Litvaks: with the accents of my father's corner of Austria (Poland). I have always liked the singing sounds made by that accent. So, apparently, did the people in that service kitchen of Fleischmann's Hotel where my father earned his first breakfast on American soil. Before the luncheon crowd started coming in my father was standing behind the oyster bar, wrapped in a white apron, his shucking knife at the ready. He had found his first American job by himself.

Not in an ill-lit, vermin-infested Allen Street loft where the victims bent over their sewing machines like serfs cringing from the lash. My father had found his first job in the Golden Land in a large room, gaily decorated with paintings and mirrors, full of the cheerful sounds of clinking glasses and laughing men, where he stood proudly upright, performing with dexterity and pleasure a difficult task that required great skill. He loved every minute of it, and his colleagues loved him.

The idyll was, of course, doomed. From his new job on Lower Broadway my father had to return at night to the congested rooming house on East Fourth Street. What he thought was his good fortune was considered, in other quarters, a threat to the community. Fellow immigrants from my father's corner of Austria (Poland) heard about the newcomer and his job. One of these was the owner of the rooming house, a man named Berlfein. He invited my father to his home on Avenue D and explained the rules by which a Jew from their area of the Old Country was expected by his fellow Jews to conduct himself in the New World. Mr. Berlfein began with oysters. Jews were forbidden by Holy Writ to eat them. To handle them was, therefore, sacrilege. Working for gentiles was not specifically enjoined. Neither was employment in an establishment that sold alcoholic beverages. The combination of the two, however, could not help but be frowned upon by God.

It was true that my father had arranged to work on Sundays, so that he would be free to attend services in the synagogue on Saturday. But the fact remained that this arrangement was made possible only because the second oysterman, who happened to be a Jew without any strong religious convictions, preferred to take his day off on Sunday. My father was, therefore, Mr. Berlfein pointed out, aiding in the destruction of the soul of a fellow Jew. And finally, of course, there was the economic argument. Shucking oysters in a saloon was not a skilled trade. It was true that my father was earning more than an unskilled operator in cloaks and suits, but he would never become more skillful, and therefore he would never earn more than he was earning now. His job had no future. Until he acquired a real skill, and was accepted in a trade where he could practice that skill, my father would never have a future. And without a future what good was a man in America? Above all, what chance did he have to find a wife? At this point Mr. Berlfein's wife led a pretty girl into the room. She was a recently arrived immigrant from Klein Berezna in Hungary.

"This is the girl you are going to marry," Mr. Berlfein said. "It is your duty."

My father did his duty. A few days before the wedding he said good-bye to his friends in the high, airy, gaily decorated, mirrored room full of the cheerful sounds of clinking glasses and laughing men. The next morning he was led by Mr. Berlfein to a poorly lighted, badly ventilated, vermin-infested loft on Allen Street. He learned soon enough how to bend over a sewing machine as though he was cringing from the lash. Perhaps there is not much to learn. For the rest of his life, almost until the day he died, he was "in cloaks and suits."

The hours he spent over a sewing machine in the Allen Street sweatshops could not have provided much in the way of a spiritual dimension to his life. Perhaps that is why he poured all of his remaining energies into the operation of what might be described as a one-man underground railway. Almost every immigrant family in those days on East Fourth Street was engaged in the process known as "bringing somebody over." The somebody was almost always a close relative, a brother or a sister, a son or a daughter, a father or a mother. And the place from which the somebody was being brought over was usually the town in Europe from which the immigrant already in America had himself or herself come. The bringing-over process required a great deal of paper work, and what would today be considered a modest sum of money. It was far from modest by the standards of those days and the people who had to earn it in the sweatshops on Allen Street.

Nevertheless, it was not the money that slowed down and often strangled the bringing-over process. It was the paper work. It was a rare immigrant who could understand or even read the documents that had to be filled in, sworn to before notaries, reproduced in varying quantities, mailed to consulates in Europe, supplemented by further documents demanded from abroad, and then, when files were lost, as they frequently were, start the tedious process over again. My father proved to be one of those rare immigrants. In addition, he was sensible enough to face the question: what good was all the paper work if after months, sometimes years, of effort, it all came to nothing for lack of passage money? Since he could not himself supply the money, my father undertook the far from simple task of obtaining it from others. Between his knowledge of how to fill out the complicated government documents, and his tireless efforts to obtain the small sums needed to implement them in the form of steerage passages from Europe, his underground railway achieved what I feel must be considered an honorable record. Coming home from his funeral, my sister Jean and I fell into a discussion of his work in those early days. Out of our heads, decades after the events, we were able to put together a list of thirty-three men, women, and children, all now alive, who had reached America through my father's efforts before Hitler's holocaust swept across Europe.

On the day in 1939 when I told him about my impending trip around the world, he was at the peak of his powers, a man about whom it had never until this moment occurred to me to wonder: Was he, too, like my mother disappointed in America?

"How about you, Pop?" I said.

"I couldn't let myself be disappointed," my father said.

"Why not?" I said.

"When I walked out of Europe into that Dutch ship I left nothing behind me that I could come back to," my father said. "Except Franz Josef's military prison."

"Franz Josef and his military prisons went out of business a long time ago," I said.

"Not inside my head," my father said.

I had a sudden recollection of moments in school when I was surprised by the receipt of a good grade on an exam I had been certain I'd flunked. One of my earliest stories—"My Father Sits in the Dark"—dealt with a boy's troubled confusion about what went on inside the head of his immigrant father who sat up late in the dark night after night, obviously brooding about something, but refusing gently to tell his son what it was.

156

"How was it in Europe when you were a boy?" I said.

"Franz Josef and his horses, that was not good," my father said.

"How about the rest of it?" I said.

My father hesitated, then the gentle smile resurfaced.

"Your mother is smarter than I am," he said.

"In what way?" I said.

"You heard what she said," my father said. "By her here in America everything is better."

"That's what she says," I said. "I'm talking about what she feels."

"How a person feels who can ever know?" he said. "All you can do is guess."

"I don't want to guess," I said. "If you feel the same way Mom does, then you're telling me not to go. Is that right?"

"How can I tell you not to do something I know you can't stop yourself from doing?"

"Pop, what do you want me to do?" I said.

"Go in good health and come back the same," my father said. "So you can tell us both, your mother and me, which one of us is right about America."

eleven

In 1940 I published an account of the trip around the world I took in 1939. It is a time that is now not infrequently referred to as "the eve of the war." *Letter of Credit* is prefaced by a short statement: "The characters and situations in this work are neither fictional nor imagined. A meticulous effort has been made to portray actual places and real people. The names of the latter have been regretfully but scrupulously changed."

Like most writers I have had some regrets after its appearance about every book I have published. There are always second thoughts, things that you could have done better or—because it is too late to undo them—it is harmless to tell yourself you could have done them better. In 1946 I gave my friend Fred Schwed, Jr., an advance copy of my about-to-be-published war novel. He stared for a few moments at the title: *Too Early to Tell*. Clearing his throat in a manner that over the years I had learned to recognize as a warning, Fred said dryly, "Yes, and too late to retract."

Letter of Credit is one book about which all my second thoughts have been pleasant. I would not, even if I could, retract a word. Somewhere in *Tender Is the Night* Fitzgerald admits us to a moment of self-revelation in the life of his hero Dick Diver: "He was twenty-seven. It was a good age for a man to be."

When I was living *Letter of Credit* I was twenty-five. I did not know then how good an age it is for a man to be when he sets out—not too much unlike Magellan and Francis Drake—to, as Magellan and Drake would surely have put it, circumnavigate the globe. When I set out I did not know, as neither

Drake nor Magellan knew, what would happen to me. I certainly did not know I was setting out on a journey that, by the time it was completed, would be obsolete: I went by ship, train, bus, bicycle, horse-drawn vehicle, whatever transportation was available within the limits of my budget. Heavier-than-air vehicles were not. Plane travel, as we came to know it after the war, did not exist in 1939. That was my lucky break. Everything that happened to me happened the way it happened to Magellan and Francis Drake: at the level of the human eye.

That is the way I recall all of it because that is the way I still see all of it: at eye level, the way they—the people and the places—looked to me then. Then was 1939. Today is 1985. My mind, as I shave, tells me I am scraping lather from the same face I carried around the world forty-six years ago. My inner eye, however, sees clearly the face that forty-six years ago did not yet have to be shaved every day. I feel like the hero of *Berkeley Square*, a play about the mystery of time and its passage to which Miss Merle S. Marine took the members of the De Witt Clinton High School Playgoers Club.

The hero is struck by the fact that the passage of time is like the flow of a winding river. If you are rowing down the river, the bend you have just left behind is the past. The bend up ahead which you have not yet reached is the future. And the piece of river into which you are now dipping your oars is the present. If you were up in an airplane, however, your vision would not be limited to the piece of eye-level river on which you are now rowing. From an airplane you would see all of it. The entire river, the part through which you have just rowed, the part on which you are now rowing, as well as the approaching part around the bend that you have not yet reached. In other words, looking down from high up you could see more than the piece to which at eye level you are limited, namely, the present. From up in the air you could see all of time: the past, the present, and the future. The plot of the play, as I recall, deals with the playwright's speculation about whether this simultaneous overall view—of the past, the present, and the future—is a good thing for the human condition. I don't recall the side of the argument on which the playwright comes

159

down. As a storyteller, however, I know the side on which, to make his play succeed with a large audience, he would have to come down.

Leafing through *Letter of Credit* in 1985 to refresh my recollection of the events through which I lived in 1939, I was surprised by an unexpected feeling of excitement. I felt somewhat like the hero of *Berkeley Square*. I was up in an airplane, looking down at the river of my time. I could see the bend in the river I had left behind forty-six years ago. I could see the stretch of river above which I was at present flying. And I could see ahead to the bend of the river I would not—if I were on the ground at eye level—be able to see. The excitement did not last long but it did not disappear. It took a different turn.

Obviously I could not see into the future, meaning beyond 1985. I could, however, look back into the future. To parts of it, anyway. Some of the people in my 1939 past had not made it to my 1985 present. They were no longer alive. The period, therefore, from our shared 1939 past when we met, to the year when they died, had been their future. Not knowing when they were going to die, they had not known the period was their future. But I knew it. I knew it because I was still alive. Or I would know it if I did a bit of work.

I made a few phone calls and wrote a few letters. As a result I am pleased to be able to do something with *Letter of Credit* that I have never been able to do with any of my other books. I can add a few postscripts.

The book was made possible by a habit I had fallen into soon after I began to publish. I discovered that my mind kept churning out story ideas at all sorts of places and all hours of the day. I was sure I would remember them. It upset me to learn that by the time I got around to jotting them down, they had fled my mind. I had nothing to jot. The solution, it seemed to me, was not to wait until I could get around to jotting my ideas down. The solution was to set aside a part of the day for the jotting-down process. I chose the period just before I went to bed. It was the only part of the day over which I had complete control, the time when I was no longer subject to the whims of Mr. Geschwind or the demands of my instructors at C.C.N.Y. and N.Y.U. Law School. When I decided to take the trip around the world it occurred to me that the jotting-down process was the only way to preserve a record of my journey. In addition there was the task of keeping my family at home informed about my progress. Why not combine both jobs in one operation? Why not send home at regular intervals a few pages typed on my portable? Or even every day if I had something of sufficient interest to report? In this way I would be relieved of the nuisance of carrying an ever-fattening journal with me all the way around the world. The journal would accumulate at home and wait for my return. All that was required was a competent assistant. I offered the assignment to my kid brother. He accepted with gratifying promptness.

"I suggest you address the envelopes to me," he said.

"Why?" I said.

"So I can read the stuff first and do a little editing."

"What kind of editing?" I said.

"Don't get your blood pressure up," Leon said. "I'm just making a suggestion."

"Okay," I said, "make it."

"If this thing is worth doing, you'll want to do it right," my kid brother said. "Right?"

I looked at him with interest. I'd known him since the day Dr. J. Morris Slutzky brought him into the world. I had never before noticed in my kid brother any of the traits I had come to associate with the editorial process. Why, all of a sudden, did he sound like Mrs. Katharine White at *The New Yorker?*

"Get to the point," I said.

"You'll want to write it all down the way it happens," he said. "Leaving nothing out, I mean. Otherwise, when you get back home and read it, it won't be much good to you as raw material. Right?"

"Stop saying 'right,' " I said. "Just tell me what you have in mind."

"I'm putting myself in your shoes," Leon said. "If I'm sending home a true account of everything that happens to me, I'm not sure I'd want Mom and Pop to read it as is. Right?"

"Oh," I said.

"Exactly," my kid brother said. "On the other hand, I'm sure you don't want to tarnish your rep as a dutiful, loving son.

So you'll have to be writing long letters home telling Mom and Pop all about it the way the *New York Times* tells it, all the news that's fit to print and only the news that's fit to print. Which coming on top of keeping a detailed daily journal with all the news that really happened, fit to print or not, grinding out those Dear Mom and Pop letters could really become a swift pain in the ass. Right?"

"If you say 'right' once more—"

"I won't if you say you'll address the envelopes to me," Leon said. "In that way I'll be reading them first, and I can decide what to leave out when I read them aloud to Mom and Pop over the evening blintzes."

"What about Jean?" I said.

"Your sister is the private secretary to a senior partner in one of this city's most prestigious law firms," my kid brother said. "She also is no dope. For Jean, since you're not exactly a dummy yourself, I'm sure you'll know how to do your own editing."

"Right," I said. "Any other suggestions?"

"What kind of paper did you plan to use?" Leon said.

"What would you suggest?" I said.

"Onionskin," my kid brother said. "For a garrulous reporter it's the only way to beat the international airmail rates."

The journal starts with a garrulous description of the bon voyage party on board the S.S. *Washington* that sent me on my way. I don't know if the *New York Times* would consider any of it fit to print, but I pluck from the unedited pudding two favorite plums. Andrea and Dick Simon's farewell present was a neat little basket containing a flashlight, a pair of sunglasses, and a cashmere pullover. Peter Schwed, younger brother of my friend Fred Schwed, Jr., brought me a small tin globe to which he attached a note: "Jerome Weidman, his oyster."

After forty-six years they still arouse a pleasant glow.

The journal pours a not unexpected contribution into the stream of the "eve of the war" reporting that, for a couple of decades after V-J Day, was responsible for a major contribution to the book publishing industry's annual gross.

In London I looked up Charlie Evans of Heinemann, my English publisher, to whom I had been introduced in New York by Dick Simon. Charlie introduced me to his son Dwye, who, perhaps at his father's suggestion, undertook the task of showing the visitor from New York around. I did not realize, until I arrived in London, that the cornerstone of the curriculum of the New York City public schools of my day was English literature. Stepping out of the boat train on the first fragment of the continent from which both my parents had fled with revulsion, fear, and anger, their son had the surprising feeling that he was coming home. These were the streets on which my oldest friends from the Hamilton Fish Park Branch of the New York Public Library had been born and raised and lived their absorbing lives. During my sight-seeing hikes I walked along with David Copperfield and Becky Sharp. At the monument in Pudding Lane the other tourists were interested in the details of the Great Fire, but I'd known those details since I was ten. What I was interested in trying to track down was Todgers Lodging House where the Pecksniffs lived.

One morning my sight-seeing program was interrupted by Dwye Evans. He called me at my hotel, told me he had to meet some people at Waterloo Station, and asked me to come along. In the taxi Dwye explained about the people we were meeting. They were the three children of a business friend in Germany. The parents had been denied the right to leave the country by the Nazi government. Dwye and his father had succeeded, however, after posting bonds and going through a good deal of red tape, in obtaining permission for the children to come to England. Charlie Evans had arranged for them to enter a private school in Surrey. They had landed at Southampton early that morning and were due on the boat train at Waterloo Station in half an hour. Dwye was going to pick them up, take them to his home for the night, and then drive them down to the school in Surrey the next day.

The boat train was on time, and we had no difficulty locating the three German children. They were standing in a bewildered huddle on the platform. I was shocked by their appearance. From Dwye's use of the word "children," and because they were traveling alone, I had imagined them to be somewhere around the age of fifteen or sixteen. They proved to be two little girls, one aged six, the other eight, and a boy of eleven.

Dwye explained the children were not allowed to take any money with them out of Germany, so their parents had equipped them with the finest products that could be purchased in Berlin. (Their luggage, for example, was beautiful.) The money would have been futile otherwise. The arresting thing about them, after I recovered from the shock of seeing how young they were, was the expression on their faces. Their bewilderment was not a thing of the moment. It was permanent, a sort of mental deformity that was as obvious as a clubfoot. The six-year-old was plump and pretty, with a mass of bright yellow hair woven into braids. Her eight-year-old sister was almost fat. And the boy of eleven was far from lean. Yet they had a shrunken, almost shriveled appearance. I had never seen children who looked like that. Not even on East Fourth Street. It took several moments before I could think clearly enough to explain to myself that these children had spent most of their lives in a constant state of terror. Fear had been with them so long that it had warped them.

Dwye introduced himself and me. We were both effusive. It was the only way we could think of acting in the face of so much chronic fright. They were polite and respectful, but I could see they were unimpressed. The boy understood English and spoke it fairly well. He had studied the language at school in Berlin. Everything we said he repeated in German to his younger sisters, and he translated his own replies for their benefit. He stood between them, his small arms across their shoulders, and listened soberly to Dwye's reassurances. They were in England now, he told them. There was nothing to worry about. They were safe. Nothing bad could happen to them here. The expressions on the faces of the two little girls did not change. They were watching their brother. He clicked his small heels together and bobbed his little head in a brisk, formal bow.

"Thank you," he said politely, and he smiled for a moment. The little girls smiled, too. But they did not take their eyes from his face. When his smile disappeared theirs went with it. I was glad when they did. The smiles on the faces of those children were not pleasant to look at. Dwye signaled a porter, who came up and carried their luggage out to a taxi. I tried to take the hand of the little six-year-old girl, but she pressed closer to her brother's side. There was no intensification of the fear on her face. She had no occasion to fear me more than any other man. It was merely that in her six years of life she had learned it was safer to hold on to her brother's hand.

In the taxi they huddled together in one corner. The boy sat in the middle, his arms still placed protectingly across the shoulders of his little sisters. Dwye and I looked at each other. There didn't seem to be anything we could say or do for these children. They stared out at the people and automobiles in Piccadilly without interest or emotion. If they had been hungry or cold or thirsty, it would have been simple. We could have bought them food or drink or clothes. But they didn't need anything like that. They needed reassurance and safety. At the moment they actually had that. The thing that was making Dwye and me feel the way we did was the knowledge that it was beyond our powers of persuasion to convince them that the reassurance and safety were actually theirs.

The taxi turned from Piccadilly into Park Lane and moved down the handsome thoroughfare that flanks Hyde Park. The smooth green lawns and lovely trees were spread out in the sun on our left. People were taking advantage of the excellent weather. Hundreds of men and women were sitting on those small, spindly green chairs that rented for tuppence an afternoon, reading newspapers, smoking placidly, dozing in the warm sunlight. The three children looked out at the pleasant scene. As we neared Hyde Park Corner Dwye smiled at them.

"Perhaps after lunch," he said, "we'll take a stroll in the park, shall we?"

"Is it allowed?" the boy asked politely.

"Why, of course it's allowed," Dwye said. "You're in England now. Nobody can hurt you here. Don't you understand that?"

The boy bobbed the respectful, polite bow with his small head. He turned back to the window.

"Yes, thank you," he said in his flat, expressionless child's treble. "I understand. In England you have green chairs for the Jews to sit on. In Germany we have yellow chairs."

165

Letter of Credit was published a year and a half later. We were not yet in the war, but the European participants had begun to take it seriously. The period known as the Bore War had just ended. France fell on the day *Letter of Credit* was published. A week later I had a note from Edna Ferber.

"While reading your new book I recognized the three children you and Dwye Evans met at Waterloo. They are members of my family. It was as a favor to me that Dwye and his father Charlie Evans, who are my very old friends, did all the considerable work involved in getting those children safely out of Germany. I would so much like to talk to you about it. Would you come to dinner next Thursday at eight?"

I rang the doorbell of Miss Ferber's apartment on Park Avenue at 7:59.

"I suspected from your work that you would be prompt," she said as she opened the door. "So I made sure I was dressed."

I was surprised. Not because she, too, was prompt. Knowing Miss Ferber's work, I had assumed the author (with George S. Kaufman) of *Dinner at Eight* would set an example for her guests. What surprised me was her appearance.

In the days when I was using my first borrower's card to the Hamilton Fish Park Branch of the New York Public Library the name Edna Ferber was already—on the shelves for the contents of which I competed every Saturday morning—as prominent as the names Dickens and Thackeray. I read *So Big* when I was in J.H.S. 64. I saw *Show Boat* when I was a member of Miss Marine's De Witt Clinton High School Playgoers Club. Many years later, when I was president of the Authors' League of America, and we were fighting for a new copyright law, Edna Ferber figured prominently in the testimony prepared by Irwin Karp, the League counsel, for me to deliver in Washington before the Senate committee: even though Miss Ferber was still very much alive, several of her earliest books had already entered the public domain because she had exhausted the inadequate copyright period then allowed by the old law.

When I met her for the first time the one thing for which my experience with Edna Ferber's work had not prepared me was her size. In my mind the creator of Emma McChesney was

166

strong, forthright, powerful, and therefore large. The woman who opened her Park Avenue door for me on that night in 1940 was tiny.

"I'm so glad you came early," she said. "It will give us time for a talk about my nieces and nephew before the other guests arrive."

After the war, when Peggy and I were living in Westport, Connecticut, Edna Ferber rented a nearby house for the summer. She asked us to dinner and I asked her what had happened to the boy and his two little sisters Dwye Evans and I met at the boat train in Waterloo Station in 1939.

"With the help of Dwye Evans and his father we managed to get them to America before Pearl Harbor," Edna Ferber said. "You will be pleased to know that, in spite of their still-tender years, they are living happily ever after."

Scotland was Dwye's idea. He was driving up to Edinburgh on business and asked if I would like to come along. I said yes if we could stop at Kirriemuir.

"What for?" Dwye said.

"I'd like to take a look at James M. Barrie's birthplace," I said.

"Any special reason?" Dwye said.

"*Sentimental Tommy*," I said. "When I was a kid it was the first book I borrowed from the Hamilton Fish Park Branch of the New York Public Library."

Kirriemuir looked like an illustration from Pierre Loti's *Pêcheur d'Islande*, the text we used in second-year French at De Witt Clinton. There were, however, no signs of the sea or fishermen. Just clusters of decaying stone cottages baking in the sun. The cottage we wanted looked no different from its neighbors but was easy enough to identify. There was a metal plaque on the wall beside the door. As soon as Dwye stopped the car the door was opened by a toothless old woman with uncombed white hair for whom the word "slatternly" had obviously been invented.

"I'm Mrs. Thompson," she said. "You'll be wanting to see the house?"

"If we may," Dwye said.

"This way, please."

She held the door for us. We stepped into a low-ceilinged room with an earthen floor. It was full of the smell of boiling cabbage and the shrieks of several tumbling small children.

"All yours?" Dwye said.

"My daughter's," Mrs. Thompson said. "This way to the room, please."

The room was a museum on the floor above. The walls were covered with inexpertly framed photographs of Barrie taken at different periods of his life, souvenirs of his youth in Kirrie-muir, and mementos of his career, including playbills and in-scribed portraits of famous actresses who had performed in his plays. Copies of his books were racked on a sagging shelf above an old kitchen table.

"He did his early writing on that," Mrs. Thompson said.

"How do you know?" Dwye said.

"He told me so," Mrs. Thompson said.

"You knew him?" I said.

"Came up here for a last look, he did. A few months before he died. Gave me this."

Mrs. Thompson took down a picture from the wall. It had the only frame in the room that seemed fairly new. It contained a full-face picture of Barrie staring directly into the camera. He looked like a man who had just lost a bundle at the track and was trying to pretend it didn't matter. In one corner, in a strong slanting script, was written: "To Mrs. Thompson of the tene-ments, from J. M. Barrie, late of same."

"He must have liked you," Dwye said.

"No reason he shouldn't," Mrs. Thompson said. "I don't get a shilling from the National Trust for keeping his memory green, just free rent and whatever the trippers are kind enough to leave as a tip."

On the table under the pictures, near a jumble of dusty knickknacks, I saw a playscript bound in pale blue covers. It was a copy of *The Boy David*, Barrie's last play, his only attempt at a Biblical subject.

"He wrote that special for this actress Elisabeth Bergner," Mrs. Thompson said.

I flipped the pages. It was probably an early version. There were many handwritten corrections. I was surprised to note that most of these were amplifications of statements the author had apparently felt were too brief. The typed "Who are you?," for example, had been crossed out. Above was inked in: "Who is it, pray, that I have the honor of addressing?" I wondered if the author was trying to slow down the scene, or if he was having difficulty achieving what he thought was a correct Biblical tone.

"Is this his handwriting?" I said.

I thought perhaps the corrections might have been inked in by a director.

"See for yourself," Mrs. Thompson said.

She pointed to the corrected page, then at the inscription in the corner of the picture Barrie had given her.

"They certainly look alike," Dwye said.

"Why shouldn't they?" Mrs. Thompson said. "They were done by the same hand."

She opened a drawer in the table and pulled out a battered little history book. On the flyleaf, in the still not completely firmed-up handwriting of a schoolboy, was written in pencil: "James M. Barrie, 1874." Mrs. Thompson opened the book and very carefully slid out several tattered sheets of ruled notepaper. They were covered with neatly written lists of famous battles, dates, kings, and historical places. We thanked Mrs. Thompson, tipped her, and left.

"When you were examining the picture you had an odd look on your face," Dwye said in the car as we drove away. "What were you thinking about?"

"Mrs. Sandys," I said.

"Who was she?" Dwye said.

"Sentimental Tommy's mother," I said.

When I left England Dwye's farewell present was a copy of *Tommy and Grizel*.

I read it on the way to Paris, where I was met at the Gare St.-Lazare by a young reporter named Leigh White from the *Paris Herald*. After the interview we picked up his wife and I took them to dinner. They were an attractive couple. He was blond, husky, cheerful, and garrulous. An American college-football-player type. His wife, Mariecruz, was dour and taciturn, the lean, dark, good-looking daughter of an Andalusian coal miner who spoke no English and even less French than I did. They met in Spain when Leigh White was covering the civil war for an American news agency. They were married during the retreat from Barcelona because it was only as his wife that he as an American citizen could get her out of Spain. They were almost penniless when they arrived in Paris but, through the influence of Vincent Sheean, Leigh got a job as a reporter on the *Paris Herald*. The pay was low, but so was the franc. As a result, with the generosity of Jo Davidson, who solved their housing problem by turning over to them his studio on the rue de Cicé, they were managing to scrape along while they tried to plan their future. This, I learned, was true of quite a few young people in Paris who had come out of the Spanish civil war. The city seemed a good place to pause for catching one's breath. Even those who did not have to do it in Paris managed somehow to get there for the attempt.

Mel Auerbach, for instance. He came out of Spain with Leigh White after the collapse of the Republic, and was rewarded by his syndicate with a good job on the A.P. desk in London. Soon after I arrived in Paris, however, I learned from White that his friend Auerbach was coming to Paris with his wife.

"Why?" I said.

"He says he wants to find his sea legs," Leigh White said.

I don't think White was doing anything more than using a popular euphemism for the situation in which he and so many of his colleagues found themselves. Soon after I got to know Mel Auerbach, however, I realized the phrase was more apt than Leigh White had probably intended it to be. Auerbach was obsessed by the image of a sailboat.

He was born in Hackensack, New Jersey, the son of a grocer. Even as I on East Fourth Street, so Mel Auerbach in Hackensack found his life guided very early by his borrower's card from the local public library. Almost as soon as he started to read he started to dream about becoming a writer. Soon the dream began to take on sharper definition and specific equipment. The chief piece of equipment was a sailboat. On it, at the appropriate moment, Mel Auerbach planned to set out down the Intracoastal Waterway for Florida, writing the Great American Novel as he went. He intended to keep sailing until he completed his masterpiece. The dream persisted through the discouraging reality of trying to earn a living after college as an A.P. stringer on space rates in the Hackensack area.

Auerbach was so broke that he sought out expense-account assignments because of the opportunity they provided for picking up a few extra dollars by padding the swindle sheet. Thus, when he learned that the dirigible *Hindenburg* was on its way from Germany to Lakehurst, he called the A.P. office in New York and applied for the assignment of covering the arrival because it meant he could probably beef up his gasoline and meal vouchers. When he got to Lakehurst he found there were so many reporters—many with nationally and internationally known bylines, all of them more important than the A.P. stringer— that Auerbach decided it was pointless to join the crowd out on the field. They all wanted interviews with the dirigible's V.I.P. passengers. Against that kind of competition Mel Auerbach felt his chances for an interview were slim, so he decided to stick close to his wire, which was almost half a mile from the mooring tower but had a clear view of the landing field.

The *Hindenburg*, of course, surprised the world, as well as the Lakehurst press, by never making it to the mooring tower. The zeppelin blew up instead, killing many passengers and members of the ground crew. The disaster, as it turned out, took place practically under Mel Auerbach's nose. He was the only reporter on the scene who was anywhere near his wire, so he got the disaster flash off first, enabling the A.P. to scoop the world. He followed up with the standard A.P. routine, sending the bulletins required for keeping the story on the front pages of all A.P. clients. He added, however, an improvisation of his own. There were several reporters on the scene who worked for small local papers. All these papers had gone to press before the disaster occurred. Mel Auerbach, acting without authority, hired them all as his legmen. All night long, while the fire slowly burned itself out and the list of casualties grew longer, Auerbach's legmen chased all over the field and brought the fresh details to him. Auerbach rewrote steadily through the night, and fed the results into the A.P. wire. His boss in New York was delighted.

"All of a sudden from an unknown stringer out in the boon-ies I was King Shit," Auerbach told me in Paris. "My boss asked me what I wanted as a reward. I said I wanted to be transferred to Europe. They gave me a big raise, added a nice fat bonus, and shipped me to Spain."

The assignment was exciting and lucrative. In addition to his salary Auerbach had an expense account and received a monthly bonus for working in a war zone. His expense account was so liberal, and his Hackensack tastes were so modest, that he was able to bank his entire salary as well as his bonus money. As a result, when he was on his way out of Spain during the retreat from Barcelona, he had saved enough to turn his dream into reality. He could go home to Hackensack, buy that sail-boat, and start writing his novel.

"Just before I crossed the border into France," Auerbach told me, "I stopped to do one last story on a concentration camp, and that's where I met Pepita. I'd known her parents in Barce-lona. They'd been killed in the final fighting, leaving her alone and penniless, which was how she got scooped up with all the other refugees in this camp. She's just a kid, and she looked so helpless I couldn't walk away and leave her there. The only way I could get her out was the way Leigh got Mariecruz out."

"You married her," I said.

He reared back as though I had hurled an accusation at him.

"What else could I do?" he said.

It seemed sensible to treat this as a rhetorical question.

"Didn't you like London?" I said.

"You married?" Auerbach said.

"Not yet," I said.

"When you get married you won't ask that question," he said.

"Why not?" I said.

"It's not what you like," Auerbach said. "It's what your wife likes."

"Your wife didn't like London?" I said.

"My wife is seventeen years old," Mel Auerbach said. "If you've just spent your whole seventeen-year life as a coal min-er's daughter in Spain, starving and hiding in shell holes, and

172

at the last moment, when everybody else in your family has been killed, you get saved from a concentration camp by a lucky break, how can you not like any place with a roof over your head, decent food to eat, a clean bed to sleep in, and a husband to take care of you?"

"I've just spent some time in London," I said. "It struck me as a place that at the very least meets those basic requirements."

"You bet your ass it does," Mel Auerbach said.

"Then why did you and Pepita leave?" I said.

"We got ourselves pregnant," he said.

"Oh," I said.

"Yeah," Mel Auerbach said.

I thought about that for a few moments. According to H. L. Mencken a great city is a place where you can get anything you want at any hour of the day or night.

"Can't it be done in London?" I said.

"Probably," Mel Auerbach said. "But Leigh White says for an abortion Paris is better."

I did some more thinking.

"Why does it have to be London or Paris?" I said. "You just told me you're pretty well fixed financially. You've got enough socked away to buy that sailboat and start writing your novel. Why not go home and do it there?"

Mel Auerbach gave me a funny look.

"You're a nice Jewish boy, right?" he said.

"Right," I said.

"Then like the British say, let me put you in the picture," Mel Auerbach said. "You're me. Your family keeps kosher. They live over the grocery store in Hackensack, New Jersey. Their darling son, they haven't seen him over a year, he comes home from Europe with a prize package: a *shicksa* wife. While they're still trying not to drop dead from the shock, little Melvin breaks the news his *shicksa* wife is knocked up and he's got to arrange for an abortion."

Pause.

"You've answered my question," I said.

"So let me ask one," Mel Auerbach said.

"Shoot," I said.

"What are you doing tonight?"

"You have something in mind?" I said.

"Yes."

"What?"

"Chez Flammbaum," Mel Auerbach said.

"What's that?" I said.

"A kosher restaurant in Montmartre," Mel Auerbach said. "Leigh White says it's very good."

To a nice Jewish boy there are no bad kosher restaurants. Chez Flammbaum, however, lingers in my mind not for the food, which was excellent, but because of our waiter, who was named Pinchas. He could have been transplanted from Ratner's on Second Avenue: thin, stooped, hollow-cheeked, his mournful eyes sunk deep, his naked skull decorated with pencil stripes of white hair carefully combed over from a still-fertile tuft behind the opposite ear, weighing somewhere between 100 and 110, and ready to supply, along with the food, the definitive opinion on whatever subject is under discussion at his table. On the night of my visit to Chez Flammbaum the subject was Danzig. Leigh White had brought news from the *Paris Herald* city room of a new development in the mounting crisis. He and Mel Auerbach compared it with the rumors in Barcelona just before the end.

"Were you in Spain?" Leigh White said.

"Long before you got there," Pinchas said.

He had been everywhere. He was born in Antwerp, where he was trained as a diamond cutter. He was hounded out of Holland by anti-Semitism. He tried Poland and Austria and Belgium with similar results. Finally he came to Paris from Spain and found his job with Chez Flammbaum. He spoke French, Spanish, German, Russian, Polish, English, and of course Yiddish. Mel Auerbach and I tried to speak Yiddish to him but he insisted on replying in English.

"What difference does it make whether tonight in Danzig the crisis is better or worse?" Pinchas said. "It's what we do about the crisis that matters. If we do like we did before, which was nothing, we know already what will happen. The same like it happened in the Ruhr and in Austria."

"Doesn't that upset you?" Leigh White said.

"What upsets me is everybody is so afraid of war that nobody understands that a thing like Danzig is a chance to finish him off, but once more, like in the past, we won't take the chance," Pinchas said. "No matter what Hitler does, or how many times he does it, everybody acts like it's a great big surprise, like he's never done anything like it before. So when the crisis is over, everybody says see, it's just another bluff he pulled off, like all the other bluffs, and because this time again there was no war everybody is happy. Why can't they understand that so long as an animal like Hitler is still alive there's nothing to be happy about?"

"A bluff is better than a war," Leigh White said.

"How long can we let him kill people and children in their homes and call it a bluff?" Pinchas said. "Why can't we look at the truth and face the fact that from each bluff he comes out stronger? Now is the time to stop it. Not tomorrow. Now, today. No more hoping for another bluff. There's only one way to finish him and that's with a war. It has to come. Better the war should come now over Danzig while he's still a little bit weaker than he'll be after he pulls off tomorrow's bluff."

"That's a strange point of view for a Jew," Leigh White said.

"If you were a Jew, you wouldn't think so," Pinchas said.

"How about my friends?" Leigh White said. "They're both Jews." He turned to me and Mel Auerbach. "Do you agree with this guy?"

I hesitated. So did Mel Auerbach.

"Don't answer," Pinchas said. "Because you're Americans, and Americans they don't know the answer. They've never had to live through what we over here we've had to live through all our lives. You think what he's doing today to the Jews in Germany is something new? Of course not, but I'll tell you what's the only thing that is new."

"What's that?" Leigh White said.

"This crazy *momzer* he thinks he's so smart because we let him get away with all these bluffs one after the other," Pinchas said. "But the truth is he's stupid, so stupid that he has no idea what he's up against."

"What is he up against?" Leigh White said.

"Me," Pinchas said, slapping his narrow chest. "Them." He pointed to me and Mel Auerbach. "All of us all over the world. The Hitlers they've been trying to wipe us out for thousands of years, but do I look wiped out? How about these two American friends of yours? Do they look wiped out? We're still here, aren't we? And we'll always be here. So don't worry about Danzig. If it turns out this time it's not just another bluff, if tomorrow we wake up and find out this time it's war, so all right, good, we'll fight him like we fought all the others, and it'll come out the same way it's always come out. Me, look, I'm serving you chopped liver. You, you're eating chopped liver. We, the chopped-liver eaters, we'll live to pee on that bastard's grave."

Some of us did. About Pinchas, I can only hope.

The crisis followed me to Juan-les-Pins, where it took a different form. I met an English girl named Beriton and her older brother. We were all staying at the Hôtel-sur-Mer for the same reason: it was modestly priced. The Beritons were on holiday, Rita from her job as a shorthand-typist with an advertising agency on Oxford Street in London, her brother Hugh from his job in the London office of a firm of automobile manufacturers with whom, before the First World War in which he lost a leg at the Marne, Hugh had been a successful salesman. The loss of his leg meant the end of his career as a salesman, but the automobile firm took him back at a modest salary as their foreign-letter translator. He knew several languages. He was a large man of forty-six, with a strong face that was beginning to settle into jowls, close-cropped black hair going gray at the temples, a stolid manner, and a pleasant smile. He heaved himself about easily enough with his crutches, but it was obvious that without Rita he would not have been able to move about as freely as he did. Edward Gibbon brought us together. I noticed that every day after breakfast, when his sister helped her brother settle himself on the beach for the morning, she left him with a fat book. I am always curious about what people read, so I sneaked a look. Hugh Beriton's constant beach companion was a copy of the Modern Library edition of *The Decline and Fall of the Roman Empire*. I'd been nibbling away at it for years but always, before long, I found something to distract me. This did not stop me from starting a conversation one day about Gibbon, which led where I had hoped it would: an introduction to Rita. I didn't realize we had become good friends until Bastille Day. Monsieur Gruno, the proprietor of the Hôtel-sur-Mer, laid on a special dinner. An orchestra played, we all sang the "Marseillaise," "God Save the King," and "The Star-Spangled Banner." Toasts were exchanged and there was a fireworks display on the beach.

"Let's go down and watch them being touched off," Rita said.

We stood up and waited for Hugh, but he shook his head.

"You two run along," he said. "I'm a little tired. I'll have Gruno fetch my Gibbon and catch up on a bit of reading before I turn in."

Rita kissed him good night, and we walked down through the noisy, bright streets toward the beach. Music came pounding out of the dance halls and nightclubs around us. By the time we reached the end of the pavement the fireworks display was over and people were coming back toward the dance halls and nightclubs. We stepped down onto the sand and walked along toward the little wooden jetty from which we swam every day. Near it was a dinghy drawn up on the beach. It belonged to one of the yachts anchored offshore. We climbed in and sat down. It was very dark and there was a small, comfortable breeze. Behind us were the sounds of music and laughter and an occasional raucous scream. But the noises were filtered through the night and seemed far away. In front of us the sea was black and smooth. To the right we could see the dotted line of tiny lights that was Cannes and to our left, farther away, the faint yellow glow that was Nice. I lit a cigarette and handed it to Rita and then lit one for myself. We smoked in silence for a while.

"Well," Rita finally said. "It's back to Brompton day after tomorrow. I don't see that I have cause for complaint, though. I've had a ripping time. Haven't you?"

"Yes," I said.

She looked at me quickly as she poked her foot back into her silver slipper, using her forefinger for a shoehorn.

"What's the matter?" she said. "Anything wrong?"

"No," I said. "Yes. I don't know, really. I sent a wire to the travel agency in Marseilles this afternoon, asking them to book my passage on a ship going to India."

"Oh," she said; then, "You lucky dog."

"I suppose I am," I said.

She looked at me again. She had taken off the second shoe and was shaking out the sand. She stopped and balanced it on her palm.

"Homesick?" she said.

"A little, but it's more than that," I said. "You know all those things I told you about this trip. How I've looked forward to it, what I thought it was going to be like."

"Yes," Rita said.

"Well, it hasn't been like that at all," I said. "I've had fun, but it hasn't been— Well, things like tonight. Gruno making that speech about peace, those two little girls trying to sing 'God Save the King' and 'The Star-Spangled Banner'—it's no time to be taking a pleasure trip. They have to be here, it's their home. You have to be in London, it's your home. But I shouldn't be here. I should be in New York, that's my home."

I waited for her to say something, but she didn't. She sat on the crossboard of the little boat, her elbows on her knees, and looked out at the sea.

"I can cut my trip short right here," I said. Now that I'd started, I wanted to get it all out. I was finally saying the things with which my mind had been wrestling for weeks. "I can catch a ship and be back in New York in a week or ten days. Or I can go over to Marseilles and take the ship going to the Far East, which means I won't be home for months. If I had the guts," I said, "I'd take the ship back home to New York, because that's what I want to do."

"Do you have a cigarette?" Rita said.

I gave her a cigarette, took one for myself, and struck a match for both of us. She inhaled deeply.

"You're the same age Hugh was when he went to war," she said. "Nobody knows what will happen in the next few months, perhaps in the next few weeks. You have a chance to do something that most people would give years of their lives to do. If the war comes and you have to fight, you'll have to fight whether you took this trip or went home. If you fight and something happens to you, the way it happened to Hugh, at least you'll have something to look back on and remember. Surely you don't want to spend your life like Hugh, poor darling Hugh, translating letters about motor parts at four guineas a week, going to the bios on crutches every weekend, and reading Gibbon before bedtime. Six months from now you may be in the trenches or whatever they'll be called this time. Next year you may be a cripple for life. There are enough of us who must do the things we don't want to do. Hugh and I must go back to Brompton. We don't want to but we must. But you don't have to go back."

She paused, and for a moment she scowled down at the burning end of her cigarette. Then she smiled and threw the cigarette into the water.

"Look at it this way," she said. "You've got something every damned one of us wants, and you have it right there in your hands, and you're thinking of throwing it away. Doesn't make much sense, does it?"

"No, it doesn't," I said, and it didn't.

I never saw Rita again. She and her brother Hugh were both killed in 1944 when a V-1 rocket—a.k.a. buzz bombs or doodle bugs—hit their house in Brompton.

I sailed for Bombay from Marseilles on July 21, 1939, aboard the P. & O. liner S.S. *Rajputana*. Two days later, when we docked at Malta, we were not allowed to go ashore. Security reasons. I was leaning on the rail, looking across the harbor at warships lined up in double rows, huge guns pointing directly at us, when someone on my left said, "Curious the effect of late-afternoon light on battleship gray, isn't it?"

I turned. Beside me, leaning on the rail, was one of the Indian students who were returning from school in England to their homes in Bombay and Calcutta. What had impressed me about them was the precision with which they aped the ways and manners of Englishmen. If you listened to them talk, without glancing at their faces, it was almost impossible to distinguish them from the Englishmen on board. They all wore blazers that bore on the left breast the coat of arms of some English public school. They joined industriously in the organized deck sports. They never laughed indecorously or raised their voices in argument. They were polite and gallant and gentlemanly always. They dressed for dinner every night and diligently chain-smoked Players and Craven A's. Only in one respect did they differ. The English men and women on board were all reading *No Orchids for Miss Blandish* and back numbers of *Esquire*. The Indian youths were all reading Penguin editions of *A Philosophy for Modern Man* and *A New History of England*. I turned from the young man beside me to look again at the battleships in the dying sunlight.

"Well," I said, "they say the sun never sets on the British Empire."

The young man gave me a slanting glance.

"Do you know why they say that?" he said.

"No, why?" I said.

"Because God doesn't trust an Englishman alone in the dark."

He may have been right, but I've known quite a few Englishmen I would trust at any time of day. In London, for example, there had been Dwye Evans and his father Charlie. In Juan-les-Pins there had been Hugh Beriton. Two months later, in Singapore, there was Bramwell Ormiston.

He said, "Are you planning to make any stops between here and Australia?"

I looked up from my oysters. Mr. Ormiston's prominent front teeth were pulling one of the small brown lumps from the slender silver fork. The Englishman's eyes looked troubled. I wondered if the oysters could be as big a disappointment to him as they were to me.

"Batavia, yes," I said. "I've got Charlie Evans's letter to Himmelsdyck at the Nederlandsche Indische Handelsbank." I paused, hesitated, then said, "I told you that, I'm sure I did."

Mr. Ormiston's oyster came free. He chewed with obvious pleasure. The troubled look, then, was caused by something else.

"So you did." He swallowed the oyster and poised the fork over his plate for another assault. "So you did," Mr. Ormiston said again.

Something, it seemed to me, had gone wrong during the last few minutes. Bramwell Ormiston had insisted on giving me a farewell lunch at Le Bistro before my ship sailed. It was the new "in" place. It would be a shame if, after two weeks in Singapore, I left town without sampling the oysters for which the restaurant was famous. They were flown up twice a week from Australia. Oysters, which after a struggle I'd learned to like, have never been a passion. They tend to remind me of Burton Rascoe and his snails. Like Lou G. Siegel's Specials, I can take them or leave them alone. Furthermore, I had learned on this trip that, just before boarding a ship, I hated to be separated from my luggage. I'd suggested, therefore, that we have our farewell lunch at my hotel. This would have made it possible for me to check out, leave my bags in the lobby, and eat my lunch in peace. Besides, in my fifteen days at the Raffles, I had learned that the food in the Grill Room was not only as good as any food I'd had in Singapore. For a boy from East Fourth Street it was probably too good. My pants were beginning to feel tight.

Bramwell Ormiston, however, insisted. In view of the hospitality I had enjoyed from his predecessors in the publishing business I had met thus far on my trip, it seemed elementary politeness to agree. Mr. Ormiston was the senior sales representative in the area for a number of British publishers, including Charlie Evans of Heinemann, who had published my first three books. Charlie had advised Mr. Ormiston to be on the lookout for me. Mr. Ormiston was determined to see that I had a good time in Singapore. His determination had proved one of the more pleasant aspects of the visit. So here I was at Le Bistro, digging sandy oysters out of what looked like shells of halved walnuts, and wondering what had happened to the cheerful Englishman whom, after two weeks, I had come to think of as a friend.

"You've got something on your mind," I said.

"Yes," Mr. Ormiston said.

"Maybe you'd better tell me," I said. "I'm due at the dock in forty minutes."

"Quite," Mr. Ormiston said. "Before coming over to meet you for lunch I read through the wires at the office."

I could feel my stomach muscles tighten. I had sailed from New York in February. Now, near the end of August, I knew exactly what Mr. Ormiston meant when he said he had been reading through the wires at the office. From Charlie Evans in London to Mr. Ormiston in Singapore, all the men I'd met had started their business days by reading through the wires at the office.

"What were they like this morning?" I said.

"On the bad side, rather," Mr. Ormiston said.

"Old bad?" I said. "Or new bad?"

"I don't think there's much chance of holding him," Mr. Ormiston said. "The show is about to start."

My stomach muscles eased. The show had been about to start in London, in Paris, in Marseilles, in Bombay, in Kuala Lumpur. So long as here in Singapore it was still about to start, I was sure I would get back to New York before anything actually did start. After all, Dr. Slutzky had said I would. And hadn't I promised my mother and father they could count on it?

After the oysters Mr. Ormiston and I shared something out of a casserole, we had coffee, and, to my great relief, I found we were rolling down to the dock in his Daimler.

"Please don't hang around," I said. "You've got things to do."

"Nonsense," Mr. Ormiston said. "I'll just see you safely on board."

A few minutes later I was following him down the corridor of B Deck on the S.S. *Nieuw Zeeland* in Singapore harbor. Mr. Ormiston was following a Chinese steward. He carried my two bags. The steward opened the door with a key dangling from a large metal hoop around his neck. Mr. Ormiston moved past him, circled the cabin, and poked sharply at the spotless linen spreads on both carefully made berths. One was under the porthole. The other was at the corridor side of the cabin, set at right angles to the berth under the porthole.

"Any preference?" Mr. Ormiston said.

"No," I said. "I can sleep anywhere."

"Lucky chap," Mr. Ormiston said. "Steward."

"Sah?"

"One case here."

Mr. Ormiston's forefinger stabbed at the space under the berth against the corridor wall. The steward dipped down and shoved my brown suitcase into the space.

"Most people choose the berth under the porthole," Mr. Ormiston said. "A common error. You'll be steaming south. The berth under the porthole will get the morning sun. Nobody sleeps through a sunrise in the Timor Sea. The other case here, Steward."

He dropped some coins into the steward's hand.

"Thank you, sah."

"Quite," Mr. Ormiston said.

The steward went out.

"Well," I said.

"Well, then," Mr. Ormiston said.

He clapped his hands as though he was summoning a coolie in a movie about the Far East. With a small shock I realized we were not in a movie. Mr. Ormiston and I were in the Far East. It seemed as improbable as the awkwardness of farewell.

"I have a confession to make," Mr. Ormiston said.

"What's that?" I said.

"I may have saddled you with a bore on this trip," he said. "I have a friend who is sailing with you and I said it was all right to look you up."

"I can't believe any friend of yours is a bore," I said.

I have made dumber remarks in my day, but not many.

"It's very kind of you to say that," Mr. Ormiston said. "But it's not true, of course. Even if it were, I should have asked your permission first."

"Let's say you did," I said. "Who is he?"

"It's not a he," Mr. Ormiston said. "She's a Mrs. Killian."

She was the wife of a man with whom Mr. Ormiston had been at Cambridge. After graduation Howard Killian was invited to Australia as editor of a new daily newspaper in Sydney. He did a brilliant job. The paper became a huge success. Killian's financial rewards were large. He married the daughter of a prominent Sydney banker. They had a son who was sent to Cambridge.

"It's been a happily ever after story, truly it has," Mr. Ormiston said. "Until six months ago, when Kate suddenly stunned Howard by telling him she wanted a divorce."

Killian couldn't believe it. There had never been the slightest hint of any difficulty. He was still very much in love with her, and he'd assumed she was in love with him. He tried to talk her out of it, but he couldn't. Kate Killian was a very forthright person. Perhaps a bit too forthright. Ruthless, Mr. Ormiston suggested. She maintained she was just as upset as her husband was, but she couldn't help herself. She'd fallen in love with another man and that was all there was to it.

"Who's the other man?" I said.

"That's the puzzling thing about it," Ormiston said. "Nobody knows."

He meant, I gathered, nobody who knew the Killians. According to Mr. Ormiston, Kate Killian refused to tell her husband. A few months before I arrived in Singapore Howard Killian called Ormiston from Sydney and told his friend Mrs. Killian was going to Japan for a divorce. She'd be coming through Singapore and Killian wanted Ormiston to be on the watch for her. Ormiston had gladly done this because he and his wife had always been fond of Kate Killian. When she stopped off on the way to Tokyo, however, she said nothing to the Ormistons except that she was sorry it had to happen, but she felt absolutely helpless. She was in love with another man, and in her view divorce was the only way to be fair to her husband Howard. A week before Ormiston and I had lunch at Le Bistro, Kate Killian called from Tokyo. She told Ormiston she'd be coming through Singapore again, divorce in hand, and she was booked out on the *Nieuw Zeeland* for Sydney. She had a two-day stopover in Singapore and she wondered if she could spend the time with the Ormistons. She did and, on this morning, when Ormiston offered to drive her down to the ship Mrs. Killian said no, Mrs. Ormiston had already offered to take her and she'd accepted because Mrs. Ormiston had told her Mr. Ormiston was seeing off a friend on the same ship.

"Me," I said.

"Quite," Mr. Ormiston said. "At breakfast this morning, when we were saying good-bye, I felt a bit sorry for her, going back to Sydney on her own. Since nobody knew who the other man was, all their Sydney friends were on Howard's side. My wife and I couldn't help thinking she might find the return to Sydney a bit sticky."

"How did I get into it?" I said.

"My wife, I'm afraid," Mr. Ormiston said. "She's read your stories, and she's liked them, especially the ones about East Fourth Street and your mother. My wife thought what Kate probably needs at the moment is the sympathetic ear of a stranger, and what ear could be better than yours? After all, you'd both be on the same ship, you're both traveling alone, and, well, before I'd quite thought it through I gave her your name and suggested she look you up. I do hope you'll forgive me."

"Not until I find you need forgiveness," I said. "Right now all you've earned are my thanks."

"For what?" Mr. Ormiston said.

"For the opportunity to repay you and Mrs. Ormiston for the kindness you've shown me," I said.

They don't—my kid brother once observed sardonically to my sister about their brother the storyteller—they don't call him Gentleman Jerome for nothing.

"That's very kind of you," Mr. Ormiston said. "I hope you don't find Kate too boring."

He clapped his hands again, and seemed to realize no coolies would come running. He stuck out his hand.

"Good-bye, old chap, and good luck." Then he was in the open doorway, one foot out in the corridor over the raised sill. "I don't mean to frighten you, old chap," Mr. Ormiston said. "But do get home as quickly as you can."

I was still trying to think of something to say when I realized I was alone. I decided to unpack. I got as far as putting my toilet kit on the shelf under the shaving mirror when there was a tap on the door.

"Come in."

In came a woman who looked not unlike my mother. If, that is, my mother had a standing weekly hair appointment with Mr. Kenneth, and her clothes had been made for her by Molyneux. The visitor was not exactly old, certainly not old old but definitely no longer young, like my mother once beautiful now handsome, and by any yardsticks very appealing.

"Mr. Weidman?"

"Yes."

"I'm Kate Killian," she said with a smile. "Brammy Ormiston said if I looked you up, you wouldn't throw me out."

"He spoke no less than the truth," I said. "He just left here a few minutes ago."

"I know," Mrs. Killian said. "His wife just left me."

"In that case," I said, "why don't we go up on deck and watch the ship get under way?"

"If you don't mind, I'd rather not," Mrs. Killian said. "I don't want to run into any more Singapore people I know. They make a career of these sailings. They seem to equate missing a bon voyage party with excommunication. After forty-eight hours of houseguesting with the Ormistons I've had enough of Singapore."

"I thought you might like a drink," I said.

"I would," Mrs. Killian said.

"Unfortunately I have nothing down here," I said, "so we'll have to go up to the bar."

"No we won't," Mrs. Killian said, opening her large alligator purse. "I thought being an American you might still be functioning under Prohibition mentality, so I came prepared." She pulled out a bottle of J. & B. "A couple of tooth mugs would do very nicely."

I got them down from the shelf under the shaving mirror.

"Say when," Mrs. Killian said, and poured.

"When," I said.

"Surely you can do better than that," Mrs. Killian said.

"Thanks, no," I said. "This will do me fine."

"Not for me," Mrs. Killian said, and poured herself a belt. "Now, then, why don't you sit here." She pushed me toward the bunk under the porthole. "And I'll sit here."

She moved to the other bunk against the facing wall, sat down, and raised her glass.

"Here's to sin," Mrs. Killian said. "I'm sure Brammy Ormiston filled you in on the scarlet woman his Cambridge classmate married."

186

"Only about the divorce," I said.

Mrs. Killian laughed.

"That's as far as he could go," she said. "He doesn't know the best part."

"The other man?" I said.

She laughed again.

"The other man," she said.

"He said nobody knows the other man," I said.

"How silly of Brammy," Mrs. Killian said. "Obviously I do."

"But nobody else," I said.

"If you mean my husband, no, he does not," Mrs. Killian said. "I've always found that if you don't want people to know something about you, the sensible thing is not to tell anybody. At the moment the other man, as he's come to be known in Sydney and Singapore, the other man and I are quite enough."

"You seem to be having fun keeping it that way," I said.

She gave me a sharp look.

"Brammy tells me you're a writer," Mrs. Killian said. "You know that nothing you do is fun unless you have an audience."

"A story doesn't exist until somebody reads it?"

"Precisely," Mrs. Killian said with the sort of smile that was my mother's very effective substitute for Mr. Kenneth and Molyneux.

"Am I your audience?" I said.

"You could be," Mrs. Killian said.

"How?" I said.

She tossed off her drink and stood up.

"Meet me in the bar before dinner," she said.

When I got to the bar it was jammed. I worked my way toward Mrs. Killian. She was sitting at a small table with a tall, handsome man in a spotless white uniform.

"You know our purser," Mrs. Killian said. Then she saw the look on my face and she laughed. "No, no, this is not the other man. This is Mr. Van Zuylen, our purser. He was telling me the latest on the ultimatum."

"What ultimatum?" I said.

"I was just about to find out," Mrs. Killian said. "Sit down.

187

Mr. Van Zuylen is the only one on board who can be relied on for accurate information."

"Thank you," the purser said. "The situation is not simple. Our radio communications with Europe are always erratic when we are at sea because of the wide fluctuation in atmospheric conditions. At times like this we must also face the fact that London and Warsaw and Berlin are not paying very much attention to a small Dutch vessel steaming south from the equator for Sunda Strait. We must scramble for our news, as one were to say. More accurately, what we get are fragments combed from the air by our wireless room which we then try to put together into some sort of comprehensible pattern."

"Tell us the pattern," Mrs. Killian said.

"The sequence of our wireless room fragments have been put together as follows," Mr. Van Zuylen said. "First, two days ago, on one September, German troops cross the Polish border. Yesterday, on two September, while we are still docked in Singapore, all is confusion. The Singapore newspapers are incoherent. The wireless reports on shore the same. The ship's wireless, of course, sealed as always while in port. So of yesterday we can truly say we know nothing. Therefore, today, three September, we sail from Singapore, and we begin here on board the familiar combing of fragments from the air by our wireless room. Thus we learn, or from the fragments we have managed to put together we believe we learn, that this morning, on three September, the British prime minister sends an ultimatum to Hitler. Withdraw from Poland in twelve hours or face war."

"When are the twelve hours up?" I said.

"The point is that we are ignorant as to precisely when the twelve hours are up," Mr. Van Zuylen said. "In addition to the normal complexity of varying time zones, we are faced with a totally new and unusual—"

The purser's voice stopped. He was staring across my head. I turned. A white-haired man in white uniform had come into the bar. He looked around, saw the purser, and came toward our table in a half trot. He was carrying a sheet of pink onion-skin paper. He looked as though a doctor had just told him he was bleeding internally.

"Sir," he said when he reached our table.

Mr. Van Zuylen took the onionskin. His hand shook. The paper made a faint but clearly audible rustling noise. The purser pulled from his pocket a pair of black horn-rimmed glasses. On his nose they unexpectedly made an unpleasant caricature of his until this moment woodenly handsome face. When the purser looked up from the paper I realized with a sense of shock that the room had been totally emptied of sound, as though every fragment of noise, however tiny, had been sucked out of the air. Everybody in the room was watching Mr. Van Zuylen.

"Ladies and gentlemen," he said, standing up.

He paused, as though unexpectedly he had become aware that something was wrong. He removed the glasses from his nose.

"Ladies and gentlemen," the purser said again. "I have here a transcript of a statement just broadcast by shortwave to the English people by the prime minister of Great Britain Mr. Neville Chamberlain."

The purser replaced the glasses on his nose and read aloud to the silent audience in the bar of the S.S. *Nieuw Zeeland*.

" 'I am speaking to you from the Cabinet Room at 10 Downing Street. This morning the British ambassador to Berlin handed the German government the final note stating that unless we heard from them by eleven o'clock that they were prepared to withdraw their troops at once from Poland, a state of war would exist between us. I have to tell you now that no such understanding was received, and consequently this country is at war with Germany.' "

The purser removed his glasses, opened his mouth, closed it and hurried away. The hushed voices around us began to grow louder. People started to get up and move. They headed for the door, then stopped and, after a moment of hesitation, moved in another direction. They seemed uncertain about where they wanted to carry the shocking news or to whom. I had the same feeling. I turned to Mrs. Killian, and had another shock. She looked as though she had just been advised she was the winner in a national lottery.

"Are you okay?" I said.

"Why shouldn't I be?" she said. "After all, I called it right."

"I don't understand," I said.

"For more than a year everybody's been full of gloomy guesses about when the war was going to start," she said. "I didn't have time to join the guessing game. I had to make a decision."

"About what?" I said.

"The man I'd fallen in love with," Mrs. Killian said. "He's been training in England with the R.A.F. Last year he came home to Sydney on leave. As soon as I saw him I realized when he went back to England I would probably never see him again. I wanted him to carry with him the memory of what we both wanted. We couldn't have it while I was married to Howard. It was obvious to me that our only chance for something worth remembering had to be squeezed in between the time I could set myself free and the time he was called up. If I started on a divorce at once, I could be free in six months. I went to Japan almost exactly six months ago. As soon as I had the divorce I cabled him to meet me—"

"The other man?" I said.

Mrs. Killian smiled and nodded.

"I arranged for him to meet me in Singapore," she said. "I booked passage for both of us on the *Nieuw Zeeland* from Singapore to Sydney. I came into Singapore two days early and went to the Ormistons'. He flew up from Sydney yesterday and went to the Raffles. he came aboard ship a half hour before I did. I didn't want Sally Ormiston, who was seeing us off, to run into him."

"She would have recognized him?" I said.

"Of course," Mrs. Killian said. "So we stayed out of each other's way until the ship sailed."

"Where is he now?" I said.

"In our cabin," Mrs. Killian said. "Dressing for dinner."

"Are you going to introduce him to me?" I said.

Mrs. Killian laughed.

"A story doesn't exist until it has an audience," she said. "Here he comes now."

I turned. A handsome young man in R.A.F. uniform was coming across the bar toward us. I had a moment of surprise. Mrs. Killian was looking at him the way my mother looked at

190

me the day I delivered the valedictory address to my graduating class at De Witt Clinton High School. The surprise was followed by the shock of comprehension.

"Mr. Weidman," Mrs. Killian said. "I want you to meet my son Chips."

We shook hands. Up through the tangled emotions that were suddenly tumbling through my mind, a hard fact shouldered its way: this good-looking boy in R.A.F. uniform could have been one of my kid brother's classmates at C.C.N.Y.

"Let's go up to the wireless room and see if we can get some later news," Chips Killian said.

The three of us went up together. Mrs. Killian and her son walked hand in hand. There was no later news, but the wireless officer handed me a long cable. It was from Max Schuster in New York offering me a job at Simon & Schuster.

In 1943 I had a letter from Mrs. Killian in Sydney. After a good deal of sardonically funny gossip about war on the Australian home front, she wrote, "You will want to know about Chips. Molotoff was in London. The Russians were clamoring for a second front. We were not ready to open a second front. So we staged an enormous raid on Hamburg, to impress Molotoff with our seriousness, and to stop the second front talk. We sent up everything we had, including crates that never should have flown. Because of his experience and skill Chips felt he had a better chance in a crate than some less experienced kid would have. He was wrong, but it was an important political gesture. They had to impress Molotoff, and to do it they threw Chips' life away like a used envelope, but I'm not asking questions. I'm merely telling you because I felt you'd like to know. Chips did what he had to do, and he did it happily because I had done what I felt I had to do. He took with him the most wonderful memory a man can carry into battle, and he left me with the most wonderful memory the mother of a gallant soldier can want. If you disapprove don't write. If you do approve . . ."

I wrote.

191

twelve

At our first meeting Max Schuster said to me, "I'm writing a cookbook called *Nobody Knows the Truffles I've Seen*," and he giggled. Six years later, at our last meeting—I was on my way into Doctors Hospital to visit my wife and our brand-new firstborn son; Max was on his way out after a visit with his dying mother—he said to me, "Have you heard about the chorus girl who was generous to a vault?" His hand flew up and delivered a sharp slap to his forehead and he said, "My God, what am I doing? Upstairs my mother is dying, and here downstairs her son makes jokes!" And he giggled. Both giggles were laced with the same troubling threat of hysteria that became for me the signature of the strange man to whom for two years I tried to be a paid assistant.

I would like to record that I earned my salary. I don't think I did. Not, however, for want of trying. We both tried. Unfortunately the cards were stacked against us. I should have known this from the fact that my duties as assistant to M. Lincoln Schuster were explained to me not by Max but by his partner.

"What we've got on our hands is a personality problem," Dick Simon said. "In the beginning, when we started our business, it didn't show up as a problem because we were a small operation and Max and I did everything ourselves. As the staff got bigger Max and I began to divide the responsibilities. Max's interests were mainly editorial, so he more or less took that department under his wing. Since my interests have always been mainly sales and promotion, I more or less took charge of those functions. I say more or less because, as you may have noticed, we don't really stick to departmental lines. What makes Simon and Schuster work is that all of us pretty much work at everything. Even people in the bookkeeping department come up with ideas for books, and if anybody has an advertising idea, no matter what department he or she works in, the idea gets a hearing, and if it's good, we use it. This sort of freewheeling operation has suited me fine, but I've begun to feel that Max isn't very happy with it. Maybe because I like tennis and bridge and so do most of our associates, whereas Max is not a games player. For a man who publishes books I'm really not much of a reader, whereas Max is a scholar. What's happened is obvious. Most of the staff seems to gravitate toward me rather than to Max. What's developed unconsciously but naturally is that I've come to have what you might call a team, but Max hasn't got anybody but Max, and that worries me. I've talked it over with him, and while he says he doesn't mind one bit, because all he's interested in is that the firm should function well, I think he minds it very much. I hate to have him feel left out. So I suggested maybe the solution would be to hire someone just to be Max's team. He was surprised by the suggestion, but also pleased. When we discussed possibilities your name came up right away. We both agreed you'd be perfect for the job because we've both come to know and like you, and you seem to like us, so we decided to send that cable and offer you the job."

"As Max's team?" I said.

"More or less," Dick Simon said.

It did not strike me as a very clear directive, so I decided to ask my team captain.

"The main thing is that I don't want to interfere with your career as a writer," Max said. "That comes first and should be your main preoccupation. What I'm interested in hiring is only your free time. You can have a desk in my office or an office of your own or, if you prefer, you can have both. The job I have in mind for you has never existed before. There are no rules or boundaries. I'd like you to make up the job for yourself as you go along. The best way to do that, I think, is to immerse yourself in the shadow of the throne, so to speak. See if you can catch my rhythm and begin to accompany me in whatever key

193

it makes you feel comfortable to play. Before long I think you'll be able to fill in your own way, at your own pace, what people who insist on titles might call the job of Max Schuster's right-hand man, his ambassador with and without portfolio, his alter ego, his chief cook and bottle washer, or even his doppelganger. Does it sound interesting?"

It was not the word I would have chosen, but I could think of none better, so I said, "Very."

"Then I'm sure this marriage will work," Max said with, of course, that giggle. "Any questions?"

"Not at the moment," I said.

"I'm having lunch with Fulton Sheen," Max said. "Would you like to come along?"

"Not this time," I said. "Later, when I've got into your rhythm, and you've got a lunch date with Sheen but something more important comes up, maybe I could take the lunch for you."

"You're catching on," Max said. "I'm sure this is going to work."

I hoped so. His offer came at a time when I felt like an apple that had been broken in two. One part was all of my life before the publication of *I Can Get It for You Wholesale*. The other part was what had happened since. The space in between was the trip around the world I had undertaken with the hope that it would bring the two parts together in a seamless whole to form a solid place, a platform on which I could recapture my balance for dealing with the years ahead. On the last leg of my journey—getting to Australia during the Japanese submarine scare and then across the Pacific while the war was being fought in Europe—it became clear to me that, so far as my basic objective was concerned, the trip had already failed: the outbreak of war had shot the bottom out of the business of building platforms on which to stand for dealing with the years ahead. There might not be many years ahead. I would have to take my chances, postponing final decisions until the war ended, continuing the day-to-day balancing act by which, I was able at last to see clearly, I had managed my life up to now. I began at once to plan the book about my trip, which I published a year later as *Letter of Credit*.

I could have financed the project by asking Simon & Schuster for an advance, but I had been trained never to spend unearned money. When I was a boy the installment plan as a way of life had begun to make some inroads on East Fourth Street, but not in the Weidman household. I gathered from what I heard my parents say about neighbors who indulged in the practice that they considered all the people involved, buyers as well as sellers, participants in a criminal act. In a small, admittedly irrational way, it is a conviction their son still shares. I had already made up my mind to finance *Letter of Credit* by continuing to do what I had been doing for several years, namely, write short stories, when I received Max Schuster's cable on board the *Nieuw Zeeland* in the Java Sea.

Accepting his offer did more than solve an immediate financial problem. It allowed me to join on a more intimate basis a group of friends I had come to know with the publication of *I Can Get It for You Wholesale*. Soon after these friends began to surface in the telephone messages my mother took for me, she pinned on them the name that, after half a century, remains my family's identification tag for the group: "Jerome's Simon & Schuster bunch."

They were attractive people, lively, witty, talented, and young. For me they were a new and pleasant departure from the ambience of East Fourth Street, Monroe Geschwind & Company, C.C.N.Y., and N.Y.U. Law School. And they seemed to like me as much as I liked them. Rising from the writing table after the daily stint was done to join my friends in the Simon & Schuster offices, and being paid for doing so, was a pleasant prospect. Perhaps too pleasant, as it turned out. I was soon having so much fun that I scarcely noticed an important point: the man I had signed on to serve as ambassador with or without portfolio, alter ego, and chief cook and bottle washer was not having any.

Max Schuster and his hired doppelganger came from pretty much the same background. We were both first-generation Americans, sons of Jewish immigrants from Central Europe who had settled in New York at the turn of the century. We were both raised in twin cultures: at home, the *shtetl* and Yiddish; outside the home, the city streets and English. When we achieved success we both treated our parents in the same way. I moved mine from the Bronx to West Eighty-seventh Street in Manhattan. Though Max Schuster's success was in degree, of course, vastly greater than mine, it was not unlike mine in kind. He moved his parents into a large house in the posh suburb Scott Fitzgerald in *The Great Gatsby* called East Egg. Here, with the help of appropriate servitors, they lived in what I don't think I exaggerate by calling considerable splendor. I am equally certain, because Max's parents were so very much like mine, that here they also lived in exile. This was relieved, of course, when Max—who had an apartment on East Seventy-third Street in what had been the Joseph Pulitzer mansion—came out to visit on weekends.

In the neighboring house lived a well-known landscape architect named J. J. Levinson and his family. It was inevitable that the Schusters and the Levinsons would meet. Perhaps what happened was also inevitable. Mr. Levinson was a quiet man dedicated to his family and absorbed in his work. Mrs. Levinson was a vivacious lady with a White Russian accent who was absorbed in her growing daughters as well as in the arts and their practitioners, not necessarily in that order. If the word "inevitable" had not already worn out its welcome in this paragraph, I would use it here to describe what happened to Mrs. Levinson and Max Schuster. They fell in love.

The consequences, which may not have been inevitable, were to Max's doppelganger very surprising. Max's mother was a deeply religious woman with fiercely held convictions. One of these was that it was her duty to enforce her son's compliance with the Biblical injunction against coveting his neighbor's wife. In the hope that time would work the cure over which it is so widely credited with having total control, Max's mother exacted from her son a promise that he would not see or talk to Mrs. Levinson for five years. Max made the promise and he kept it. Five years later to the day he walked across the lawn and claimed his bride.

How his mother felt about this I never learned. How Mr. Levinson felt about it was not so difficult to discover. The divorce proceedings were awkward. To some extent because of Mr. Levinson's profession. Among other properties owned jointly

196

by Mr. and Mrs. Levinson, for example, were what the press identified as "several hundred thousand dollars' worth of fir trees in Canada." When the legalities were settled, the principals, who had both by now achieved what Trollope calls a certain age, got married.

I knew nothing of all this when I got back to New York from my world trip. When he met with Max Schuster and accepted his not very sharply defined job, the doppelganger was unaware that his principal was a newly minted bridegroom.

The day after my conference with Max Schuster I finished Chapter 1 of *Letter of Credit*. I read through the eleven handwritten pages I had started setting down at five in the morning, put them into my manuscript box, and rose from the worktable. It was eleven-thirty. I felt I had earned my lunch. I looked forward to sharing it with one or more of my friends who were now my colleagues on the Simon & Schuster staff. I took the subway down to Grand Central and walked to 386 Fourth Avenue. It was a few minutes after twelve when I came down the corridor to Max Schuster's office. Hazel Jacobson, his senior secretary, gave me a big smile.

"Welcome to the Inner Sanctum," she said. "Mr. Schuster said you'd probably be dropping in around noon."

"Is it all right to go into his office?" I said.

"Of course," Hazel said. "Mr. Schuster said you'd probably want to use his desk while he's away."

"Away where?" I said.

"His honeymoon," Hazel Jacobson said.

A few moments of what's-going-on-around-here dialogue were enough to bring the whole romantic background down on me like one of those sudden viral infections for which the medical profession seems to have been unable to find a better name than There's a Lot of It Going Around. My temperature was just returning to normal when Dick Simon poked his head into Hazel Jacobson's office.

"Hi, alter ego," he said with a grin. "What are you doing for lunch?"

"I haven't had a chance to check," I said, and turned to Hazel. "What's on the schedule?"

She held out Max Schuster's appointments calendar for the

day. The first item, next to the printed "9:00 A.M.," read in Max's scrawl: "Honeymoon, Hawaii." A diagonal pencil line was drawn down the page through all the blank spaces until the middle of the page. Next to "2:00," in the same scrawl, was written: "Lunch, mother, here." I looked up at Dick Simon.

"Not today," I said. "I've got a date."

"Who with?" Dick said.

"Sorry," I said. "I can't say until I've reported the meeting to the captain of my team."

Dick Simon nodded solemnly.

"Okay," he said. "I think we're on the right track."

When I came into Max's office I suddenly wondered if we were. The Simon & Schuster offices at 386 Fourth Avenue were neither opulent nor unpleasant. It was the sort of commercial space in which dress manufacturers of the second rank functioned successfully on Seventh Avenue. There was no reason why a company engaged in a not dissimilar business should in it do less well.

Max Schuster and Dick Simon had the two largest private offices. Even though both rooms were the same size, only Dick's room could be used for meetings. Max's room was so cluttered that there was space for only two chairs. One behind the other beside his desk. Every inch of the large couch against the wall, and the sitting spaces of two upholstered chairs that flanked the couch, was covered with stacks of newspapers and magazines. Max Schuster subscribed to more publications than my old boss Monroe Geschwind. Like my old boss he had no time to read any of them, but he went through them all the way he went through all seven New York daily newspapers: skimming the headlines and, with a black crayon, scrawling a code number across the first paragraph of each. The code was something he had devised himself, a complex personalized variation of the Dewey decimal system. It broke down all human knowledge into categories of Max's own invention that only he understood and Hazel Jacobson and her assistant, after much trial and error, had finally mastered. Thus they were able to clip the newspapers and magazines their boss marked every day, and file the clippings in the bank of green metal filing cabinets behind Hazel's desk where they waited for the day when Max Schuster would find the time to sit down and assemble his multivolumed treasury of man's knowledge. It would be, he told me, to all other encyclopedias previously compiled what Mommsen and Gibbon were to all other histories of Rome.

When I came into Max Schuster's office on the day he took off on his Hawaiian honeymoon and I took up my duties as his team, I stopped short and stared. In the cleared space at the center of his desk, where Hazel Jacobson always deposited the morning mail, the familiar stack of opened correspondence had been replaced by something I had seen only twice before: on East Fourth Street when I was a boy, and in Woolloomoolloo, a suburb of Sydney, Australia, when I was waiting for my ship to San Francisco. It was a workman's lunch kit that consisted of a nest of white enamel bowls fitted snugly one on top of the other. They were held together in the shape of an outsize test tube by a metal basket handle to keep the food in the bowls warm as long as possible and to prevent spilling when carried.

Sitting patiently in the chair beside the desk was a very small old lady. She wore a good dark cloth coat. Her white hair was wrapped in a gray silk bandana tied under a determined chin. The folds of the bandana framed a bright, eager face on which many emotions moved restlessly around a central core of unmistakable suspicion.

"You're Max's new Jerome," she said in Yiddish.

"You're Max's mother," I said in English.

"You don't speak Yiddish?" she said.

"How could I not speak Yiddish?" I said in Yiddish.

Responding to my accent with obvious pleasure, she said, "You're a Galitzianer!"

"What else?" I said, responding to hers.

She looked across her shoulder, at the closed door behind which Hazel Jacobson and her assistant were clipping and filing the sections of the newspapers and magazines their boss had marked with black crayon before he left on his honeymoon. Bringing her glance back to me, his mother's voice sank to a conspiratorial whisper.

"There's Litvaks working here," she said.

"You must be kidding!" I said.

This, in Yiddish, is the traditional response that one Galitzianer is expected to give to another upon making the horrified discovery that there are Litvaks in the vicinity. It is also quite a mouthful to translate into four English words. I am not sure that in the above four I have done it. Max Schuster's mother, however, to whom I was now speaking in Yiddish, obviously felt I had done it successfully. She giggled. The sound evoked the faint whine of hysteria that, between puns, punctuated her son's speech.

"It's true," she said.

"I didn't know that," I said.

"With Max you've published already three books," Mrs. Schuster said. "You know the Simon and Schuster people. How long does it take for a Galitzianer to smell out a Litvak?"

"Publishing books with people is different from working in the same office with them," I said. "This is my first day on the job."

"For a smart Galitzianer that's long enough to smell out a Litvak," Mrs. Schuster said. "My Max tells me you're no dope."

"Maybe I'm not so smart as he thinks," I said.

"My Max says before you became a writer you were an accountant," the old lady said. "You shouldn't have too much trouble smelling out a bookkeeper who is also a Litvak." She looked at her wristwatch. I noted that it was more expensive than the one I had given my mother when *I Can Get It for You Wholesale* was published. Mrs. Schuster said, "This is a time to come to work? When the whole world it's going to lunch?"

I explained the terms under which I had accepted the job. The small, bright, suspicious face framed by the gray silk bandana shook slowly from side to side.

"You're trying to eat kosher while at the same time you have on the same table meat and milk," Mrs. Schuster said. "It can't be done. If you like the job here in the office, you'll spend less time at home with your writing, and if you like the writing better than the job, you won't be earning the money the Litvaks in the bookkeeping department will pay you."

I could not tell her I agreed with her. It would have meant

revealing that I had taken the job as part of the balancing act by which I felt I had to live until the war decided for me what thus far I had not been able to decide for myself: how I was going to spend the rest of my life.

"Max and I figure why don't we try it out for a while and see how it works out?" I said.

"Not on an empty stomach," the little old lady said.

She stood up, bent over the desk, and separated the white enamel bowls from the metal handle that held the lunch kit together.

"Blintzes," Mrs. Schuster said as she set two places with paper napkins.

"My favorite fruit," I said.

In Yiddish the joke works. Anyway, my Galitzianer hostess got it. She laughed.

"What kind does your mother make?" she said.

"Both," I said.

"That's what I figured," Mrs. Schuster said, handing me a bowl and a fork. "Here's on this side with cheese and on this side with the potatoes. Eat in good health."

"You, too," I said.

I ate. She nibbled.

"Good?" she said.

"Very good," I said.

"Better than your mother's?"

The answer was no, but they were good enough.

"I can't tell the difference," I said.

Mrs. Schuster laughed again.

"A Litvak wouldn't have the brains to say that," she said. "A favor it's all right for me to ask?"

"Of course," I said.

"Don't tell Max I was here."

"Out in the reception room the girl at the switchboard, and next door Hazel Jacobson and her assistant," I said. "They all saw you come in. They'll tell him."

Mrs. Schuster shook her head.

"Nobody tells Max anything," she said. "That's why he wanted you to come work for him. I read in the *Jewish Daily*

Forward about your book, the review said a dope a book like yours couldn't write. You're smart. You hear things. You could tell Max a lot that goes on here in the office."

I could, but I didn't. It was not the way I interpreted the functions for which I was being paid by the Litvaks in the bookkeeping department for the hours I spent away from my writing table. More important, I learned soon enough that nobody could tell Max Schuster anything he did not want to hear. I spoke to Dick Simon about this.

"When I first became aware of the personality problem between us," Dick told me, "I was afraid it might begin to affect the way we functioned as partners, so I took it up with my analyst. My thought was that maybe the solution to the problem would be for Max also to be analyzed. Martin knew all about Max through me, of course, but they had never met. In fact at that time I don't think Max even knew I was being analyzed. Martin suggested he have a talk with Max. I told him Max was so hostile to analysis that if he knew Martin was an analyst, he wouldn't go near him. So Martin suggested I invite them both to a dinner party. Martin felt if he had a chance to observe Max in a group of people, he might get some slant on how to approach the problem."

"Did he?" I said.

"Yes and no," Dick said. "After the dinner party Martin told me he felt Max was disturbed enough to need help, but he was so skillful at covering himself that analysis would be a complete waste of time. He's already set up too many defenses, and he's so brilliant at manipulating them, Martin said, that no analyst would have a chance to get through to him. Martin feels it's hopeless to try."

On the theory that perhaps Martin meant it was hopeless for Martin to try, I decided it might not be a bad idea to see if I could find a pattern in Max's behavior that would simplify the job of being his assistant. It was not easy.

I discovered soon enough, for example, that one of the reasons Max Schuster had no team on the Simon & Schuster staff was that while he talked a good deal about team play, he had no idea what the phrase meant to other people. Very soon after they went into business Dick Simon and Max Schuster had established the fame of their corporate name as well as the fortunes of the founders with a series of spectacular successes that affected the two men in different ways. Both enjoyed being white-haired boys who had been profiled in *The New Yorker*, but only Dick Simon was able to laugh at the humorous aspects of the achievement. He used to make jokes, for example, about the crossword puzzle books which were Simon & Schuster's first commercial success and gave the brand-new firm an almost instant international reputation. Max, on the other hand, when the crossword puzzle books were mentioned in his presence, gave me the impression that he was currently preoccupied with projects so much more intellectually elevated that he had to be reminded he had once been associated with a Ford fashion that had swept the country and left him rich.

One day soon after I came to work at Simon & Schuster, while Max was still in Hawaii on his honeymoon, to help break me in as his partner's team, Dick Simon took me on a walking tour of New York bookstores. In those days, before Penn Station was torn down to accommodate the new Madison Square Garden, there was a large Doubleday bookshop in the arcade that ran from Seventh Avenue to the main waiting room. Dick was a tall, handsome man who tried to diminish his height by walking with what in the John Held, Jr., era was known as a debutante slouch. Instead of diminishing, he and the trained debutante both succeeded in enhancing their physical presence. In every bookstore we entered all eyes turned immediately to the door. If the clerk happened to be free, he came hurrying across with a welcoming smile to meet the newcomers. If the clerk was busy with a customer, he called down the store, "Be with you in a minute, Mr. Simon." He pretty nearly always met his own deadline, usually by giving the customer short shrift. What Dick Simon had in abundance is what is today identified, not always with accuracy, as charisma. On East Fourth Street it was known as the hots. There were no bookstores on East Fourth Street, so I cannot say from my own experience what having the hots got you in places where reading matter was sold. There were, however, plenty of girls on East Fourth Street, and an on-the-spot observer can state that what it got you on my block was the pick of the lot.

When Dick and I came into the Doubleday shop in Penn Station the clerk was helping a customer at the far end of the store. He glanced up, recognized Dick, and called cheerfully, "Be with you in a minute, Mr. Simon." Dick and I examined the displays on the counters around us. One of these was a rack of Modern Library books. Dick took down a copy of Machiavelli's *The Prince* and riffled the pages. When the clerk reached us Dick introduced me to him. The clerk said he'd done well with my books and, having seen the announcement in *Publishers' Weekly*, wished me luck in my new job as Max Schuster's assistant. He and Dick discussed the current state of the book business and Dick gave him the titles of the forthcoming Simon & Schuster publications for which the clerk might be well advised to keep an eye open. Dick suggested the clerk would be especially well rewarded not to overlook my forthcoming travel book *Letter of Credit*, which would be published early next year. As we turned to leave, Dick held up the copy of the Modern Library Machiavelli.

"This is new, isn't it?" he said.

"Came in yesterday, Mr. Simon," the clerk said.

"May I have it, please?" Dick said.

"By all means," the clerk said. "Shall I wrap it?"

"No, I'll carry it as is, thank you," Dick said as he tucked the book under his arm and, from his breast pocket, pulled out a wallet.

"No, no," the clerk said quickly. "With our compliments, Mr. Simon, please."

"I insist on paying," Dick said, extracting a dollar bill from the wallet. In those days Modern Library books retailed for ninety-five cents a copy. The clerk continued to protest. Forcing a dollar bill on him, Dick said, "I've always wanted to read Machiavelli, but I've never got round to it. If I pay for this copy, I know I'll read it. If I get it free, I'll invent another excuse not to get around to reading it. I want very much to read it, so I insist on paying for it."

"I never thought of that," the clerk said, ringing up the sale and handing over a nickel. "I hope you enjoy it, Mr. Simon."

"I'm sure I will," Dick said.

Out in the arcade, heading toward Seventh Avenue, he held the book out to me.

"You can have this if you like," he said.

"I thought you always wanted to read it," I said.

"That's what I wanted the book clerk to think," Dick said. "Now he'll remember both of us. It's not always easy to make that big an impression for ninety-five cents."

I never got around to reading Machiavelli, either, but I still have that Modern Library copy of *The Prince*. Every time I see it on the shelf I am reminded of the incident when it came into my possession and how it demonstrated for me the difference between the characters of the Simon & Schuster partner about whom I still think with affection, and the partner for whom I signed on to become a team member.

The same dedication Max devoted to the accumulation of newspaper and magazine clippings for this projected encyclopedia was applied to every facet of his business on which he could impose a system. Especially on those facets that nobody had ever been able to subject to a system. The making of a best seller, for example. The fact that nobody had ever been able to reduce the elements that go into the fashioning of a predictable best seller has long been illustrated by the classic story of an expensive book-business survey that produced the three categories of books that had always proved most popular: books about Lincoln, books about doctors, and books about dogs. The only thing predictable about this survey was that some publisher was bound to act on it, and not long after the survey was completed some publisher did. He brought out a book called *Lincoln's Doctor's Dog*. It was—predictably—a disaster.

This did not, however, stop M. Lincoln Schuster from continuing the search for a predictable formula for the making of a best seller, and of course, he came up with a formula. Max found it by studying the publishing history of every Simon & Schuster book that had ever appeared on the best-seller lists. It was not unlike producing a history of every human being who had ever appeared on the scene as an occupant of the White House. Max started from the moment of contact between the sperm of the occupant's father with the egg of the occupant's mother and moved on, relentless step by relentless step, until the moment when the occupant took the oath of office from the chief justice of the Supreme Court. All these histories of all these Simon & Schuster best sellers were neatly typed up by Max's secretary and bound in a handsome black leather notebook. It was kept on a Moorish tabouret in Max's office, where it was available for consultation and study by one and all. One and all included every new Simon & Schuster employee, including the more aggressive Litvaks in the bookkeeping department. When I was added to the payroll Hazel Jacobson indicated discreetly that my time had come to study the black book.

I did it with care, and I made a fascinating discovery. No matter what the subject of the best seller, regardless of the author's sex, age, nationality, size, wealth, height, fame, obscurity, girth, color, education, creed, degree of literacy, or previous condition of servitude, every member of this richly—one could say wildly—varied crew of men and women who had written the long list of Simon & Schuster best sellers had shared one common experience. At the moment of fertilization, no matter where it took place, always present either at stage center with a blank contract and a filled fountain pen, or concealed in the prompter's box hissing instructions to an underling about how best to guide the author's pen, was M. Lincoln Schuster. As Casey Stengel used to say, you could look it up. In the black book on the Moorish tabouret in Max's office. I did.

I then collected comments about the black book from all my friends on the Simon & Schuster staff. From their unbuttoned remarks I decided I had finally found a way to approach my boss on the subject I considered central to the task I had undertaken, namely, becoming Max Schuster's team. I now saw clearly that, unless I could teach him to be aware of what other people meant by team play, the task was impossible. A lecture was, of course, out of the question. My approach, I decided, would have to be the method Max himself used to keep the world at bay: humor.

"It's an astonishing record," I said the day I brought the black book back into his office and replaced it on its Moorish plinth. "I honestly don't see how you managed it."

206

"Managed what?" Max said.

"To be right there, on the spot, when every one of these best sellers was born," I said.

Max giggled. In the faint touch of hysteria that suddenly stained the air I heard the death rattle of my plan.

"Did you hear the one about the old farmer who was interviewed by the press on his hundredth birthday?" Max said.

"I don't think so." I said.

"The reporters wanted to know about the rumor that he was the father of almost two hundred illegitimate children all over the country?"

"What did he say?" I said.

"When the reporters asked how he had managed it," Max said, "the old man said, I had a bicycle."

thirteen

The war, which had caught up with me in the Java Sea, caught up with Somerset Maugham in the South of France. He had been trapped on the Riviera by the German breakthrough in the summer of 1940. Driven from his home on Cap Ferrat, he made his way on a small freighter to England. The Ministry of Information promptly assigned him to the United States as a goodwill ambassador for the embattled Empire. Nelson Doubleday, Maugham's American publisher, arranged to build a modest house for him on the Doubleday family plantation at Parker's Ferry in North Carolina. While the work went forward Maugham and his longtime secretary-companion Gerald Haxton put up at the Ritz-Carlton in New York. Maugham spent his time working on a novel called *The Hour Before the Dawn*, which the British Ministry of Information had asked him to write. Between chapters he dined out.

After I met him at one of these dinners in Dick Simon's house, Maugham asked me to lunch at the Ritz. When we were leaving the dining room he showed me a letter he had written in longhand to the Internal Revenue Service in answer to an inquiry the I.R.S. had made about a sum of money he had earned in Hollywood in 1912. Maugham asked if I would be good enough to have the letter typed because Gerald, who did all his typing, was in Washington for a few days. I said I would be glad to, and took the letter back to the office. Hazel Jacobson's assistant typed it, and I sent it over to the Ritz by messenger. It was the beginning of a friendship that lasted until Maugham's death in 1965.

A couple of months after I had the letter typed, by which

time we had shared several meals, including a dinner at the Elbow Room with a girl I was dating—I thought she would be impressed if I produced Somerset Maugham as a dinner companion; she was—I had a call from my mother. Because of my now agreeably busy social life downtown, I was spending several nights a week away from the family apartment on West Eighty-seventh Street. I made it a point, however, never to miss the Sabbath dinner on Friday night. When I got to the office on this Friday morning I found a message from my mother. I called her.

"Are you coming home tonight?" she said.

"I always come home on Friday night," I said. "Why shouldn't I come home tonight?"

"Because I want to go downtown this morning to buy my spring coat," my mother said. "If you meet me in front of Klein's to help me pick out the coat, you could skip coming home for supper tonight."

"Why can't I do both?" I said.

"Because seeing a son twice a day is for some mothers just as much too much as it is for some sons," she said. "For today it's enough you should meet me in front of Klein's."

I did, and we bought her spring coat. Out in the street it occurred to me that she knew quite a bit about the Lower East Side of Manhattan, and—now that we had moved down from the Bronx to Eighty-seventh Street—she was learning about the Upper West Side, but she knew almost nothing about midtown Manhattan.

"If you're in no hurry," I said, "we could walk uptown to the subway at Grand Central and on the way I'll show you some of the important buildings."

She liked the idea. This pleased me because I was now living so much of my life downtown that just about the only opportunity I had for pleasing her was on Friday night when, for the Sabbath meal, I always brought her a cake. It was always the same cake, and it always came from Cushman's: a lemon concoction that consisted of two slabs of golden-yellow sponge cake filled with some kind of darker-yellow custard. I don't know when or where my mother acquired her passion for this creation, but I do know it was not a passion difficult to satisfy:

there were Cushman bakeshops all over town, and this dreadful little number cost only twenty-nine cents.

Fortunately, after buying her spring coat, as we walked uptown on Fourth Avenue, we came to a Cushman's bakeshop. I went in and bought one of the twenty-nine-cent cakes she adored. As we were passing under the marquee of the Ritz-Carlton, a taxi pulled up at the curb. The doorman twisted the handle, stood aside politely, and out of the taxi stepped Somerset Maugham. We exchanged greetings and I introduced him to my mother. Her English had improved considerably since the days on East Fourth Street. It was probably inadequate for complex business talks or intellectual discussions, but she was not one to dwell on her inadequacies. In the scene that follows I have, for the sake of clarity, done a bit of tidying up. In substance and tone, however, it is an almost exact rendition of what my mother wanted to say in the way she thought she was saying it.

"I am glad to meet you," she said to Somerset Maugham. "My Jerome tells me you are a very famous writer and you and he you've become friends."

"That is true," said Maugham in his most courtly manner. For the benefit of the rare reader who may be unaware of his international reputation for ill-tempered invective, I add that when it came to courtly manners, Edwardian variety, Maugham was no slouch. Always assuming that it was not one of those moments when he chose to disregard them. This was definitely not one of those moments. My mother, I could see, was bringing out the best in him. It made me slightly nervous.

"I hope you don't mind I'd like to ask you a question," my mother said. "My husband and I we always thought Jerome was going to be a lawyer. In law school, like always in school, he got very high marks. But a few years ago he surprised us. All of a sudden he became not a lawyer but a writer. My husband and I we don't have any complaints, but like any mother and father we can't help worrying a little. So my question, what I want to ask it's this. Do you think our Jerome he did the right thing, Mr. Mawg-ham?"

Mr. Mawg-ham, which is the way my mother pronounced his name, looked thoughtful.

"On the whole, Mrs. Weidman," he said finally, "I would say yes. The lad has a bit of talent, as much as many, I should say perhaps more than most, and the way the world seems to be going in this fifth decade of the twentieth century, I am inclined to think the pen would lead to a happier life than the law, possibly even a more lucrative one as well. Yes, Mrs. Weidman, I believe your son has made a wise decision."

As I translated into Yiddish the few words of this impeccably enunciated speech with which I thought she might have some difficulty, my mother's face began to glow. Her smile had always been extraordinary. Somerset Maugham was having a chance to see it at its best.

"Thank you very much," my mother said. "When I get home and I tell my husband what you just told me, I wish you could be there to see his face how happy it will make him to hear it. Here, Mr. Mawg-ham, as a small thank you, I want you should please have this."

She handed him the twenty-nine-cent lemon sponge cake from Cushman's.

"You are very kind," said Maugham with a bow. Courtly, of course. "It has been a great pleasure talking with you."

He bowed again, tucked the cardboard box under his arm, and walked off into the revolving doors of the Ritz. As my mother and I turned and walked off to the subway, I let her have it.

"Do you know what you've just done?" I said. "This man is not only one of the world's most famous writers. He is also one of the world's great authorities on food. He pays his chef in the South of France more money each year than I've earned in my whole life. By giving him that twenty-nine-cent piece of junk you've broken up our friendship."

At the subway kiosk my mother took from me the box containing her spring coat and she smiled again.

"Just wait till he takes a bite," she said.

I did not have to wait long. When I came into the Simon & Schuster office Hazel Jacobson said, "Mr. Maugham called a few minutes ago. He wants you to call him back right away. Shall I get him?"

"Yes," I said, and Oh Jesus, I thought, here it comes. What

came was Somerset Maugham's voice, crisp and businesslike as always.

"Jerome," he said. He pronounced it Jeddum. "Could you give me the address of the bakeshop in which your mother purchased that lemon tart?"

"Why?" I said.

"It's Gerald," Maugham said. "He now wants a whole one for himself."

What Maugham wanted, the next time he invited me to lunch, was to celebrate the resolution of the tax problem to which I had been introduced when he asked to have typed his handwritten letter to the I.R.S. In 1912, he explained, he had stopped in Hollywood on his way to San Francisco where he planned to board a ship on which he had booked passage to China. During the brief stopover in Hollywood he sold a story to Carl Laemmle for $10,000. In San Francisco, before boarding the ship to China, Maugham left the check for investment with a stockbroker friend, and forgot all about it. So did the friend. After the friend died, when the executor of his estate went through the stockbroker's papers, he discovered that the original $10,000 Maugham had turned over to the deceased for investment had grown to almost $400,000. The I.R.S. impounded the money and notified Maugham that he would receive what was left after he signed a waiver to cover the government's tax claim. Since Maugham's original reply, which I had asked Hazel Jacobson's assistant to type, there had been a lengthy exchange of letters between Maugham and the I.R.S. When the matter was finally settled, the I.R.S. claimed a little more than $100,000 in taxes. The balance, which came to almost $300,000, was remitted to Maugham. It was not surprising to find him, at our celebration lunch, in a good mood.

"What we have here," he said, "is a perfect illustration of a point on which I have been insisting for years, namely, when it comes to making money, writers, far from being the feckless ink-stained wretches they are painted by businessmen, are actually every bit as acute as their detractors. Indeed in some cases, such as this one, they are far more competent than the so-called industrial tycoon. The process of making money in

212

the stock market has no more mystique to it than a bowl of radish tops. Your average penny-a-liner can do it as well as your average stockbroker. In fact, as I have just demonstrated, your average writer by applying simple common sense can do it infinitely better than any stockbroker."

I sensed from this somewhat formal introduction that I was being enlisted by a skilled playwright in the construction of a scene. Since he was also a friend, I cooperated.

"You've got a system?" I said.

"Indeed I have," Maugham said.

"Is it a secret?" I said.

"Not from a friend," he said. "Do you remember those long pins women used to wear to anchor their hats to their complicated hair arrangements?"

"I've seen my mother use them," I said. For the benefit of latecomers who might still be coming down the aisle toward their seats, I added, "What do these pins have to do with your system for making money in the stock market?"

"They provide the best way for choosing a stock that will increase in value dramatically," Maugham said.

"How?" I said.

"In one hand you take the stock-market page from your morning newspaper," Maugham said. He illustrated by picking up a Ritz menu. "In your other hand you take your mother's hatpin. You close your eyes, stab one into the other, and whatever stock has been impaled on the pin, that's the stock you buy immediately to the full extent of your financial resources."

"Then what?" I said.

"You place the stock in a shoe box, put the shoe box under your bed, and forget about the whole thing," Maugham said.

I assumed the expression of an actor registering a moment of puzzled thought before uttering his next line.

"That's all?" I said.

"That's all," Maugham said.

"Haven't you left something out?" I said.

"Why do you ask?" Maugham said.

"It seems to me something is missing," I said.

He frowned at his plate, tugged an earlobe, and for several

moments seemed genuinely troubled. Then, abruptly, his face cleared.

"Ah, yes, of course, you're quite right," Maugham said with a smile. "What I forgot to mention is that you must be absolutely certain that you do this only in the spring of 1912."

I laughed, of course. It is not difficult to grasp what your response to a joke is expected to be if you pay attention to the way it is set up. Or rather the way you, the auditor, are being set up. It was obvious from the third or fourth line of the exchange recorded above that I was being led into the role of straight man. I played it dutifully. I was, after all, a guest and my host was a man I admired. I saw now that he was also a humorist disappointed in his audience response.

"That joke wasn't very successful, was it?" he said.

I braced myself. I was suddenly reminded of my host's international reputation for ill-tempered invective. I decided to take a chance.

"I thought it needed cutting," I said.

Maugham laughed. He did not laugh often. When he did, it seemed to change his appearance from that of a mathematician preoccupied with the creation of a difficult equation to a malicious prankster enjoying one of his more successful efforts.

"When in doubt about a scene I have learned there is only one rule to follow," he said. "Cut, cut, and then cut some more."

"Would you like to try it again?" I said.

"Thank you, no," Maugham said. "But I would like to ask a question."

"All right," I said.

"Was it better or worse than the M. Lincoln Schuster average?" Maugham said.

Astonished, I said the first thing that popped into my head: "You know him?"

"I recently spent an evening in his presence at the home of Mr. Harold Guinzburg," Maugham said. "Do you know Mr. Guinzburg?"

"The president of Viking Press," I said. "Max Schuster introduced me to him a couple of years ago."

"A charming man," Maugham said. "With a charming wife. They seemed quite patient with your boss."

"Did you like him?" I said.

"Do you?" Maugham asked.

"He's my boss," I said.

"I should think you earn your money," Maugham said.

"What worries me is that I don't think I do," I said.

We discussed my job, the conditions under which I had taken it, and my doubts about whether I was making it work.

"Nobody can make it work," Maugham said.

"Why not?" I said.

"In addition to my observation of the man at dinner," Maugham said, "Mr. Guinzburg later filled me in on some of Mr. Schuster's activities, including his frantic gathering of material for an encyclopedia that it seems to me quite clear will never be written. Surely you understand what you are dealing with?"

"I'm not sure I do," I said.

"This clawing at scraps of the past and the present," Maugham said. "It strikes me as a perhaps unconscious attempt to build a wall against the intimations of mortality to which we are all doomed. With most people it comes rather late in life. Mr. Schuster seems to have been struck very early. I have a feeling that he's making a career out of holding off the inevitable. Working as his assistant in such an attempt can hardly be called a career at all."

"What would you recommend I do?" I said.

"When a sensible writer finds himself trapped in a bad scene there is only one thing he can do," Somerset Maugham said. "Cut."

fourteen

There are two ways to cut. The writer can leave it to his editor, the playwright to his director: or the author can do it himself. When I finish a story or a chapter or a scene, among the strongest feelings by which I am assailed is a sense of astonished relief that I managed to get it finished at all. As a result I have always been afraid to tamper with it. At *The New Yorker*, of course, tampering went with the territory. It was my story, but it was their magazine. I got the message. I forced myself to learn—and with the help of my editors at *The New Yorker* I did learn—how to handle the sort of salutary tampering that is a practical necessity in a great deal, if not all, of creative work. If the editor who wants a cut will mark where he wants it, I can almost always do it myself.

The lesson, unfortunately, does not always carry over into real life. On the Simon & Schuster scene Maugham had marked clearly where he felt I should make my cut. There was no editor, however, peering sternly over my shoulder, waiting for me to do as I'd been told, so I put off the decision. I have always looked upon procrastination with contempt, especially in myself. I was not happy with this particular delay because I was intensely aware of the reason. I was hoping almost childishly for the equivalent of an editor to come along and say make this cut or else. Not for the first time in my experience, indecision paid off. What I was waiting for showed up.

"Leonard Lyons' secretary called," Hazel Jacobson told me about a week after my celebration lunch with Somerset Maugham. "Mr. Lyons says to meet him at the Alvin at seven-thirty. It's an early curtain."

I was introduced to Leonard Lyons by Walter Winchell. My introduction to Winchell was a direct result of Max Schuster's genius for spotting the best seller of tomorrow. I started to read Winchell's New York *Daily Mirror* column in 1927, when I was a freshman at De Witt Clinton High School. Max Schuster started to read Winchell the day he and Dick Simon opened their first publishing office, on West Fifty-seventh Street. Max read the column to see if the birth of Simon & Schuster was noted by the man who can be said to have invented the gossip column, certainly the gossip column as we have come to know it in this century. The birth of Simon & Schuster was noted, all right. Winchell missed very little. At once Max went to the only typewriter the brand-new firm owned—a stenographer had not yet been hired—and hunt-and-pecked a letter to Winchell. Max thanked the columnist for noting in print the birth of Simon & Schuster, and he offered him a contract for a book to be called *The Private Papers of Walter Winchell.*

"The son of a bitch," Winchell told me years later with as much admiration for somebody other than himself as I had ever been able to discern in his voice. "Not only did he give me the thrill of a chance to see my name on a book like Sinclair Lewis and all those other double-domed boys. He also handed me the best subhead I've ever had."

The thrill of the offer and the gratitude for the gift proved to have just about the same life-span as a Winchell column. Soon after he signed the contract and deposited the $500 advance check Winchell forgot all about both. Not Max Schuster. He started a file. Twelve years later, when I came to work as his assistant, Max turned the file over to me.

"Everybody here at Essandess thinks it's a dead duck, and I must say it looks that way," Max said. "Winchell doesn't even answer my letters anymore, but if I can get you together with him I think it might move the project into the active column."

"Why?" I said.

"You're a new face," Max Schuster said. "It's the only thing that sparks him."

That night Max took me to dinner at the Stork Club. Sherman Billingsley—the founder and owner of what was then New York's most famous nightclub—made a fuss over him. He gave us a table in what was at that time the club's "in" spot: the Cub Room. Everybody who came in seemed to know Max. Or, after a fast pun and a slow giggle, was led to believe he or she knew Max. He introduced me to all of them but they made no impression, not even the ones with famous names. It was like being introduced in rapid succession to the members of a receiving line moving past to the beat of a Sousa march. When Winchell came in everything changed. His arrival did to the Cub Room what John the Baptist must have done to Herod's throne room when the section of his body Salome had specified was carried in to fill her order. Winchell paused and swept the room with his restless, flinty, suspicious glance. I had the feeling everybody in the room was holding his or her breath until Winchell made his choice. When he did I felt rather than heard a faint mass expulsion of breath. He came across the room like a bicycle rider sliding from his vehicle before the wheels had come to a full stop. The next expulsion of breath was mine. He had stopped at our table.

"My publisher!" Winchell said in the voice that always sounded like pebbles hurled at a window.

Max came to his feet. Winchell buried him in a bear hug, pushed Max free, and sat down. I reached out involuntarily to grab him. There was no chair in the empty space down which his body was moving. My grabbing hands met each other. A chair, swung on one leg in a pivoting arc from a nearby table by a swiftly moving waiter, was in place when Winchell's rear end reached sitting position.

"Max, for Christ's sake, what the hell are you doing here?" he said.

"Waiting to introduce you to my right-hand man," Max Schuster said. "He's been assigned to stick to you like a mustard plaster until *The Private Papers of Walter Winchell* get to the printer. Until then did you hear about the obstetrician who spent a hard day at the orifice?"

Mustard plasters have gone out of fashion. Down on East Fourth Street they were considered very effective for the treatment of lobar ailments. Even though, because my boss asked me to do it, I did my best to imitate a mustard plaster, my performance did not help Simon & Schuster get *The Private Papers of Walter Winchell* to the printer. In the attempt, however, I learned a few interesting things that, without direct experience, I would not have believed. For example, I learned it is possible to spend the hours from midnight to six in the morning on the front seat of a radio-equipped prowl car being driven through the streets of New York City by the world's most famous gossip columnist chasing police calls and learn absolutely nothing but the columnist's vitriolic version of his latest feud with a rival columnist. I also learned how to sit up until dawn at a table in Lindy's watching the world's most famous gossip columnist settle the claims of three contenders—a world-famous bandleader, a nationally famous first baseman, and a member of the House of Commons—as to which had been the first lover of an aging diva who had just shifted her not inconsiderable charms from the scion of a huge tobacco fortune with a passion for backing Broadway shows to a Chicago traction magnate under indictment for stock fraud who had jumped bail to seek asylum in Greece.

The situation improved somewhat when Winchell introduced me to Leonard Lyons. Not because the ego of the latter was smaller than that of the former. Lyons was easier to take because his pretensions were modest, whereas Winchell's could be bloodcurdling. Crossing Leonard Lyons involved no more risk than crossing the street. If you took ordinary precautions, such as not telling him anything you did not want printed, or looking both ways before you stepped off the curb, the chances were good that you would not get hurt. Crossing Winchell was always dangerous, even when the crosser was unaware he had done so, because Winchell had no sense of proportion. He demanded total loyalty, on every level. Even a moment of harmless forgetfulness on a minor matter was treated like a declaration of war to which the only response was the only one Winchell understood: total annihilation.

There was also, of course, another area—more important than character—in which the men differed. Lyons had industry, Winchell had talent. Lyons was a conscientious legman. Winchell was an original with a touch of genius. Lyons used the language indifferently. Winchell wrote English as though he had invented it. Some of it, of course, he did invent, as Mencken points out in *The American Language*. In memory, where the only judgments that matter take up permanent residence, Winchell remains a vivid experience, Lyons an amiable drone. Even though for a time Lyons and I were treated as relatives.

This was due to the fact that his wife was a deeply religious woman. Mrs. Lyons would not go to the theatre on Friday night or the eve of any major Jewish holiday. Her husband shared Mrs. Lyons's religious convictions but, as a Broadway columnist, he felt there were permissible exceptions to the rigidity of his observance. He saw it as part of his duty to his readers, for example, to cover all Broadway first nights. As a nice Jewish boy from an area south of East Fourth Street he found it impossible to waste one of the two free tickets he always received for a Broadway opening. For plays that opened on a Friday night or the eve of a Jewish holiday, therefore, he cast around for a substitute to fill the seat that, on all other nights, would have been occupied by his wife. Late one Friday afternoon his secretary called and asked if I would like to fill in for Mrs. Lyons at the opening scheduled for that night. I said I would, and I did, and a tradition was born.

Before long, at Broadway openings on Friday night or the night before a Jewish holiday, I became known as Mrs. Leonard Lyons. It was a mixed blessing. There are, of course, opening nights and opening nights. But it takes only one *Our Town* to erase the memory of a string of disappointments. They came along often enough, however, to make me feel grateful for my brief tenure as the Friday-night Mrs. Leonard Lyons.

A week after the celebration lunch with Somerset Maugham, at which he advised me to cut myself out of the Simon & Schuster scene, I was pleased when I came into the office and Hazel Jacobson told me, "Leonard Lyons' secretary called. He says to meet him at the Alvin at seven-thirty. It's an early curtain." The opening that night was *There Shall Be No Night* with Alfred Lunt and Lynn Fontanne. I did not know Lunt and Fontanne, but I did know the author of their play. We had met at the time when I was still playing mustard plaster to Winchell in the hope of getting *The Private Papers of Walter Winchell* to the printer. I was sitting with Winchell and several of his cronies in the Cub Room when an extremely thin, very tall man with an unbelievably melancholy face stopped at the table to say hello. He seemed to know everybody at the table except me. Winchell introduced us.

"I liked your story in this week's *New Yorker*," said Robert E. Sherwood.

This was indeed what F.P.A. used to call praise from Sir Hubert, and without thought but a great deal of delight I said, "You did?"

"Knock it off!" Winchell rapped out angrily.

Startled, I said, "What?"

"In this league we don't stretch compliments into double bows," Winchell said. "He said he liked your story. You say thanks and shut up."

The unbelievably melancholy face did not change but it came closer as the tall man leaned down over me.

"Let's try it once more and get it right for Walter," Robert Emmet Sherwood said solemnly. "Ready?" I nodded. Mr. Sherwood said, "Mr. Weidman, I liked your story in this week's *New Yorker*."

"Thanks," I said. "I am now shutting up."

Mr. Sherwood nodded and moved off, unaware that he was carrying with him the feelings of a casually met fan who had just become his dedicated admirer for life. The prospect of being present at the opening night of his new play made me for the first time feel more than casually grateful to Mrs. Leonard Lyons for the depth of her religious convictions.

I don't remember much about *There Shall Be No Night* except that it struck me as being one of those plays I had come to believe were the special province of Maxwell Anderson: an intensely explosive democratic-versus-fascist struggle in an unidentified country has reached crisis proportions in a divided family; after two acts of passionate debate the third act always ends when the hero goes off to certain death at the hands of the overwhelmingly superior fascist forces because he is convinced that only a symbolic martyrdom can arouse his listless countrymen to a full realization of the nature of the enemy and thus turn what seems a hopeless tide of despair into a powerful wave of the future; after a burst of off-stage gunfire establishes that the hero has indeed achieved martyrdom, his wife, who is the play's heroine, reads aloud for his hesitant followers, as well as the theatre audience, a letter of hope for all men everywhere that the heroine's husband left behind. In the lobby during the first intermission I ran into Harold Guinzburg.

"Are you liking this?" he said.

"Very much," I said firmly.

"So am I," Harold Guinzburg said dryly. "Instead of going back for the second act, I wonder if I could persuade you to take a walk with me?"

I hesitated. I did not know him very well, but from what I did know I had no reason to believe he was a practical joker. He seemed to understand what was going through my mind.

"Willie Maugham suggested we have a talk," Harold Guinzburg said.

The editor for whom I had been waiting, the man who would say make this cut or else, had finally arrived.

"I'll be glad to take a walk with you, Mr. Guinzburg," I said.

He was a member of the group of bright young non-*shtetl* Jewish boys—Horace Liveright, John Macy, Dick Simon, Bennett Cerf, Donald Klopfer, Robert Haas, Alfred Knopf—who appeared on the New York publishing scene in the twenties and jolted from its riverbed the course of a business that had been chugging along contentedly in a tweedy, pipe-smoking way without much basic change since Gutenberg invented movable type. They all came from families with money that could be traced not only to good solid generalizations like Brooklyn real estate or costume jewelry, but also to brand names such as, in the case of the Guinzburgs, Kleinert's Baby Shields. To my knowledge none of them ever laid claim to membership in the Grand Street Boys. The fact that it was Somerset Maugham who suggested to Harold Guinzburg that we have a talk brought to mind a British equivalent of the American Guinzburg family: the Rabensteins in Maugham's story "The Alien Corn." Maugham writes of Ferdy Rabenstein in his seventies: "He had kept his figure and he held himself as gallantly as ever." Harold Guinzburg was still far from seventy when we took our walk after the first-act curtain of the *There Shall Be No Night* opening performance, but the words "he held himself gallantly" fits the picture of him on that night that has remained in my mind. He was a slender, compact man with black hair and a peculiar but attractive smile that was the result of an apparently irregular formation of his front teeth. His voice was low and deep and he spoke haltingly, as though he was giving a quick editorial look at the words he was about to utter before he released them to the world. He chain-smoked cigarettes in a way that suggested he enjoyed more the process of getting them to his lips for lighting than the pleasure of inhaling the smoke. As soon as we left the Alvin I realized he was not a stroller. Harold Guinzburg walked.

"I was going to call you," he said. "Then I saw on my calendar I had tickets for this opening and it seemed better if we ran into each other."

"How did you know I'd be at the Alvin to be run into?" I said.

A low chuckle emerged around the cigarette he was arranging between his lips.

"It's a Friday night," Harold Guinzburg said. "So I knew the real Mrs. Leonard Lyons would be staying at home."

"That sounds like something out of Maugham's Ashenden stories," I said.

Without breaking his stride, but with a perceptible change in his voice, Guinzburg said, "What makes you say that?"

"You said it was Maugham who suggested we have a talk," I said, "and I assume you know his British agent stories."

"I do," Harold Guinzburg said, bringing a lighter flame to the end of the now properly settled cigarette.

"What you said about the real Mrs. Leonard Lyons," I said. "It's the sort of comment Ashenden is always making in those stories."

We reached the corner of the street.

"Let's go this way," Harold Guinzburg said.

He turned into Seventh Avenue. I took two quick catch-up steps. Side by side we headed north toward Central Park South.

"No matter what you decide to do about what I tell you," Harold Guinzburg said, "I must before I say a word have your promise that you understand you must not repeat any of it."

"All right," I said.

"Not to anybody," Harold Guinzburg said.

"I understand," I said.

I thought Ashenden would have done this part of it—whatever "it" was—more adroitly.

"Do you know William Joseph Donovan?" Harold Guinzburg said.

"Wild Bill?" I said.

Harold Guinzburg nodded. "Do you know him?"

"I read the newspapers," I said.

"That's all?" Harold said.

"If there's more than I saw in the papers earlier this year," I said, "I don't know it."

What I saw in the papers early in the year, during the period known as the Bore War, was that FDR had sent the famous hero of World War I as his personal envoy on a tour of the European capitals for a series of private talks with the leaders of the combatant nations in the hope of reaching some sort of agreement for ending the war before it escalated to a point where it would no longer be possible to contain it. In a Budapest nightclub, the newspapers reported, Donovan got into a drunken brawl, lost his passport, and was asked to leave the country.

"That's all true enough," Harold Guinzburg said, marching swiftly along Seventh Avenue toward Central Park South. "Now I'll tell you what didn't get into the papers."

When Donovan got back to Washington he reported to FDR that none of the combatants was in a mood for compromise. The escalation of the war was inevitable, and he looked for the eruption to take place within a matter of months. Asked by the president if he had any ideas for improving the preparations this country was already making, Donovan suggested the immediate creation of a worldwide secret intelligence-gathering agency, an area in which he felt the Europeans were far ahead of us. FDR asked Donovan to undertake the job of setting up such an agency and Donovan accepted.

"It's called the Co-ordinator of Information and that's all the public has been told or will be told," Harold Guinzburg said. "The C.O.I. is being set up and staffed in secret. Congress has not been asked for money because neither FDR nor Donovan wants the boys on the Hill to know what's going on. The necessary expenses for setting up an office and a secretariat are coming out of unvouchered funds under the president's personal control. The reason why I was at that opening tonight is Bob Sherwood. He's been writing the president's speeches for some time, as you probably know from the newspapers, and FDR wants to tie him more closely to Washington. So he's made Bob the deputy director of the C.O.I. and Bob has appointed me his special assistant in charge of staffing. Everything is still shapeless. We don't know where we're going or how we'll get there, but we do know it's going to take a staff to do the work, so I've been ordered to round up a staff."

We had reached Central Park South.

"Let's go this way," Harold Guinzburg said.

He turned right. I made my two catch-up steps to fall in beside him and we headed toward Sixth Avenue.

"Because of his background in this sort of thing during World War I," Harold Guinzburg said, "I asked Willie Maugham to come to dinner and we discussed the problem of staffing. He recommended you."

"Why?" I said.

"You're a freelance writer," Harold Guinzburg said. "Which means you can support yourself on royalties, so that an organization like the C.O.I., which has no funds for salaries, can use you without having to answer to Congress."

"How about answering to my landlord?" I said.

"Willie had an advance copy of *Letter of Credit* which you'd sent him and he'd just finished reading it," Harold Guinzburg said. "He passed it on to me. Willie feels between the performance of this new book of yours in the stores, and your *New Yorker* stories, you won't have to answer to your landlord until this unpleasantness in Europe is over."

"You're a book publisher," I said. "Would you give that piece of advice to one of your authors?"

"Certainly not," Harold Guinzburg said. "But I want very much to have you join us and so does Bob Sherwood."

"Aren't you pushing it a little?" I said. "Mr. Sherwood doesn't even know I'm alive."

"You're quite wrong," Harold Guinzburg said. "Bob told me you joined him once at the Stork Club in giving Walter Winchell a lesson in manners. Any further questions?"

"Aside from his confidence in my being able to live on my book royalties," I said, "did Maugham have any other reasons why he felt I should join you?"

"He told me you're fed up with your job as Max Schuster's assistant," Harold Guinzburg said.

He reached into his pocket and pulled out a small envelope.

"Sorry about tearing you away from *There Shall Be No Night*," he said. "If you really want to know how the play comes out, here are two down in front for tomorrow's performance. Take a girl."

fifteen

I took Peggy.

If my relationship with her had been chronicled by Max Schuster the way he tracked the history of every Simon & Schuster best seller, the final entry in the black book on the Moorish tabouret in his office would have indicated that he was personally responsible for what happened to Elizabeth Ann (a.k.a. Peggy) Payne and Jerome (a.k.a. Yeedle) Weidman. In a way, of course, Max would have been right: the way Icarus would have been right if he had claimed to be personally responsible for the invention of the Wright Whirlwind motor.

In June of 1940 a man named Ralph McAllister Ingersoll placed on the newsstands of New York City a new daily tabloid called *PM*. Mr. Ingersoll's original name for his publication was *Newspaper*. His theory was that most people when they approach a newsstand do not ask for the *Times* or the *News* or the *Mirror*. They say, Mr. Ingersoll said, "Gimme a newspaper." As a result, Mr. Ingersoll felt, if he produced a newspaper called *Newspaper* everybody who approached a newsstand would walk away with a copy of his new publication, and soon the *Times*, the *News*, and the *Mirror* would be out of business. This idea, like a good many others put forward by Mr. Ingersoll, was discarded after a paid survey indicated that among the people surveyed not a single one had uttered a word when he approached a newsstand. The people who were surveyed snatched the newspaper of their choice from the top of a pile, dropped their coins on the pile or into an outstretched palm, and kept moving, usually on the run.

That was what Max Schuster did after he invested some money in *PM*. He kept moving, leaving his right-hand man or doppelganger to attend as his representative Mr. Ingersoll's planning sessions. Many of these were held in the newspaper's Brooklyn quarters. As a result I got to know many *PM* staff members who were working on dummies in preparation for the paper's opening date.

Among these was Henry Simon, younger brother of Simon & Schuster's Dick Simon. Henry was an intelligent, unaggressive, concave-chested type with an overall grayish look. He was a professor at Columbia University's Teachers College, and shared the Simon family's knowledgeable passion for music. Henry wrote about it with wit and what he wrote was read with interest by close friends such as Irwin Edman and Otto Klemperer. When I met Henry Simon he had just been hired as *PM*'s music critic, and he was between marriages. One day, over a hamburger in the gin mill down the street from the *PM* building, he told me he was interested in a girl who was a reporter on the city desk. Henry had asked her several times to have dinner and accompany him to concerts he was covering for the paper, but she had pleaded previous engagements. Henry Simon's experience with women, I soon learned, had taught him how to perceive at once the difference between a girl who is actually overwhelmed by an excess of previous engagements and a girl who uses that as an excuse because she does not find him attractive enough to accept his invitations.

"This girl falls into the latter category," he said with a self-mocking smile and the professorial manner that were his signatures.

"How can you tell?" I said.

"She's beautiful," Henry said.

Even when he made a joke there was something sad about him. If you listened carefully, however, you discovered that he made very good jokes. Unfortunately, by listening to him carefully, you also learned that beautiful girls were not among Henry Simon's careful listeners. I am not the only Henry Simon friend, I learned later, in whom he evoked a vestigial atavistic parental impulse to lend assistance.

"I wish there was something I could do," I said.

"There is," he said.

"What?" I said.

"If I could tell her you'd be there, I'm sure I could get her to come to dinner at my house," Henry said.

Neglecting the Winchell rule that "in this league we don't stretch compliments into double bows," I said, "You told her I'd be there?"

"Not yet," Henry Simon said.

"Then how do you know it will work?"

"She's a Sarah Lawrence girl, and we were talking about the Teachers College attitude toward the Sarah Lawrence curriculum, when she happened to mention among other things that in one of her economics classes at Sarah Lawrence *I Can Get It for You Wholesale* was assigned as outside reading."

"Did she like it?" I said.

Nuts to Walter Winchell.

"Very much," Henry said.

"So you told her I'd come to your party?" I said.

"I couldn't do that without asking your permission," Henry said. "Will you come?"

"How big a party is it going to be?" I said.

"So far just the three of us," Henry said. "You could bring a date, of course."

Of course. But all at once I saw something more interesting in the invitation.

"Remember the party you gave about a month ago?" I said. "The big one for that conductor?"

"Otto Klemperer?" Henry said.

"That's the boy," I said.

"What about him?" Henry said.

"There was a tall, dark girl there," I said. "She came with some little guy who's a vice president at Chase Manhattan. I never got a chance to talk to her, but since then I've given her some thought. I don't know her name, because we were never introduced, but—"

"She wore her hair like this?" Henry said.

Without releasing his two-fisted grip on his hamburger he made a circling motion around his head with both hands.

"That's the girl," I said.

"Olga Calloway," Henry said. "What about her?"

"Is she married to that shrimp from Chase Manhattan?" I said.

"Olga is one of my students," Henry said. "She's not married to anybody, and if anybody has any brains she won't be. Why do you ask?"

"If you get her to come to your dinner party as my date," I said, "I'll be there to play John Alden to your date. By the way, Miles Standish, what's her name?"

"Peggy," Henry Simon said.

Henry lived on West Fifty-ninth Street, between Eighth and Ninth avenues, in the Beaux Arts Mansions, a building popular with musical people, many of them performers. They liked the location because Carnegie Hall was within walking distance. When I arrived Henry was making drinks for his date and Olga Calloway. He introduced me to his guests and made a drink for me. There was a great deal of talk about *PM*, none of which I remember. What I remember is my feeling of disappointment. Olga Calloway was still tall and good-looking, and her hair was still done in the halo arrangement that had caught my eye at the Otto Klemperer party, but something was missing. By the time Henry announced that we would be having dinner at the Stockholm, a Swedish restaurant across the street, it occurred to me that what was missing was the vice president from Chase Manhattan. He was, I clearly recalled, a colorless shrimp. Perhaps it was because of her proximity to him that the shrimp's date had looked more glamorous at the Otto Klemperer party than she was looking in her role as my date at Henry Simon's party.

After cocktails, crossing the street to the Stockholm, Henry and his date led the way. I followed with Olga Calloway, who did not seem to be aware of my disappointment. She talked away with a disorganized vigor that, at the Klemperer party and at a distance, had seemed sexy. In the dimly lighted Stockholm, flanked by an apparently endless variety of artfully arranged fish—most of which turned out to be basically East Fourth Street matjes herring—Olga Calloway's sexiness had either vanished or been obscured by the smorgasbord odors in which we were all being marinated.

I didn't exactly heave a sigh of relief when Henry signaled for the check, but my eagerness to get into the fresh air may have been the reason why, when we paired off out on the sidewalk for the trek back across Fifty-ninth Street to Henry's apartment for coffee, Henry was up front with Olga Calloway, and his date and I were a few steps behind. After a few moments I became aware that the smell of herring had vanished. I looked down at Henry's date.

"Do you really want to go back to Henry's place?" I said.

"Not particularly," she said.

I took her arm and slowed our pace, widening the gap between us and Henry and Olga Calloway. By the time I felt they were a safe enough distance up ahead of us I demonstrated a skill I had learned as senior patrol leader of Troop 224 on East Fourth Street. I put my touching middle finger and thumb into my mouth and blew. A shrill blast went out on the night air. A taxi screeched to a stop at the curb beside us. I opened the door, handed Henry's date into the cab, and climbed in beside her. As I write this, it occurs to me that, during the forty-four years that have passed since the moment when I sat down beside her in that taxi, there have been remarkably few occasions—a war, for example—when the space between us has been much wider than it was on that night. I am pleased, but not surprised.

Before I met her Henry Simon had told me Peggy was beautiful. When we did meet I could see at once that Henry had spoken no less than the truth. She was beautiful, however, not the way any girl I had previously considered beautiful had been beautiful. Peggy did not hunch over the handlebars about it. She didn't distract you with all the fuss other beautiful girls I had known made about their beauty. Here was, in my dealings with girls, an entirely new approach to the subject, plus an acute intelligence that in all my previous experience had surfaced only in girls who tended to look like ZaSu Pitts. The combination caught my attention at once and held it: thus far, as I have already indicated, for more than four decades. Such things do not, of course, happen without cause. In exploring this particular cause, I discovered something striking: it is possible that the longevity of our marriage, if it can be traced in part to Max Schuster and Icarus, can with a similar degree of legitimacy be attributed to George Horace Lorimer and "the weekly founded by Benjamin Franklin."

In 1899 the owners of the *Saturday Evening Post* were troubled by the declining popularity of their publication. For the task of lifting the magazine across the doorstep into the twentieth century they reached halfway across the continent for the young press agent then serving the Armour meat-packing interests in Chicago. Lorimer took with him to Philadelphia a young newspaperman from Paw Paw, Michigan, named Will Payne. He proved to be remarkably versatile. Before long Will Payne was writing the *Post*'s editorials and financial articles, contributing short stories and romantic serials, and covering major news events such as the Peace Conference in the Hall of Mirrors at Versailles. Years later, when I came to know Will Payne, he told me about the variety of his work for the *Post*. "One week," he said, "I had seven signatures in a single issue." He also had a son named Whitney. Shortly after Whitney Payne got out of college he followed his father to Philadelphia to become the *Post*'s director of advertising. The family Whitney Payne brought with him to Philadelphia included an infant daughter, born in Evanston, Illinois, named Elizabeth Ann (a.k.a. Peggy) Payne.

Elizabeth Ann Payne was raised on the Philadelphia Main Line, educated at the Phoebe Anna Thorne School located just outside the gates of Bryn Mawr College, and went on to Sarah Lawrence. Here the family interest in journalism began to assert itself and, during a winter in Florida, she did her first professional newspaper work as a reporter on the St. Petersburg *Times*. This was followed by a job on *Newsweek*, then back to Sarah Lawrence to get a degree in economics. In the course of this she won a national contest open to economics majors, sponsored by the Department of Labor. The prize was a one-year job in Washington. After the excitement of the contest, however, the prize seemed less attractive: it had nothing to do with the field in which Elizabeth Ann Peggy Payne now knew she wanted to work. A few months before her graduation Ralph McAllister Ingersoll started rounding up a staff for *PM*. After graduation Elizabeth Ann Payne was tapped for the city desk. All the ingredients were now in place for this brilliant, modest young beauty from the Philadelphia Main Line to fall in love with this nice Jewish boy from East Fourth Street.

A week after we met it dawned on me that I was beginning to acquire what I had hoped but failed to get from my trip around the world: the cement to hold together the years of my life up to the publication of *I Can Get It for You Wholesale* and the formation of a platform on which I could hope to stand for all the years up ahead. I began to sense that Elizabeth Ann Payne was not only bringing out the best in Jerome Weidman. Soon it became obvious that she had a talent for aborting without difficulty the worst in Jullyiss Widdermuenzer. Today I see it all clearly in a quatrain by E. B. White that has been snaking in and out of my mind for almost half a century:

> *Couples who call each other darling*
> *Are always quarreling.*
> *Couples who call each other "Hey!"*
> *Live in peace from day to day.*

When Elizabeth Ann Payne and Jerome Weidman began to call each other "Hey!" I began to hear the echoes of a phrase I had been hearing and seeing in print for years but had never associated with myself. The phrase was "mixed marriage." It was not unlike looking at a sheet of postage stamps and suddenly becoming aware that somewhere in the middle of the one hundred identical pictures of a former president, or an internationally acclaimed athlete, one of the pictures had suddenly changed into someone familiar. A startled voice inside me was suddenly asking, "Who, me?"

"Who else?" the voice of my parents came back quietly, not in English translation. The words came back like the echoes themselves, in the language the three of us had shared at the beginning, before any of us learned English. The language in which phrases for "mixed marriage" could not be put into words: they existed only as emotions. If you learned the language when I learned it, for use with the people from whom you learned it, you understood that there were things for which it was better not to have any words. All at once the storyteller son of Annie Falkovitz was discovering that there were times in life when words did not work.

"How am I going to handle this?" I said to Peggy.

"I don't know," she said. "This is just as new to me as it is to you. How badly will it hurt them?"

"Very badly," I said. "Not because of you personally. They don't even know about you yet."

"Let's keep it that way for the time being," Peggy said. "I'm not me. I'm a girl they don't know. Any girl. Would it hurt them so much that, if you married this girl, whoever she is, they would put you out of their lives?"

"Oh, no," I said. "They'd never do that."

Peggy frowned.

"You're sure of that?" she said.

"Absolutely," I said.

Still frowning, Peggy said, "You've got some sort of power over them?"

I hesitated but I said it: "Yes."

"Money?" Peggy said.

"They depend on me," I said.

"But you depend on them, too, don't you?" Peggy said.

"Not for money," I said. "That's different."

"Would it help if they met me?" Peggy said.

"Of course it would," I said. "But that's not the point. Not now, I mean."

"Why not?" Peggy said.

"When we reach the point where they've met you and they know I want to marry you," I said, "it won't matter how much it hurts them, they won't try to talk me out of it."

"That doesn't seem to make sense," Peggy said.

"That doesn't stop it from being true," I said.

"How do you know it's true?" Peggy said.

"I know them, and I know myself," I said. "When I introduce you to them and I tell them we're going to get married, they'll see it as a test."

"What's wrong with that?" Peggy said.

"I'm afraid to put them to that test," I said.

"Could it be what you mean is you're afraid to put yourself to the test?" Peggy said.

"No, I don't mean that," I said. "I mean I'm afraid to put them to the test because it won't be a fair test."

"Because they're afraid to lose your financial support?" Peggy said.

"That's it," I said.

"And that makes you ashamed?" Peggy said.

"Well, yes," I said.

"In a way, then, you don't really have a problem," Peggy said. "All you have to be is ruthless."

"If you want to look at it that way," I said.

"But you don't want to be ruthless?" Peggy said.

"In my shoes would you want to be ruthless?" I said.

"We'll come to me later," Peggy said. "Right now we're talking about you. You don't want to be ruthless. Is that right?"

"Yes," I said.

"Maybe you wouldn't take it so hard if you stopped thinking of yourself as someone unique," Peggy said. "Actually you're no different in that respect from most people. Everybody including you wants to be loved no matter how they act."

"That doesn't change the fact that it makes me feel rotten," I said.

"You're in good company," Peggy said. "You're like that Karamazov brother, the evil one, whatever his name is. The one about whom Dostoievsky says he was a sentimental man, and then Dostoievsky puts in a comma after the word 'sentimental,' and he says of this evil brother he was wicked and sentimental. You're a nice Jewish boy, a loving son, but if we borrow Dostoievsky's comma and put it in here, we come out with you are a nice Jewish ruthless boy and a loving son."

"It's sort of scary," I said.

"It scares you to know you can be ruthless?" Peggy said.

"Not always," I said.

"But in this case yes?" Peggy said.

"This is not a case," I said. "This is real. She's my own mother. He's my own father. This is different."

"Then there's hope for Elizabeth Ann Payne," Peggy said.

"What are you talking about?" I said.

"Getting married," Peggy said. "If it makes you afraid to be ruthless with your mother and father, a girl who plans to become your wife has a right to look at it as a step in the right direction."

sixteen

"The only problem now is how to do it," I said. "Getting married is not going to be easy."

"Why?" Peggy said.

"I don't think my parents have ever met a gentile," I said.

"My parents have never met a Jew," Peggy said. "But I'm not marrying your parents, and you're not marrying mine, which leaves just the two of us to handle it."

"How?" I said.

"A civil ceremony," Peggy said. "That's what Maggie and Arthur did."

Maggie was her friend from Sarah Lawrence: Maggie Frohnknecht. Arthur was my friend from *The New Yorker:* Arthur Kober.

"The situations are not the same," I said. "Maggie and Arthur are both Jewish."

"Arthur is Jewish," Peggy said. "The Frohnknechts are rich."

"They are also Jewish," I said.

"People with that kind of money no longer think so," Peggy said.

She knew more about that than I did, so I said, "I'll talk to Arthur."

After I did, Peggy brought up the stickier point.

"We've got to do something about the Montague-Capulet syndrome," she said.

"How do we handle that?" I said.

"There's only one way," Peggy said. "When the ceremony takes place both sets of parents should be elsewhere."

"You talk to your set," I said. "I'll talk to mine."

On the morning of the wedding I called my mother and told her it would take place later that afternoon.

"Where?" she said.

"In the home of Judge Ferdinand Pecora," I said.

There was a pause. I suddenly wished he had a middle name. To my mother it would have sounded more impressive.

"A judge?" she said finally.

"That's right," I said. "Judge Ferdinand Pecora."

"The one he was in the papers?" my mother said. "With the picture that it showed a midget sitting on Mr. J. P. Morgan's lap?"

"Judge Pecora had nothing to do with that," I said. "All he was doing as a special prosecutor was conducting this congressional investigation of Wall Street. Mr. Morgan was a witness."

"How does such a thing happen?" my mother said.

"I suppose there was a press agent in the hearing chamber," I said. "He probably thought it was good publicity for the midget."

"I'm not talking about the midget," my mother said. "I'm talking about my son."

"Judge Pecora is a friend of my friend Arthur Kober," I said. "Judge Pecora married Arthur, and Arthur asked him to marry me and Peggy."

"That's her name?" my mother said. "Peggy?"

"Yes," I said. "Peggy."

"And where is he going to do it, Judge Pecora?" my mother said.

"At home," I said. "His home, I mean. Mrs. Pecora will be a witness."

"His home?" my mother said. "A private house?"

"It's an apartment," I said. "In a big building on Seventy-second Street and Broadway."

"But it's his own?" my mother said. "Where he lives?"

"Yes," I said.

Pause.

"Well," my mother said, and I could tell from the tone she gave to the single syllable that I was over the hump. "To be married by a judge, a famous man his picture it's in the papers, that's very nice. Papa and I we figure you must know what you're doing, so we both wish you happiness and good luck."

Peggy's family had a somewhat different frame of reference. When Peggy called her mother in Scarsdale and told her the wedding would take place that afternoon, Mrs. Payne burst into tears.

"I don't care what anybody says," she sobbed. "I want you to be happy, and everybody knows Ellen Mackay has had a beautiful life, so there's no reason why you shouldn't."

Ellen Mackay was the debutante daughter of Clarence Mackay, the president of Postal Telegraph, remembered by some as the Western Union rival that favored the color blue. When we lived on East Fourth Street the day-by-day—indeed the round-by-round—details of the stormy romance between the Catholic heiress and Irving Berlin, the Jewish songwriter, were read aloud to us from the pages of the *Jewish Daily Forward* by my father at the supper table.

"Jerome does not write songs," Peggy said to her mother on the phone.

In addition to Judge and Mrs. Pecora there were two other witnesses to the ceremony in the Pecora living room: my sister Jean, the first member of the family to whom I introduced Peggy; and Chandonette Norris, a friend of Peggy's from the *PM* staff. Mrs. Pecora poured sherry while His Honor smiled benignly.

"My record as a marrier is perfect," he said. "Not one of the couples I've married has ever been divorced."

Mrs. Pecora leaned close and whispered in his ear. His Honor frowned.

"I regret to say I must amend my statement," he said to us. "My wife reminds me that my record would be perfect if it were not for Victor Mature. He did get a divorce, but he's an actor, and I don't think actors should be allowed to affect anybody's statistics. Anyway, I'm proud of my record as a marrier, and I know you two nice people will not change that."

A dozen years later, on my way out of the Beverly Hills Hotel, I ran into Judge Pecora coming in. He stopped in his tracks, pointed a finger at me, and said accusingly, "Are you still married to that lovely girl I married you to?"

"Yes," I said.

Judge Pecora smiled and pumped my hand.

"That's wonderful," he said. "Give her my best greetings and tell her I consider this piece of news you have given me as a good omen in connection with my present visit to California."

"Is it indiscreet to ask what the occasion is?" I said.

Judge Pecora grinned and leaned close.

"Of course it's indiscreet but since today I consider you and your wife my rabbit's foot, if you promise to keep a secret for a few hours," he said, "I'll tell you."

"I promise," I said.

"I flew out here to straighten out Charlie Chaplin's problem with the Immigration Department," Judge Pecora said. "He's not a citizen, as you probably know, and he wants to go to England on business, but he's afraid to leave the country until he gets the Immigration Department's promise to allow him to return."

Ten days later, back in New York, I saw the front-page announcement that, while he was on the high seas heading for England, Chaplin was advised by the U.S. Immigration Department that his visitor's visa had been canceled. It would be foolish to attribute this betrayal or piece of bad luck, call it what you will, to the fact that, by seeing me in Beverly Hills a dozen years after he married Peggy and me in his apartment on Seventy-second Street, Judge Pecora in a moment of euphoria mentioned the outcome of a troubling situation before it actually did come out. It would be foolish at the same time—for a man who has felt since childhood that to boast about achievement is to invite the attention of The Man Up There who is on the constant lookout for someone to slap down—to say it seems no more than the boaster deserves. In this case, however, even if the boaster deserved it, he was spared. It was his client who was not. Years went by before Chaplin was allowed to reenter the United States.

Even now, forty-three years after our marriage ceremony, I have a twinge of sorrow about the fact that close to the time I said "I do" in answer to Judge Pecora's traditional question, I also said good-bye to Jacques Chambrun. It seemed time to move on. He had sought me out when it was almost impossible for a young writer to get an agent, and he had demonstrated almost immediately—with those three sales in one week to *The New Yorker*—that he could do well for me, and for many years he did. Yet, like Churchill the morning after V-E Day being dismissed from further service to the king and country he had led to victory, the day after my marriage Chambrun was dismissed from any further services as my agent. There were many reasons but, even if they were all good, none was good enough to excuse what remains in my mind an act of ingratitude of which I am not proud.

Quincy Howe, the editor-in-chief at Simon & Schuster, arranged for me to meet Bernice Baumgarten of the Brandt & Brandt office, considered by Simon & Schuster to be the best agents in the business. We met in the bar of the Murray Hill Hotel, where a few years earlier I had been introduced to the New York publishing world by Ken McCormick and Burton Rascoe, and we had a cocktail. No, we had two cocktails. At any rate, I did. The number is important because, until that moment, the alcoholic beverages I had consumed were the thimbleful of sacramental wine my father doled out once a year at Passover, and the occasional Scotch and soda I had learned to take during my trip around the world. What I drank at the Murray Hill tasted different. Mr. Howe called it a martini. As I left the bar after my second, I was pleased to note that I had lost much of my nervous apprehension about this meeting with the best agent in the business.

During the small, pleasant fuss over the menus, I heard myself saying to Quincy Howe, "We've been discussing contemporary American writers, and you are the editor of one of America's most important publishing houses, for which we both work, so I'd like to ask if you've ever heard of a writer named James Gould Cozzens?"

Only those who have known Quincy intimately, and have therefore learned to cherish him, will understand the charm of the confused look through which he mumbled, "Cozzens? Cozzens? No, I'm afraid I haven't."

Flushed with what I learned later was alcohol, but at the moment I believed was triumph, I turned to the third member of our party.

"I find this very interesting," I said. "We have been discussing contemporary American writers, and none of us has mentioned the man I think is the finest novelist working in America today. How about you, Miss Baumgarten? You are one of America's most distinguished literary agents. Have you ever heard of James Gould Cozzens?"

Miss Baumgarten made the gesture women always seem to make just before they sink the harpoon: she touched the invisible bun at the back of her head.

"As a matter of fact I have," she said dryly. "You see, I happen to be married to him."

An hour later in her office I became a Brandt & Brandt client, which I still am, and I began to understand that my enthusiasm for the work of James Gould Cozzens did not exactly set me apart. There were quite a few of us. It was very satisfying, on meeting another member of the cult, to stop his "You know that scene in *S.S. San Pedro* when—?" with a disdainful "Oh, sure, but do you know the part in *Men and Brethren* when Ernest Cudlipp goes into the drugstore and—?"

It was very satisfying until 1957, when Mr. Cozzens published *By Love Possessed*. Suddenly the members of the cult found themselves, somewhat irritably, part of a herd.

Their resentment cried out for a spokesman, and they had not far to look. One of our noisier and more voluble intellectual critics leaped into the breach, and from the pages of *Commentary* he sent out to the sulking faithful a nine-thousand-word attack. The spokesman had two basic objections to *By Love Possessed:* (1) most reviewers had praised the novel highly, and (2) Mr. Cozzens's syntax was on occasion almost as complex as the spokesman's own. Perhaps because the attack lacked conviction, or few people who like to read novels read *Commentary*, Mr. Cozzens survived.

This is not surprising. A man who publishes steadily for forty-five years—the first of Mr. Cozzens's thirteen novels, *Confusion*, appeared in 1924—has something that we are constantly told many American novelists lack: staying power. Every page of all thirteen of his novels bears the indelible imprint of the Cozzens intelligence. It can be felt almost physically. The printed Cozzens page looks muscular. The reader immediately feels he is in the presence of an architect. Here are none of those easy rhythms behind which many writers conceal their inadequate grasp of their material. The Cozzens sentence is put together with the precision of a Swiss watch movement. Every word has been chosen to carry its weight toward clarity. The reader's mind is jolted into careful attention and Cozzens proceeds to say what only great writers of fiction can tell us: this is the way life is, not the way we would like it to be.

The Cozzens hero is rarely heroic. Even more rarely does he resemble that convenience of the Tape Recorder School of writers: the "average" or "common" man. Cozzens clearly subscribes to the important truth embedded in Franklin P. Adams's sardonic observation: "The average man is not so average." The Cozzens hero is nearly always an acutely intelligent man born into an upper-middle-class eastern family of tradition and a comfortable amount of worldly goods. No Grand Street Boy, he. He has gone to a good prep school and an Ivy League college. He spends his life in a profession considered appropriate for men of this background and breeding: the law, medicine, the church. When war comes the Cozzens hero enlists and is, of course, commissioned. Raised to believe he is "better" than the common run, the Cozzens hero is constantly surprised to find that he is not really "better." Out of this repeated discovery, and the repeated adjustment the discovery entails, is fashioned the Cozzens drama.

A Cozzens drama is quiet-spoken. An Episcopalian minister, arranging an abortion as the only way out for a trapped parishioner, does not, quite naturally, shout his plans from the housetops. The son of a judge, who discovers at Harvard Law School that there are students smarter than himself, does not punch the smarter man in the nose. All he does is learn. And while we watch him learn, we learn. It can be an unpleasant process, not only for the hero but for us, because Cozzens sheds light in areas we always unconsciously assumed were adequately illuminated.

It comes as a shock, for instance, to a reader steeped in clichés about race relations, to discover that a highly intelligent black verger in an otherwise all-white Episcopal church will voluntarily arrange to take Communion last, so as not to embarrass a member of the ruling race by forcing him to take to his lips a cup from which the black man has drunk first. The shock is followed at once by a stab of pity: an artist has opened up for us a secret window in a human heart: he has shown us how one man worked out a way to get through his twenty-four hours in a world he never made.

The opening up of windows is a rare gift, and nobody in my time has practiced it with more dedicated brilliance than James Gould Cozzens.

He was very much in my thoughts when I went to Washington to prepare for making the cut in the script of my life that had been marked by that shrewd editor W. Somerset Maugham. Getting out into the confusion of Union Station with a sense of uneasiness, I remembered the sense of coming home with which a couple of years earlier I had stepped out of the boat train from Plymouth into the confusion of Paddington. In London I had stepped into something familiar: the world of Dickens a century after *Copperfield*. In Washington I stepped into something threatening: the world of Dos Passos a quarter century after the Armistice.

"Social Security Building," I said to the taxi driver.

All I knew about my appointment was that it had been set up by Harold Guinzburg, and the person who was presumably waiting for me was the sister of a justice of the United States Supreme Court: Miss Estelle Frankfurter. When I came into her presence I had some immediate doubts about one half of what I thought I had known about my appointment. It was obvious that it could not really be said with accuracy that Estelle Frankfurter ever waited for anybody. I had the feeling that she wanted to make it clear to her visitor that if he found her in the place where he expected her to be, it was just a happy accident for the visitor: Miss Frankfurter, her attitude stated clearly, had done nothing to make it happen.

"Who are you?" she said.

I told her. She scowled as she began to push papers around on her big desk as though hunting some clue to why I should have been allowed to interrupt her busy schedule. Irritated by not turning up anything helpful, she said, "What are you here for?"

"Harold Guinzburg said you would tell me," I said.

The scowl sank into a sly smile.

"Oh, you're one of those," Estelle Frankfurter said.

"One of what?" I said.

"Bob Sherwood's boys," she said. "What do you do?"

"You mean when I'm not keeping appointments in Washington that Harold Guinzburg makes for me?" I said.

Miss Frankfurter pursed her lips, opened her eyes wide, and rolled them the way Eddie Cantor used to in the early talkies. She did it so well that it occurred to me her face in repose bore a distinct resemblance to the off-screen Eddie.

"Hoo-hoo-hoo," she said, her voice climbing like Eddie's in pursuit of a laugh. "What we have here is one of Bob Sherwood's geniuses. I mean, what do you do for a living?"

I told her. The Eddie Cantor smile became a sad little dribble of mock sorrow.

"I'm sorry to disappoint you," Estelle Frankfurter said. "I'm a grown-up person with a job to do and a lot of important outside interests, none of them connected with being the sister of a Supreme Court justice, I might add. So I don't have time to read smart-aleck slick kindergarten stuff like those *New Yorker* short stories."

"In that case," I said, getting up, "I guess I'd better go back to New York."

"But you haven't been here long enough to get anything out of the talk Harold sent you down here for us to have," she said.

"I've got enough to make my report," I said.

"On what?" Estelle Frankfurter said.

"Our interview," I said.

Spry as a sparrow, which on her feet she resembled, the sister of Supreme Court justice Felix Frankfurter came darting from behind her desk in a wide circle and headed me off at the door.

"Please go back to your chair and sit down," Estelle Frankfurter said, poking my chest with her palms.

"Why?" I said.

"I think we can use you," she said.

It was my first hint that Harold Guinzburg had sent me to Washington to be put through an entrance examination. I went back to my chair, she went back to her desk, and we stared at each other across the untidy mess of papers and fabric swatches piled between us. It occurred to me that I could have been visiting an interior decorator who had spread out samples from which she would help me make my choice.

"Why do you think people like Harold Guinzburg send young people like you around to see a woman like me?"

"Because they can't get to see your brother as often as they can get to see his sister," I said.

"You have a mother?" Estelle Frankfurter said.

"Yes, why?" I said.

"How come she let you become a writer and not a lawyer?"

"I asserted myself," I said.

"You couldn't have done it in the Frankfurter household," she said.

"I could if the Frankfurters had come from East Fourth Street," I said.

"Don't pull rank on me," she said, and then she abandoned the Eddie Cantor bit. High time. Eddie himself had left it behind years ago. She went back to straight smiling, and I saw where it would not be difficult to like this woman. She said, "What's that great big grin for?"

"I think I've got you figured out," I said.

"Want to bet?" she said.

"Never on a sure thing," I said. "Want to hear?"

"I'd better," she said. "Or I'll end up in one of those *New Yorker* stories."

"Why should you care?" I said. "You don't have time to read smart-aleck kindergarten stuff."

"I read some of it," she said.

"Then you didn't tell me the truth," I said.

"Harold Guinzburg and Bob Sherwood have me sitting in this office for a purpose," she said. "If I have to tell a lie or two to accomplish my purpose, I'm just doing my job."

"If you don't stop interrupting me, I'll never get around to telling you how I've got you figured out."

"I'm waiting," Estelle Frankfurter said.

"You're proud of your brother but he annoys you," I said. "Why?"

"His eminence gets in the way of something that's more important to Estelle Frankfurter than being the sister of a Supreme Court justice."

"What's that?" she said.

"Living your own life," I said.

She hiked her small body up into the protective arms of her huge leather chair. She reminded me of pictures I had seen of Shirley Temple, in a movie about the Old South, sitting on the porch of a plantation mansion almost completely enveloped in the vast frame of a peacock chair.

"What do you know about Irita Van Doren?" Estelle Frankfurter said abruptly.

"Not much," I said. "Why?"

"Tell me what you know."

I knew Irita was the editor of the Sunday *Book Review* section of the New York *Herald Tribune* and she had three beautiful daughters. Before I met Peggy I used to go to the Van Doren apartment on West Seventy-seventh Street. One Sunday afternoon two friends and I were playing The Game with the three Van Doren girls when Irita came running out of her study where she had been working on a manuscript with Wendell Willkie.

"Quick!" Irita said. "The papers!"

It was a very hot day—this was before air conditioning had become popular in private homes—and Irita and Willkie had been working at a card table near one of the large open windows that looked out on the Seventy-seventh Street side of the American Museum of Natural History. An unexpected gust of wind had blown the curtains in across the card table. In retreating to their normal position the curtains carried several pages of the Willkie manuscript out the window. We could see them sailing across Seventy-seventh Street toward the park that surrounds the museum.

"Let's go!" said Tom Bevans.

Peter Schwed and I followed. There was no time to wait for the elevator. We took the stairs and ran out into Seventy-seventh Street. It is one of Manhattan's main east-west arteries and a busy one. When Tom, Peter, and I erupted into the street, the traffic was heavy in both directions. The manuscript pages were sailing lazily high in the air like a group of kites. The light at the Central Park West corner turned red.

"Okay, now!" Peter said.

We raced out into the gutter, keeping our eyes on the floating pages and, nervously, on the traffic zipping by on both sides of us. We froze and waited, watching the sailing pages. When the light at the Central Park West corner turned red again, we went back to work. It took three red lights before we retrieved seven pages. The eighth was easier. It had sailed across the park fence into the museum grounds. Tom Bevans, more agile than his colleagues, went over the fence. When we got back up to the apartment Irita and Willkie checked the manuscript.

"Got 'em all," Willkie said. "Thanks, men."

He and Irita went back into the study. Peter, Tom, and I and the three girls went back to The Game. A year later, in her Washington office in the Social Security Building, Estelle Frankfurter scowled at me across her cluttered desk.

"You sound as though you'd recovered the manuscript of Magna Charta," she said.

"There were those in the Van Doren apartment on that Sunday afternoon who felt we had," I said.

"What was it?" Estelle Frankfurter said.

"The first draft of the speech Willkie delivered three days later in Elkhart, Indiana," I said. "Accepting the nomination of the Republican party to run against FDR for his third term."

"Do they think Willkie's got a chance?" Estelle Frankfurter said.

"They're betting on it," I said.

"How about you?" Estelle Frankfurter said.

"I'm taking their bets," I said.

Estelle Frankfurter swung her enormous leather chair toward the window. For several moments she stared out at the Washington Monument. Then she picked up one of the cloth swatches from her desk and ran her hand back and forth across the fabric as though it was a puppy.

"Thank you for coming," she said with a smile. "I'll advise Harold when we'll want you to come down for your first briefing."

When I got back to New York late that afternoon I stopped in at the Simon & Schuster office.

"Mr. Schuster had a call from the hospital and had to go back out to Sea Cliff," Hazel Jacobson said. "His mother."

"Serious?" I said.

"It doesn't sound good," Hazel said. "He's staying the night so he won't be able to keep his date with Fulton Sheen tomorrow. Could you cover for him?"

Covering for Max Schuster was like going on a blind date. It didn't matter how many questions you asked in advance, the answers were never any help. When you met the girl you had to start from the beginning.

"Do you know anything about this Sheen business?" I said.

"A little," Hazel said, which meant she knew nothing. Until he got around to writing the history of a Simon & Schuster best seller for the black book on the Moorish tabouret in his office, Max tended to be vague about details. "I think it's about those radio broadcasts Sheen has been making from Washington," Hazel said. "Mr. Schuster's been sending him notes."

"What kind of notes?" I said.

"Oh, you know," Hazel said with the small, troubled frown that always accompanied her efforts to answer specific questions about her boss. I had worked with her long enough, however, to be able to grasp from her expression and intonation something of what she could not—or out of loyalty to Max she preferred not to—put into words.

"Notes of congratulations about the radio talks?" I said.

"Sort of," Hazel said.

"Did he say anything in these notes about a book based on these broadcasts?" I said.

Hazel's frown grew deeper.

"Not exactly," she said.

She had answered my question.

"Is this a lunch date?" I said.

"Yes," Hazel said. "I made a reservation for two at the Cloud Club."

I thought for a moment, then said, "Cancel it." I was uneasy about Sheen. I'd heard a couple of his broadcasts. I said, "Call Sheen's office and tell him the meeting will be here in Mr. Schuster's office."

"Mr. Schuster is not going to be here tomorrow," Hazel said.

"His right-hand man will be," I said. "I'll wait for Sheen in Mr. Schuster's office."

"But Mr. Sheen will be expecting lunch," Hazel said.

"That's okay," I said. "I'd like to see him in the office first."

The next day I came into Max Schuster's office early. I'd worked out a plan of attack. At five minutes to twelve I poked my head out into Hazel Jacobson's room.

"I have a feeling Sheen is going to be prompt for this appointment," I said. "When he arrives—"

Hazel's phone rang. She picked it up.

"Hello? One moment, please." She turned to me. "He's in the reception room."

"I'm ready," I said.

That's what I said, but I wasn't sure that I was. The whole idea of Fulton Sheen made me uncomfortable. It was like meeting the principal of a rival school. You knew he had no authority over you, but you also knew he had the same authority over others that your principal had over you, so it was hard to think of him as a buddy. The meeting, however, had come at a good time for me, so I didn't duck it. When Hazel showed him in, my first reaction took me by surprise. I had never before realized how handsome clerical clothes can be if they are worn by a man who is built to do them justice. Fulton Sheen's figure was to the collar-worn-backwards set what Sally Rand's was to the bikini. He could have been wearing shining armor. His presence was so imposing that, when he entered Max Schuster's office, it was as though everything in the room was at once forced back against the walls to provide adequate space for this outsize visitor. I could almost feel myself being shoved out of his way. It was not only the impressive height of the athletic figure for which a good Savile Row tailor had done one of his better jobs. It was also the look. I was reminded of a character on Fred Allen's radio show, "Allen's Alley," who was constantly backing away from his detractors by whining, "Take dem eyes from offin me!" Sheen's glance was like a cowcatcher on a locomotive. It swept into the room, clearing everything out of the way for its owner: the fierce glare of a comic strip Savonarola pouring out like a searchlight beam from the ascetic face of an El Greco hangman. I understood instantly something that had puzzled me for a long time: how he had managed to convert people like Heywood Broun and Clare Boothe Luce. Monsignor Fulton Sheen had quite obviously done to them what he was now doing to Max Schuster's doppelganger: scaring the you-know-what out of him.

"I'm sorry to hear about Mr. Schuster's mother," Sheen said as we shook hands.

"So am I," I said. "But I must say I'm pleased by the opportunity it has given me to meet you at last, sir. Will you sit here, please?"

I indicated the chair beside the desk in which Max Schuster's mother had been sitting when I first came into this room almost two years ago.

"Thank you," Sheen said.

He did not sit. He lowered himself into the chair and arranged the skirt of his coat around his knees like the coachman folding an ermine wrap around the knees of Norma Shearer playing Marie Antoinette.

"I suppose Max told you the purpose of this meeting?" Sheen said.

"Only in a general way," I said. "If it's not too much trouble, I wonder if you'd be good enough to tell it to me now in your own words?"

"Certainly," Sheen said. "You have been listening to my broadcasts from Washington, of course."

Something told me it was better not to admit it. I wanted to keep the field clear.

"I'm sorry, no," I said. "I haven't had the chance. On instructions from Max I've been eff-yewing a series of broadcasts by Rabbi Stephen Wise that we are considering for publication in book form."

Sheen's eyes went up like a couple of window shades snapping free from their restraining ratchets.

"Eff-yewing?" he said.

"Following up," I said.

"Oh, yes, of course," Sheen said. The eyes of Savonarola shifted slightly to get their victim more clearly on target. "I seem to have missed the Wise broadcasts. What are they about?"

"The position of the American Jew in the perilous political world of today," I said.

"Odd," Sheen said.

"In what way?" I said.

"That's what my broadcasts from Washington have been about," Sheen said.

"How about some lunch?" I said.

"Mr. Schuster's secretary said there would be no time for lunch," Sheen said.

"She meant no time to go out to lunch," I said. "I've brought a snack to keep us going while we talk."

From under the desk I pulled the workman's lunch kit I had picked up on my way to the office from the delicatessen around the corner. I separated the white enamel bowls from the metal handle that held the lunch kit together.

"Blintzes," I said as I set two places on the desk with paper napkins. "I didn't know which you prefer, so I had my mother make some of both. The ones with cheese are on this side, potatoes on that side. As my mother would say, Monsignor Sheen, eat in good health."

I dug in. He lifted a forkful from the cheese side of his plate and took a nibble. After a pause he took the whole forkful. Neither of us spoke until both plates were clean.

"Allow me," I said, and refilled both. After a while I said, "Another helping?"

"My diet says quite firmly I must not," Sheen said.

"So does mine," I said. "If I don't squeal on you, sir, can I count on you to do the same for me?"

"You can," Sheen said. "If there's any more of the cheese going, I'd prefer that."

I gave him the last two cheese blintzes and took the last two potato for myself.

"Thank you," Monsignor Sheen said. "I must say this has

been an improvement over the lunch I would have had at Sheed and Ward."

"You've approached them about a book of your talks?" I said.

"No, of course not," Sheen said. "From the very start I've had my heart set on Simon and Schuster."

"I'm sorry," I said. "I think you understand why as a Jewish house we couldn't do your book."

"On the contrary," Sheen said. "I fail to understand how you of all people can fall into the conventional trap of racist thinking."

"Me as in Simon and Schuster?" I said.

"You as in *I Can Get It for You Wholesale*," Sheen said.

"What do you know about that?" I said.

"I know what I read in the papers," Sheen said. "Don't you realize that you are treating me the way only recently you were yourself treated by Mr. Nate Spindgold of Columbia Pictures?"

It occurred to me that staring at him with my mouth open would accomplish nothing. I set it in motion.

"How did you know about that?" I said. "It never got into the papers."

"When I'm interested in a subject," Sheen said, "I seek out the things that don't get into the papers. You realize, of course, that by turning me down you are providing me with ammunition for a public accusation of anti-Catholicism by one of America's leading Jewish publishers?"

For several moments the eyes of the El Greco hangman held the eyes of the boy from East Fourth Street. It was no contest. I took a deep breath. The time had come to make my move.

"Are you interested in making a deal?" I said.

"Always," said Monsignor Fulton Sheen.

"You know Father Charles E. Coughlin of Royal Oak, Michigan?" I said. "The head of the National Union for Social Justice?"

"Not personally," Sheen said.

"You know his broadcasts?" I said.

"I've heard one or two," Sheen said.

"That's about as many as I was able to take," I said. "If you guarantee to get Father Coughlin's sewage off the air, I guarantee to get your book published by Simon and Schuster."

"You have the authority to make that promise?" Sheen said.

I'd never have a better chance than this one to find out.

"My job was defined by Max Schuster himself," I said. "I am his ambassador with and without portfolio, his alter ego, his right-hand man, and when necessary his doppelganger."

"Unfortunately," Monsignor Fulton Sheen said, "Father Coughlin's diocese is beyond my reach."

"If you stretch a bit the way you just stretched for my mother's blintzes," I said, "I think you'll manage to reach him."

Sheen stood up and held out his hand.

"I'll see what I can do," he said. "And my compliments to your mother. Her blintzes are much better than any I've ever had in Lindy's."

I had an afternoon editorial date about a new story with Mrs. White in the *New Yorker* office. When we finished, shortly after five o'clock, I walked back to Simon & Schuster. I wanted to make my report to Max on my meeting with Sheen while the scene was still fresh in my mind, as it fitted into my plan for making the Maugham cut in my Simon & Schuster script. When I walked into Hazel Jacobson's room I never had to ask if her boss was in. I could always tell from the way she sat at her desk. If Max was out she crouched over her typewriter, trying to put a dent in the pile of work he had given her before he left the office. If he was in, she did not work harder. Hazel Jacobson was incapable of working harder. Every moment on the job she stretched herself to the limit. When Max was on the premises she didn't crouch over the typewriter. She cowered.

"When did he get in?" I said.

"A few minutes ago," Hazel said.

"His mother okay?" I said.

"I think so," Hazel said. "He—"

I did not hear the rest. Eager to get on with my report, I had already moved past her and pushed open the door into Max's office.

"Oh," I said, and stopped in the doorway. I had the feeling

I had stumbled into a movie still. Max was behind his desk. Dick Simon was slouched down in the chair beside the desk from which a few hours earlier Monsignor Fulton Sheen had been leaning forward over his plate to avoid dropping blintzes crumbs on his Savile Row lap. This, I could see at once, was not the moment to report my Sheen meeting to Max Schuster. Still holding the doorknob, I said, "Sorry, I didn't mean to interrupt," and I started to back out of the room, pulling the door as I went.

"No, wait!"

I stopped moving before I realized the call that had stopped me had come from Max. Now motionless, I found myself wondering if it had been a shout or a cry. The sound had certainly been loud, and it had sounded like an order, and it had brought Max to his feet behind the desk.

"It's not important," I said. "I'll catch you some other time."

Dick Simon's long body stirred. He smiled as he pushed himself up out of the slouch.

"Catch us with what?" he said.

"Nothing important," I said. "It can wait."

"Why should it?" Dick said. He turned to Max. "Any reason why we can't hear what Jerry has to say? I mean if we're finished with what we were—?"

"Yes, of course, sure, come on in, Jerry," Max said, and he made a beckoning gesture with his pipe. He was not a smoker, but he kept a straight-grain brier stuck stem-down among the needle-sharp pencils in the leather cup on his desk. Perhaps unconsciously—I was never quite sure he knew he was doing it—he would pluck the pipe from the cup during meetings and play with it as he listened. Now, dropping back into his chair, he poked the pipe at his lips and said, "What's on your mind, Jerry?"

"You're sure I'm not interrupting anything?" I said.

"You're not," Dick said. "Is he, Max?"

Max blinked rapidly several times, and then he giggled.

"Of course not," he said. "Which hat are you wearing, Jerry? Alter ego? Ambassador with and without portfolio? Right-hand man?"

254

"I'm trying on a new one for size," I said.

"Which one is that?" Max said.

"Publisher," I said.

Describing the Fulton Sheen session, I talked directly to Max. That was what I had intended to do when I came into the room. As I talked, however, I kept an eye on Dick. He had not figured in my plan to report to Max, but I was aware that Max alone was no longer my audience. I had no way of knowing, of course, what had been going on between these two men when I interrupted them. I knew them both well enough by now to be able to judge that what I had brought into the room to tell Max was not being received the way it would have been received if I had been able to lay it before Max at a time when he and I were alone together. I could feel both of them listening to me not for the meaning of my Fulton Sheen report as a publishing venture. They were listening like men who, in the middle of a battle, had both run out of ammunition. During the unexpected lull in the firing an armed man had blundered into the area. The combatants saw at once that the one who could put his hands on the weapons of the innocent newcomer could resume and probably win the interrupted battle. When I finished my report Max spoke first.

"Excuse me, Jerry," he said. "I'm not sure I understand. Did you say you committed the firm to this thing? You gave Fulton Sheen your promise that we would definitely publish a book of his radio talks? Is that what you meant?"

Dick Simon said, "Of course that's what he meant. He couldn't have made it clearer. Anyway, that's what I understood him to mean. Was I right, Jerry?"

"Of course, yes," I said. "That's exactly what I meant."

"But, Jerry," Max Schuster said. "How could you do a thing like that?"

"How could I not?" I said. "I was acting as your personal representative. I felt I'd run into what I believed was a good book. It was my job—if I understand my job as you made it perfectly clear to me when I took it—to make sure at once that the book did not go to some other publisher."

"Without consulting us?" Max said.

"By us do you mean you?" I said.

Max Schuster shot a glance at his partner. I did the same and said to Dick Simon, "Do you think I should have consulted you?"

Dick smiled pleasantly.

"Certainly not," he said.

"Why not?" Max Schuster shot the words across the desk like Tilden returning a serve. "You're my partner, aren't you?"

Dick Simon shrugged, still smiling pleasantly.

"Yes, of course, Max, but Jerry is not my right-hand man or my ambassador with and without portfolio," he said. The smile became a grin. "Or even my doppelganger. Are you, Jerry?"

"It's not the sort of assignment anybody would invent for himself," I said. "You take it on when you're asked to take it on. Max asked me to take it on and I accepted. This afternoon I did something I believed the assignment authorized me to do. If I was wrong, Max—"

My boss cut me off by yelling at Dick Simon, "You see? There you go again, turning my words around and making me look like a liar. I didn't say you and Andrea deliberately left me and Ray off the guest list for the Klemperer party. I said if you were really my friend, the way you keep saying you are, you would have seen to it that Ray and I could not be left off that list by accident, because everybody would know if you left your partner and your partner's wife off the list it means—"

"It means that only because you want it to mean that," Dick Simon said quietly. "I'm not turning your words around. What's happening is what always happens when we have a discussion. You're the one who is turning my words around. I told you Andrea and I did not give that party. Henry gave it. Otto Klemperer is Henry's friend, not ours. Henry wanted to give this party for Klemperer but Henry's apartment is too small, so since he's my brother we let Henry use our house. That's all we did, Max. We let Henry use our house for his party and he made his own guest list."

"And you made no effort to see that Henry included me and Ray on his guest list."

"For Christ's sake, Max, will you stop being silly?" Dick Simon said, even more quietly, almost in a whisper, as though he was trying to coax a child out of a tantrum. "I can't go around checking my brother Henry's guest lists."

"Why not?" Max shouted. "Is that too much to ask from a partner?"

It occurred to me that perhaps it was too much to ask from a doppelganger.

"Can I get a word in here?" I said.

Max Schuster turned. For a few moments, he stared at me as though he couldn't remember who I was. The pipestem slid back and forth across his lower lip. It was not easy to look at him head on for very long. He had no neck. His head met his body at the shoulders, there was nothing in between, so that the points of his shirt collar did not slope down his chest. They pointed straight at you, like a fanged accusation. Dick Simon broke the silence.

"The question, Jerry, is may you get a word in," he said with a smile. "And the answer is yes, you may."

"I don't want to get involved in a personal fight between you and Dick," I said, talking directly to my boss. "What I want to know is do you approve or disapprove of what I told Fulton Sheen."

The pipestem stopped dead in the middle of the lower lip. The eyes blinked slowly, as though their owner was making an effort to get them back into focus, and suddenly Max Schuster seemed to see clearly who was talking to him.

"I'm sorry, Jerry," he said. "I must have missed something. What did you tell Fulton Sheen?"

I repeated the terms of the deal I had made.

"You promised Sheen we would publish his book of radio talks," Max said. "In exchange for his promise to get Father Coughlin off the air."

"That's right," I said.

"Do you think the Sheen book will sell?" Max said.

"I thought that's what you thought because of those encouraging notes you've been sending him about his broadcasts," I said. "As your doppelganger my answer to your question is I don't see why the book should not sell. I'm pretty sure Sheen has had plenty of experience with getting loyal Catholics into bookstores."

"Then your decision was strictly commercial?" Max said.

"No," I said. "I had another reason."

"What was that?" Max said.

"I thought your mother would like the idea," I said.

Max came up straight in his chair.

"What does my mother have to do with this?"

"As much as my mother has," I said. "I'm sure they'll both think muzzling Father Coughlin is good for the Jews."

Dick Simon said, "Do we make decisions as publishers on whether or not what we publish is good for Jews?"

"When did we stop?" I said.

"When did we start?" Dick Simon said.

"The day you called me down from the Bronx to a meeting in your office with Nate Spindgold."

I walked out and pulled the door shut quietly. I was glad to leave the scene I would never be certain I had cut properly. Later, of course, I had a number of opportunities to ask Somerset Maugham if he felt I had done it right, but by that time other things had intervened. Late on a Sunday afternoon, two days after my performance in Max Schuster's office, I learned that the Japanese were dropping the old Sixth Avenue "L" back on us at Pearl Harbor.

seventeen

It has been reported that, at a Round Table lunch in the Algonquin, during a discussion about family forebears, George Kaufman stated that one of his ancestors, Sir Roderick Kaufman, had served with distinction at the side of Richard the Lion-Hearted during the Crusades. Asked what role Sir Roderick had played, his descendant George said, "He was a spy."

I believe him. The only difference between New York immediately after Pearl Harbor, and London after the fall of Constantinople, was the architecture. Before the ink was dry on FDR's request to Congress for a declaration of war, the Coordinator of Information went public. Relieved from the shackling awareness that it was under the constant threat of possible congressional scrutiny, the C.O.I. boldly shifted its staff from the gray area of the president's unvouchered funds to the public trough at which the generals and the admirals did their feeding.

An office was rented on West Fifty-seventh Street in a building formerly popular with Detroit automobile manufacturers as the New York showcase for their wares. The generously proportioned rooms were soon showing something far more eye and ear catching: the antics of a large staff—almost every member of which quite obviously considered himself a direct lineal descendant of George S. Kaufman's ancestor Sir Roderick Kaufman—not quite sure of its mandate, and making a lot of noise because of the uncertainty. Much of the noise was due to the rivalry between Wild Bill Donovan, director of the agency in Washington, and soft-spoken-to-the-point-of-frequently-seeming-mute Bob Sherwood, the C.O.I. co-director in New

York. The rivalry surfaced sooner than the betting odds of the knowledgeable gossips had suggested. The eruption was handled by the president with his characteristic dexterity. To the question both of his prima donnas were now hurling publicly—Who the Hell Is Running This Agency, Anyway?—his answer was vintage FDR: "You both are."

The C.O.I. was wiped from the war agency organization slate and at the top in large letters were chalked the initials of two brand-new agencies: O.W.I. and O.S.S. Wild Bill Donovan was offered the Office of Strategic Services, and Soft-Spoken Bob Sherwood was given the Office of War Information. FDR was still heaving the sigh of relief with which he was turning to his next problem when his attention was called back to the one he thought he had just solved. Wild Bill Donovan and Soft-Spoken Bob Sherwood, digging their toes in the hot sand, announced they were both willing to accept direction of the president's two agencies, but only on one condition: from the common C.O.I. manpower pool neither of the two directors could take with him to his new fiefdom any employee who had been recruited by the other. FDR accepted the condition and insisted that the two men shake hands in his presence. They did, and left the Oval Office to check their staff lists. I had been recruited, of course, by Harold Guinzburg working as Bob Sherwood's deputy, so I was assigned to the O.W.I. As a result I found myself, some months later, seated beside a large desk in the private office of the O.W.I. director of transportation.

"Where am I going?" I said.

"London," he said.

"To do what?" I said.

"You will be told when you get there," the director of transportation said.

"How long will I be in London?" I said.

"I can't say," the director of transportation said.

"You can't or you won't?" I said.

"I can't," the director of transportation said. "It's my job to get you there, and that's the job I'm doing, so will you stop asking a lot of irrelevant questions and just listen?"

"I don't think it's irrelevant to ask how long I'll be in London," I said. "My wife might want to know."

"It's irrelevant if I don't know the answer," the director of transportation said.

"Am I going for the duration?" I said.

"Hell, no," the director of transportation said.

"For a weekend?" I said.

"Are you trying to be funny?" the director of transportation said.

"Suppose I was in your chair and you were in mine and I told you you're going to London," I said. "Wouldn't you ask me how long you were being sent for?"

"No," the director of transportation said.

"Why not?" I said.

"Because there's a war on, for Christ's sake," the director of transportation said. "If everybody asked questions about every assignment they got, how the hell would we ever get on with winning the war?"

"All right, let's get on with winning it," I said. "Am I flying?"

"Not a chance," the director of transportation said. "There's not enough air lift right now even for the guys with real important missions."

"If you can't tell me how long I'm going for because you don't know," I said, "how come you know my mission is not important?"

"I didn't say that," the director of transportation said. "Every mission is important. What I said about yours, even though I don't know what it is, I said I know it's not real important, because for the real important ones my orders are to break my balls to get air lift. In your case all I can tell you is you're going to Montreal by train, and in Montreal you'll switch to another train that will take you to Halifax."

"That means I'm going by ship," I said.

"You are brighter than all your bitching led me to think," the director of transportation said. "Yes, son, you are going by ship."

This was at the time when Nazi submarines were sinking British hulls faster than the Admiralty could commission them.

"I don't suppose you could tell me what ship?" I said.

"If I could," the director of transportation said, "our British allies would be justified in asking to have me fired out of this job and into a federal pen for the duration. All I can tell you is how to get to Halifax. That's all I can tell anybody we send over. From Halifax on, you're in the hands of the British."

"Will the British know I'm in their hands?" I said.

"For crying out loud," the director of transportation said. In moments when he was jolted from the brand-new never-never land of directing a global war to the age-old unpleasantness of facing the hard facts of daily existence, he fell back on the more elementary slang of his youth. "What the hell do you think I am?"

"Don't tempt me," I said. "Just tell me what I do in Halifax."

"You get off the train and you're met by a contact man from the British Ministry of War Transport," the director of transportation said. "He'll tell you what to do."

"How can he do that?" I said. "He doesn't know what I look like."

"Don't you worry about that," the director of transportation said. "Whoever he is he'll know what you look like."

Incredible as it still seems, Mr. Dane did.

It is true that not many people stepped off the train in Halifax with me. I seem to recall there were two or three dozen, perhaps fifty. In a large railroad station, at three o'clock in the morning, this is not exactly a crowd. It is certainly enough of a group, however, to give a man, looking for a total stranger, at least a moment of pause. I do not recall that Mr. Dane took so much as a moment. As soon as I came through the gate from the track and set down my bag for a look around, a tall young man sucking a dead pipe advanced on me with all the assurance, and some of the pleasantly relaxed deference, of a son meeting his father at the end of a business trip. It was merely the first of several surprises Mr. Dane had in store for me.

The second occurred a few minutes later. Settled on the front seat of Mr. Dane's battered Chevrolet, I turned to take my first good look at the young man who had just stowed my bags in the rear and was now maneuvering the car deftly out of the parking space in front of the station. It was not the best of looks. All of Halifax was effectively blacked out, and the only illumination inside the cold car was a faint glow from the instrument panel on the dashboard. It was enough, however, for me to see clearly the man who had picked me up. Mr. Dane looked like one of the curly-haired waiters at Barbetta's, an Italian restaurant on West Forty-sixth Street where Peggy and I occasionally had dinner when we went to the theatre.

"We're putting you up at the Newfoundland," he said in accents more appropriate to Yorkshire pudding than to minestrone.

He swung the wheel wildly for no reason apparent to me until, a moment later, as the Chevvy careened back to its side of the blacked-out street, I caught a glimpse of a sailor and a girl locked in an embrace in what must have been the middle of the road.

"Good bit of that goes on at the Newfoundland, you'll find," Mr. Dane said without a change of inflection. "Hotel rooms are scarce, however, and needs must when the devil drives."

He brought the car to a slithering halt against what appeared to be a totally blacked-out stretch of sidewalk.

"This is it," he said, managing to enunciate with surprising clarity in spite of the cold pipestem that seemed to be a part of his face. "It's not Claridge's but in a primitive way they do you rather well. Avoid the coffee. I shan't go in with you. Best not to be seen together too much. Ask for your room and nothing else. You won't be asked anything. If you are, the askers have no right to the answers, so don't make any. You want to know, of course, when we'll be able to get you off. I can't tell you. We'll try not to keep you hanging about too long. Sleep late, if you can. It's getting on toward fourish right now, and there's nothing to get up early for. If you want me for any reason, ring this number." I took the slip of paper. "If I want you for any reason, I'll find you in the lobby."

He did, twice during the afternoon of the following day, once in the evening, and twice again on the morning following that. Except for the first visit—which resulted in Mr. Dane's suggesting my acquisition of a sheepskin-lined canvas coat and hat in a seamen's outfitting shop on Barrington Street—the other visits by the young Ministry of War Transport official seemed a trifle pointless. Mr. Dane would wander in from the street. Sucking his dead pipe and keeping his hands thrust far down in the pockets of his shabby dark blue overcoat, he would stare through a small, pained frown across the Newfoundland's crowded lobby, looking very much like an unemployed musician hunting, without much hope of success, for a colleague who might just possibly know about a temporary job. Then, catching sight of me in one of the chairs near the bank of potted aspidistras that partially concealed the flow of prostitutes moving in what seemed an endless double stream in and out of the elevator, Mr. Dane would wander over, pause beside my chair, dislodge the pipe from his mouth, tap me absently on the shoulder with the damp stem, replace it between his thin lips and invisible teeth, and wander on again, out into the street.

Except for that first visit, when he suggested the shopping trip for the sheepskin-lined coat, and the last visit, when he suggested that I get my bag, Mr. Dane said nothing. Not even about the series of hourly telephone calls which, I realized later, must have been something of a nuisance to Mr. Dane's unidentified female assistant at the other end of the wire.

The performance was not nearly so theatrical as I would have imagined if I had heard it described rather than seen it. It gave me, as I soon guessed it was designed to give me, a sense of complete confidence. From the moment Mr. Dane first touched my shoulder with the damp stem of his dead pipe I knew I was in good hands.

Toward the end of the fifth day Mr. Dane called for me in his car. He took away several of my documents, gave me a few new ones, drove me down to the waterfront, advised me to do something about my head cold, helped me into a small launch, and waved good-bye in the gathering darkness. Night fell rapidly as we chugged and bumped our way through the floating ice in the harbor to the ship that was to carry me to England. It was completely dark when I was put aboard, and we were at sea when I came up on deck in the morning for a look around. This did not take long.

The S.S. *Celtrover* was a vessel of some thirty-two hundred tons. Even a man whose training and predilections ran to pavements could circle her decks, from stem to stern and back, in eighteen seconds flat, as I soon found out. She had been built in 1893 to carry freight on the Baltic run. As a concession to one of the owners, who liked to go to sea with his wife every now and then for his gout, two passenger cabins had been constructed aft. In 1915 the *Celtrover* was armed and converted into an auxiliary cruiser. In 1933, when she was forty years old and had served her stockholders and her country well, she was junked.

After Dunkirk the U-boat successes against British shipping were helping to pose the grim question of England's survival. The Admiralty issued a desperate call for every hull of British registry that could float. Since this is the approximate equivalent of calling to arms every citizen who can breathe, a considerable number of ships were able to meet the Admiralty's rather basic requirement. The *Celtrover* was hauled from her muddy pasture on the Clyde, hurriedly if inadequately refurbished, and sent back to sea.

The fact that, when I came aboard, she had run for nearly two years without mishap through the submarine-infested waters between the Mersey and the Nile was not in the least reassuring. In addition to her long record of honorable service, the *Celtrover* had a permanent list of fifteen degrees, a maximum speed of eight knots, no running water, and a larder that seemed to contain nothing but beans and a thick, gummy soup made from frozen turnip tops. Also, she had twelve passengers in the two cabins originally built for the gouty stockholder and his wife, three lifeboats that had not swung free of their davits in twenty years, four hastily improvised gun pits fitted with weapons that jammed even in practice, a flank position in the convoy we were to join the following day, a mutinous crew, and one toilet that worked.

My tastes, like those of most boys from East Fourth Street, are not even remotely sybaritic. The homes I knew in my youth were indifferently equipped with sanitary facilities. I found the inconveniences of the *Celtrover* annoying but far from lethal. It was impossible to shave or bathe. The cement floor of the single toilet was constantly awash with a thick, grayish slime: the accumulation of years of uncleanliness dissolved by saltwater leaks from several pipes and a porthole that refused to close. The food was unpalatable and, as I discovered in the inevitable long run, indigestible. You could not brush your teeth or wash your hands without the desperate conviction that your body had gone completely numb from your gums up, or your wrists down. It was impossible to buy or borrow or cadge a drink. And even if there had been room, in the cabins built for one but now shared by six, to change your shirt, the strict order from the bridge was that everybody was to sleep in his clothes and his life belt. Everybody did, for twenty-one days.

It was not the accumulation of discomforts that caused uneasiness. What I found depressing was the fact, obvious even to me and underscored by everybody on board with whom I talked, that if the *Celtrover* got us safely through the North Atlantic to England, it would be only with the help of God. Assistance from any other quarter—the Royal Navy, the crew, the passengers, the equipment of the ship—seemed a possibility so remote that it could be safely disregarded in any computation of betting odds.

The crew was mutinous because its members had not received so much as a day's leave to visit their homes since they had joined the ship, even though the *Celtrover* had touched U.K. ports several times during the past two years. Also, the ship, despite its size, was undermanned and the living quarters available for the crew were even worse than those provided for the passengers. During our first boat drill, which was held at eleven o'clock on our first morning out, I noticed that, in addition to the life preservers that the passengers wore, several members of the crew carried on their hips a flat oilskin package. After the drill I asked one of the deckhands what these packages were. Submersion suits, he said, made of thin rubber. The waters of the North Atlantic at this time of year, he explained, were so cold that, if you were fortunate enough to find yourself a floating survivor after your ship was torpedoed, you would probably freeze to death within ten minutes. The submersion suit would keep you reasonably warm for several hours, no matter how cold the ocean. I asked when these suits would be issued to the passengers.

"Passengers?" the deckhand said. "Look, chum, there ain't enough of these things to go around even among the crew."

The other passengers were even less reassuring than the crew. Each of the eleven was a D.B.S.—Distressed British Seaman— a merchant mariner who, after being torpedoed, had been fished out of the ocean by a passing vessel and carried to the rescue ship's nearest port of call. These eleven men were being returned to England, at the expense of His Majesty's government, for new assignments. None of them had met the others before he was put aboard the *Celtrover*. They had a good deal to say to each other. I was not particularly interested in hearing too much of it but the *Celtrover* was not the sort of ship on which you could be alone. Besides, I was bunking with five of them. I heard it all, several times.

Since all of them had been torpedoed at least once, most of them twice, and four or five had been blown into the sea with almost monotonous regularity—always at different intersections of longitude and latitude—there was almost no square inch of what, in their interminable bull sessions, they called the Western Ocean that might be regarded, by a person hunting straws of reassurance, as a safety zone: a strip of sea into which U-boats could be counted upon not to venture because to do so was either foolhardy or unprofitable. Speed, my fellow passengers said, was the only protection against submarines, and the *Celtrover*, which could do eight knots when hard-pressed, was crossing in a six-knot convoy, the slowest type, designed especially for revived derelicts like the *Celtrover* that had answered, from their muddy beds of retirement, the Admiralty's frantic call.

We were for it, these experts grimly assured each other and me. On the morning of the second day—when simultaneously we reached the convoy rendezvous and ran into the heavy weather that stayed with us for three weeks—it was difficult for me to believe with any conviction that they could be wrong.

Because the *Celtrover* was undermanned, all twelve passengers were impressed by the second mate, who doubled as gunnery officer, for gun watch in the pits on the top deck. I drew three tricks of two hours each—4:00 A.M to 6:00 A.M., noon to 2:00 P.M., and 8:00 P.M. to 10:00 P.M.—in a pit mounted on the roof of the radio room and fitted with a set of twin Marlins. According to the worn engraving on their barrels, the guns had been manufactured in 1913, the year of my birth. According to the gunnery officer, when they were added to the *Celtrover*'s improvised arsenal they had not been fired for twenty-two years.

"I shouldn't worry about their jamming if I were you," the gunnery officer said when he was showing me how to operate the Marlins and they jammed. "Machine guns are no bloody good against submarines, anyway."

The watches were mounted, I learned, not to inflict damage on attackers, but to provide the ship with extra pairs of eyes. I used mine industriously during my first watch, from noon to 2:00 P.M., and whatever last shred of unreasonable hope the D.B.S. bull sessions had left in my subconscious was converted immediately to what I hesitate to call prayer but for which I cannot with honesty provide a euphemism. From my flimsy aerie built on the roof of the radio room I was able to make out sixty to sixty-eight ships in our convoy. The total varied with each computation because the seas were so rough that it was difficult to count with accuracy. I had no such difficulty with our escort. No matter how often I counted, this total always came out the same: three four-stackers, the all but obsolete destroyers we had transferred to England in the swap for Atlantic bases before we entered the war, and four Canadian corvettes.

The pitiful inadequacy of this escort for a six-knot convoy of sixty or more merchantmen was pointed out to me by all eleven D.B.S. passengers. Each one accompanied his demonstration with a stream of bitterly obscene recriminations against His Majesty's government for failing to provide him with swifter and safer passage. I assured them, with a conviction I did not feel, that they had made their point. It was demonstrated for me conclusively twenty-four hours later, when our convoy was sighted by a U-boat wolf pack. We were under submarine attack of varying intensity for sixteen days.

When our convoy split up—four days before we reached Liverpool, the destination identified in my many and complicated documents as "a U.K. port"—and the *Celtrover* swung into the Irish Sea, I was unable, no matter how many times I counted from the gun pit on top of the radio room, to reach a total of more than forty-eight ships. We had lost to the German raiders about one-third of the vessels we had met almost three weeks before at the rendezvous point near the Canadian coast. In addition, the four tables in the *Celtrover*'s tiny dining salon had broken loose from their moorings and, along with the sixteen chairs, had been smashed to bits by the violence of the sea; for the last eight days of the journey we took turns, standing up, eating the thick, gummy soup made from frozen turnip tops out of the six bowls that were all that remained of the *Celtrover*'s crockery; I learned to distinguish between the sounds made by a distant torpedo finding its target and the explosion of a depth charge; and I discovered to my considerable astonishment that it is possible for the human nervous system to survive sixteen consecutive days of being scared stiff.

I attribute this survival, in equal parts, to a member of the *Celtrover*'s crew of whose existence I did not become aware until the attack by the undersea raiders had been in progress for almost a full week, and to the unquenchable self-interest that is a part, probably a necessary part, of every writer's equipment. One day I noticed a boy, who looked about thirteen and upon inquiry proved to be four months short of his fifteenth birthday, making his way skillfully, and with apparent unconcern for the buffeting seas and the surrounding detonations of high explosive, across the pitching, slippery deck, toward the bridge. He was carrying a tray, balanced neatly on the flat of one hand, loaded with all the complicated paraphernalia necessary to an English tea. When I came down from my midday watch I asked a D.B.S. who the boy was, and why I had not seen him before.

"That's the captain's tiger," the D.B.S. said. "Doesn't have much time to hang about. He's kept pretty busy, you know."

I didn't know, so I asked several more questions. The captain's tiger, it seemed, was ship's slang for the boy who served as personal servant to the master of the vessel. His duties were difficult to define because they varied with each captain. Some masters didn't like to have anybody hanging about. Others did. Some captains preferred to do things for themselves. Others liked to be waited on hand and foot. The master of the *Celt-*

rover, a pudgy little man with a crapulous face and a poorly fitted set of dentures, whom I had seen only once, the day before the wolf pack caught us, was of the latter type, I was told. He drank vast quantities of tea, particularly when the going was rough and he was forced to remain almost constantly on the bridge, and he kept his tiger hopping.

The next day, during my noon to 2:00 P.M. watch, the boy looked up and saw me following him with my eyes as he crossed the deck. He grinned shyly. I waved from the gun pit. He stopped, hesitated, then scrambled up the ladder nailed to the side of the radio room. Balancing his loaded tray on one shoulder, he asked if I would like a cup of tea. My attitude toward tea is hardly one that can be described as open-minded, and there was nothing about the black, bitter brew that went by that name on board the *Celtrover* to dissipate this perhaps unreasonable prejudice, but a man who has been scared stiff for the better part of a week does not always remember his peccadilloes when faced with a display of spontaneous generosity. I said I would love a cup of tea and the captain's tiger, with an exhibition of dexterity the equal of which I had not seen since Houdini stopped playing the Hippodrome, poured one for me, said he had to be getting on to the bridge, and dropped nimbly to the deck without so much as upsetting the arrangement of the crockery and silver on his tray. Later, when he came back for the cup, we chatted for a few minutes. Every day after that the boy stopped at my gun pit on his way to the bridge, gave me a cup of tea, and hurried away to complete some errand for the captain.

I was surprised by how much these daily chats helped me. I began to look forward to them. I think this was because the boy, the only person on the *Celtrover* younger than I, brought back memories of my friend Natie Goodman, whose father owned the grocery store on East Fourth Street. Natie and I had helped Boy Scout Troop 224 to get started on East Fourth Street. Unexpectedly, without warning, the captain's tiger brought that time back out of the past into the terrifying present on the Western Ocean.

The weekly meetings. The new skills. The merit badges.

The useless knowledge picked up for the fun of it. I don't know why, but I still enjoy knowing that the large-tooth poplar tree, known as tremuloides, can also be properly identified as the trembling aspen. Or that the square knot is used for tying ropes of equal thickness. If they are of unequal thickness, you'd better try a sheet bend, and I still do. Morse code? I can wigwag ten words a minute with a single flag, assuming there is still anyone around who can read wigwagged Morse. If there isn't, I can send it electronically, almost as fast as A.P. bulletins come in on a news ticker. I haven't stopped much arterial bleeding lately by calling on my knowledge of the proper pressure points. However, not long before the director of transportation sent me off to Montreal to be met by a representative of the British Ministry of War Transport, who put me on a train to Halifax, where Mr. Dane arranged for me to join the *Celtrover,* I was spending a weekend in Connecticut. We were playing softball when a neighbor's son, chasing a long fly across my host's lawn, crashed through a kitchen window. When the ambulance arrived an intern complimented me on the spiral reverse bandage I'd put around the kid's forearm. Just a few of the things I learned on East Fourth Street when I was about the same age as the captain's tiger.

The best things, however, were the Sunday hikes. That's what came back to me most clearly. The Sunday hikes. Getting out of the bed I shared with my kid brother, and out of the house without waking him or my mother. She thought my scoutmaster was an American militarist working to turn me and Natie and the other boys of Troop 224 into pogromniks, her word for all people large or small who wore uniforms, whether they worked for the New York City Sanitation Department or Czar Nicholas II. Meeting Natie in the grocery store, which would not open officially for another hour (we sneaked in with a key Natie was not supposed to have). Stuffing our knapsacks with stale rolls, a small jar of butter scooped out of the big wooden tub in the icebox, a block of silverfoil-wrapped cream cheese known as a "Philadelphia," and a can of beans. (No, let's take two, baked beans are the best. But what about your old man? Aah, I'll push the other cans to the front of the shelf. He won't notice we took two.) It occurred to me in the gun pit on the *Celtrover* that Mr. Goodman did notice, but I also realized that he probably didn't mind. He was proud of the way Natie's merit badges were piling up. Mr. Goodman had come to America when he was still a young man. He was not as scared as my mother.

Knapsacks loaded, there was the long walk across town to the Astor Place subway station. Except that it never seemed long, not at seven o'clock on those Sunday mornings. The streets empty and quiet, except for the sparrows squealing their heads off as they fought over the horse droppings in the gutter, their battling noises somehow making it all seem quieter. On First Avenue, the sun coming across the "L," putting golden covers on the garbage cans. On Seventh Street, beyond Second Avenue, the young priest getting ready for early Mass, sweeping the steps of the church, his skirts hiked up to avoid the dust. On Third Avenue, in the slatted shade from the "L," the sleeping drunks known as "bimmies" looking innocently childlike and curiously clean. And the sky, like a long gold-braided canopy stretched over the tenements, smooth and blue as Waterman's ink. Mornings at seven. Browning knew. Natie Goodman and me and Robert Browning. And now, on the Western Ocean, the captain's tiger.

When I got to know the captain's tiger better, I was not surprised by these recollections. He had been born in Bootle, a slum area in Liverpool that from his description sounded very much like East Fourth Street. He had gone to sea as a cabin boy at the age of twelve. He had never gone beyond grade school. In many ways he was as innocent as a child half his age, but he had a warm, spontaneous gaiety mixed with a quick, ageless, almost terrifying shrewdness that cannot be taught and has never been learned in any classroom. By indirection, because he would not have known how to express it in words even if I had been stupid enough to ask the question, I gathered that he had not the slightest doubt the *Celtrover* would survive because he had not the slightest doubt that he would live forever. Death was a concept that had not yet reached him, as it had not yet reached me when I was twelve in that crowded little seaside village on the banks of the tidal estuary called the East River. It was helpful and refreshing to recall this at a time when the concept seemed momentarily on the verge of becoming hard fact.

One day, when he was collecting my empty cup, he asked what I did when there was no war. With that odd and insincere self-deprecation common to many members of my profession—as though I were announcing that I stole pennies from the cups of blind men, not because I liked to do it or because I was particularly adept at it but because I had to make a living—I said I was a writer. It was obvious at a glance that the boy was impressed, even awed, and, of course, at once I liked him better.

He had never met a writer, he said, although he read a good deal. I asked what he read. Oh, he said, anything, magazines mostly, and he named a few and asked if I wrote for them. I said no, they were British publications, and I wrote only for American magazines. He said shyly that he would like to read some of my work, and he asked what kind of stories I wrote. I was astonished to discover that, after all these years, I could not answer this question. I stalled for time and asked him what kind of stories he liked. He seemed to have as much difficulty with my question as I had experienced with his.

"Well," he said, hesitating as he balanced the tray against the pitch of the ship and looked thoughtfully into the distance. "I don't know," he said slowly, and then his small pinched face broke into the disturbing smile that was at once shrewd and yet very appealing. "I like them to come out nice in the end," he said.

My heart sank. I remembered that, when my first collection of short stories was published, a weekly newsmagazine of enormous international circulation had captioned its review with a single disdainful word: Sourball.

My stories, quite clearly, did not measure up to the standard set by the captain's tiger. I lacked the courage to tell him so. I did not want him to think ill of me and thus challenge the fates who were in charge of getting the *Celtrover* safely to that unidentified U.K. port. The fates were clearly, because of this boy's youth and innocence, on his side, and I was in the same boat. If I got back to America safely, I said hastily, I would send him some of my stories and let him judge for himself. By the time we docked in Liverpool I had forgotten my promise.

A year and a half later I was sent to England again. Neither I nor my second mission had increased in importance, but the war was going better. The transportation problem was less acute. Air lift was to be had almost for the asking. If the asking, that is, was in the hands of the director of transportation for the O.W.I. This time I flew. I landed at an airport near Liverpool late in the morning and learned that the next train for London would leave at five o'clock. Six empty hours faced me. I remembered the captain's tiger and, with a feeling of remorse, my neglected promise. I thumbed through my pocket notebook and found his address. It was just barely legible because I had scrawled it in the gun pit on top of the *Celtrover*'s radio room, and I had neglected to jot down his name. I was certain, however, that I could find him without it. I caught a bus into Liverpool, checked my bags at the railroad station, and took a taxi to Bootle.

We stopped in a devastated area that had once been part of a crowded slum. The street in which the boy from Bootle had lived was gone. Weeds were growing in the piles of ugly rubble that had been picked bare of every household article worth salvaging. The address in my notebook no longer existed. There were no neighbors.

At a pub on the edge of the wrecked area I described the boy I was looking for and asked when the bombs had struck. The publican shook his head dubiously at my description, but he was able to tell me that the neighborhood had been hit during the worst part of the blitz, early in 1941. I made a hurried calculation and, with some relief, reached a conclusion that I still think is sound.

When I met him on the *Celtrover* the boy from Bootle had not had so much as a single day's leave in two years to visit his home. When the bombs destroyed the house in which he was born, the captain's tiger could not possibly have been in it. And since, no matter where he might be, probably at sea in the

274

Celtrover or another of the ships that had answered the Admiralty's call, he was still young enough to retain unshaken the conviction that he would live forever, there was a fair chance that I could yet fulfill the promise I had made in the gun pit equipped with a set of twin Marlins that were ineffective against U-boats even when they did not jam.

To my next published collection of short stories I gave the only name by which I ever knew the boy from Bootle. It seemed a small and inadequate payment for friendship rendered in the bad days on the Western Ocean. Because I was aware that the standard I set for myself was not one he would have chosen or approved, I added several stories that, whatever their faults, met the standard by which he judged: they come out nice in the end. I sent a copy of the book to Somerset Maugham, who was now living in the house Nelson Doubleday had built for him on the Doubleday plantation in North Carolina. Maugham liked the collection but he felt he should call my attention to an error I had made in the title.

"You were understandably led astray by the Liverpudlian accent," he wrote. "The cabin boy on a ship who serves the master of the vessel spends most of his time tagging along after the captain. As a result he is known to the crew as the captain's tagger. As is so often the case with writers, however, your confusion resulted in an improvement. *The Captain's Tagger* would not have been nearly so good a title as your accidental invention."

eighteen

"War," according to General Karl von Clausewitz, "is part of the intercourse of the human race. We may say that war belongs not to the province of Arts or Sciences, but to the province of social life. It is a conflict of great interests which is settled by bloodshed, and only in that is it different from the others. It would be better, instead of comparing it with Art, to liken it to business competition, which is also a conflict of human interests and activities; and it is still more like State politics, which again, on its part, may be looked upon as a kind of business competition on a great scale. Besides, State politics is the womb in which War is developed, like the qualities of living creatures in their embryos."

Exactly. Except that it took some time before I caught on. How long? About thirty-six hours, I would estimate, following my arrival in Liverpool after my convoy crossing from Halifax. About one-third of these thirty-six hours went into the first hot bath and good night's sleep I'd had in a month. The rest were devoted to the ministrations of a Liverpool barber and an overnight train ride south. The next morning, in London, I reported as directed by my documents to a Miss Fortescue, an English girl of refreshing efficiency and endless patience. She exercised both in a cubbyhole on the top floor of the U.S. Embassy on Grosvenor Square.

"We're not putting you into a hotel as yet because you may not be staying in London," she said. "You will find out at one o'clock in the Waldorf Bar, where you have a lunch date. If you hurry along immediately, a taxi should get you there in plenty of time. You can leave your kit here until you get your next move sorted out."

"Who's my date in the Waldorf Bar?" I said.

"I haven't a clue," Miss Fortescue said. "But don't fret. He'll find you."

He did, but for a few minutes I didn't realize I'd been found. I stood in the doorway of the Waldorf Bar, sending my glance around the crowded room, as though I was trying to pick out a familiar face. This was nonsense, of course, because I knew there wasn't a chance that I'd recognize anybody in the Waldorf Bar. Only I, however, knew it was nonsense. What I was doing was placing myself on public view in the place where my lunch date had told Miss Fortescue he would find me.

"Mr. Weidman?"

I turned and found myself facing Mr. Alexander Musaius, my P.S. 188 physical training teacher. Or his spitting image.

"Hackett," he said, putting out his hand.

"How did you recognize me?" I said.

He held out a copy of *Time* magazine.

"I found this in the file," Mr. Hackett said. "It's not current, of course. Three years old, actually. But it has a review of your first book of short stories, *The Horse That Could Whistle 'Dixie.'* The reviewer refers to the author as balding, chipmunk-cheeked Jerome Weidman, and the picture shows you wearing a shirt clearly made of oxford cloth with a button-down collar. I brought it along on the chance that you hadn't grown any more hair since the picture was taken, and the button-down-collared shirt is, of course, as much a definitive American trait as your Ralph Waldo Emerson felt tea was a quintessentially English trait. Would you like this?"

I looked down at the copy of *Time*.

"Is the review captioned with a single word?" I said.

Mr. Hackett flipped the pages and checked.

"Why, yes, it is," he said.

"In that case, thank you, no," I said.

Mr. Hackett's thick eyebrows went up over the gold frames of his glasses, exactly as the eyebrows of Mr. Alexander Musaius used to go up in P.S. 188 when he was taken by surprise. Then, as though Mr. Hackett knew what was going on in my mind and he was determined not to disappoint me, he did what Mr. Musaius always did after the ascent of the eyebrows: his large solid body erupted in a rumbling chuckle.

"I see what you mean," Mr. Hackett said.

The word that captioned the review was the word that had come back to me when the captain's tiger asked me in the *Celtrover* gun pit what my short stories were like. The word was Sourball.

"I should have realized it might be a sore point," Mr. Hackett said, rolling up the copy of *Time* and stuffing it down into one of his already so overstuffed pockets that he seemed to be wearing not a rumpled brown tweed coat but a set of saddlebags. "I assure you I was not trying to bait you," he said. "Let's get on with the business at hand, shall we?"

The business at hand took no more than five or ten minutes, but we spent two hours over that lunch table. I can't remember what we talked about, but I enjoyed every moment of it. Maybe it was no more than the reaction to a month on the Western Ocean in the company of eleven D.B.S.s. Maybe it was much more. I was willing to let that decision wait so long as Mr. Hackett's beautifully cadenced sentences rolled on. Finally, however, they ground to a halt. A glance at his watch, a shuffling but fruitless hunt among the contents of the saddlebags, and the conversation became a crisp set of a,b,c directions.

"That's clear, then, is it?" Mr. Hackett said when he finished giving me my orders.

"Yes," I said.

With the help of two powerful thrusts of both hands, palms down, he brought his large, muscular body up from the table. I followed. We started across the crowded room. Halfway to the door Mr. Hackett stopped.

"By the way," he said casually. "You'll be wanting a name, of course, won't you?"

For a moment I didn't understand. Then I got it.

"Of course," I said.

"Anything you've decided on?" Mr. Hackett said.

"Yes," I said, making the decision as—it occurred to me for the first time in my life—most of my decisions were always made: on the spur of the moment.

"Slutzky," I said. "J. Morris Slutzky."

nineteen

The sign on the first station platform out of Euston read "Hovis." Twenty minutes later so did the sign on the second station platform out of Euston. When the train pulled out on its way to the third, I left my compartment and hunted up a conductor.

"The last two stations were marked 'Hovis,' " I said.

"That's right, sir," the conductor said.

"You mean both places have the same name?" I said.

"What is your destination, sir?" the conductor said.

"Bletchley," I said.

"I'll let you know when we get there, sir," the conductor said.

"Thanks," I said, not quite sure what I was thanking him for. I went back to my compartment. Fifteen minutes later we pulled into our third stop since Euston. The station sign read "Hovis." After the train pulled out of Hovis Number Three I went looking for the conductor again. He saw me coming and pulled out his watch.

"Bletchley in twenty minutes, sir," he said. "I'll let you know."

"How many Hovises to go?" I said.

He didn't seem to hear my question.

"When we come to Bletchley, sir, I'll let you know," he said.

He slid the watch back into his pocket and moved on. I went back to my compartment and kept an eye on my own watch. The train went through three more stations with Hovis signs before the conductor stuck his head into my compartment.

"Bletchley next, sir," he said.

I took my bag and followed him to the front of the car. As the train pulled into the station I saw the sign: Hovis.

"Bletchley," the conductor said.

"Are you sure?" I said.

"This is Bletchley, sir."

The train stopped. I climbed down with my bag and looked around. I was the only passenger on the platform. I started up toward the ticket office. On the way I passed another Hovis sign. A short distance beyond the sign a British sergeant in battle dress was waiting.

"Mr. Slutzky?" he said.

"Yes," I said. "Is this Bletchley?"

"Yes, sir," he said. "Here, let me take that, sir." He took my bag. "This way, sir."

I fell in beside him.

"If this is Bletchley," I said, "why do the platform signs say 'Hovis'?"

"It's a leftover from the invasion scare after Dunkirk," the sergeant said. "Parachutists were the problem. When they come down out of the sky, if they see place names on a railroad station, they can compare them with the maps they're carrying and figure out where they've landed. So we took down all the station signs from here to Land's End and put Hovis signs in the empty spaces."

"What's Hovis?" I said.

"Bread," the sergeant said.

He put my bag in the back of an old Ford, went around the front, and climbed in behind the wheel. I slid in beside him. We drove in bright sunlight, along a deserted country road, under a cloudless sky against which birds swooped and wheeled and made chirping noises as though they were working for Walt Disney. Neatly cultivated green and yellow fields, separated by trimmed hedges and rows of bright red flowers, stretched away on both sides of the road. It was picture-postcard country. The war, to which I had just been carried in convoy across the submarine-infested Western Ocean, didn't seem very real. The Ford turned from the road into a long, winding driveway that led up to a large, sprawling, handsome old house on a hill. The Ford stopped on the gravel path under a porte-cochere. From the top step a girl in uniform watched us arrive.

"Who's that?" I said.

"Lieutenant Dundas," the sergeant said. "Our adjutant."

I got out of the Ford and came up the steps.

"Hello, Mr. Slutzky," Lieutenant Dundas said. "Major Hackett called from London and told us to expect you."

Her voice was round and firm and fully packed. A Roxy usher would have been proud to borrow it. She apparently wanted, by the way she sounded, to correct any misconceptions a newcomer might draw from her size. Miss Dundas was a very pretty, but also very small, girl. I didn't yet know what an adjutant did at Bletchley but I had no doubt who was in charge. Lieutenant Dundas addressed, almost formally, the sergeant standing beside the Ford.

"Put Mr. Slutzky's gear in the De Gaulle room."

"Yes, ma'am," the sergeant said.

Lieutenant Dundas opened the front door and held it wide. I stepped past her into a high, wide hall, and stopped. It was as though I had suddenly been reminded that it was Friday night, or the eve of an important Jewish holiday. For the next few hours I would be Mrs. Leonard Lyons accompanying her husband to a Broadway opening. The curtain had just gone up. From one of the two aisle seats to which an important gossip columnist was entitled, I was staring into the set, trying to guess from the scenery what the play would be about.

It was a large drawing room to which much had been done to make it more functional for purposes other than sipping tea. On the right a bulletin board hung near a bookcase that could have been the prize centerpiece in a Parke-Bernet auction. On the left there was a fireplace into which the auctioneer could have walked without stooping and, next to it, a heavy walnut door. Beyond the door French windows opened into a formal garden. Something had been done to the windows. After a moment I saw what it was: blackout curtains. To the left of the

281

fireplace a massive sideboard was stocked with rows of glasses, bottles, a pitcher of water, and what Mr. Geschwind would have called a cash payments book. On the wall, flanking a map stuck full of colored pins, were a couple of pen-and-ink caricatures of FDR and Winston Churchill.

"You would like a cup of tea I'm sure," Lieutenant Dundas said.

I did not want to start off on the wrong foot by disobeying what was clearly an order.

"Yes, thank you," I said.

Lieutenant Dundas walked to the fireplace. She reached up and pulled a brocaded bell rope. As though he had been waiting in the wings for his cue, in came a heavyset, bald-headed old man. His scalp and face were flushed. He wheezed as he moved. He wore a soiled black tailcoat. Pinned on the left lapel was a frayed but still colorful campaign ribbon.

"There will be two for tea," Lieutenant Dundas said.

"Very good, ma'am," the old man said and slowly wheezed his way out.

Lieutenant Dundas sent her glance around the room. She could have been checking its contents to see if anything of value had been removed since her last inspection. Apparently satisfied that everything was in place she said, "Major Hackett asked that you wait here for him."

He showed up while I was in the middle of my second cup of tea.

"Are those muffins hot?" he said.

"They were a few moments ago," I said.

"Good," Major Hackett said, snatching one from the tray as he heaved himself into a corner of the couch facing my chair. "I suppose you've been indulging in the mental process that your *I Can Get It for You Wholesale* hero would describe as wondering what the score is."

"More or less," I said.

"I assume you weren't provided with very much in the way of helpful information before you left New York," Major Hackett said, pouring himself a cup of tea.

"No, I was not," I said.

282

"Perhaps it's just as well," Major Hackett said.

Into my head came a picture of the director of transportation for the O.W.I., seated behind his big belly at the big desk, in his big office on Fifty-seventh Street. It was probably better than just as well.

"I hope you'll tell me what they left out in New York," I said.

"Gladly," Major Hackett said. "Once you chaps got yourselves sorted out—I mean breaking up the C.O.I. into a couple of separate playpens for Bob Sherwood and Wild Bill Donovan—it occurred to both of them that two completely new staffs had to be trained. I have no idea what Wild Bill decided to do about the problem but I was told Bob Sherwood, being an intellectual type, grasped at once that training meant schools. I don't know how it was arranged, but apparently one of your more patriotic millionaires, I believe his name is Field, Marshall Field, would it be?"

"Yes, it would," I said.

"Well, Mr. Field agreed to turn over his Long Island estate to the O.W.I. for the duration as a site for such a school. Three chaps who had been recruited by Bob Sherwood and brought over to the O.W.I. from the C.O.I. were chosen to go to England to study our M.O. methods, and then return to New York with a plan for how to use Mr. Field's property."

"Am I one of those three?" I said.

Major Hackett's eyebrows made their Alexander Musaius ascent above his gold-rimmed glasses and were followed by the roar of laughter.

"Good God, didn't they tell you even that?"

Since I hadn't been told a damn thing about anything I was pleased to be able to hear myself saying calmly, "No, they did not."

"Well, no matter," Major Hackett said. "The other two chaps managed to get air lift. They flew over, spent a month with us here in Bletchley, and flew back."

"What are their names?" I said.

"I'll have to look it up, and I will if you like, but at the moment they're irrelevant," Major Hackett said. "You're the man in hand at the moment, so it's to you I'll address these introductory remarks."

"Okay," I said.

"What we're engaged in here is what we British call M.O.," Major Hackett said. "Short for Morale Operations."

With the entire continent sealed off by the Germans the only contact the British had with what was going on in occupied Europe were the various underground resistance movements. They were surprisingly extensive and superbly coordinated. The main problem at the British end was staffing. A constant stream of volunteers kept pouring out of the continent—French, Belgians, Scandinavians, Poles, Czechs—all eager to be absorbed into the British network and return to the continent to fight Nazis under M.O. direction. The big problem for the British was that they could never be certain about how these men managed to get to England. Without corroboration M.O. could not trust their explanations even though the British were aware that many of these men, perhaps even most of them, were telling the truth. To function properly M.O. had to work on the totally unsentimental assumption that every man who came out of the occupied continent was a Nazi agent until he was able to demonstrate by standards set up by M.O. that he was not. These standards were the core of a debriefing period that could take weeks, often longer. The man was sent from school to school, all secret, scattered across the landscape from Land's End to John o'Groat's. The trainee was taught everything from the use of small arms and high explosives to how to drop by parachute into an enemy-occupied area. Once trained they were sent back to the continent on all sorts of missions, from blowing up a railroad center and getting out immediately, to settling down for the duration to edit an underground newspaper. In theory there were no rules and yet, in actual fact, every operation was enmeshed in a network of rules without which it would have been impossible to conduct this form of irregular warfare. Many trainees dropped out somewhere along the line. For those who survived the sometimes invisible hazards of the training period, Bletchley was the end of the line.

"Do you have any designs on that last muffin?" Major Hackett said.

"I was saving it for you," I said, pushing the tray toward him.

"Thank you," Major Hackett said, scooping up the muffin. "By the time one of those bodies arrives at Bletchley he is fully trained, ready to go back to the continent on a mission. The nature of the mission is what he learns here. When he arrives he has no idea what it is. Neither do I until I receive the instructions from M.O.H.Q. in London. When the man assigned to the mission gets here, he is turned over to a British officer who has been assigned by M.O. to work under my supervision. They work in secret, just the two of them with me doing a bit of over-the-shoulder peering, until he and the briefing officer are convinced the man who is going back is ready. When he is, an R.A.F. detail comes for him at the appointed time. They drive off, and we never see or hear from him again. Sometimes we get word that he's made it. More often we don't. There's no time for speculation because the next body has already arrived for his instruction period."

Major Hackett heaved himself up out of the couch, crossed to the fireplace, and hauled on the bell rope. Again, as though he had been waiting just outside the door, the old man in the black tailcoat came wheezing into the room.

"More tea, sir?" he said, heading for the tray.

"Please," Major Hackett said. "And if the muffins could be induced to attain a somewhat higher temperature—?"

"They will be, sir," the old man said as he wheezed his way out with the tray.

"Is that a campaign ribbon on his lapel?" I said.

"Boer War," Major Hackett said. "He was at Mafeking with Baden-Powell. Two hundred and seventeen days. Remarkable that he can still manage a tea tray. Where was I?"

"I think you were about to tell me why I'm here?" I said.

"So I was," Major Hackett said, coming back to the couch. "At this end we, of course, don't know yet what the plans are at the American end. All we know is that the O.W.I. is setting up a school on the Marshall Field estate, and we have offered to train three of your men to serve as a cadre of instructors for that school. The training we've given your two colleagues who preceded you at Bletchley was exactly the same we give the bodies that go through this place on their way to actual missions on the continent. It seems highly unlikely that the people you will be training at the Marshall Field estate will be dropping into *Festung Europa* by parachute to blow up a railroad-marshaling yard or settle down to edit an underground newspaper for the duration. On the theory, however, that if you train a man to carry a donkey on his back he'll have no difficulty carrying a toy poodle, we feel if the instructors at your O.W.I. school on the Marshall Field estate are made aware of what our students here at Bletchley are called on to do, yours will probably be better equipped for the probably less demanding work they will be asked to do overseas. You see the point, I'm sure?"

"Yes," I said. "And now that I'm here I will get the same training my two colleagues got?"

"Quite," Major Hackett said. "Except that in your case there is something more."

"What's that?" I said.

"We understand that you know Dr. George Gallup," Major Hackett said. "Is that correct?"

"Yes," I said.

We met in 1940 when I was working for Max Schuster. Gallup's eminence as the founder of the then still small but already potent polling business had erupted on the American scene when the *Literary Digest*, which conducted a nationwide poll, predicted that Alf Landon would beat FDR in his run for a second term. George Gallup, then almost unknown to the public at large, announced that the *Digest* was wrong. He predicted that FDR would win and by how much. He was right, of course. As a result the *Digest* went out of business, Gallup became an international celebrity, and he attracted the attention of the Inner Sanctum. Gallup signed a contract with Simon & Schuster for a book that would take the reader behind the scenes of what at that time still seemed to the public an activity touched by magic, not unlike fortune-telling and reading the future with

286

cards. The manuscript arrived while everybody at Simon & Schuster was still trying to think up a snappy title for what we all saw as more or less an accumulation of peppy anecdotes about encounters between Gallup's pollsters and the citizenry being polled. The title Gallup chose for his book, as well as the fact that on the title page he gave credit to his Ph.D., was a measure of the difference in his approach to the material and that of his publishers. The publication of *The Pulse of Democracy* by Dr. George Gallup was greeted with a respectful sale and went the way of what at Simon & Schuster was known as a "succès d'estime and a flop de fiasco."

Not until I arrived at Bletchley, and had my indoctrination meeting with Major Hackett, did I realize that Dr. Gallup had reached an audience he may not have been aware existed. It certainly came as a surprise to me that Britain's psychological warriors, under the umbrella of Morale Operations, had taken Dr. Gallup's text to heart. At that time one of M.O.'s greatest challenges was to learn how the different peoples of occupied Europe would feel about, among other things, an Allied landing on their different beaches. Would they rise up and assist the Allied troops? Would they help their Nazi occupiers to fight off the invaders? Would they be indifferent? The answers, if they could be obtained, might differ with every occupied country, possibly with different beach areas in the same country, but on one point they would be identical: the information contained in the answers, if accurate, would be invaluable to the Allies probing, as they prepared for a second front, for favorable landing areas. The problem was how to obtain such information. The obvious way—to send in a team of Gallup's pollsters with a series of carefully phrased questions—was of course preposterous. To M.O., however, as I learned from Major Hackett, the preposterous was the raw material for achievement. Studying *The Pulse of Democracy*, they worked out a series of questions that could be asked in any language, about matters totally removed from even the hint of an amphibious operation, that would nonetheless be helpful to the informed reader of the results turned in by the secret pollster.

"Among the exercises we schedule for all our students here

at Bletchley," Major Hackett said, "we send them out on an actual Gallup poll in the field."

"You mean—?" I said.

Major Hackett laughed.

"No, of course not," he said. "By the time one of our trainees goes off on his mission, it is too late to put him through any more tests. While he is here at Bletchley, however, he is sent out to some neighboring area in the countryside, a small city, perhaps, to do a secret poll, using the assumed name and identity he has been using here at the school, on a subject we choose for him. We will, of course, put you through all the things we have put your two preceding colleagues through, but because of your connection with Dr. Gallup we are going to call on you for a bit extra."

"What's that?" I said.

"We'll go into it in detail when the time comes for you to take the field," Major Hackett said. "With your consent, of course?"

"Of course," I said.

"Good," Major Hackett said. "Then let's get squared away on everything else first."

The squaring-away process took twenty-six days. Working alone with a different instructor in each subject I went through a curriculum of eleven crash courses, including leaflet writing, clandestine document photography, carpentry, electric wiring, typesetting, karate, and polling techniques. During the twenty-six days I came to know Major Hackett, Lieutenant Dundas, and Mullin the butler who had been at Mafeking with Baden-Powell. I was never sure how many students were living in the house—just as I was never sure how many ships accompanied the S.S. *Celtrover* in the convoy that carried me across the Western Ocean—because nobody stood still long enough to be counted: they came and went at all hours of the day and night. Every day I passed at least one person in the halls I was certain I had never seen before. Sometimes they were in civilian clothes, sometimes in khaki battle dress without insignia. We never spoke or, except for an occasional noncommittal nod, acknowledged each other's existence. The day before I was scheduled to go off on my polling field trip I was crossing the lawn from the printshop with my instructor. He stopped to talk with a man I had never seen before. They spoke in French for a few moments and then my instructor turned to me.

"Oh, by the way," he said, "this is Henri Chenevier. He'll be your Number Two on tomorrow's exercise. Chenevier, this is J. M. Slutzky."

We nodded and shook hands and, in the few hurried moments, exchanged looks. I carried away the impression of a tall man in a dark suit with reddish-brown hair and a thick, neatly trimmed mustache. He seemed to be about forty. After lunch I was driven to the station marked "Hovis" by the sergeant who twenty-six days earlier had picked me up there. I took the train to London and checked into the Park Lane Hotel, where a room had been reserved for me. After dinner I took a walk. When the air-raid sirens went, I looked around for a shelter. I had stopped in front of the Cambridge Theatre. *Heartbreak House* was playing, with Robert Donat as Captain Shotover, Edith Evans, Isabel Jeans, and a twenty-year-old newcomer named Deborah Kerr. I bought a ticket and went in and in a few minutes I forgot about the air raid. It was one of the most absorbing evenings I've ever spent in a theatre. The next morning I left the Park Lane at 9:45, took a taxi to Kings Cross, and bought a first-class round-trip ticket to Cambridge: eighteen shillings. The train left at 10:15 and arrived in Cambridge at 12:45. Henri Chenevier was waiting on the platform. He was wearing the same dark suit.

"Hello," he said.

"Hello," I said.

We waited quietly, watching the passengers move down the platform. A man wearing a dirty raincoat and a green porkpie hat stopped in front of us.

"Have you seen my wife?" he said.

"Not yet," I said.

"She said she'd be waiting at the car," Chenevier said.

I wondered which of us had got it wrong. The line I had memorized was, "She told me she'd be waiting in the car." The man in the porkpie hat didn't seem to notice the discrepancy.

"Let's join her, then, shall we?" he said.

That meant, or should have meant, that we had been met by Dr. William Grew, director of the Ministry of Information in the area who, it said in my briefing paper, would serve as our "coordinating liaison." He led us out to a blue Rover and opened the front door. Chenevier gestured politely for me to get in first. I did. Dr. Grew slammed the front door and opened the rear door. Chenevier got in. Dr. Grew slammed the door, went around the car and slid in behind the wheel. Sitting beside him, I became aware of the smell of clothes that had been worn a long time without laundering or dry cleaning. The war had nothing to do with it. Englishmen had smelled that way in peacetime, when I came to London on the first leg of my *Letter of Credit* trip. Dr. Grew drove us to the Garden House Hotel, a modest establishment without an elevator. There was a desk clerk but no other employees in the small lobby. A double room had been reserved for us. Dr. Grew waited while we signed the register, then we had lunch in the shabby but serviceable dining room. The talk was about the weather, which was good, and the food, which was not. Powdered eggs and bangers. They were known in the Bletchley students' dining room in several languages as "those fucking sausages." Wartime bangers in England were stuffed with many grains, some not readily identifiable, but none was meat. After lunch, for which, according to our briefing papers, each of us paid his own check, Dr. Grew drove us around the city. He pointed out places of interest, identified main thoroughfares, and suggested areas where we might have luck picking up interviews for our assignment. At three o'clock we stopped at Dr. Grew's office, a neat little two-story brick building on a cul-de-sac around the corner from a Gaumont British movie theatre that was showing *The First of the Few*, with Leslie Howard and David Niven. When Chenevier and I were settled on chairs in front of Dr. Grew's desk he picked up the phone.

"We're about to start," he said into it, and hung up. "I've asked my wife to join us. She is my assistant."

Mrs. Grew came in, and the atmosphere changed at once. The way it changed in *The Thirty-nine Steps* when Robert Donat, on the run from the murderous gang of World War I spies, knocks on the door of a lonely farmhouse somewhere on the Scottish moors, and the door is opened by the farmer's wife, the young—then very young—Peggy Ashcroft. Up to now, from the moment in the morning when I left the Park Lane Hotel in London, the day had been not unlike an attempt to cross a snow-covered field without revealing my presence by stepping carefully in a previous crosser's footprints. Chenevier, Dr. Grew, the hotel, lunch, the talk about the weather, the tour of the city in Dr. Grew's Rover, all had been footprints on a briefing sheet into which I had been stepping with care to make sure I was obeying precise instructions designed to conceal my presence from others who might come along later. I had been rubbing elbows cautiously with passing strangers. Chenevier, about whom I knew nothing except that he was one of Major Hackett's "bodies." Dr. Grew, about whom I knew less. Now, all at once, with Mrs. Grew's entrance, everything seemed to come to life. Chenevier became a human being preparing for a mission to occupied Europe in the course of which the odds were good that he might lose his life. Dr. Grew, a Ministry of Information bureaucrat, became the meticulous, strict, efficient, unsmiling, fussy clerk who had somehow managed to bring to his desolate home this lovely, shy bride from the big city, a girl much younger than her husband who was not equipped to cope with the harsh drudgery and frightening loneliness of a sheep farm on which it was obvious her jealous husband was virtually keeping her prisoner.

"Mr. Chenevier, Mr. Slutzky," Dr. Grew said. "My wife."

As we acknowledged the introduction, I sensed that Chenevier was experiencing a reaction not unlike my own. He seemed to move forward a little into the room, as though slipping out of a heavy coat because he had suddenly became aware that the room was warmer than the street he had just left behind.

"Mrs. Grew has been in charge of all these operations since M.O. started sending them our way," Dr. Grew said. "The duties of this office are too heavy and complex for me to abandon them completely when we are handed one of these assignments, so I've been forced to limit my participation to that of supervision. Mrs. Grew's experience with these polls has been extensive and you will find her most cooperative. Major Hackett informs me that you are in charge, Mr. Slutzky, and Mr. Chenevier is your Number Two?"

"That's correct," I said.

Dr. Grew turned to his wife.

"Mrs. G.?" he said.

She didn't move, yet she seemed to come forward in her chair, as though she, too, like Chenevier, had become aware that the room had taken on a more comfortable climate, and she was moving out of a heavy outer garment.

"May I suggest, then, Mr. Slutzky," she said, "a method of procedure during your stay in Cambridge?"

Her voice was like her manner: shy but firm.

"Please," I said.

"Would you state, then, the nature of your assignment as you understand it?" Mrs. Grew said.

"Without identifying ourselves as the conductors of a poll," I said, quoting from our briefing papers, "our task is to find out how the people of Cambridge feel today about the way Germany should be treated after the Allies have beaten her in the field. Specifically, we want to know how the people of Cambridge feel about Lord Vansittart's plan to colonize Germany after the war the way in the past Britain colonized India and France colonized Indo-China. If the Vansittart plan is too harsh, what alternative would the people of Cambridge suggest? As a point of departure to precipitate discussion this poll will use Noël Coward's new song 'Let's Not Be Beastly to the Germans When Our Victory Is Ultimately Won.' " I turned to Chenevier. "You agree?"

He nodded and said, "Completely."

"That is also our understanding of the assignment," Dr. Grew said as he turned to his wife. "Am I correct?"

"Yes, of course," Mrs. Grew said.

"In that case, gentlemen, will you be good enough to accompany my wife to her office upstairs?" Dr. Grew said. "She will provide you with reading material that will give you a picture of the city, and answer any question you may have, while

I carry on with my other duties. I would suggest that you dine early, because I will be picking you up in my car at the hotel at seven-thirty for an evening meeting at my home."

We thanked him and followed Mrs. Grew upstairs. Her office was in one corner of a library of reference books and Ministry of Information publications. The walls were covered with war posters urging the citizens of Great Britain to conserve energy, refrain from increasing industrial haze, work hard, and keep their mouths shut about the movements of friends and family members in the armed services because the ears of the enemy were everywhere. Chenevier and I sat facing each other across a table in the middle of the room, leafing through books and studying maps of the city. Mrs. Grew, while we worked, sat at her desk in the corner. After a while I felt my attention wandering. I looked up and saw Chenevier watching Mrs. Grew. He turned and caught my eye. He raised his eyebrows and nodded toward the door. I nodded back and we both stood up.

"Is anything wrong?" Mrs. Grew said.

"No," I said. "I think we've got enough out of the books and maps so that we feel we can go out and start our interviewing."

Mrs. Grew smiled and stood up.

"Of course," she said, and walked us to the door. "You will be ready at seven-thirty when Dr. Grew comes to pick you up?"

"We certainly will," I said.

Chenevier bowed and we left. Out in the street we looked at each other.

"A pub?" he said.

"All right," I said.

We found one called the Red Lion a couple of blocks from the M.O.I. office. We went in. Chenevier ordered stout. I said I'd have the same. The waitress brought the drinks. We sipped. Chenevier cleared his throat.

"The little one, she is married to a bastard, no?" he said.

I was aware of making a conscious effort to conceal my astonishment.

"How do you know?" I said.

"How does one know it is hot or cold?" Chenevier said. "One feels."

As the leader of our two-man team I was embarrassed. I had seen nothing to justify Chenevier's reaction. I felt as though I had missed something important. Chenevier finished his stout.

"Another?" he said.

"Not for me," I said.

Chenevier pushed aside his empty glass and stood up.

"Let us go," he said.

We went back to the hotel and up to our room. We stood in the doorway and looked at the twin beds. I watched Chenevier out of the corner of my eye.

"You have a preference?" he said.

"No," I said.

"In that case," Chenevier said. He pulled a coin from his pocket. "Your call," he said.

"Heads," I said.

The coin landed on the bed. Chenevier bent over it.

"Heads it is," he said.

I picked up my bag from the floor just inside the door and set it on the bed near the window. Chenevier picked up his bag and set it on the other bed. We both looked at our watches, then at each other. The warm moment in Mrs. Grew's office when I felt we had ceased being strangers had vanished. Chenevier and I were back where we had started from when we were introduced the day before at Bletchley. Two men who knew nothing about each other except that they were both using assumed names.

"Are you greatly concerned," Chenevier said, "about not being beastly to the Germans when our victory is ultimately won?"

"Only if it's not beastly enough," I said. "Where would you like to start?"

"The cinema near the M.O.I. office?" Chenevier said.

It did not strike me as an ideal place for conducting covert interviews, but my confidence in myself as leader of the team had been momentarily shaken. I was suddenly acutely aware that I knew less about the man I was working with than I had felt I knew in the M.O.I. office. It seemed sensible not to ruffle any feathers. He had made a suggestion. We would explore it.

"Let's have a look," I said.

We walked to the Gaumont British theatre. It looked deserted. Chenevier seemed to be aware that I was not impressed.

"We must not judge by the outside," he said. "It will be better inside."

It was not deserted inside. It merely confirmed what I felt we should have known: a movie theatre under any circumstances is not an ideal place for conducting covert interviews.

"We can certainly do better than this," I whispered to Chenevier.

"We are here," he said. "We might as well see the film."

We saw Leslie Howard and David Niven in *The First of the Few* while I wondered irritably how to recapture control of the leadership of my two-man team. By seven, when the movie was over, I had thought of nothing except that now we had no time for dinner before we kept our seven-thirty date with Dr. Grew. He was pulling his blue Rover up to the curb in front of the hotel when we arrived under the marquee.

"How fortunate that I've caught you," he said, leaning out the window. "I've been called to an emergency meeting in Huntingdon, so we must cancel this evening's meeting at my home. I'm terribly sorry. I will call you in the morning and make another date."

He rolled up the car window and drove off. I decided to assert my authority.

"This afternoon," I said, "in those guidebooks we were studying in the M.O.I. office I noticed an establishment called the Rex Dance Hall. It sounds as though it might be a good place to start our interviews."

"All right," Chenevier said.

It was also a noisy place. After an hour I had accumulated four interviews and a headache. Chenevier had not been very cooperative. He drank stout in brooding silence and watched the band. After the fourth interview I told him I'd had enough and suggested we leave and get something to eat.

"We'll probably do better in a restaurant," I said.

"May I go to the W.C. first?" Chenevier said.

It may not have been intended as a sarcastic remark, but I had no idea what was going on inside his head. I decided the best demonstration of leadership at this stage was to avoid an open and public display of insubordination.

"Take your time," I said.

After a while it occurred to me he was taking more than was necessary. I went to the W.C. No sign of Chenevier. I returned to our table. No sign of my Number Two. I waited another ten minutes, then paid the check and walked back to the Garden House Hotel. It was almost two o'clock in the morning. I asked for my key and went up to our room. My unpacked bag was still sitting on the bed near the window. Chenevier's bag was gone. I did not have to sit down for my next bout of thinking. I had no idea what had happened, but I had the Bletchley briefing sheets clear in my head. There was no doubt what an operative was supposed to do when a plan went off track: call nobody, retrace steps. I took my bag and carried it down to the lobby.

"Half the bill for your room has been paid," the old man at the desk said.

I did not ask who had paid it. I paid my share and asked for a railroad timetable. There was a 6:05 train to London. Almost four hours to wait. I took a taxi to the station. A dozen or so men in uniform were already waiting. They were seated and sprawled on the benches, some dozing, others sleeping soundly. I joined them. At five o'clock I carried my bag into the washroom and shaved, then went into the restaurant and had breakfast. The train was on time. It pulled into Kings Cross at 10:35. I took a taxi to the Park Lane Hotel. The room from which I had set out for Cambridge the day before was still registered in my name. I went upstairs and called Bletchley. Lieutenant Dundas answered the phone.

"Major Hackett, please," I said.

"Mr. Slutzky?"

"Yes," I said.

"You are expected in the common room," Lieutenant Dundas said.

I took a taxi to Euston, caught the next train to Bletchley, and started counting Hovis signs. At the seventh sign I got off. The British sergeant in battle dress was waiting.

"Let me take that, sir."

I gave him my bag. He put it in the back of the old Ford, went around the front, and climbed in behind the wheel. I slid in beside him. We drove in the same bright sunlight, along the same deserted country road, under the same cloudless sky, against which the same birds were swooping and wheeling and chirping as though they were still on the Walt Disney payroll and the word had been passed that the boss was on the premises. It was the same picture-postcard country, except that this time, as we drove through it, I did not feel as I'd felt the previous time, full of anticipation for a new experience that lay ahead, whatever it might be. Now, a day later, I carried with me a feeling of discomfort. The trip had obviously been a failure. There was always the possibility that the failure had been intentional, that I had been put to some kind of test, but I didn't really believe that. I thought of British novels I had read in which it was said of a man who had failed on some military mission that he had blotted his copybook. The Ford stopped on the gravel path under the porte-cochere. Lieutenant Dundas was waiting on the top step.

"Major Hackett is in the common room," she said.

He was having tea.

"Join me?" he said.

"No, thanks," I said.

"I'll just finish, then, while you put me in the picture."

He was on the last muffin when I got to the end.

"That's the lot, then, is it?" Major Hackett said.

"Yes, sir," I said.

"Could you have it on paper by four-thirty?" Major Hackett said. "Lieutenant Dundas is waiting."

Ten years later, when with my family I was spending the summer in a rented house in Kent near the town where Major Hackett lived, he invited me up to London one day for lunch at his club. The surprise other guest was Henri Chenevier. Like the rest of us he was ten years older. Aside from a somewhat thicker waistline, however, he didn't seem to have changed much.

In the cheerful clatter of biographical fragments with which we filled in the time since we had last seen each other, I gathered that, after V-E Day, Chenevier returned to his family in Belgium, where he resumed his career as a judge, and got married. Now, as we were having lunch in Major Hackett's club, Chenevier was the father of three small children with whom he and his wife were living happily ever after in Brussels.

I kept thinking of the moment in Cambridge when we left Mrs. Grew in the M.O.I. office and, over a glass of stout in the Red Lion, Chenevier had astonished me by saying savagely, "The little one, she is married to a bastard, no?" I kept hoping he or Major Hackett would say something about Chenevier's disappearance that night from the Rex Dance Hall, but neither man referred to the Cambridge incident even casually. We could have been three old classmates having a reunion and, in the flood of remembered anecdotes, managing to avoid the only subject in which we were really interested.

To avoid slighting any of the traditions attached to reunion luncheons, I finally asked Chenevier what was the biggest difference he had noticed between present-day London and the wartime London in which we met.

He thought gravely for a moment, then said, "The sausages are no longer so fucking."

twenty

A week after Chenevier disappeared from Bletchley, Major Hackett decided I had as much in my head—written notes were forbidden—as my two predecessors had carried back to New York in theirs. The time had come to go home.

Unhampered by the efforts of the O.W.I. director of transportation in his office on West Fifty-seventh Street, depending solely on the skills of Miss Fortescue in her cubbyhole on the top floor of the U.S. Embassy on Grosvenor Square, I managed to make my return crossing of the Western Ocean by air. I was back in New York in plenty of time to take up my duties as a member of the staff for the opening of the O.W.I. training school on the Marshall Field estate at Huntington, Long Island.

The day before I reported for duty I had a meeting with Harold Guinzburg in the New York office on Fifty-seventh Street. I briefed him about my work at Bletchley, and asked when I would meet the two other men who had been trained by Major Hackett for the instructors' cadre.

"You won't," Harold said.

"Why not?" I said.

"They are no longer with us," Harold said. "Which leaves us with the problem of what to do with you."

"I thought that was settled by my last six weeks at Bletchley?"

"I thought so, too," Harold said. "But in your absence we've had a few more growing pains."

"A reorganization?" I said.

"You could put it that way," Harold said.

"I see," I said, or rather I saw what General von Clausewitz had intended his readers to see. "Fill me in," I said.

"Bob Sherwood doesn't want you nailed down to the school for the duration," Harold Guinzburg said. "He wants you overseas."

"So do I," I said.

"Then you'll cooperate?" Harold said.

"With what?" I said.

"The administrative setup at the school that has been taking shape while you were in England," Harold said. "You won't have to fuss with executive responsibility. All you'll have to do is take your place on the teaching staff."

"For how long?" I said.

"Until your overseas assignment opens up," Harold said.

"May I ask what it is?" I said.

"Of course not," Harold said. "None of us knows yet. But the plans for the second front are moving along, and Bob wants all our best people in on that."

"You're telling me that I'll be in on it?" I said.

"You have my promise," Harold Guinzburg said.

The next day I was driven out in an O.W.I. station wagon to the Marshall Field estate. I was greeted at the front door by my friend Fred Schwed, Jr.

"What are you doing in this place?" I said.

I was not aware, when I left for England, that he had joined the O.W.I.

"Helping the staff get ready for our first group of students," Fred said. "I've been here almost a week, which makes me an old hand, so I've been assigned to show you around."

It was not unlike being shown around the New York Public Library at Fifth Avenue and Forty-second Street. When I stepped out of the car that brought me to Huntington my hand went by instinct to my hip pocket. The automatic check of any East Fourth Street boy to make sure he had remembered to bring his borrower's card.

"Architecturally speaking," Fred said, "the operative word here is vast."

For a half hour we tramped along what seemed miles of

corridors that looked like autobahns, and acres of ballrooms from which every priceless antique and world-famous painting had been stripped and sent into storage for the duration. We paused for breath in what had been Mr. Field's bedroom and stared into a marble amphitheatre that, in time of peace, served as the master's bathroom.

"Lose something?" Fred said.

I stopped swiveling my head.

"Where do they hide the shower?" I said.

"There is no shower," Fred said.

When I left East Fourth Street for uptown the first luxury I encountered that made me understand the gap between the have-not and the have was the bathroom shower.

"How come a man with Mr. Field's kind of money doesn't own a shower?" I said.

"Can you picture a man saying, 'Jeeves, draw me a shower'?" Fred said.

The reply did more than answer a question. The arrangement of words bore the unmistakable signature of Fred Schwed, Jr. For those who were fortunate enough to know him, almost everything he did or said was as unique as a fingerprint. So was Fred's life. His father, Fred Senior, had been a stockbroker in the days when the word was still synonymous—to a boy from East Fourth Street, anyway—with great wealth. I don't know how great Mr. Schwed's wealth was. The poet Newman Levy, however, who served in the same unit with Fred's father during the First World War, once told me that Fred Senior spent most of his time on K.P. duty describing for everybody within earshot the feats of the horses in the racing stable he had been forced to leave behind when he was drafted.

"Did your father really own a racing stable?" I once asked Fred.

"Not by the time I was old enough to be aware of the family's physical possessions," Fred said. "It's not the sort of thing you can tuck away in a closet. I do remember that my father always carried two tightly folded one-thousand-dollar bills wadded into his watch pocket."

"Why?" I said.

301

When Fred was doling out fragments of autobiography it was not a waste of time, I had learned, to feed coins into the gas meter.

"My father," Fred said, "lived in terror of running into a bet during the working day and not having on him the cash to cover."

By the time I met Mr. Schwed Senior his working day, according to Fred, was spent at the track. Not, I would have guessed even if Fred had failed to point it out, with great success. Mr. Schwed was a compulsive gambler. According to his son it was ironically in character, therefore, that Mr. Schwed should have been ruined financially by being made the innocent victim of a scam that had been set in motion by one of his closest friends: Arnold Rothstein.

"I have had a great deal of experience with moneyed families that lost their money," Fred once told me. "It is a human activity that is accomplished with grace only in Civil War novels."

The grace that preceded Mr. Schwed's financial ruin included a passion for Kipling, and sending his sons to Lawrenceville and Princeton. While Fred was at Princeton his father asked Fred on the eve of one of the Big Games to pick up his tickets. The son forgot. The father did not. "I've stood you an education," Mr. Schwed wired Fred Junior, "and what have you done for me?" No member of the Schwed household, which was trained to share the family head's passion for Kipling, had to be reminded that the telegram was a quotation from the Master's bitter ballad "The Mary Gloster," in which the dying shipping tycoon Sir Anthony Gloster upbraids his wastrel son for his frivolous life.

Christian Gauss, the Princeton dean of whom Scott Fitzgerald thought so highly, was also a Kipling fan. This may have had something to do with the way he handled an unpleasantness caused when, during a football weekend in his junior year, Fred was caught with a girl in his dormitory room. Going by the book, the punishment was expulsion. Going by the author of "Recessional," Mr. Gauss tempered the book with the quality of mercy. He kicked Fred out, but he gave him a foot in the door for coming back. If, after a year out in the world on his own, the dishonored son of Old Nassau could prove to the satisfaction of the dean that he had earned the right to make another try for his diploma, Fred Schwed, Jr., would be read-mitted to Princeton as a senior. Fred spent the year selling ad-vertising space for the *New York Times*. Christian Gauss was impressed. Fred was readmitted. He spent an uneventful year back on campus, and earned his degree. He carried it into the arena where his father had once been a mover and shaker, and where many of Fred's classmates were now making their ca-reers. So did Fred but, like everything else he did, Fred did this in his own inimitable way. Even the things he did not do on his own tended to take on a touch of the inimitable: A. J. Liebling, with whom Fred grew up, told me that, because of a slip of the scalpel during Fred's circumcision, he was known to his contemporaries at summer camp as "Home Made Schwed."

After a number of years as a successful stockbroker he de-cided to become a writer. He began by composing a valedictory to the corner of Broad and Wall: an impressively perceptive and wildly hilarious minor classic called *Where Are the Customers' Yachts?* It was published by Simon & Schuster in 1939, which is when Fred and I met. In 1966, when Fred Schwed, Jr., died, he was my closest friend. I wrote a note to Peter Schwed, Fred's younger brother, then the executive editor at Simon & Schus-ter. The note ended with sixteen words that, on bad days, still sound in my head: "He made it easier for me to get through the last thirty years of my life."

The process of helping me get through all kinds of days started on the Marshall Field estate in 1943. Taking over the Field estate to turn it into a school struck me as not unlike taking over the Duchy of Luxembourg to turn it into a parking lot. Along with the useful space came a complex hierarchy of managerial servants. All of them civil, of course: they came from England. Perhaps that is why they slid so easily into their new roles as American civil servants. Under the umbrella of the O.W.I. table of organization a bright young Cockney named Ogg—who had started as a Marshall Field footman when he was imported at the age of eighteen from the London area within the sound of Bow Bells—became at twenty-five the O.W.I. school steward. He went on the civil service payroll as a CAF 11 when Bob Sherwood cut himself free from the C.O.I. and Wild Bill Donovan.

"Ogg is the key to the whole enterprise," Fred Schwed said. "Sherwood writes Pulitzer Prize plays in American, but Ogg speaks the mother tongue of the Marshall Field staff."

"What's that?" I said.

"The language of Shakespeare and Milton," Fred said. "Field servants are all sired and bred in England. When ripe they are brought over under quotas fixed by the U.S. immigration laws. The kitchen staff were all, like Ogg, born within the sound of Bow Bells. The gardeners are Scotch. The chauffeurs are Glaswegians. They take orders from nobody. Ogg, however, makes inaudible suggestions to them in accents to you and me totally incomprehensible, and they respond like Paavo Nurmi to the starting gun. If we funnel everything through Ogg, we'll have no trouble getting our job done."

"Which is what?" I said.

"Receiving from New York every second Saturday afternoon a delivery of twenty or thirty untrained amateurs and, every second Saturday morning, sending back to New York twenty or thirty thoroughly trained professionals ready to be ticketed, stamped, and shipped out to staff our outposts in the far corners of the world."

"Trained for what?" I said.

"The curriculum is not quite firmed up," Fred said. "We've been waiting for your report on your M.O. tour of Bletchley."

"It will be handed in tomorrow," I said.

"Ticketyboo," Fred said.

"Meaning what?" I said.

"Okey doke," Fred said.

It was. Thanks largely to Fred Schwed, Jr. He had no discernible dedication to efficiency. His inefficiency, however, like his approach to life, was completely original. As a result, what in other four-thumbed hands might have appeared a hopeless foul-up, coming from Fred seemed a refreshingly new and helpful approach to an old problem.

What made the main house on the Marshall Field estate the ideal physical setting for a school was that it had been built to accommodate the owner's way of life. On the second floor, in addition to Mr. and Mrs. Field's private suites, there were four guest bedrooms. All huge, of course, but nonetheless only four. The servants' wing, however, consisted of a long, spacious corridor with thirty handsomely decorated bed-sitting-rooms on each side. Between every two rooms there was a large, beautifully equipped bathroom. The sixty Field servants who in peacetime occupied these attractive quarters were reduced to twenty and transferred to the O.W.I. payroll. The remaining forty were moved to other parts of the twenty-three-hundred-acre estate. It included, among other things, a prizewinning dairy farm; kennels in which Labrador retrievers were raised in hordes; pheasant runs; grouse-shooting facilities; an indoor tennis court; a heated outdoor swimming pool; a private beach; and other specialized areas Fred and I never found time to penetrate. The sixty vacated bed-sitting-rooms in the servants' wing became our students' dormitory.

The O.W.I. school, which soon came to be known to its students as Lloyd Neck Tech, opened for business in March, a time of year when the North Shore of Long Island is more often than not still in the grip of winter. To keep the huge house comfortable when Mr. and Mrs. Field were in residence the basement furnaces burned four tons of coal every day. The O.W.I. budget, which, like the budgets of all wartime agencies, tended to be drawn up by people far removed physically from the place where their appropriations were to be spent, allowed for only two tons of coal per day. Complaints from the student body began to trickle—then pour—in. One day, on our way from the lecture hall to the Faculty Lounge, Fred and I were surrounded by a group of militant complainers. We listened to the protests. I told them we would take up the problem with Mr. Ogg. This did not satisfy the protesters. They grew louder. In a sudden explosion of fury Fred roared, "Stop bellyaching! Many are cold but few are frozen!"

The curriculum was divided into three sections. Morning workshops in the use of radio equipment, portable printing presses, and document photography. Afternoon lectures on leaflet writing; the history of the causes of the war; the nature of the Nazi and Japanese enemies; the function of propaganda in an overall war effort; the gathering of intelligence; the dissemination of information in neutral and hostile environments.

The most interesting part of the curriculum was the series of evening lectures. Not necessarily because of their subject matter, but because of the visiting lecturers who delivered them. Their names were, more often than not, household words. Occasionally, it must be admitted, not in the more important households. Not everybody, however, shares Caesar's preference for being first man in an Iberian village to being second man in Rome. I learned at Lloyd Neck Tech that celebrity, like beauty, is not infrequently in the eye of the beholder.

Once we set the machine in motion it gave off encouraging signs of life. When the signs became clear indications of gathering strength, the Washington office sent a directive to Bob Sherwood in New York. He passed it along to us with a penciled marginal note in office code: "DTNI." Translation: "Do The Necessary Immediately." Adding this marginal code to the contents of the decoded memorandum we found ourselves faced with a direct order: "Add a course in physical training to the curriculum immediately."

A staff meeting was called at once in the Faculty Lounge. The room had been Mr. Field's study. The magnificence of the former furnishings—which had gone off to join in storage for the duration the Rembrandts and signed Hepplewhites from other parts of the house—had been described for us by Ogg. It was the sort of description that the reporters arriving on the scene immediately following the destruction of Pompeii might have received from the sole survivor if he had been an intelligent and sensitive man, overwhelmed by the horror of what he had just seen and lived through, who unfortunately for history was limited to repeating over and over, as he wrung his hands, the word "indescribable." From Ogg's not always coherent—but never less than enthusiastic—repetition, I gleaned a few hard facts.

Built into one wall of the completely paneled room was a large stained-glass compass face. On it colored lights never stopped winking on and off. This was a gift from a group of Mr. Field's British friends who had been his guests a few years earlier for a month of grouse shooting. As a thank-you present they commissioned a firm of Swiss clockmakers to install a weather vane in Mr. Field's study. I did not realize why the ceaseless, and apparently senseless, performance of wildly winking colored lights looked familiar until Fred Schwed, who was guiding me through the house when I saw it for the first time, turned to me and cried, "Tilt!" The contraption looked like a pinball machine.

The fireplace was, in the cliché I had learned at Bletchley, big enough for a tall man to walk into without bowing his head. Playful Lloyd Neck Tech students frequently did. Once, when he was describing the uses to which in the past the room had been put, Ogg said, "When Mr. Field was divorcing his first wife the lawyers for both sides sat around the fire in that study day after day for almost eight months."

"What took them so long?" I said.

"The first Mrs. Field was a Phipps," Ogg said. "Nobody had ever divorced a Phipps before, so they didn't quite know how to go about it."

The faculty of Lloyd Neck Tech, trying to deal with the directive Bob Sherwood had sent out from New York, had the same difficulty. None of us had ever conducted a physical training course. Volunteers were called for. None responded. Somebody suggested drawing lots. Everybody thought this was the best solution. Everybody except Fred Schwed.

"The only man in the room who can do the job has never won anything in his life except a high school oratorical contest," he said. "If we draw lots, we'll lose him. The only way to nail him down is to appoint him by direct order."

"Appoint who?" the commandant said.

Fred nodded in my direction. The group glance that followed his could without modification have served the witnesses who watched the woman taken in adultery.

"You must be kidding," the commandant said.

Fred placed his hand on an imaginary Bible and raised the other to the heavens.

"God's truth," he said.

The commandant gave me another look and turned back to Fred.

"What makes you feel he's qualified for the job?"

"He's a closet gymnast," Fred said.

It was true, so I took the assignment. There was, however, no room on the already crowded daily schedule for a calisthenics class. The only solution was to schedule the class for the time of day when I was accustomed to taking my workout in the privacy of my room.

"What time is that?" the commandant said.

"Five A.M.," I said.

The groans went unheeded. If Mr. Sherwood's directive was to be followed, it would have to be followed at five o'clock in the morning. It was. Out on the front lawn. How this part of the Lloyd Neck Tech curriculum—which was treated with unconcealed loathing by all participants except its instructor—developed into a passion for late-afternoon softball may be difficult to understand. In view of the consequences, I have resisted making the attempt. The facts speak for themselves.

Soon after the calisthenics class at 5:00 A.M. got under way, a 5:00 P.M. softball game materialized as the high point of the day. Everybody came out to watch, including the Cockney kitchen staff, the Scotch gardeners, and the Glaswegian chauffeurs. All our students, the girls too, insisted on playing. To satisfy all demands, I worked out a schedule on which, by a system of almost insanely complicated rotation, everybody got a chance to play. Even if, because of the size of a particular class, it meant keeping two games going simultaneously. Several members of the faculty, including the commandant, insisted on participating. Fred Schwed and I limited ourselves to the roles of umpires. Until one day, when two games were in progress, and one of the teams, in the fourth inning, lost its right fielder: a sprained ankle. The cry went up for a substitute. Fred and I, as umpires, were the only nonplaying faculty members available. The captain of the suddenly shorthanded team came trotting across the field and asked one of us to step in.

"You go," Fred said, giving me a shove toward the captain.

"Why not you?" I said.

308

"I'm a southpaw," Fred said.

"What difference does that make in right field?" I said.

"If you knew anything about baseball, you wouldn't waste everybody's time by asking dumb questions," Fred said. "Hurry up, they're yelling for you."

A chant had started out on the field, but all I could make out were the words "Play ball!"

"I'm not very good at this game," I said to Fred. "You go."

Fred turned to the impatient captain.

"Which would you prefer?" he said. "A middle-aged, flat-footed, overweight, myopic ex-stockbroker, or an eagle-eyed, wiry, muscular, fit-as-a-fiddle young calisthenics instructor?"

The captain took my arm.

"Let's go," he said.

We trotted to the place where the injured player had dropped his glove when he was helped off the field. I picked it up, slipped it on, punched the pocket in the palm, and dipped down into the traditional eye-squinting, hands-on-knees crouch. The crowd cheered. I thought I detected a trace of Cockney in the ovation, or it may have been a faint Scots burr. No matter. The point is I could feel my spirits make a totally new kind of upward move. A sort of spurt, actually. I am not, as a rule, a despondent person. On the other hand neither am I the kind of horse's ass who, when like Macbeth he hears the skirling of the bagpipes, finds he cannot hold his water. Why, then, on this occasion, hearing the cheers from the sidelines, did I suddenly hear myself yelling wildly, "Play ball!"?

The pitcher responded. The batter swung. The crack of oak meeting cowhide rang out across the field like a gunshot. The ball came hurtling right down the old alley. Both the first and second basemen were so concentrated on frustrating what looked like a certain two-bagger that neither realized they were galloping head on toward each other. When they found out, the crash that hurled them apart would have done credit to a couple of heartily banged cymbals. The ball paid no attention to this diversion. It kept right on in long hard hopping leaps, heading I suddenly realized straight at me. I came up out of my crouch, started forward to scoop it up, then hesitated. Wouldn't it be

safer to wait and scoop it up when it reached me? The momen-
tary hesitation performed hesitation's customary function: it
proved fatal. When the ball did reach me I was off balance. I
snatched at it wildly. I found myself clutching air. The ball
sped between my legs. A groan went up from the crowd. I
wondered, as I whipped around and started after the ball, if I
had detected a touch of Cockney in the groan. Or could it have
been a faint Scots burr? Before I could decide which, I stepped
on the ball. It had unexpectedly stopped dead. I sprawled forward, ploughing up with my nose several inches of neatly
trimmed lawn before I stopped moving.

Picking myself up, I realized the groan from the crowd had
changed tone. It had become a roar of derision. I didn't bother
working out whether the derision was tainted with a touch of
Cockney or stained by a Scots burr. In any language, regardless
of accent, the sound would have conveyed its unmistakable
message. Feeling my face grow hot, I stumbled after the ball. I
got my glove on it, stood up, and clawed at the alternatives.
Should I throw to first and try to catch the batter? Or should I
throw in the opposite direction and try to cut off the man who
had left first and was heading for second? The moment of clarity, during which I was frantically weighing the choice, vanished in a flood of horrified realization. There had also been a
man on third! I could see him streaking for home. From the
depths of my humiliation came the surge of fury that I felt
would give me the strength to pluck from this nettle danger the
beckoning flower of victory. Pulling together every scrap of energy in my eagle-eyed, wiry, muscular, fit-as-a-fiddle, calisthenics instructor's body, I did something that a kindergarten
child would have known Joe DiMaggio in his prime would never
have attempted: from deep right field, throwing overhand, I
tried to cut off a runner at the plate not with a hurled walnut,
but with a softball. Even as it left my hand I sensed that what
I was trying to throw felt as big and heavy as a medicine ball.

The last thing I remember was a loud, sharp, snapping crack.
I thought of Natty Bumppo, squatting concealed in a James
Fenimore Cooper forest, hearing a clumsy paleface reveal his
presence to the enemy by stepping on a dry twig, and then my

thinking stopped. When I opened my eyes I was coming out of the ether in the office of Dr. Jason Clerihew in Cold Spring Harbor. Fred Schwed was sitting at my side.

"Don't move," he said. "Around your chest you're wearing forty pounds of slowly drying damp plaster."

"Why?" I said.

"Dr. Clerihew says it's the only way to keep your right arm immobilized," Fred said. "It's broken in three places between your elbow and your shoulder. The hope is that if you can't move the arm, the breaks will heal and you will learn an important lesson."

I fed the expected coin into the gas meter.

"Which one?" I said.

"Never try to reach home plate from right field by throwing a softball overhand," Fred said.

In the average lifetime the occasion for applying this bit of wisdom is not likely to be repeated. Once encountered it can be said to have made its mark. As of this writing it has certainly not been repeated in my lifetime. I still remember, however, and will probably never forget the state of depression into which the incident threw me. It centered around the promise Harold Guinzburg had made about my overseas assignment. We were then at the stage of the war when all the attractive assignments tended to look as though they would be connected with the preparations for opening the second front on the Nazi-occupied European continent. If I got back to London sometime toward the end of 1943 or the beginning of 1944, Harold said, the chances seemed good that I would in some way get in on the operation. My attempt to reach home plate from right field by throwing a softball overhand put an end to that chance. Dr. Clerihew felt that if I proved to be a good healer, he should be able to remove the forty pounds of plaster from my chest within two or three months, and replace it with a smaller cast restricted solely to my arm, which I could then carry without too much difficulty in a sling.

"For how long?" I said.

"Six to eight weeks," Dr. Clerihew said.

"And then?" I said.

"A smaller cast for perhaps another month."

"After which will I be able to travel?" I said.

"If you don't do anything foolish," Dr. Clerihew said.

Wondering in the back of my head how it was possible to do anything to help open a second front without doing at least something that was bound to be foolish, I kept the front of my head working on some unpleasant arithmetic. The three casts Dr. Clerihew had mentioned added up to a six months' incarceration in plaster. I broke my arm in October of 1943. If my arithmetic and Dr. Clerihew's guess were correct, it meant I would—no, I might—be ready to go back to London in April of 1944. I could not help feeling that General Eisenhower would have been justified in feeling he could hardly count on my help in time to do him much good, but it seemed wise to keep that opinion to myself. All at once I was having enough trouble carrying out my duties as a member of the Lloyd Neck staff. Not to mention performing normal functions such as sleeping, brushing my teeth, and shaving with my right arm immobilized in a vertical position. Fred Schwed said I looked as though I was playing The Game and trying to get the other participants to guess an appropriate quotation from the poetry of Emma Lazarus by giving an imitation of the Statue of Liberty. Nor was I, cosmetically speaking, a particularly entrancing sight. The commandant felt, however, that my lack of mobility made me the perfect member of the faculty to play host to the school's visiting lecturers.

The duties involved were simple: meet the visitor's train at the Huntington railroad station in a car chauffeured by one of the Marshall Field Glaswegians, keep the visitor company until the time of his lecture, and then, if he was not staying the night, see that he was delivered to the Huntington station in time to catch the last train back to New York. It was the sort of chore that obviously depended for its boredom quotient, as well as its entertainment content, on the personality of the visiting lecturer, or on both personalities.

Louis Fischer, the internationally known journalist who was widely held to be an important authority on Russia, was not the outgoing type. He did not speak during the drive from the station. We reached the school three hours before the guest speaker was due on the lecture platform. It was a sunny day. There was a pleasant breeze from the Sound. I asked Mr. Fischer if he would like to take a walk.

"Yes," he said.

We walked in silence among some of the most expensively and beautifully landscaped acres in the Western Hemisphere. Mr. Fischer did not comment. I made several attempts to point out the striking features of Mr. Field's domain, such as Moloch III, the prize bull Mr. Field had just added to his Caumsett Farm herd at a cost, according to the New York *Daily News*, of $160,000. Mr. Fischer did not even follow my pointing finger. He continued his purposeful forward stride, eyes fixed on the ground, face set in a brooding scowl. Suddenly he stopped.

"Turn your back, please," he said.

"Why?" I said.

"I want to micturate."

Douglas Miller was a refreshingly different type. He was tall and shapelessly plump, with a fringe of white hair at the edges of a totally naked scalp. He wore a relentless smile built around a pipe that seemed to be permanently fixed between his teeth. He was one of our most popular lecturers. He showed up whenever asked with his charming German wife and the cheerful look of a man arriving at a party at which he expects to have a good time. He always did, and so did his audience. The cheery twinkle in his eyes gave you the feeling that their owner had lived one of those rare, fortunate lives that had never brought within his field of vision an unpleasant sight. This was strange because Douglas Miller had spent all of his adult life in Germany as the U.S. commercial attaché at the American Embassy in Berlin. He had watched at close range the horror of the Nazi takeover. Out of this experience he had written *You Can't Do Business with Hitler*, a best seller that had done much to change the unrealistic attitude of the American business community toward the nature of the Nazi enemy. As the plaster-encased Grover Whalen of Lloyd Neck Tech, I learned to stick close to Douglas Miller during his visits. On the lecture platform he was formidably convincing without being pompous. Off stage he was endlessly and unexpectedly entertaining even under the most surprising circumstances. One day, while a group of us were chatting in the Faculty Lounge, Fred Schwed came in with a yellow strip he had torn from the news ticker, known at Lloyd Neck Tech as the verb knocker. Fred was carrying the first news the people in the Faculty Lounge had heard about the assassination of Mussolini's son-in-law Count Ciano. Douglas Miller pulled the pipe from his mouth and released one of his infectious little boyish laughs.

"An assassin's bullet never found a more worthy target," he cackled gleefully.

George Gallup was equally entertaining, but in an entirely different way. He was solid and friendly but never frivolous. He did not make jokes. He made statements. Most of them parsed. Because I had known him at Simon & Schuster, during my stay at Lloyd Neck Tech—in and out of plaster—it was never a chore to meet Dr. Gallup when he arrived or to see that he was put back on the train to New York when he departed. His talks were models of lucidity. Working with a blackboard, using a vocabulary as simple and direct as a grocery list, he made the technique of the weighted sample clear to everybody in the lecture room including, I learned later, some of the Glaswegian chauffeurs who enjoyed sitting in on the lectures. Like any actor who has worked out the technique of his performance to achieve his best effects, Dr. Gallup always ended with an anecdote that brought down the house. One day I wrote it down in Pitman shorthand.

"In conclusion," Dr. Gallup said, "I would like to tell you about something that happened to me a number of years ago, when polling techniques were just beginning to capture the attention of the public. Young and Rubicam, for whom I was then doing commercial surveys, suggested that I give a series of talks all over the country to familiarize the public with the process. I enjoyed these talks very much, especially the question-and-answer periods with which they always ended. One day in Chicago, when I was taking questions from the floor, a white-haired old lady raised her hand. 'Dr. Gallup,' she said, 'I have listened to your talk with interest, but I am puzzled. I am ninety-four years old,' she said, 'and I have been practicing medicine in this area for sixty years, and yet never once have I been approached by one of your pollsters for my opinion on any question.' 'Well,' I said patiently, 'I have just explained to the audience how the technique of asking properly weighted questions makes it possible to obtain a very large answer from a very small sampling. As a result, the chances of your being approached by one of my pollsters are approximately the same as the chances of your being struck by lightning.' 'But Dr. Gallup,' the little old lady said, 'I have been struck by lightning twice.' "

So have I. It happened one night at Lloyd Neck Tech when Fred Schwed came storming into my room at one o'clock in the morning. It was not, of course, my room. It was Marshall Field's master bedroom suite, but I was occupying it for the duration of my assignment at Lloyd Neck Tech. It was like occupying Radio City Music Hall by being granted permission to curl up in an aisle seat when the theatre is closed to the public. Ogg had, of course, described the former splendor of the empty shell, but it was a little difficult under the circumstances of my occupation to believe the vast space had ever been cozy. The circumstances of my occupation consisted of a canvas army cot and a straight-backed kitchen chair on which I hung my clothes when I retired for the night. Since my attempt to cut off a runner at the plate with a softball thrown from right field, retiring for the night had become a dismantling process that reminded me of a performance I had once observed in Cyril Ritchard's dressing room when he was playing Captain Hook in *Peter Pan*. I did not have to remove a peg leg from my knee, of course, or an iron hook from my wrist or a patch from my eye. But I did have to peel myself and a forty-pound plaster cast out of chino pants and a khaki shirt, then climb into pajamas and brush my teeth, doing all this with one hand because the other had been locked into an overhead Statue of Liberty position by Dr. Clerihew. By the time I got through this performance, and had managed to arrange myself on the canvas cot, I had the feeling that I had earned my rest. I don't think Fred Schwed disagreed. It was just that by the time I was ready for sleep he was ready for a bull session.

Somerset Maugham once stated that he had no doubt when

he died he would be admitted to heaven because every day of his life he had done two things he did not want to do: he had got out of bed in the morning, and he had gone to bed at night. Fred Schwed felt the same way. Having known both men, I feel as I write that somewhere up there they should be having a good time burning the midnight oil. Unless, of course, one of them tries to reach home plate from right field by throwing a softball overhand. Forty pounds of plaster tend to diminish one's enthusiasm for talk, even good talk, especially after midnight. It was not Fred, however, who was carrying the plaster, and since I had been listening to him with enthusiasm for years at all hours of the day and night, there was no reason for him to assume that, just because there was a war on, I had tired of his performance. In fact, I hadn't. Until his wife Harriet sent out from New York an advance copy of a forthcoming novel called *The Lost Weekend*.

Fred tended to be a noisy reader. If he liked something, he urged everybody within sight or earshot to get in on the pleasure, and he documented his reason with copious quotations from the text. His performance was not dissimilar if he disliked something except that the accompanying decibels of sound were higher. *The Lost Weekend* was the first book that, in my experience, Fred read as though it was a serial appearing in very short installments and, because of his enthusiasm for the story, he couldn't refrain from filling the waiting time between installments by buttonholing an audience of potential converts. In the case of *The Lost Weekend* his enthusiasm was greater than I had ever before seen or heard it, and his audience was limited to one: me.

"Listen to this," he would shout as, book in one hand, glass in the other, he would kick open Marshall Field's expensive— perhaps priceless—door, and start reading aloud before he crossed the threshold. His booming voice carried him like a schooner under full sail straight for the cot on which I lay powerless, nailed to the canvas by my plaster cast like an onionskin memorandum held to a desktop with a bronze paperweight. When he finished the excerpt from *The Lost Weekend* Fred would turn, stalk out of the room and kick the door shut, presumably to study the next installment of the novel for his upcoming performance.

This went on for a week. During the day he did not mention *The Lost Weekend* except to say, "I'm getting close to the end, and then I'll turn it over to you so you can see for yourself how really extraordinary this book is."

I gathered soon enough that my friend's absorption in the book was caused by the parallel the author had unconsciously drawn between his hard-drinking hero and a man he had never met: Fred Schwed, Jr. The detail was, I must say, surprisingly similar: the games the man in the novel and Fred Schwed played, the foods they liked, the types of women they were drawn to, the prejudices they shared and, finally, their preference among current American writers.

"Listen to this!" Fred shouted as, carrying the book and his glass, he kicked his way into my room on the tenth or twelfth night of his serial performance. "The son of a bitch he's writing about even thinks the way I do that the greatest living American novelist is James Gould Cozzens. What do you think of that?"

Even though I shared this view of Cozzens' status among my contemporaries, what I thought of the revelation had nothing to do with the work of a jointly admired novelist. What I thought was that in all the years I had known Fred and cherished his friendship I had obviously overlooked one—probably the most significant—of all the facets of his character. Contemplating the untidy figure in bathrobe and slippers towering over my canvas cot, shaking the copy of *The Lost Weekend* as though it was a flyswatter, and spilling whiskey down his chin as he took crudely managed gulps from his glass, I found myself wishing the moment could be shoved back in time to any moment before I tried to reach home plate by throwing a softball overhand. I wanted desperately to get up from that cot and run out of the room. Instead, I writhed under the plaster cast like that memo under the bronze paperweight caught in a draft from an electric fan. Astonished as well as upset I heard myself saying, "Fred, are you an alcoholic?"

His eyes blinked rapidly. Like a ballet dancer winding down

from a difficult leap, both his hands—the one with the book and the one with the drink—descended slowly to his sides. The pause in which we were both suddenly trapped was a horror. I thought he was going to throw the glass in my face. I wouldn't have blamed him if he had. Instead, however, Fred's body suddenly seemed to grow taller inside the bathrobe.

"No, of course I'm not an alcoholic," he said coldly. "I just happen to be the biggest Jewish drinker in the Western Hemisphere."

He turned and stumbled out of the room. I rose from my cot the next morning with a sick feeling that I had lost my best friend. When I saw him an hour later in the downstairs hall, however, Fred was waving a copy of the day's schedule over his head in a gesture of triumph.

"Telephone for you in the office!" he yelled. "Harold Guinzburg calling!"

When I got to the phone in the office Harold said, "How's the arm?"

"I have a date with the doctor this afternoon," I said.

"What do you think?" Harold said.

"I think he's going to remove the cast," I said.

"Good," Harold said. "Who've you got scheduled for the graduation exercises tonight?"

"Doug Miller is coming up from Washington and Joe Liebling's coming out from New York. Why?"

"Bob Sherwood just got back from Iceland," Harold Guinzburg said. "He wants a policy meeting, but he's due in Washington tomorrow, so he's pressed for time. It might solve Bob's problem if you're sure about Miller and Liebling."

"I arranged to have a car pick them up at the New York office at three-thirty," I said.

"I'll see that Bob goes out in the same car with them," Harold said. "Which will solve everything including you."

"What about me?" I said.

"Bob wants to tell it to you himself," Harold said. "Make sure the Faculty Lounge is available when they get there, and, Jerry?"

"Yes, Harold?"

"I haven't said anything about a policy meeting."

"Of course not."

"And call me as soon as you get back from the doctor," Harold Guinzburg said. "It's important."

At the midday break Fred Schwed drove me into Cold Spring Harbor. Dr. Clerihew took X-rays, cut away the forty-pound plaster cast, and replaced it with a plastic device that covered only my bicep. I was able to wear it comfortably under my shirt.

"I'm not sure I like this," Fred said. "You look almost human again."

For the first time since I tried to reach home plate with a softball thrown overhand I felt human. My first hot bath in three months helped the reconversion. It did more than open my clogged pores. It released the parts of my brain that had been immobilized along with my broken arm. Suddenly free and alive, my thought processes darted about, circling and sniffing at Harold Guinzburg's guarded phone call, seeking hints about the nature of what was coming up in my immediate future as a result of Bob Sherwood's impending visit. Why did he have to tell it, whatever "it" was, to me in person? Why couldn't Harold Guinzburg have told me about it on the phone?

"I see in the papers where the General Accounting Office is bitching about how much money the O.W.I. is wasting," Fred Schwed said. "Sherwood is probably trying to set an example for cutting down on our phone bills by coming out to deliver his message in person."

"That doesn't sound very sensible," I said.

"It wasn't intended to be," Fred said. "It was intended to get you to stop trying to overthink something that in all probability doesn't require any thought at all. You're dealing with a playwright who has won four Pulitzer Prizes, and in his free times advises presidents when to come in out of the rain. Why don't you just relax until he shows up and let it come as a pleasant surprise."

"If it is pleasant," I said.

"It's bound to be," Fred Schwed said. "Sherwood is famous for his curtain lines."

It was a talent about which I did not have to be reminded. I became a fan of Bob Sherwood's curtain lines when Miss Merle S. Marine, director of the De Witt Clinton High School Playgoers Club, arranged for herself and the twenty-eight club members to see Robert Emmet Sherwood's *The Road to Rome* from fifty-cent seats in the second balcony.

The Road to Rome is a dramatization of an historical guess. Every schoolboy knows that Hannibal beat the togas off the Romans at Cannae, but nobody knows why the next morning, instead of sacking the city he had just rendered powerless, Hannibal turned his armies around and, leaving Rome intact, started the long march back home to Carthage. In any situation where nobody knows, anybody can guess, and Bob Sherwood's play is one of the most successful historical guesses in the modern theatre. The plot of *The Road to Rome* assumes that the beautiful wife of the defeated Roman general, Aemilius Paulus, sneaks into Hannibal's tent during the night and, with the sort of persuasive argument that women before and after Mrs. Aemilius Paulus have employed when dealing with military men all through history, she succeeds in making Hannibal give up the prize that now lies within his grasp. The next morning, in the final scene of the play, Hannibal is saying good-bye to the Roman general, who is overcome with joy by Hannibal's inexplicable generosity and has no idea what caused it. Hannibal is also saying farewell to the Roman general's sexy wife who has, of course, more than an idea. She knows damn well why Hannibal is going home. So does the audience, thus setting up one of those delicious stage moments that only a superb craftsman knows how to create: a situation in which the audience knows all, but the people on stage divide up into some who do, and one who does not.

Raising his hand in a farewell salute to the Roman general, Hannibal says: "Peace to your sons!" With innocent surprise the Roman general—who falls into the category of humans identified by P. G. Wodehouse as dim bulbs—says: "But I have no sons." Hannibal: "You may have." Curtain.

This talent, against which I brushed so innocently at De Witt Clinton High School, had become—when I encountered

320

it in person at the C.O.I. and then, in 1943, at Lloyd Neck Tech—a formidable figure on a stage much larger than the one from which *The Road to Rome* was released to the world. When he was not accepting Pulitzer Prizes, Bob Sherwood was writing FDR's speeches; ghosting the full-page ads for Convoys Now!; appearing at rallies in Madison Square Garden and in debates at Town Hall in which his denunciation of the America First Committee was usually the high point of the evening; and his name was listed among the members of the official party on the presidential train during the swing through the West and Midwest shortly before the 1940 election.

When I first met Bob Sherwood I was impressed by his physical presence. It was reported that Winston Churchill, after their first meeting, described the playwright as "three meters of a walking disaster." His long, narrow face always looked as though he was picking his way through the debris of a train wreck, hunting the remains of his loved ones. His voice was low, his manner stumbling, his words almost unintelligible. The impression he created of almost pathetic helplessness was painfully vivid. It was also, of course, as misleading as the instruction sheet that comes with a Japanese Erector Set.

This shy man, who looked as though even Scrooge would lack the heart to send him out into the street unattended, had earned more money on Broadway than Billy the Kid had lifted from waylaid stagecoaches; he had written the "quarantine the aggressors" speech; and he was the president's personal emissary to the world's mightiest states. And yet, because all of these unbelievable facts were as true as the scales in a Quaker butcher shop, Bob Sherwood cast a spell on people in his presence not unlike expressions I have seen in the newsreels on the faces of visitors to the shrine of Our Lady of Lourdes. I know whereof I speak. Fred Schwed and I were two of those people. Fred was waiting for me outside the closed door of the Faculty Lounge with a finger on his lips.

"When did he arrive?" I whispered.

"When you were in your leaflet-writing workshop," Fred said.

"Did he ask for me?" I said.

"Yes," Fred said.

My heart skipped a beat.

"By name?" I said.

"I guess when you've known him long enough to qualify as a member of the coterie you get a number," Fred said. "Right now you're still just plain Jerry Weidman."

"How about you?" I said.

"I've known him since I was at Lawrenceville," Fred said. "He used to go to the track with my father."

"What are you doing?" I said.

"Turning the doorknob," Fred said. "Ogg says that even when Marshall Field is in residence it's the only way to get this door open."

"I mean the policy meeting," I said. "Are we allowed to go in?"

"Bob asked me to wait for you and bring you in," Fred said.

"You call him Bob?" I said.

"Only behind his back," Fred said.

"What does he call you?" I said.

"I can't think of it offhand," Fred said. "It has six digits."

twenty-one

Sherwood was called away from the policy meeting to take a call from the White House. It was the first of several that kept punctuating his movements during the next few hours.

"Don't worry," Fred Schwed whispered to me in the main lecture hall while Sherwood was making the valedictory address to the graduating class. "If Harold Guinzburg said Sherwood wants a few minutes alone with you, he'll find them. All you have to do is stick close to him."

This was not easy. Especially during the graduation party, which spilled out all over the house. The students wanted to hear about Lunt and Fontanne, who had starred in *Reunion in Vienna* and *Idiot's Delight*. Did he really model Irene, the heroine in the latter play, on Greta Garbo? Was he quoting Shelley or did he actually write the poem that Bette Davis recites in the last act of *The Petrified Forest?* Was the Roman general played by Philip Merivale in *The Road to Rome* supposed to be a homosexual? Was it true that Raymond Massey had hesitated about accepting the lead in *Abe Lincoln in Illinois* because he was a Canadian?

Sherwood obliged with a talent for anecdotage that made much of his success in the theatre immediately comprehensible. He was a natural actor. Still later, in the Faculty Lounge, where he was surrounded by the Lloyd Neck Tech staff and the visiting lecturers who had addressed the graduating class, the talk was so concentrated on the war that I decided to abandon the attempt to get a moment alone with him that night. Knowing what was involved on a Saturday morning in getting a graduating class off to New York by train, and then putting the house in shape for the arrival of the new class late in the afternoon, I decided to get some sleep. Sherwood and the visiting lecturers were all staying the night. If Sherwood really did have something to tell me, it would have to wait for morning. I went up to my room. While I was brushing my teeth Fred Schwed came in.

"Where were you?" he said. "Bob's been looking for you all night."

"I've been keeping myself in his sights," I said. "But there was too much competition."

"He says meet him for breakfast in the dining room at six-thirty," Fred said.

"He'll never make it," I said.

"Maybe not, but you'd better," Fred said.

I did. When I got to the dining room, however, Sherwood was already deeply engrossed in a discussion with Douglas Miller and Joe Liebling. Everybody murmured good morning and went back to the discussion. I was in the middle of my first cup of coffee when Fred Schwed arrived. More murmured good mornings. Fred sat down next to me and leaned close.

"Bob say anything to you?" he said.

"Not yet," I said.

"He's probably still brushing up the dialogue," Fred said. "I'll keep an eye on him for you. Ogg wants you at the door right away."

The steward was standing on a chair in the vestibule, caught up in what looked like a small mob scene from a newsreel of a subway accident. The students milling around in front of Ogg had lost the appearance of people I had come to know during the two weeks we had been living together in slacks and sports shirts. They were all wearing city clothes.

"Please give me your attention," Ogg was saying in a loud voice. "I have here a set of instruction sheets made up by the New York office. They tell you what your program is to be from now on, which people you are to see, where you are to go, and so on before you step on that ship or plane that will take you overseas. There's one of these sheets for each of you.

324

Read them carefully and do what they tell you to do. This is very important, because otherwise you'll just wander about in the New York office for days and nobody will pay any attention to you."

He stepped down from the chair, started handing out the instruction sheets, and signaled to me. I climbed up on the chair.

"Don't read them now," I said. "Put them in your pockets and read them on the train. The cars are outside. There's very little time. Please get your bags and put them and yourselves into the cars as fast as you can. We don't want to miss that train. Step on it, please."

Fred Schwed showed up in the hall behind the crowd and signaled to me. I came down from the chair and pushed my way out to him.

"Bob wants you at the tennis court," Fred said.

"Now?" I said.

"Now," Fred said.

The tennis court was an imposing fieldstone structure that housed an indoor tennis court under a glass-domed roof and, at the far end, quarters for the commandant and four guest rooms. When I came down the path I saw Sherwood standing beside an O.W.I. station wagon at the front door. He was chatting with Douglas Miller, Mrs. Miller, and Joe Liebling.

"Thank you all very much," Sherwood said, shaking their hands as they climbed into the station wagon. "And do come again."

The driver closed the doors and came around to the front. He got in behind the wheel. The motor coughed. More good-byes from inside the station wagon. Sherwood waved. So did I. The station wagon pulled away.

"Are you free now?" Sherwood said.

He was talking to me, of course. Somehow, however, because his words sounded like part of the farewell ritual in which he had just been engaged, I didn't realize he expected an answer. Before I could make one a long, sleek limousine came purring down the driveway and stopped in front of us.

"I mean are you due back at the house?" Sherwood said.

"Not right now," I said. "But I could check."

"I already have," Sherwood said.

The chauffeur, who wore the livery of a New York limousine rental service, got out of the front seat, came around the car, and opened the rear door. Sherwood touched my elbow.

"I'd like you to drive into New York with me," he said. "Is that all right?"

"Of course," I said.

I waited while he jackknifed his long body into the car, then I followed and sat down beside him. The chauffeur slammed the door.

"Harold Guinzburg tells me you're one of Harold Freedman's clients," Sherwood said as the car got under way.

Harold Freedman was the head of the Brandt & Brandt Dramatic Department.

"I am, yes," I said.

"So am I," Sherwood said.

I was, of course, aware of this. Harold Freedman—who is one of the main characters in my novel about the theatre called *Word of Mouth*—represented many of the most important playwrights working in the American theatre at that time. Among these, in addition to Robert Emmet Sherwood, were Maxwell Anderson, Sidney Howard, S. N. Behrman, and Elmer Rice. One day, the story went, while they were at lunch in the Algonquin cutting up—along with their steaks—the producers with whom they were forced to deal to get their plays on the boards, Sherwood is supposed to have said to his colleagues, "What the hell can Gilbert Miller do for us that we can't do for ourselves?" The answer was the Playwrights Company, an organization founded by the five authors with the help of Harold Freedman which, for the next decade, seemed to have a monopoly on the production of Broadway hits.

"I wonder if you'd do me a favor?" Sherwood said.

"Of course," I said.

"Elmer Rice recently went through a divorce, as you probably know from the newspapers," Sherwood said. "Last year he got married again, to a much younger woman, and they've just had a baby. Elmer has written a play about the experience. It's called *A New Life* and, under the terms of our agreement to produce our own plays, the Playwrights Company is of course obligated to do this new play by Elmer. Before I catch my plane to Washington this afternoon I have a lunch meeting with the Playwrights and Harold Freedman at which we must make a decision about this script. Do you have any trouble reading in a moving vehicle?"

"Trouble?" I said.

"Some people get dizzy," Sherwood said.

"No, I don't have that trouble," I said.

"Would you do me a favor and read this script for me now?" Sherwood said. He pulled a blue-backed playscript from his briefcase. "I'd like to have an additional opinion before I go to that lunch."

"I'll be glad to read it," I said.

"That's what Harold Freedman said you'd say," Sherwood said.

I took the script. He took some O.W.I. documents from the briefcase. We read in silence. When I finished the script I looked up. We were crossing the Fifty-ninth Street bridge into Manhattan. Sherwood looked up from his documents.

"What do you think?" he said.

I told him. He thanked me. The limousine pulled up in front of the O.W.I. offices on West Fifty-seventh Street. The driver came around and opened the door. Sherwood climbed across me and got out.

"Take Mr. Weidman back to Huntington," he said to the driver, then dipped his long body to look in at me. "I hope you like your next assignment," he said.

"But I have no assignment," I said.

"You may have," said Robert Emmet Sherwood.

twenty-two

I did and I didn't. By the time I arrived in London, Montgomery was dug in at Caen—refusing to budge until Eisenhower supplied more air cover—and, on his way to the Rhine, Patton slapped a wounded G.I. The crusade in Europe was clearly under control. I was ordered to Washington to "learn the Pacific show."

Eighteen years later, when my son John entered Harvard, he was invited to tea at the home of Professor John King Fairbank. When they were introduced by Mrs. Fairbank the host asked John if the invitation had surprised him. John admitted it had. The distinguished authority on Far Eastern affairs explained the invitation by saying, "Your father and I won the war together."

The manner of delivery, John reported, was deadpan. John's reaction was not. His you-must-be-kidding-sir response was not returned in kind. It was clear to John that for one of the world's great authorities on Chinese-American relations the subject of Fairbank-Weidman relations was not open for discussion. It seemed to me, when John tried to reopen it with his father, I could do no less than emulate the man under whom I had served.

"If Professor Fairbank doesn't want to talk about it," I said, "I'm afraid I have to do the same."

"Don't be afraid," John said. "Someday you'll probably write your memoirs. I can wait."

As I write he is still waiting, and I find myself tugged in two directions: the desire to set down something that will make John's long wait seem worthwhile, and my father's advice about lying.

"Before you do it," he once told me, "give yourself a minute to figure out what you will gain by doing it. You'll be surprised by how much of the time it doesn't add up to enough to take a chance on being caught and looking like a damn fool."

My relationship with John King Fairbank is nothing I care to risk staining. The truth is for eighteen years I was unaware that we'd had a relationship. He was my superior in Washington. I did what he told me to do. When I finished what I'd been told to do John King Fairbank said, "Thanks." As a storyteller I was not struck by the thought that this exchange carried within it the kernel of a yarn that might in the hands of a more alert writer become a sequel to the saga of Damon and Pythias. What I had been told to do was make a survey of our Japanese propaganda effort and compare it with what I had observed of our similar effort in the E.T.O. All I remember about the project is a single sentence, and I remember it only because of the comment it aroused.

The sentence: "What we have set up thus far amounts to a Barmecide's feast of propaganda."

The comment: "What in Christ's name does that mean?"

The comment was not made by John King Fairbank. Eighteen years later I felt I was reasonably correct in drawing the inference that he had understood what I meant.

Another man who understood was Owen Lattimore, with whom in Washington I shared an office. What made Owen a pleasant office companion was his habit of looking up from his work and, without preliminary, launching into an anecdote that had apparently just crossed his mind. Somewhere in what seemed to me the middle of my report, which I had asked him to read and catch any errors I may have made, Owen looked up with a grin. I had been watching him nervously. I assumed what had brought his head up was my reference to a Barmecide's feast.

"Did I tell you about Hemingway at Emily Hahn's wedding reception in Hong Kong?" he said.

"I don't think so," I said.

"Mickey Hahn had been living in Hong Kong for some time before she met this Englishman Colonel Boxer," Owen Lattimore said. "Hemingway arrived in town on assignment from

PM and, being an old friend of Mickey's, she invited him to the wedding reception. A lot of toasts were made. When Hemingway's turn came he raised his glass and said, 'Here's to bigger and better Boxer risings!' "

I think of this anecdote as the conclusion of my efforts to learn the Pacific show. Owen Lattimore told it to me on August 5, 1945. I remember the date because Owen's account preceded by twenty-four hours the date much of the civilized world has never been able to forget: August 6, 1945.

The day we dropped the bomb on Hiroshima was the first time I began consciously to think of myself as a family man. Peggy and I had been married for almost three years, and six months earlier we had become parents. In spite of the complications that becoming parents brought into our lives, in one respect it seemed perfectly normal: it was no more hectic than the rest of wartime life. On August 6, 1945, however, jolted into awareness that wartime life was ending for everybody, we began for the first time to think of ourselves as a family in search of a peacetime home. I was astonished to discover the search was not easy.

Choosing a home had, of course, never been my business. Until I got married the choice had always been made by my parents. After I got married I moved out of my parents' home and into Peggy's apartment at Eleventh Street and Fifth Avenue. It was perfectly adequate until Jeff was born. Before the inadequacy could become more than an inconvenience, I was ordered to Washington to learn the Pacific show. John King Fairbank's staff helped us find a place on Constitution Avenue. It was, I must say—if anything must be said for it—at least adequate. Now, however, we were finished with Washington. Where to go? A swift survey proved that what we had been hearing as gossip all through the war was hard fact: adequate apartments in New York City were difficult to come by, meaning they were beyond the financial reach of a wartime bureaucrat returned abruptly, with a wife and a six-month-old son, to prewar life as a freelance writer. Aunt Ethel came to the rescue. Peggy's Aunt Ethel, that is.

She was a divorcée living on her property settlement in a

profitable Mount Vernon apartment house and weekending on a tax-deductible Black Angus cattle farm up in Dutchess County near a town called Millerton. In addition to the large main house, which was occupied by Aunt Ethel when she was in residence, there were two smaller human habitations: a tenant farmer's prefab, and an attractive Cape Cod guest cottage. Aunt Ethel employed only one tenant farmer to run the place. When we arrived he and his family were living in the prefab. The guest cottage was unoccupied. Peggy and I rented it from Aunt Ethel for fifty dollars a month.

The farm was on top of a mountain. From Aunt Ethel's acres, and our cottage windows, four mountain ranges were clearly visible. From Aunt Ethel's kitchen garden, which was tended by the tenant farmer, came a steady flow of golden corn as tender as custard and fresh strawberries as large as golf balls. Unlimited access to both came with the rent. We settled into the cottage with the intention of awaiting the arrival of our second child. While waiting we concentrated on the hunt for a home closer to New York. Peggy had grown up on the Philadelphia Main Line. She knew about suburban living. I did not. She worried about how I would adjust to an existence, however temporary, on a cattle farm two and a half hours by train from Grand Central Terminal. Fred Schwed warned her what to expect, but Peggy did not repeat to me Fred's warning until the initial shock was over.

"The thing to remember about your husband," Fred told Peggy when he and Harriet drove up to have a look at our temporary home, "is that until he was well into his twenties the only green things he'd ever seen were the faces of his fellow students in English composition class in P.S. 188."

Peggy remembered it when we discovered we were facing a diaper crisis. It had not occurred to us that the diaper service, which had relieved much of the civilized world from the drudgery through which my mother suffered, had not yet penetrated to our corner of Dutchess County. In the local supermarket we bought the equipment used by the local farmers: a large bucket and the biggest available carton of detergent. The local farmers, however, rinsed their diapers at the level on which they planted their crops. I rinsed ours on the top of Silver Mountain. The wind-chill factor almost did me in.

In the early hours our mountaintop was whipped by winds that found me every morning trying to hang out freshly rinsed diapers in below-zero temperatures. It was not easy but, to an old East Fourth Street holder of the Pioneering Merit Badge, it was a challenge. The problem was that, by the time I got the clothespins into the last diaper on the line, the diapers I had hung at the beginning of the line were no longer flopping lengths of wet cloth. The wind-chill factor had turned them into lethal sheets of plate glass. I learned soon enough never to go back, to continue moving forward, plucking the wet diapers from our laundry bucket as swiftly as I could shove clothespins into place. Above all, I learned never to pause for an examination of my progress. One day I forgot. That morning, when I reached the end of the clothesline, I turned and looked back. Like Lot's wife, who had disregarded a not dissimilar injunction, I paid the price. A clothespin had worked its way loose from a diaper near the beginning of the line. It was whipping wildly in the wind. When Peggy got me down from the mountain on our prewar retreads, the local doctor managed, with seven stitches, to close the gash the rogue diaper had opened in my cheek.

"That settles it," Peggy said. "We've got to find a place to live where the holder of the Pioneering Merit Badge does not have to put his life on the line every morning just to keep the offspring in clean diapers."

We found the place in Westport, Connecticut. Westport had many things to recommend it in addition to a good diaper service. To begin with, it was not completely foreign terrain to either of us. For almost a decade before the war, while she was at Sarah Lawrence and later, when she was working at *Newsweek* and *PM*, Peggy had been visiting friends who lived or had summer homes in Westport. During the same period, before I met Peggy, I had discovered in Westport, through my friends at Simon & Schuster, the pleasures of the country weekend. During the early part of the war, after we were married, when I was not overseas and before I was sent to Washington to learn the Pacific show, we had spent weekends with friends in Westport and the surrounding area. We settled into what was, therefore, a familiar and congenial place. It was also, although we were not of course aware of this at the time, what we and our surviving contemporaries now think of as Westport's golden age. We got there before it was overrun by the TV aristocracy. When the television screen began to invade the American home, Madison Avenue advertising and network executives discovered the pleasures of living fifty minutes from Grand Central in a town with good schools, low real-estate taxes, and what was at that time still the best short-line railroad in America: the New York, New Haven & Hartford.

Before the TV invasion Westport was still a small country town with a population that broke down into three social groups. In my novel about this period, called *The Third Angel*, I have a character based on Fred Schwed—who with his wife Harriet lived in nearby Rowayton, known to Westporters as the Athens of South Norwalk—identify these three social groups as the commuters, the geniuses, and the clam diggers. The commuters were the Madison Avenue TV big shots. The geniuses were writers, painters, magazine illustrators, and other creative people including Wanda Landowska and her internationally acclaimed harmonium. The clam diggers were the grocers, butchers, artisans, lawyers, doctors, hardware merchants and other shopkeepers without whose services life in Westport would not have felt as right for me when we came to live there as life on East Fourth Street had felt when I lived on the Lower East Side. Valuable acreage, purchased for peanuts in the days when an order of scrambled at Jack's on Sixth Avenue was still made with three eggs, was registered at Town Hall in the name of Philip Dunning, who wrote *Broadway* with George Abbott, and John Held, Jr., who drew in the pages of *College Humor* the quintessential flapper before Scott Fitzgerald put her into words. And, of course, many of the streets were still unpaved country lanes.

Why this should linger in the mind of a boy from East Fourth Street as a symbol of an idyllic time, I am not sure. I suspect it has a lot to do with the boy's age. Peggy and I were young when we came to Westport. We were up to our ears in all the good things that are a part of being young, including neighbors who were doing what we were doing. Raising children, finding our feet in our professions, living comfortably with the belief that there was time for everything because the notion that we were not going to live forever had not yet entered—as it had not yet entered that of the captain's tiger on the Western Ocean—our consciousness. Obviously this sort of thing has been happening for a long time, to all sorts of people, but for me they are characters in books I never seem to be able to accept as real. I accept what I know or get to know. What I know best and miss most are my kind of people, the people with whom I grew up, and the people with whom Peggy and I were young.

Inevitably among these latter, given what I do for a living, were magazine editors. Among those who have for me a special glow is Herbert R. Mayes. He was, when we met, the editor of *Good Housekeeping*. I came to know him when he was living in New York and we had just moved to Westport. Later he moved his family to Stamford, a few miles away. A line from a biographical note I wrote at that time for the De Witt Clinton High School *Alumni Bulletin* comes to mind: "As a household headed by a free lance writer the Weidmans are constantly aware of the existence not of one boss but of many."

The employees who worked for Sinclair Lewis's Zenith, Minnesota, hero had to worry only about the whims of George Folansbee Babbitt. The head of the Weidman family in Westport had to worry about the moods of Wolcott Gibbs and his successors as my editors at *The New Yorker*; Stuart Rose and his colleagues at the *Saturday Evening Post*; Kenneth Littauer and Max Wilkinson and God alone knows who was in charge of buying fiction during the final sorrowful confusion at *Collier's*; plus a gallery of others that I have a notion any freelance short-story writer of the period would prefer not to have brought out of the mists of memory with sharper definition than that provided by the phrase Too Numerous to Mention.

Also unmentionable, of course, was the subject of rejections. Even though it is a condition of existence among short-story writers as endemic as dental caries, it is to polite conversation among writers what the self-serving declaration is to a court of law: inadmissible as evidence. Writers prefer to be known to the world only by their appearances in print. We all know about the trunk in which our best work is forced to blush unseen because the cynosure of neighboring eyes to which its contents were submitted belonged to people who. And we all know how to fill in the space after the word "who."

In those days it was always possible for a *New Yorker* short-story writer to identify a rejection by another *New Yorker* short-story writer. It was possible, that is, if the rejected story was sold elsewhere, because elsewhere was always *Mademoiselle* or *Glamour* or *Seventeen*, the only publications that seemed to buy *New Yorker* rejects. When they bought mine I was, of course, grateful. It is the sort of gratitude, however, that has sharply defined limitations. These three magazines could not buy all *New Yorker* rejects. They certainly did not buy all mine. Which is how Herbert R. Mayes came to occupy his prominent place in the Weidman household's private pantheon of heroes.

When we were still living in Washington—and the bomb dropped on Hiroshima signaled the cancellation of my orders to learn the Pacific show and forced me to contemplate life as a family man who before the outbreak of hostilities had been a freelance writer—I faced the problem the way a Boy Scout who had earned thirty-six merit badges on East Fourth Street had been trained to face all problems. I rolled up my sleeves, sat down, and in five days wrote five short stories. Carl Brandt, my agent, sent them all to *The New Yorker* because, like most *New Yorker* regulars, I had a first-reading contract with the magazine. The contract was also—and of course more accurately— known as a first-rejection agreement. In this instance *The New Yorker* demonstrated the greater accuracy of the latter definition with a posting of such dexterity that I felt almost physically assaulted. The five stories were rejected, as they had been written, on five successive days.

My long ambivalence about making the decision to become a freelance writer was crystallized abruptly by a knot of panic. For fifteen years, from the sale of my first story to the *American Spectator* until the bomb was dropped on Hiroshima, writing had been for me an enjoyable sideline, not an occupation on which I depended for my living. During all of those fifteen years, while I earned some money by writing, the bulk of my modest income had come in the form of a weekly salary: first from Monroe Geschwind, then from Simon & Schuster, finally from the O.W.I. On August 6, 1945, it was obvious that my O.W.I. salary would stop almost immediately. I was about to become a freelance writer whether I was ready for the role or not. All I could now depend on for supporting my family were my writing skills. I did not realize, when I wrote those five stories in the first days after the bomb was dropped, that I was putting to the test my capacity to support my family. When *The New Yorker* turned down all five stories the realization that struck me was shattering: I had failed the test. I saw now that the success I'd had thus far as a writer was due largely to the peace of mind I'd been earning with those weekly salary checks. With the supporting salary gone I had demonstrated promptly and conclusively—five rejections in a row!—that without the peace of mind provided by what Mr. Musaius in P.S. 188 used to call a nice steady flow of Yankee bean soup coming in over the windowsill, I would never again be able to write anything.

Into this moment of desperation came a phone call from New York. Peggy took it while I was pulling from our Washington mailbox what proved to be the last of the five rejection letters from *The New Yorker*. I read it on the way upstairs, and handed it to Peggy without a word. She read it in silence and handed it back to me.

"Do you know a man named Ziff?" she said.

"I don't think so," I said. "Why?"

"He just called from New York," Peggy said. "He wants you to call him back."

"Did he say what it's about?"

"Only that it's important," Peggy said. "He's waiting for your call."

"Can we afford long-distance calls?" I said.

"Mr. Ziff asked you to call collect," Peggy said.

She gave me the piece of paper on which she'd written Mr. Ziff's number, and went into the bedroom to give Jeff his bottle. I called Mr. Ziff. It was a long call. After I hung up I sat near the phone and stared out at Constitution Avenue. When Peggy came back into the room she was carrying Jeff.

"What did Mr. Ziff want?"

"He offered me a job," I said.

"Doing what?" Peggy said.

"Editor in chief of a brand-new publishing firm he's about to start," I said. "Ziff-Davis, Inc."

Peggy crossed the room and put Jeff in his bassinet. She did it slowly. Her mind was clearly on something else. Finally she said, "Did Mr. Ziff say why he called you and not somebody else?"

"He knows something about my work for Max Schuster before the war," I said. "From what he's heard he told me he felt I was just the man he's looking for."

"How do you feel about it?" Peggy said.

"I told him I'd have to talk to you first," I said.

"I don't really know what good that will do," Peggy said.

"We're broke," I said. "A man's just offered me a job. How many ways are there to feel about a situation like that?"

"Just one, I suppose," Peggy said. "If all you're thinking about is immediate cash."

"What else is there to think about?" I said.

"How about what you've been doing these past fifteen years?" Peggy said.

I stared at her with interest. We had known each other for four years. I'd been thinking I knew everything about her. More accurately, I hadn't been thinking at all. It occurred to me that if I was going to keep up with her, I'd better start.

"You mean you believe I've got a choice?" I said.

"Isn't that what you believe?" Peggy said.

"I've just had five rejections in a row," I said. "From the magazine for which I've been writing since I was a kid."

"Maybe that's why you've had five rejections in a row," Peggy said.

"What do you mean?" I said.

"Maybe you're not a kid anymore," Peggy said.

It was a new thought. At the moment I did not feel equipped to examine it. So I raised my voice.

"Mr. Ziff is offering me more money than I ever made at Simon and Schuster," I said. "And when I told him to take on a job in New York we'd have to find a place to live in New York, he said he'd arrange that, it's part of the deal."

"Did Mr. Ziff sound any better on the phone than that cable from Max Schuster sounded when you received it on the *Nieuw Zeeland* in the Java Sea?" Peggy said.

Pause. I wished it had been created by her, not me. She waited quietly.

"You don't want me to take this job," I said finally.

"I don't want you walking into a situation where you'll end up having to lean on a friend like Somerset Maugham to help you make another cut in a scene that's gone wrong."

Another pause.

"I don't have to call Mr. Ziff right away," I said.

A flicker of something I'd never seen there before crossed her face. It could have been disappointment.

"If you have any doubts," Peggy said quietly, "maybe you'd better."

The phone rang. She answered it.

"Yes, he is," Peggy said, and held out the phone. "It's Carl Brandt."

My feelings about Carl Brandt are an important part of my novel about the publishing business called *The Sound of Bow Bells*. Those feelings include the conviction that Carl's tendency to become a father figure to most of his clients was richly deserved. He never waited for an office visit to probe for the place where a client was hurting. Carl always knew. In this case he knew my immediate need was cash to get me out of Washington, and back into the real world which, for me and Peggy, meant New York. Without asking my permission, or even hinting at his intentions, Carl had sent one of the five rejected stories to Herbert R. Mayes at *Good Housekeeping*. Mr. Mayes bought it and sent Carl Brandt a check for $1,250. At that time, after fifteen years as a regular contributor, the highest price I had ever received for a story from *The New Yorker* was $750. The Weidman family was on a north-bound train the next day. When we arrived at Aunt Ethel's farm in Dutchess County a letter from Carl Brandt was waiting.

"Herb Mayes bought the second of those five stories this morning for fifteen hundred dollars. He'd like to have lunch with you. Let me know your plans and I'll fix a date."

It was the first of a series of lunches that took place at intervals of five or six months over a period of a dozen years. We always met in the restaurant attached to the *Good Housekeeping* testing kitchens on the top floor of the Hearst Magazine Building at Eighth Avenue and Fifty-seventh Street. The lunches were almost ritualistically identical. Mr. Mayes and I were usually the only people in the room, always at a corner table reserved for him. The waitresses were always motherly gray-haired ladies who wore bright gingham aprons. I was always served a generous helping of whatever it was the motherly ladies were working on in their testing kitchens at the request of the magazine's editorial staff, which had the authority to issue or deny the issuance of the much sought after *Good Housekeeping* Seal of Approval. After I had consumed whatever it was that had been placed before me, my opinion of what I had eaten was asked and recorded by the motherly ladies in the gingham aprons. I cannot remember now any of the concoctions that were placed before me. I do not remember any of my opinions—that is to say, the opinions I delivered to the motherly ladies—except that they were uniformly favorable. I remember clearly what, while I worked my way through the day's lab specimen, Herb Mayes had for his lunch. It was always the same: a minute steak, medium rare. He was never asked for his opinion of the steak. He was always too busy with the business that brought us together: short stories for *Good Housekeeping* magazine.

At every meeting I would present him with eight or ten ideas. He listened carefully, asked a few questions, then chose five or six, sometimes more. Herbert Mayes did not choose what he thought he could use. When he made a choice he was not unlike a purchaser placing an order with a salesman who had called with a sample case and spread his wares. Herbert Mayes was firm about the content of the stories he chose, and definite about the number he wanted. When he turned down an idea it was never because he felt it was bad, even though he may have thought so. When he turned down an idea it was always because "I can't use that." He never said, "I can use that if you write it the way it sounds in your verbal outline." He didn't have to. I didn't have to be told that his acceptance was conditional on my delivering the story on the pages that came to his desk the way it had come to him in my description across his minute steak. Carl Brandt made sure I understood that. After I delivered the third story Herb Mayes told Carl Brandt he was pleased that I understood it, and he doubled my price. I was, of course, pleased. Carl Brandt, however, did not want me to be merely pleased. He wanted me to understand why Mr. Mayes was pleased.

"A man who edits a monthly magazine lives through twelve crises a year," Carl said. "He wants good stories, naturally. But even more than quality he wants reliability. A writer who can deliver regularly is worth more to his peace of mind than a writer who can deliver only occasionally."

It was a two-way street, of course. An editor who accepted what he ordered from the sample case was worth more to the peace of mind of a writer's family than an editor who was not sure of what he wanted until it was delivered to him in finished form and said, probably with complete sincerity, that it wasn't at all what he felt he had ordered. The capacity of Herbert R. Mayes to see clearly in my spoken outline the story he wanted to see in his magazine, plus my capacity to reproduce my verbal account on paper, made it possible for me to spend my days writing novels, which had always been a financial gamble, and my evenings writing short stories that I could count on with relaxed confidence to pay the rent. From the moment I ate my first test recipe across the corner table in the *Good Housekeeping* restaurant I never had another rejection slip. Also, my short-story price trebled and my change in status was reflected in the food I ingested: when I sat across the table from Herb Mayes for one of our editorial conferences, the little old lady in the gingham apron finally served us both the same lunch: minute steak, medium rare.

Steak was a popular part of the Westport scene. For most of us inflation was still something that had happened in Germany during the period after the First World War when Christopher Isherwood was gathering the material for his Berlin stories, and the outdoor barbecue was beginning to edge the Sunday brunch for the number one position on America's list of favorite meals. I remember with special pleasure one such meal that followed a telephone call from Katinka Loeser, wife of Peter De Vries.

She told Peggy that Kingsley Amis and Mrs. Amis would be passing through Westport in a few days on their way home to England from Princeton, where Amis had just finished a writer-in-residence stint. They would be staying overnight and Amis would like to meet the author of *I Can Get It for You Wholesale*, so Katinka wondered if Peggy and I would come to dinner to meet the author of *Lucky Jim*. The result was a delightful and memorable evening. Mr. and Mrs. Amis provided the delight. I provided the part that was memorable. At any rate, my difficulty with spelling did.

The next day I hurried around to the public library. After a frustrating half hour I hurried around to a public phone booth.

"Peter," I said. "Last night at your house you and Kingsley Amis mentioned a British novelist."

"Mentioned?" Peter said. "I thought what we did was rough out a first draft of his citation for the Nobel Prize."

"Well, don't send it to Stockholm until you get the library in this town to put some of his books on the shelves," I said. "I have just spent a half hour with the catalogues and I can't find even one of his books listed."

"That's funny," Peter said. "Last year, during the book drive, I personally gave the library five of his books. They were my duplicates."

"Maybe this library has some peculiar rules," I said.

"How do you mean?" Peter said.

"Maybe they don't list duplicate copies in their catalogue."

There were a few moments of silence at the other end, and then Peter chuckled.

"How were you trying to look him up?" he said.

"Under *P*," I said.

"And then?" Peter said.

"*O, l, e,*" I said. "How would you spell Pole?"

"I've learned to spell it *P, o, w, e, l, l,*" Peter said. "It's not unlike Xerox. If you try to find it under Z, you might miss your dividends."

So I went back to the catalogue, and found a batch of cards for a novelist named Anthony Powell. I took down the three books that were on the shelf at the moment, and I haven't missed a dividend since. In fact, over the years I have collected more dividends from Anthony Powell than from Xerox. These dividends are difficult to define, the way economists who make their living trying to explain their kind of dividend always start to mumble when asked a simple question like "When somebody has a loss does that mean somebody else picks it up as a profit?"

Dividends from reading require no explanation. True pleasure of any kind resists definition. Cataloguing the obvious does not help. It merely pares away—and leaves what? The sense of well-being, for example, which is so great a part of pleasure, is for some people just as intense while eating a hot dog in the bleachers at a baseball game in which the Mets are ahead as it is when attending the graduation exercises at a son's school at which he is named Head Boy. There are many ball games, of course, but for each boy only one graduation. Yet the stab of pleasure is the same. I would probably experience it again if I owned any Xerox and it divided five for one as it once did when I did own some Xerox. Over the years, however, I have found Anthony Powell more reliable. I think it is this reliability that sits at the core of my pleasure in his work. Like true love it was a slowly mounting awakening.

On that day when I learned how to spell Mr. Pole's name the first of his books I opened was *Afternoon Men*. I remember a sense of puzzlement. After all, I had been reading novels for a long time, and writing them for a dozen years. I was accustomed to their infinite variety. Then I found myself laughing, and I began to suspect I had been puzzled because I had never before been stirred to laughter in quite this way.

The next book I read was *Venusberg*. The suspicion grew that I had stumbled into something unique. By the time I reached the "A Dance to the Music of Time" series I was convinced of it. The conviction troubled me. I am inclined to apply some of the basic virtues not where my mother tried to teach me they belong but in areas where they make me feel comfortable. I am, for example, fiercely loyal to writers whose work I like. For years before I encountered the work of Anthony Powell I was convinced that the greatest British novelist was Evelyn Waugh. Now I was being crowded by an odd uneasiness. A newcomer—to me, anyway—had come across the horizon. I devoured Mr. Powell's books. I realized I had fallen in love with his work, and it made me feel awful. My mounting passion made me feel disloyal to Evelyn Waugh.

I had a few bad years. Then Mr. Waugh died. As a private tribute to him I spent a month rereading all his books. My conviction that he had been the greatest British novelist of his day remains unshaken. But his day was done. The lion was gone. I was free to face the conviction that had been nudging at my conscience for years. That conviction, it pleases me to record, is that the greatest British novelist now is Anthony Powell. The difference between these two extraordinary writers, it seems to me, is one of method. Casting his cold eye, Waugh follows through with an almost terrifyingly honest, even malevolent, rendition of his vision. Take it or leave it. While you're taking it you are laughing your head off. Powell's eye is just as sharp, and just as terrifyingly honest. His rendition, however, is deceptively gentle. Waugh takes careful aim at the bull's-eye and, with an economy that is one of the glories of English prose, pulls the trigger. Wham. Right on the nose. Powell seems to shrink from the bull's-eye. He circles gracefully. Almost apologetically he backs into the firing area. You don't realize he has taken aim, or even pulled the trigger, but wham. Right on the nose.

So much for trying to explain the inexplicable: genius. In the end all explanations are inadequate. Because in the end the creative act is, at its heart, a mystery.

So is the creator. Some years later I was asked to join a symposium on Powell. Apparently what I said pleased him because he wrote me a thank-you note. He added that he was surprised to learn from a mutual friend about the difficulty I had with his name in the Westport library the morning after I met Kingsley Amis at the home of Peter De Vries.

"I see nothing unique about the way I pronounce my name," Powell wrote. "After all, you don't identify your great transcendentalist poet as James Russell Lowell," and he indicated that he was pronouncing the first syllable of Lowell's name as though it rhymed with cow. I felt it was only fair to write back and point out that neither did we refer to the author of *The Rise of Silas Lapham* as William Dean Holes. "True," Powell replied, "but I must tell you I feel you should."

twenty-three

Shortly after my oldest son Jeffrey received his doctorate, and assumed his duties as director of the Clarence Ward Art Library at Oberlin College, he sent me a disturbing message. The director of the Special Collections division of the main library had run across a piece I had written during the war for a publication issued under the imprint of the Black Sun Press of Paris. If I was interested, Jeff wrote, the director of the Special Collections division would be pleased to send me a Xerox. Was I interested?

It was like asking the poet Enoch Soames, one of Max Beerbohm's *Seven Men*, if he was interested in restructuring the pact he had made with the Devil for a glimpse of the British Museum's catalogue of a hundred years hence. As Mr. Beerbohm's readers are aware, what Enoch Soames got for selling his soul to the Devil was posterity's verdict on his poetry. It consisted of a single word: "labud."

What could I have written for the Black Sun Press of Paris during the war? Did I dare find out? More to the point, did I have the courage not to? After I dropped my note of acceptance into the mailbox I had a bad time.

As I remembered the literature of the American expatriate occupation of France during the twenties, the Black Sun Press had functioned contemporaneously with Sylvia Beach's Shakespeare & Company; Gerald and Sara Murphy; the Dadaists; Diaghilev; Picasso; Sir Charles Mendl; Zelda and Scott; Papa and Bumby; the Querschnitt; Darius Milhaud; and Jean Cocteau. I remembered reading somewhere that, while Miss Beach was helping to keep James Joyce afloat during the composition of *Finnegans Wake*, and Hemingway was accusing Fitzgerald of the long count in his boxing match with Morley Callaghan, the Black Sun Press, which was owned and operated by Caresse Crosby, was dedicated to the publication of the poetry of her husband Harry Crosby. While this legend was being put together and polished, I was bucking for the Pioneering Merit Badge on East Fourth Street. What in God's name could I have written during the Second World War that had found its way into the pages of a publication that was part of this legend from the First World War? When I opened the envelope from the director of Special Collections at the Oberlin Library I found out.

It was a biographical sketch of the artist that I had written not for the Black Sun Press of Paris but for the catalogue of a 1943 exhibit of drawings by a friend of mine named Sam Rosenberg. The exhibit was hung at the Caresse Crosby Gallery in Washington, D.C. The same Caresse Crosby who, in the twenties, had owned the Black Sun Press of Paris. The brief biography of Sam Rosenberg, which had appeared in the exhibit catalogue, had apparently been republished by Mrs. Crosby in the next edition of the *Black Sun*, which had been brought out in Washington. I read it with the sort of absorption usually devoted to a last will and testament in which the reader hopes to find substantiation for a not very definite rumor that he is a legatee. It reminded me of the day *I Can Get It for You Wholesale* was published.

I had been told by Dick Simon that the advance word on the book in the trade was good. Simon & Schuster, he said, expected good reviews. So did I. On publication morning, therefore, I did not wait as I always did to pick up the morning papers at the end of my subway ride downtown to work. At that hour I had my choice of the neatest discards of New York's four morning newspapers. The Times Square I.R.T. subway platform, where I got off, was always littered with them. No discards for me, however, on May 5, 1937. I invested four cents in fresh copies of the *New York Times* and the *New York Herald Tribune* from the newsstand at the 180th Street–Bronx Park South subway station. This was the end of the line, or the beginning, depending on whether you were going to or coming from work. In the morning, on my way to work, there were always plenty of empty seats, or at least they were plentiful for the first few minutes. I found one at the window side of the caboose, and settled down with my papers. I did not look up until, fifty minutes later, the train pulled into Times Square.

I don't know how many times during those fifty minutes I read those reviews. I do know that, by the time I looked up, I had those reviews memorized. Almost, anyway. Ralph Thompson in the *Times* was very good. Lewis Gannett in the *Trib* was better. Crossing the platform in a pleasant daze, it occurred to me that I might as well take a look at the *News* and the *Mirror*. These papers did not, of course, have regular book columns, but I suddenly found myself thinking that perhaps in a special case the editor asked one of his reporters to do a review. It was a long shot, of course, I didn't really know why the editors of the *News* and the *Mirror* should consider my book a special case, but the discarded papers scattered all around me were mine for the picking up. I chose a *News* and a *Mirror* in reasonably good condition, jogged the pages into alignment, and sat down on a platform bench to have a look. I tried the *Mirror* first. Nothing. I opened the *News* and started flipping pages. At Sidney Skolsky's column I stopped.

I had started reading his Broadway column when I was a boy in J.H.S. 64. I liked his two features "The Gossipel Truth" and "Times Square Tintypes." On this morning of May 5, 1937, I liked them even better. They were devoted to a review of *I Can Get It for You Wholesale*. It was embedded in a paean of praise to De Witt Clinton High School, from which Skolsky had graduated ten years before I did, and to which he apparently felt we were both a credit. Later in the day I wrote Mr. Skolsky a note of thanks. I addressed it in care of the New York *Daily News* on East Forty-second Street. A reply arrived three weeks later from Mrs. Sidney Skolsky in Hollywood, where it seemed the Skolskys had taken up permanent residence a few years earlier. Mrs. Skolsky wrote that Sidney was pleased with my letter but, because he never wrote letters himself, he had

347

asked her to thank me for him, which she herewith did. I didn't feel I could allow the correspondence to stop there, so I wrote a thank-you note to Mrs. Skolsky for her thank-you note. Her next letter was addressed to dear Jerry and my next reply was addressed to dear Sidney and Estelle. It was the start of a triangular correspondence that has never stopped, even though its participants were reduced to two when Sidney died in 1984. In 1939, on the last leg of my trip around the world, when my ship from Australia docked at San Diego I called Sidney in Hollywood. His wife answered, of course. In addition to the letters he never wrote she always answered the calls he never took. Estelle invited me to spend a few days with them. I did, and had a pleasant time. On one of those days Sidney took me on a tour of the Warner Brothers lot. It included a visit with Jack Warner.

As soon as we came into his office Mr. Warner stood up and came around his desk to shake hands with us. It was obvious, of course, which one of us he was eager to see. In a few minutes I understood why. I gathered from the talk between Sidney and Mr. Warner that the studio was locked in a battle over money with Bette Davis, who was then the studio's biggest and most lucrative star. The day before, her press agent had issued an ultimatum: unless the studio met Miss Davis's demands by midnight of the following day, which was the day Sidney had chosen to take me on a tour of the Warner lot, she would leave Warner Brothers and sign elsewhere. Jack Warner laughed heartily, meaning he was putting a lot of effort into the not exactly pleasant sounds he was producing, and told Sidney he felt the cunt was bluffing. Didn't Sidney agree?

"No," Sidney said.

Jack Warner's hearty laugh stopped dead. In a voice stiffly laced with shock he said, "You know something I don't know?"

"I've seen a letter," Sidney said.

"From whom?" Jack Warner said.

"You know I never reveal a source," Sidney said.

"Shit, Sidney, after all these years, for Christ's sake, you know you can trust me," Jack Warner said.

"So does the lady," Sidney said.

"Bette?" Jack Warner said.

"Who else?" Sidney said.

"You can at least tell me if it was a letter to her or a letter from her," Jack Warner said.

"She doesn't write letters," Sidney said. "She pays a lawyer to do that for her."

"Then it was a letter to her, right?" Jack Warner said.

"Right," Sidney said.

Jack Warner scowled. At nobody in particular, which made it worse. Unfocused, directed at the world in general, the scowl made it clear that in Mr. Warner's eyes everybody was responsible for his present state of mind. I suddenly found myself wishing I was somewhere else.

"Did the letter mention money?" Jack Warner said.

"Of course," Sidney said.

"How much?" Jack Warner said.

"Ten," Sidney said.

Jack Warner moved sharply in his chair.

"A week?" he said.

"What else?" Sidney said.

Jack Warner's face changed color. It took on a shade I had seen before only on the eggplants my mother used to bring home from the Avenue C pushcart market. The head of the Warner Brothers studio reached for the phone, then seemed to become aware that he was not alone. The hand dropped back. Jack Warner smiled. Oy!

"It was nice seeing you, Sidney," he said.

"Likewise," Sidney said, touching my arm as he pushed himself up out of his chair. I watched Jack Warner as we crossed the large room to the door. He watched us. As the door closed behind us his hand was moving back to the telephone. At the end of the corridor I asked Sidney what the letter had actually said.

"How should I know?" he said.

"You made it up?" I said.

"Why not?" Sidney said.

"He's calling someone right now to check, isn't he?" I said.

"Of course," Sidney said.

"But if there is no letter—?" I said.

"Then there isn't much he can check," Sidney said.

"When you said ten, did that mean some other studio has offered Bette Davis ten thousand dollars a week?" I said.

"That's what she's asking Warner's for," Sidney said. "Why shouldn't some rival of Warner's give it to her?"

"Suppose Mr. Warner finds out there is no such letter?" I said.

"I'll make up something else that will fit," Sidney said.

"Fit what?" I said.

"The new situation I've created," Sidney said.

"What situation?" I said.

"I've got Jack Warner shitting bricks," Sidney said. "That's got to help Bette."

"Did she ask you to help her?" I said.

"Sure, but she doesn't know it yet," Sidney said.

I thought about that for a few moments as we walked along.

"When she does get to know it," I said, "it will be because you remind her?"

Sidney grinned.

"You've seen her on the screen, and you've just seen him in his office," he said. "Of the two, which one do you think is likely to show some gratitude for a friend's help?"

I didn't answer that, but I thought about it. I was still thinking about it a couple of years after we settled in Westport, on the day when Sidney called me from Hollywood.

"I hear you're coming out to do the Bugsy Siegel story for Jerry Wald," he said.

"What else have you heard?" I said.

"It's for Joan Crawford," Sidney said. "She's going to play Virginia Hill."

"It's not settled yet," I said. "Carl Brandt is still working out the details."

"They were all worked out ten minutes ago," Sidney said. "Carl is probably trying to get you on the phone right now."

"In that case I'd better hang up," I said.

"All right," Sidney said. "But when you find out when you're coming out make sure you call and let me know."

"Why?" I said.

"I want to meet you at the airport," Sidney said.

twenty-four

Just as he never learned how to answer a letter or return a phone call, Sidney Skolsky never learned how to drive a car. When he met me at the Los Angeles airport, therefore, I was not surprised to see Estelle at the wheel of the family Buick.

"It's safer," she said.

Sitting between her and Sidney on the front seat I soon saw what Estelle meant. She was an excellent driver. She had to be, not only to move safely through the terrible traffic, but to do it at all while Sidney barked a constant stream of orders at her across my lap. She didn't say a word until we reached Linny's.

"When do you want to be picked up?" she said.

"Wait for my call," Sidney said.

I followed him into the restaurant and across to a corner booth, where Eddie Cantor was waiting.

"I understand you two know each other," Sidney said.

"Know each other?" Eddie Cantor said. "Listen to him. Jerry and I are old friends, for God's sake."

As friends went in Eddie's world, it was true enough.

"Are you doubting Eddie's word?" I said.

"Not anymore," Sidney said. "So sit down and act friendly."

We shook hands and I sat down.

"Will Ray Stark be joining us?" I said.

"He got you here," Sidney said. "What more can you expect from an agent?"

"We'll bring Ray into the picture when we need him," Eddie Cantor said. "In the meantime it's just you and Sidney and me, kid."

When I first met Eddie Cantor it had been just you and Max and me, kid. Max was, of course, Max Schuster. We were not yet in the war, but it was being fought in Europe, and Congress had just passed the Draft Act. Like a great many citizens Eddie saw it as an opportunity to serve his country. Simon & Schuster had done very well for him with his autobiography, *My Life Is in Your Hands*, and even better with his book about the Wall Street Crash: *Caught Short*. As soon as the draft became law Eddie flew into New York from Hollywood to see Max Schuster. Max was unavailable. His doppelganger met with Eddie. What Eddie had in mind was a joke book about the draft. He showed me five pages of one-liners written for him by the team that wrote his Chase & Sanborn radio show.

"That's just a sample," Eddie said. "But I'm sure you get the idea."

I did, and I promised to "see how the boys feel about the project." The Japanese attack on Pearl Harbor relieved me of the necessity to keep that promise. Ten years later, across the pastrami sandwiches in Linny's, I could see that Eddie was not holding the defection against me.

"Jerry," he said, "you're the only one who can pull me out of this."

"This" proved to be the story of his life, a filmed biography with which he planned to bring his long career to an appropriately distinguished close. He had chosen his old friend Sidney Skolsky—who had made motion picture history with his production of *The Jolson Story*—to produce *The Eddie Cantor Story*. To bring the film to the screen Eddie had entered into a fifty-fifty profit-sharing contract with Warner Brothers. The project had been under way for two years. According to Eddie's contract with Warner Brothers the cameras were scheduled to roll exactly six weeks from the day we were meeting at Linny's.

"What's the problem?" I said.

"No script," Eddie said.

"That's not true," Sidney Skolsky said. "We've got a script."

"It stinks," Eddie Cantor said.

"A script that stinks is better than no script," Sidney Skolsky said.

"In what way?" I said.

"It can be fixed," Sidney said.

"Which is where you come in," Eddie Cantor said.

"I'd like to help you, but I'm afraid it's impossible," I said.

"Why?" Sidney Skolsky said.

"I've just arrived in town," I said. "Tomorrow morning I report to Jerry Wald at Warner Brothers to write the Bugsy Siegel story for Joan Crawford. I've got to get it finished in six weeks."

"Why?" Eddie Cantor said.

"Peggy and I have rented a house for the summer in Kent," I said. "We sail for England on the *Liberté* on June eighth, the day after the kids get out of school."

"According to my Warner contract," Eddie Cantor said, "the eighth is the day filming must start on *The Eddie Cantor Story*."

"That's my point," I said.

"It's not mine," Sidney Skolsky said. "You'll be working for Jerry Wald on the Warner Brothers lot. My office as producer of *The Eddie Cantor Story* is on the floor below him. Everybody knows we're old friends. Everybody knows you and Eddie are old friends."

"How does everybody know that?" I said.

"I've paved the way in my column," Sidney said.

"So nobody on the Warner lot is going to think anything is suspicious if they see us passing the time of day in the corridor," Eddie Cantor said.

"Or having a sandwich together in the commissary," Sidney Skolsky said.

"How is that going to solve the time problem?" I said. "I just told you I'm sailing on the *Liberté* on June eighth."

"You're not planning to sail before you finish the Bugsy Siegel story for Jerry Wald," Sidney Skolsky said.

"Of course not," I said. "That's why we put the June eighth date in my contract. I'm sure I can finish the job on time."

"So am I," Sidney Skolsky said.

"Why should the Eddie Cantor story take you longer to write than the Bugsy Siegel story?" Eddie Cantor said.

"It shouldn't," I said. "Unfortunately, after I finish the Bugsy Siegel story I can't stay on."

"Who said anything about staying on?" Sidney Skolsky said.

"Then what are we talking about?" I said.

"We're talking about you doing here in Hollywood what you did on Seventh Avenue," Sidney Skolsky said. "When you were running Lou G. Siegel Specials for Monroe Geschwind during the day and at night you were writing *I Can Get It for You Wholesale* for Simon and Schuster."

"Now wait a minute," I said.

"We can't wait," Eddie Cantor said. "They're bastards, these Warner Brothers. If the cameras don't roll according to the contract, Jerry, they'll throw me and the contract out on my ass."

"I can't help that," I said.

"You've got to," Eddie Cantor said. "We're both Grand Street Boys."

"No, we're not," I said. "I'm an East Fourth Street boy."

"Didn't I tell you to lay off with that Grand Street Boys shit?" Sidney Skolsky said.

"I was just trying to appeal to his finer instincts," Eddie Cantor said.

"De Witt Clinton boys don't know from finer instincts," Sidney Skolsky said. "They have only one kind. They never let another De Witt Clinton boy down."

The Bugsy Siegel story, which appeared on the screen as *The Damned Don't Cry*, went into national release almost simultaneously with the Eddie Cantor story, which appeared on the screen as *The Eddie Cantor Story*. I appeared on the *Liberté* with Peggy and the kids on June 8. I slept all the way to Plymouth.

twenty-five

On August 29, 1971, soon after Bennett Cerf died, his son Christopher called me in Florida. He asked me to write something for the funeral service that was to be held in St. Paul's Chapel at Columbia University.

He hated to inconvenience me, Chris said, but could he have it immediately. Immediately? Well, in a couple of hours at most? They were really jammed for time. Would I call back as soon as I could and read it to him on the phone? I did, and had no idea what I had written until, along with other tributes, it was read aloud at the service. The reader was John Daly, the master of ceremonies of "What's My Line?," the highly successful TV show with which Bennett had been associated for many years. If there were any complaints about what the audience heard, therefore, they could not be lodged against the manner of the delivery. Every syllable was heard clearly in every corner of the chapel.

I listened to all the tributes with interest. Mine was the only one to which I listened with discomfort. Until Chris made his request I had never written a tribute for a funeral service. I had, of course, listened to many, but I remembered almost nothing about them, frequently not even the names of the central characters. The piece about Bennett was my first effort in the genre. Listening to what I had written in haste I was not surprised to find myself repenting at leisure. I wished my maiden effort had not been so maiden. A few warm-up sessions would have helped. Preferably on another central character. For someone who had known Bennett long and well, someone to whom

355

his life had meant more than I realized until he was gone, my performance was bound to be inadequate. Bennett Cerf was not a subject suited to three hundred words dictated hurriedly on the telephone from half a page of Pitman shorthand notes. Or maybe, it occurred to me fourteen years later as I studied my Pitman squiggles, that is precisely the way a man like Bennett should be dealt with.

In any case, after a good deal of thought, I decided to reproduce that 1971 moment and then, in Wordsworth's tranquillity of recollection, add a few footnotes. The hope is that the real man—or, more important, the man who was real to me—will emerge. First, what I dictated to Chris Cerf on the phone on August 29, 1971:

"Mustard makes the meal." So it says on all those huge signs that flash by on the sides of London buses. It certainly does. If, that is, you like mustard. I do. And it has been quite a meal. I sat down to it in 1933. For anybody who is not a quick reckoner, I will do the arithmetic. That was thirty-eight years ago. I feel sorry for those who did not know Bennett in 1933. Everybody who knew him later knew him at his best. But I knew him when the ingredients of the mustard were still being put together. On that first day in 1933 I did not realize I had been privileged to join a select circle: The Bennett Watchers. I merely pulled up a chair and turned to the girl on my right. A long, bony finger tapped me on the left. I turned again. It was Bennett. Tall, handsome, slender as an asparagus spear, yet looking as though he was occupying three chairs.

"Young man," he said sternly, "for a non–Random House author I am not going to tell this story twice."

He never did. He was too busy working on the recipe for that mustard. When the special flavor it added to so many areas of our time became apparent, people would ask me, "How does he do it?" I never told them. I kept the secret. It was part of the privilege of having known Bennett in 1933. The secret was simple: he was a life enhancer. Every minute of the day he had fun. And he passed the mustard pot. So you, too, had fun. In thirty-eight years I never knew a moment in his presence that was not made brighter by the flavor he added. The moments will continue. Some flavors last. Renaissance men were built to last.

Leaving aside the hyperbole that is an inevitable part of all commemorative oratory, there is in this sample of the genre a basic truth about Bennett that does not emerge on a first hearing or even reading. A truth that in 1971 I had no idea I had learned about Bennett but now, on reflection in 1985, seems to me to be central to his character.

One day, when Bennett was telling us about something William Faulkner had done, he said to Peggy, "You know how he is when he's been drinking."

"I've heard, but I don't really know," Peggy said.

Bennett seemed shocked.

"You mean you've never met Bill Faulkner?"

"Never," Peggy said.

"How about you?" he said to me.

"I make it a point never to know any authors Peggy doesn't know," I said.

"We'll have to correct that," Bennett said.

The next day Phyllis Cerf called and invited us to dinner with Faulkner the following week. We met at the Côte Basque, Phyllis and Bennett, Peggy and I, Faulkner and his date for the evening, Nancy Olson the actress. Faulkner reminded me of Maugham. Both men were small and neatly made, with sharp, watchful eyes, unobtrusive mustaches, and a quiet manner. Neither spoke until addressed, and both replied with seeming reluctance, as though they didn't want to overwhelm you with more information than they felt you could handle. Both also gave me the idea they were content but not particularly impressed to find themselves in the company they were at the moment keeping. The strongest similarity was a feeling I had that both men lived around a core of total self-sufficiency. They had something going on inside that sustained them, something on which they had learned they could count, something that was none of the rest of the world's business. They even dressed the same way. Dark, faintly pinstriped, conservatively cut suits, and both carried their crumpled handkerchiefs stuffed into the left cuff of their jacket sleeve.

Bennett asked Faulkner to order the wine, which he did after studying the list for a long time in a manner that seemed to earn the approval of the sommelier. Bennett watched the performance with obvious pleasure, as I'd seen him watch his sons Chris and Jonathan when they did something admirable in public. After ordering the wine Faulkner seemed to retire into that private place within himself for the rest of our time at table, but it was the sort of retirement that did not affect the other dinner guests. It was as though a priest, who was expected to do it, had absented himself from the festivities long enough to perform some important private ritual. When we broke up to walk over to the Cerf house on Sixty-second Street I stepped into the men's room. Like the men's rooms in many expensive restaurants all over the world this one in the Côte Basque was not spacious. The small room was equipped with only two stalls. Faulkner had already taken his place at one. I stepped into position at his side. Not a word was spoken until we finished. Then, as we were both working on our zippers, Faulkner broke the silence.

"Ah know what you do," he said in a low, musical voice. "Ah think you should keep right on doing it."

In 1970 I published the first volume of my trilogy about a boy named Benny Kramer who grew up on East Fourth Street and, at seventeen, moved to the Bronx. The third volume is called *Tiffany Street*. When he read my outline for the second and third volumes of the trilogy, Bennett asked me, "When was the last time you set foot on Tiffany Street?"

"Nineteen-forty," I said. "The day we moved back to Manhattan."

"Before you sit down to write *Tiffany Street*," Bennett said, "would you like to take another look at Tiffany Street?"

"Why?" I said.

"From this outline you make it sound like a place where you and your family were happy," Bennett said.

"That's the point of the trilogy," I said.

"I'd like to take a look at Tiffany Street," Bennett said. "Will you come with me?"

"Of course," I said.

"Let me arrange for transportation," Bennett said.

The transportation proved to be a police car. All during the

358

planning of the trilogy I had not connected Tiffany Street with the newspaper stories I'd been reading about the South Bronx. When Bennett and I reached Tiffany Street I told the policeman at the wheel to take us to number 1075.

"House numbers don't mean much up here anymore," the policeman said. "What does it look like?"

"Four floors," I said. "Yellow brick with a sandstone stoop and two big maple trees on the sidewalk in front with a fire hydrant in between."

"Let's try for the house number," the policeman said. "Can't go by the trees up here anymore."

When we got there I saw why. Two holes in the broken sidewalk were all that remained of the maple trees. Much of the building had crumbled. It looked like some of the bombed-out houses I saw in London during the blitz. There was no glass in the few window frames that remained more or less intact. The front door was gone. The fire hydrant was still there but it was cracked and sagging, as though it had been hit with a sledgehammer. A thin trickle of water dripped down from one side. An old woman wrapped in rags was on her knees in front of the hydrant, catching the dripping water in an old gasoline tin.

"That's all the drinking water they've got until four blocks over that way," the policeman said.

He waved up the deserted street I used to walk twice a day when I took the subway downtown in the morning to my job with Monroe Geschwind and came home at night after my classes at N.Y.U. Law School.

"What are you thinking?" Bennett said.

I didn't seem to be able to put my feelings into words, so I shied away from them and asked a question instead.

"What made you suggest we come up here?" I said.

"I have a very good feeling about the Benny Kramer trilogy," Bennett said. "I wouldn't mind seeing it grow into a tetralogy."

In 1969 Random House published my novel *The Center of the Action*. It is a thinly disguised story of the destruction of Richard L. Simon by the forces he had unwittingly set in motion when he sold Simon & Schuster to Marshall Field.

"Poor bastard," Bennett said sadly after he read the manuscript. "He was such a bright guy, how could he have done a thing like that to himself?"

Sometime after this, Random House sold itself to RCA. Two years later, a few months before Chris Cerf called me about writing a piece for his father's funeral service, Peggy and I were spending a weekend with the Cerfs at their country place in Mt. Kisco. I am an early riser. On Sunday morning, leaving the household asleep behind me, I went down to the pool for a swim at five-thirty. Coming around a clump of trees that shielded the pool area from the house, I heard a sound that stopped me in my tracks. In the early-morning light I could see through the trees a man wearing pajamas and a robe slumped in a beach chair. His large body was shaking with sobs. I turned and tried to back off, but Bennett had seen me.

"It's okay," he said, wiping his eyes with the heel of his hand. "Come on in, the water's fine."

The cackling laugh with which he always greeted one of his own jokes rang through the trees. Except that this time the sound was not a happy ring. It was an uneasy tinkle. I broke into a run, greeted him as I emerged from the trees the way he liked to be greeted, with a boisterous shout, and dove into the pool. I did five laps before I felt it was safe to come out. When I did Bennett was drying his eyes again. This time he did not make a joke. He just stared at the puddle I was dripping in front of him.

"I'll get coffee," I said.

"Sit down," Bennett said.

I sat down.

"Don't tell Phyllis," he said.

I shook my head.

"She doesn't know how bad it is," Bennett said. "Or maybe she does. She's very smart. But I don't want her to know you caught me crying."

"Caught you doing what?" I said.

"All right, wise guy," he said. "But you didn't see me."

"Okay," I said.

"You won't believe the shit they're putting me through," Bennett said.

"Sarnoff?" I said.

"Who else?" Bennett said. "He's the chairman of the God-damn board. He *is* RCA, for Christ's sake. Everything they've been doing to us, he acts as though he has no idea what I'm complaining about, but I know he's doing it. Old Smiley. He doesn't even give me a chance to open my mouth. I'm just one member of the big gang, the board. We're chicken feed, Random House. Every other Goddamn thing they own has more votes. All I can do is sit there and take it. You know what they did at yesterday's meeting?"

"What?" I said.

"Random House is not pulling its weight, Sarnoff says. They thought they were buying a red-hot concern, but what did they get? A nickels-and-dimes novelty shop. He's putting their accountants on the Modern Library. A thing like that, they'd been told it's a gold mine, why isn't it showing a decent profit? The accountants say because we keep a lot of crap on the list for sentimental reasons, titles that were hot maybe in the twenties, but now who reads them? They have to go, he said. All that shit has to go, he said. *The House with the Green Shutters* by George Douglas Brown, that has to go. *The Complete Poetry* of Samuel Hoffenstein. *The Education of Henry Adams. The Enormous Room* by E. E. Cummings. Who else? Yeah, *Casuals of the Sea* by William McFee, *The Old Wives' Tale, Ten Days That Shook the World*, all that, he says, has to go. I tried to argue, but he shut me up with You feel that way about things like those books, why did you sell a thing like Random House to an outfit like RCA?"

Bennett's voice stopped. The question hung in the air between us. I let it hang. Bennett squinted, as though the answer to his question was somewhere up there and he was trying to read the words, and then I saw the tears running down his face again.

"Why did we?" he said to nobody in particular.

"I think maybe coffee—?"

Bennett pushed me back into my chair.

"You know what Donald and I are thinking?" he said. "Don't say anything about this, not even to Peggy, it's still a secret, but Donald and I we've been talking of buying Random House back from them. We'd begin all over again. Just the two of us, me and Donald, the way it was at the beginning. Very small. The way we started. Taking our authors with us, our friends. O'Hara, Michener, Red Warren, Truman—" He paused. "You'd come, wouldn't you?"

"You know I would."

I think he did know, which is why I'm trying now to edit the crap out of what I dictated to Chris on the phone in 1971. His father was better than that.

How much better tended to be obscured by a trait of character that is widely considered amusing: Bennett liked winners. Not the way we say of people that they like Hershey bars or Ronald Reagan. Bennett liked winners the way Nathan Hale liked his country. With a passion so deep that he never questioned it, or tried to understand it, or was even aware of its existence. It does not, at first glance, seem something to which a man can be as dedicated as Romeo was to Juliet, something that can be at the core of an adult existence, something around which a man's whole life can be built. At first glance, no, it certainly does not seem so. A second glance, however, if you devote fourteen years to it, convinces me it was a pursuit to which Bennett, most of the time unconsciously, of course, did dedicate his life.

He liked winners. I don't mean his own winnings. Of course he liked that. Everybody does. What Bennett liked was the ambience of the winners' circle. The way autograph collectors like to hang around locker rooms and stage doors. No matter who entered the circle to pick up a prize, regardless of the nature of the achievement, whether magnificent or trivial, Bennett—like a salmon fighting its way upstream to spawn—made his way to the scene, and could be seen within camera range, watching, applauding, sharing in another's—anybody's—glow of triumph.

Scott Fitzgerald pointed out that very little of life is lived on beaches. I would suggest that, numerically speaking, even less of it is lived in the winners' circle. There are more losers than winners. Spending your entire life with winners inevitably cuts you off from the larger number of your fellow men. Bennett did not grasp this until—through what he clearly interpreted as no fault of his own—Bennett himself became a nonwinner. When

362

it happened there were no white blood corpuscles in his emotional bloodstream to fight off what he did not recognize as a universal condition. So the disease spread undeterred, and he was destroyed.

Still in all, as we used to say on East Fourth Street, still in all.

twenty-six

For a long time after I became a professional writer I had a strong feeling that, in view of my East Fourth Street provenance, I had chosen an odd way to earn my living. This feeling has, with the passing years, tended to diminish in strength. Not counting my immigrant parents, the inclinations of the rest of the family would seem to dilute my earlier conviction.

My son Jeff, after years in pursuit of his doctorate in art history, can be read today by anybody willing to spend thirty-five dollars for a copy of *The Art Institute of Chicago Centennial Lectures*. My son John—putting behind him Harvard College and Yale Law School—hung in his den as an ornament the shingle admitting him to practice at the New York bar, and turned to the theatre: *Pacific Overtures*. My wife Peggy, whose passion is archaeology, has had on the Random House list for twenty years more active titles than her husband and sons put together: *The Pharaohs of Ancient Egypt, Meet the American Indians, Meet the Pilgrim Fathers*. Her grandfather, Will Payne, after his early years as a newspaperman in Chicago, came to the *Saturday Evening Post* with George Horace Lorimer in 1900 and for forty years helped fill its pages with short stories, romantic serials, articles on economics, and most of its editorials. My brother Leon, an intensely private person, has under a pseudonym the rest of the family has yet to penetrate published at least one novel. My sister Jean, an accomplished sculptor, took a somewhat different but more dramatic route to the world of letters: she married the son of Upton Sinclair.

David Sinclair is not a writer. He is a research physicist.

Among many other accomplishments he is the central character in my favorite retirement story. After serving during the war on the Columbia University campus in a classified unit that may or may not have been working on the development of the bomb, David moved on to the research department of Johns-Manville. In 1965, coincidentally with the age of the century, he reached retirement age. David was given the farewell luncheon, the gold watch, and what might have been a severe case of depression if he had not been cut, at least in part, from the same bolt of cloth that suited his father Upton. When he died at ninety-one Upton Sinclair was deep into a new book. His son David had no intention of stopping work at sixty-five because his number had come up on a retirement chart. He ordered stationery and announced his availability as a freelance consultant. He never had to use a single sheet of those expensive letterheads. While the printer was running them through the press, what was then known as the Atomic Energy Commission was running out of theories for the solution of its greatest problem: fallout. The builders of the bomb had been aware of the problem for twenty years, ever since on August 6, 1945, it was dropped on Hiroshima. For two decades the solution had eluded the best and the brightest. In 1965 one of the brightest decided that, if they could find a way to count fallout, they might also find themselves on a more promising road toward eliminating it than any they had thus far followed.

The A.E.C. put the question to its computers and sat back to wait. They did not have to wait long. The computers came up promptly with a surprising answer. Beginning with the first efforts late in the nineteenth century, and continuing through almost seven decades of the twentieth, approximately one hundred papers on how to count air pollution had been presented at the world's major universities and published in their scientific journals. Of these, thirty-nine had been written by someone named David Sinclair. Another question—Who is David Sinclair?—was fed into the A.E.C. computers. The answer was equally prompt and perhaps even more thorough. It included almost every detail about David Sinclair, including his telephone number, except the fact that he was the brother-in-law of a novelist named Jerome Weidman. The A.E.C. did nothing to correct this totally irrelevant omission, but they did use the telephone number. As a result, at the age of sixty-five, David Sinclair was offered and accepted a fifteen-year contract to devote his enormous research talents to the service of his country. In 1980—when the contract was about to expire and David, like the century, was entering his ninth decade—the contract was renewed.

One of the more pleasant aspects of the relationship between my brother-in-law and the Atomic Energy Commission was that, through David, I was introduced to some of the literature. In it I discovered an article about the psychological aspects of the problem written by a Major John Hackett of Ham Street, Near Ashford, Kent, England. Major John Hackett of Ham Street proved to be the same Major John Hackett who had been my C.O. during my wartime stay at Bletchley. I wrote to him at once, the letter was forwarded, and I learned that Major Hackett was now living on a farm in Kent from which he commuted five days a week to his Berkeley Square advertising business in London.

Peggy and I were then living in Westport and, like many of our neighbors, had been thinking of renting our house and going to Europe with the children for their summer vacation. I mentioned this in one of my letters to Major Hackett. If it could be worked out, I indicated, one of the pleasures of the trip for us would be a meeting of the two families. Major Hackett's reply was a cable: WILL ARRANGE EVERYTHING SEND DATES SOONEST.

We sailed in June on the *Liberté* and were met at the boat train in London by John Hackett. Coronation Week was just ending. London was still festooned with bunting. Going down to Ashford with John Hackett we could see from the train windows the Kentish hills still planted with coronation poles marking the places where, for the celebration of the Jubilee of another queen, A. E. Housman had written: "From Clee to heaven the beacon burns, The shires have seen it plain . . . Because 'tis fifty years to-night That God has saved the Queen!"

My recollections of John Hackett at Bletchley, about whom over the years I had briefed Peggy in stupefying detail, required only minor corrections to synchronize him with the man who met us ten years later at the boat train. The thick brown eyebrows were now shot with gray but still resembled a couple of vigorously used toothbrushes. The lenses of the gold-framed glasses had become bifocal. The large, muscular body was a little larger at the middle. Much of his conversation was still delivered—around the pipestem clenched tightly between the very white teeth—in beautifully cadenced sentences as though he was reciting poetry that he was making up as he went along. Almost all the sentences ended in the rumbling chuckle that was a pleasure to the ear, and the pockets of his wrinkled tweed jacket still resembled overstuffed saddlebags. His wife, who was a charmer, met us at the Ashford station. She won the hearts of Jeff and John by presenting them with coronation crowns, the special five-shilling coin minted for the occasion, each one encased in a neat little Lucite box.

"I don't know how much John has told you," Mrs. Hackett said as we settled ourselves in her Rover for the drive to the place that was to be our home for the next three months. "I do know he's probably said not a word about housekeeping. So why don't you sit here up front with me," she said to Peggy, "and I'll fill you in."

While she did that John Hackett filled me in about the place he had rented for us. It was called Capel-Orlestone. I don't know why and never got around to asking because everything else about the place seemed more interesting. It was a large working farm with a manor house and outbuildings, owned by Sir Roland Oliver, who, according to John Hackett, was the British equivalent of our Supreme Court chief justice. Once every year Sir Roland's duties called him off on the assizes.

"You know the sort of thing," John Hackett said. "He hangs a chap or two in Glasgow, then moves on to put some poor sod away for life in Birmingham. No telling what he'll find on the bill of fare, so to speak, until he gets there. Tedious business, but it has to be done."

Never before had Sir Roland rented Capel-Orlestone for the period when he was off on the assizes. When his neighbor John Hackett suggested it to him, Sir Roland's first reaction was an indignant no, certainly not, he wasn't going to have his home overrun in his absence by a horde of trippers. What in the world could John be thinking of?

"A bit of lolly, I pointed out to him," John Hackett said to me. "He detests the Inland Revenue, and he'll do anything to beat it, so after a bit of thought he said all right, he'll rent the place to these friends of mine, but only if they met two conditions."

"What are they?" I said.

"First, that I assure him these people were genuine friends and not merely casual business acquaintances," John Hackett said. "And, second, he wants the transaction kept confidential and the rent paid in advance in the form of five-pound notes."

"That's all right with me," I said. "But you say he's the chief justice of England?"

"Yes, why?" John Hackett said.

"Suppose we get nailed?" I said.

"Why should we be?" Hackett said.

"Back home nailing people for tax evasion is the only way we seem to get at our really big criminals," I said. "That's how they finally caught up with Al Capone."

"Sir Roland is a different kettle of fish," John Hackett said. "You needn't worry about him."

"I'm not," I said. "I'm worrying about myself."

"Why?" John Hackett said.

"In this country, for all I know, subverting the chief justice of England could carry the death penalty."

"No fear," John Hackett said. "Sir Roland would probably arrange to have you come up before him somewhere on the assizes, in which case you're sure to escape with a life sentence. We'll run over to the bank in Ashford tomorrow morning and get the rent in five-pound notes, shall we?"

We did, and neither Sir Roland nor I was nailed. Except perhaps to a literary discovery that belongs in what used to be known in the humor column of the De Witt Clinton High School News—called, of course, "De Wit of Clinton"—as the Raised Eyebrows Department.

Capel-Orlestone was a large, rambling structure, not exactly run down, but not precisely run up, either. It was country shabby in a comfortable, pleasant way, and the bathrooms worked adequately most of the time. When they did not Alice's husband came in from somewhere out on the farm to fix them. Alice was the housekeeper, a strong, bright, cheerful, and efficient woman with a sense of humor and two children of her own. She added Jeff and John to the brood as though they were family members who had just come home from a long stay with a colonial relative. Jeff and John clearly enjoyed the relationship. The whole place had the sort of casual, worn-at-the-edges charm that I remembered from early Hitchcock movies, and the croquet court was magnificent.

The master bedroom on the second floor was large and, at night in early June when we arrived, as cold as our tenement flat on East Fourth Street used to be on New Year's Day. The bed, however, was enormous and the blankets and comforters were plentiful. On our first night at Capel I had just managed to dig myself into a reasonably warm cocoon when I realized I had forgotten to bring up something to read. While I was wondering if I should take the long walk down the draughty corridors and stairs to the library on the ground floor, Peggy pointed to a shelf over our heads. It ran the width of the bed and was jammed with books.

I climbed out of my cocoon and had a look. What I saw was a grab bag that had obviously accumulated over the years from the things people carried upstairs as bedtime reading and never bothered to carry back down: *Good-bye to All That* by Robert Graves; *Three Weeks* by Elinor Glyn; *The Story of San Michele* by Axel Munthe; *Over the Top* by Arthur Guy Empy; *Death of a Hero* by Richard Aldington; *If Winter Comes* by A. S. M. Hutchinson; *The Four Horsemen of the Apocalypse* by Vicente Blasco Ibañez; *The Fortunes of Richard Mahony* by Henry Handel Richardson—my eyes stopped moving, caught by a volume that seemed out of place.

It was obviously older than the other books I glanced at, even though the others all dated from the twenties. I pulled this older book from the shelf. It was a copy of *Lord Jim* by Joseph Conrad. I opened it at random and the corner of a yellowed page flaked away. More gently I turned to the front of the book. On the flyleaf, in brown ink that had faded to a watery tan, was written: "For Sir Roland Oliver, With the Greatest Pleasure, Joseph Conrad."

I handed the book down to Peggy. While she examined it I ran my eye along the rest of the shelf. Among the many books arranged in no particular order I found and pulled out three more by Conrad. All were in more or less the same condition, some with pages more foxed than others, and all were similarly inscribed. The next day, when John Hackett came over for a drink, I showed him the books. He studied the inscriptions, turned the pages slowly, then came back to the flyleaves.

"Odd," he said. "I never heard Sir Roland mention Conrad. Do you know his work?"

"*Lord Jim* was assigned reading in high school," I said. "Then Peggy and I inherited a set of the Memorial Edition when her father died, and I found myself reading more and more."

I did not realize until this moment that for some time, in addition to reading more and more, I had also been doing more and more thinking about Conrad. I was keenly aware, in fact, that for several months before we came to Kent in 1953, he had been taking up more and more space in my thoughts. Now, like me and my family at Capel-Orlestone, he had taken up residence inside my head. I could not back off and pretend that Conrad—any more than I—had wandered in by mistake. The Inland Revenue could, of course, be circumvented; there was no written lease, and Sir Roland Oliver had insisted that the rent take the form of untraceable five-pound notes. There were, however, relationships that I had learned at N.Y.U. Law School had nothing to do with written documents. Common law marriage, for example. A couple who live together for a reasonable length of time cannot later maintain successfully in a court of law—merely because they have separated on discovering their feelings for each other had changed—they are absolved from any of the legal obligations their time together has created. There is, for instance, the relationship between a man or woman and his or her birthday. No matter how unpleasant it may be to face, regardless of the sums that may have been spent on the services of plastic surgeons, the relationship—which may be denied—cannot be altered. It is a matter of public record. In 1953, like everybody else who was born in 1913, I was undeniably forty years old.

It is a peculiar age for a man to be. Not like twenty-five, for which a man who happens to be twenty-five can maintain it is the perfect age for a man to be when he sets out—like Magellan and Francis Drake—to circumnavigate the globe. At forty all men are not unlike a Monroe Geschwind client at the end of his fiscal year: aware that he is expected to turn over his records to his accountant for their annual audit. How am I doing, Mr. G.? You'll have to wait, Mr. W., until we close your books and make up your balance sheet. Mr. W. did not have to wait. I had learned during my apprenticeship with Monroe Geschwind how to make up my own balance sheet. It is a brutally simple process. You start with an inventory of your assets and liabilities at the time of your last audit.

My last audit had taken place soon after the publication of *I Can Get It for You Wholesale*. When Hemingway had written me not to let them get me down because "I think you can write just a little bit better than anybody else that's around." When Fitzgerald had told his literary executor Judge John Biggs, Jr., that "among the new writers there is only one." And when the dust had settled I felt as though I'd been caught in a downpour that left me with my shirt so shrunken that I found it difficult to breathe. Which, to a man who had been taught how to read as well as how to prepare his own balance sheet, meant: get out of New York for a while. I got out.

Now, fifteen years later, without pausing for an audit, I had done it again. Why had I left New York this second time? Pausing at Capel-Orlestone for the audit I should have made in Connecticut, I had to face the fact that I had not been caught in a sudden downpour. The weather since we had settled in Westport had been extremely pleasant. Why, then, did I feel again the way I had felt fifteen years ago? As though my shirt had shrunk so badly that I could scarcely breathe? The answer, I realized at Capel-Orlestone, was not unlike the answer to the St. Paul's visitor surrounded by monuments who wanted to know where was the monument to the man who had built the place: "If you would see the monument to Sir Christopher Wren, look about you."

Looking about me I saw not only the Conrad first editions on Sir Roland Oliver's bedroom shelf. I saw all the other Conrad books I had read and all the facts about his life that, unaware I was seeking anything, had during the past months thrust their way into my mind. Among these the one that struck me almost with the impact of a physical blow was the fact that Conrad had published *Almayer's Folly*, his first novel, in 1895, when he was thirty-eight. Thirty-eight is close enough to forty to make its unmistakable point to a man at Capel-Orlestone who had started publishing at twenty: I was already two years late for catching up with the extraordinary man who had started publishing when he was twice my age. At forty there is no escaping the meaning of the figures on the balance sheet. I was shocked by the amount of capital I had unwittingly lost in the form of wasted time.

Most of this was due, of course, to the fact that the explosion of TV on the American scene had caused the collapse of the magazine short-story market. Like many of my contemporaries who began their careers by working seriously in the short-story field to underwrite their work as novelists, I had been caught by the change. The advertising dollars that American business had grown accustomed to pouring into the magazines had for decades made the writing of short stories a practical way for a serious novelist to earn his base pay. This advertising money was now suddenly channeled into TV. Magazine circulation dropped spectacularly. In the hope of recapturing it the editors stopped buying short stories and began to pour a larger share of the magazine's editorial dollar into the purchase of nonfiction. The markets for short stories as I had known them in my youth vanished. Again like many of my contemporaries I started making up the difference by accepting assignments in other fields. Not until I found myself at the age of forty making a balance sheet at Capel-Orlestone did I realize the extent of the damage. There was no doubt that writing *The Damned Don't Cry* and *The Eddie Cantor Story* helped fill the financial gap caused by the disappearance of the short-story markets. Especially if you were still able to divide your time the way you divided it at nineteen: running Lou G. Siegel Specials during the day for Monroe Geschwind, and writing *I Can Get It for You Wholesale* at night for Richard L. Simon. Working on the balance sheet at Capel-Orlestone, I saw something that perhaps shows up earlier in an auditor's work sheets than on a doctor's diagnosis: what the human body is capable of doing effortlessly at nineteen cannot be repeated at forty. The simplest arithmetical projections, applied to the most generous life-expectancy tables, come as a shock to the most primitive auditor: at forty the best part of the race has been run. It does not seem possible but, as any auditor knows, numbers cannot be denied. After forty, whatever is thrown into the race must be measured not only in expected dollars but also, and more importantly, in terms of how much the reservoir of available time up ahead will be diminished by the effort. In Capel-Orlestone it was impossible to avoid something that might have slipped by in Westport: a feeling of panic at the realization that at forty, when most people still think of themselves as young, the writer must realize that he can no longer afford the luxury of measuring out his life with coffee spoons. He must make sure he directs what is left into the channels that count.

For me what has always counted most is the novel. At Capel-Orlestone, working on my balance sheet without the distractions of New York and Westport, I became aware that up to now I had worked in my chosen field more or less at random. When I finished a novel the next one was ready, inside my head, waiting to be written—as soon, that is, as I finished whatever was at the moment my secondary commitment: a short story for Herb Mayes; a script for Jerry Wald or Eddie Cantor; a TV series for CBS.

As I stared at the Conrad first editions on the shelf over Sir Roland Oliver's bed, a crash program began to shape up in my head to replace the capital I had squandered, to recapture the time I had lost. I would not write what should have been my next novel. I would write what would be the first novel in a scheme of novels. I could suddenly see a whole series, each novel separate and complete in itself, yet each one taking its place as a panel in an overall, longer work. How much longer? Why, as long, of course, as the author remained alive to keep adding panels. What else could it mean?

"It could mean trouble," said Carl Brandt, my agent, when I got back to New York and told him what I had in mind.

"What sort of trouble?" I said.

"Almost all your work is autobiographical," Carl said. "It now consists of thirty-eight books, twenty-two of them novels. Do you plan to begin this serial novel at the point where your twenty-second published novel ends?"

"Certainly not," I said. "I plan to begin where life begins, at the beginning."

"Your beginning?"

"Of course," I said.

"How are you going to avoid repeating material that you've already used in all those already published autobiographical books?" Carl said.

"By doing what Conrad did," I said.

"What's that?" Carl said.

"Tell only the truth," I said.

"I always assumed that's what you were doing in all your books," Carl said.

"I was," I said. "Beginning now, however, I plan to put in only what I left out the first time."

On the last day of our stay at Capel-Orlestone, Sir Roland came home from the assizes. In spite of the confusion of packing and getting ready to leave, I managed to have a few minutes alone with him. This was not easy. He was a tall, broad-shouldered man who reminded me a little of Fulton Sheen. The moment he came into a room it seemed too small for everybody else who happened to be in it. His large bald head was dotted with liver spots the size of bottle caps and wisps of surviving, free-floating white hair. He had the sort of long, thin, drooping nose that would have delighted a cartoonist, who would obviously have drawn it to look like a faucet with a drop of liquid gathering slowly at the tip, waiting for gravity to shake it free. When I got close to him I saw that it was indeed a drop of liquid, and it did shake free. Sir Roland caught it with the sleeve of his baggy, double-breasted, gold-buttoned blue blazer. He wore it unbuttoned so that with every move he made the wings of the coat flapped as though he were a huge bird trying without much success to get off the ground. It was, I found, difficult to keep a conversation going with him because he kept pulling from his outer breast pocket a long thin glass jar that looked like a fat test tube. I learned later from John Hackett that the jar had once held sticks of pickled asparagus spears. Now it contained Booth's gin. According to John Hackett, Sir Roland drank steadily from the moment he got out of bed in the morning until, usually with the help of Alice's husband, he got back into it at night. When I asked him about the Conrad books on the shelf in the master bedroom he said oh, yes, they were first editions but they were not inscribed to him.

"He gave them to my father," Sir Roland said. "My father rented Capel to him several times for very small fees because he admired his work."

"Did you know him personally?" I said.

"He taught me to sail," Sir Roland said.

"Joseph Conrad?" I said.

Sir Roland grunted.

"Was he a good teacher?" I said.

"Bloody fool didn't know the first thing about it," Sir Roland said. "He almost drowned me one day, and my father discontinued the lessons."

"Where did he do his writing?" I said.

"At the table in the library, just back there," Sir Roland said, gesturing with the asparagus jar. "He sat sort of hunched over, like this—" Sir Roland's big body bent down into a loop as the wispy hair came down toward an imaginary table—"and made these awful grunting noises as though he was fighting to get the bloody words out on paper." Sir Roland took a sip and dropped the long glass jar back into his breast pocket. "Nice chap, though," he said. "Very courtly. Always kissed my mother's hand when they met."

"Did you ever see any of his manuscripts?" I said.

"Nobody did," Sir Roland said. "He was afraid to have anybody take a look."

"Why?" I said.

375

"He didn't want people catching on," Sir Roland said.

"Catching on to what?" I said.

"Well, you see, he couldn't write English," Sir Roland Oliver said.

"Joseph Conrad?" I said.

"Not a word," Sir Roland said. "He could scarcely speak the language. That was the trouble when he tried to teach me how to sail a boat. I hadn't got a word of Polish, and his version of English was Greek to me."

"Then how did he get all those books written?" I said.

"Oh, Jessie took care of that," Sir Roland said.

"Jessie?" I said.

"His wife," Sir Roland said. "She was a bookseller's daughter, and devoted to him. She did all the laundry and cleaning, when he hadn't got her nailed to the scullery with the baking and cooking, but the moment he brought in some pages she'd drop whatever it was she was doing and get to work."

"On what?" I said.

"She took what he wrote in Polish and she Englished it," Sir Roland Oliver said.

He took another sip of gin, smiled sardonically, and caught a drop from his nose on the sleeve of his blue blazer. My mind went back to the Memorial Edition Peggy and I inherited from her father. Every volume had a frontispiece that consisted of a photocopy of a Conrad manuscript page. They were all handwritten in English. I remembered having no difficulty reading the clear, even lines, including inserted corrections. I wondered if Sir Roland believed what he was saying.

"You say your father liked his work?" I said.

"Very much," Sir Roland said.

"Did you?" I said.

"Rubbish, I thought," Sir Roland said. "But of course I never told him that."

"Are there any writers whose work you do like?" I said.

"Only one," Sir Roland said.

"Who?" I said.

"An American chap named Dashiell Hammett, if I'm pronouncing it correctly," Sir Roland said. "You wouldn't happen to know him, would you?"

twenty-seven

As a matter of fact I did. We were introduced in 1937 by Arthur Kober.

When I started selling short stories to *The New Yorker*, Arthur had been contributing to the magazine for several years. We did not meet, however, until Dick Simon sent him the galleys of *I Can Get It for You Wholesale*. Arthur wrote an enthusiastic quote for the dust jacket. On publication date we were introduced by Dick at a small dinner party in the Simon house on West Eleventh Street. Arthur and I liked each other and became friends. Before he turned to writing he had been a Broadway press agent. The theatre remained the major interest of his life. My own interest went back to the days of Miss Merle S. Marine's Playgoers Club at De Witt Clinton High School. Before long I was meeting theatre people at Arthur Kober's apartment.

One day, when he was having trouble with a short story, Arthur called and asked if I could drop in for a drink and talk about the plot. He issued this invitation quite often. Not because he—or anybody else, including me—thought I was an expert on plot. Arthur asked me to come over because he believed it helped him to talk about his writing problems. I had learned from brutal experience that the worst thing I could do when I had a writing problem was talk about it. The only thing that helped, I discovered, was to let it fester, like an infection, until it burst and came suppurating out of my system onto paper. It always did. I didn't know why. I did know, however, that telling this to Arthur Kober would have upset him. It would have been a blow to his self-confidence, which was never very sturdy about anything, including his clothes and his relationship with waiters. His friends learned soon enough how important—and satisfying to them, of course—it was to prop him up.

On this particular day, when I got to Arthur's apartment, he had another guest. When Arthur introduced us I did not catch his name. This happened to me frequently during Arthur's introductions because of the way he spoke. Coming as I did from East Fourth Street I had a pretty good idea how I sounded when I spoke: I was never mistaken on the phone for Ronald Colman. Without having given much thought to the subject, I had a pretty good idea how somebody like Arthur, who came from a not dissimilar family background in Harlem, should sound. He didn't. Arthur Kober had worked out a way to sound that he felt was an improvement on what nature had handed him at birth. He sounded like a bogus Arthur Treacher trying to remember that this time he was not playing a butler. The vaudeville British accent was always threatening to break through into the indignation of an honest deez-dem-and-doze delivery that felt it was being elbowed from its rightful place by a fraudulent usurper. The invention emerged through pursed lips as a sort of fruity gargle in which crucial syllables, especially in names, tended to surface halfheartedly without any sort of clear definition.

Once in a while, annoyed by the confusion resulting from what struck me as a foolish affectation, I would ask Arthur to repeat the name of the person to whom I was being introduced. In this case I did not. There was something about the man to whom I was being introduced that made the request for such a repetition seem an admission of inexcusable stupidity. There was about him a subtly pervasive aura of regality, a touch of what in my history books was evoked by the phrase "divine right of kings." You had it, or you didn't. If you didn't have it, all your claims to it were a waste of breath. If you did have it, you didn't waste your regal breath reminding people they were in its presence. Part of the knowledge was never thinking about the crudity of having your name questioned by the occasional dumbbell. I knew at once that I did not want this man to think I was a dumbbell. Never mind Arthur's fashionable mumbling.

I would catch up with the name later. Right now it was enough to be in this stranger's presence. I decided he was probably an actor. Not only because he was tall, lean, and good-looking, with a great profile and a head of crew-cut prematurely white hair. I decided he was an actor because of the way he held his body, shoulders back, head up, keeping the better side of the profile toward the camera or the footlights. It was obvious to me that he looked good in either medium.

"Arthur told me you were coming," he said. "So I read your story in this week's *New Yorker*. One of your best."

That's when I knew I could not say I was sorry I had not caught his name. It was also the reason why I don't remember what we talked about. I couldn't wait to get out of that room before I made a fool of myself. The next day I called Arthur and asked him who was that impressive character I met at your place yesterday. He told me his name. It rang no bells.

"Is he an actor?" I said.

Arthur Kober never let me forget that moment of ignorance. It did me no good to protest that I never read mystery stories. I read the newspapers, didn't I? Like everybody else who read the newspapers I read the Broadway columns, or was expected to. The name Dashiell Hammett lived in Winchell and Lyons and O. O. McIntyre cheek by jowl with the names Dorothy Parker and Noël Coward and Marc Connelly the way the names Lou Gehrig and Bobby Jones and Gene Tunney lived in the sports columns of John Kieran, Paul Gallico, and Stanley Woodward. Soon after Arthur put me in my place I walked to where on East Fourth Street I had learned my way around. In the public library catalog, under the name Dashiell Hammett, I found cards for five novels. Only two were on the shelf. I took them home.

The Maltese Falcon met my private test for excellence: I wished I had written it. *The Thin Man* troubled me. I found it hard to believe this book had been written by the same man. I kept this opinion to myself, of course. With Arthur Kober's help I was seeing more of the author and liking him. I felt uncomfortable about not liking his last book. It would have been disloyal to voice doubts about something that was apparently universally admired and, in view of the series of motion pictures that flowed from the book, a huge financial success. Besides, after I read the three intervening novels, I felt I knew what was wrong with the last one.

The first four novels were all western in locale, centered mainly—*The Maltese Falcon* totally—in and around San Francisco. They had a sense of place that made almost physical contact with the reader, so that you felt you had been born and raised and spent your life on the streets the author brought to life. *The Thin Man* dealt with New York, a place where I had actually been born and raised and spent my life. In Hammett's pages the streets of New York seemed askew. The sense of place in *The Thin Man* was not unlike that of a travel book by a writer who had passed through on a hurried visit and later fleshed out his recollections by referring to guidebooks. It was the difference between Dickens's *American Notes* and his *Martin Chuzzlewit*. The former is an artist's sketchbook, the latter the finished masterpiece he painted when he came home and settled down to distill the essence of his art from the raw sketches made on the run.

I felt, however, as I still feel: a writer should be judged by his best work, not his poorest. Besides, I was beginning to think of this writer as a friend. I felt then, and I feel now, that a writer's faults should not be pointed out by his friends. Certainly not in public, and probably not even when he asks. Furthermore, this particular friend was at the peak of his career. The work on which I assumed he was engaged was bound to be at least as good as his earlier fine performances. It could not help being better than his last.

Furthermore, by this time Arthur Kober had introduced me to his ex-wife. Like any Winchell reader, I knew she and Dashiell Hammett were an "item." Like all inhabitants of a Winchell item, they were obviously on the verge of ankling to the altar. I have never been impressed by historical novels in which the hero is a young schmuck from the provinces named, let us say, Julien, who meets a foreign ambassador named, let us say, Benjamin Franklin, and the author begins his next chapter with: "Little did Julien know that . . ."

I am not a young schmuck anymore. Even when I was, I was not so dumb or, as we used to say on East Fourth Street, *pas si fou*. I knew as well as any reader of the New York *Mirror* the name of the girl who inhabited Winchell's item with Dashiell Hammett. I saw it as my duty to a friend, however, to cheer them on, and not cause distress by opening my big trap with totally unsolicited remarks about a friend's work. I did my duty. I kept my mouth shut.

Doing my duty provided one of the most enjoyable periods of my life. Soon after I met Peggy I introduced her to Hammett. I gathered almost at once that he approved of us. He started to inject Yiddish words into his conversation in our presence. Peggy, however, was fussy about language. I did not realize she had learned any Yiddish from me until, in our presence, Hammett referred to Hemingway as a smuck.

"I think you mean schmuck," Peggy said.

"I mean he's a horse's ass," Hammett said.

"In that case the proper word is putz," Lillian Hellman said.

"Is it?" Peggy said to me.

"I'm not sure," I said.

I knew a schmuck from a putz, but I knew something more important. Contradicting Lillian was not a rewarding activity.

"But in certain cases it is," I added diplomatically.

"Hemingway is such a case," Lillian said.

That ended that subject, as in her house many did. Hardscrabble Farm was a pleasant place, especially when Hammett was in residence. He brought out the best in Lillian, who was a superb hostess even when he was not around, but Peggy and I liked it better when he was.

Once, in one of those dangerous moments when people, who as a rule are sensibly reticent, find themselves trading unbuttoned biographical assessments, Lillian asked me if I knew what made her tick.

"No," I lied. "What makes you tick?"

"Piss and vinegar," she said.

If you were around her for any length of time, it helped to know that. What helped most, however, was Hammett. His presence diluted hers. Their feeling for each other, which was never overtly sentimental, was almost palpable the moment you came in the door. During a period of about two years, before and after our marriage, Peggy and I came in that door so often, especially for weekends, that we began to feel like members of the family. After the war, by which time we were parents living in Westport, the visits were less frequent but no less enjoyable. Hammett was extraordinary with children. He never hunched over the handlebars. Just being in his presence seemed to warm them. I have color film shot at Hardscrabble when Jeff and John were four and five that record his casually painstaking efforts to teach them how to row a boat and bait a hook. Even today, almost forty years later, I can see clearly in the two small faces on the screen what I felt that day in Arthur Kober's apartment when I saw Hammett for the first time: the desire of my sons for this remarkable man's approval. I have no doubt that much of this same feeling was at the core of Lillian's feeling for him. She always wanted to bait that hook the perfect way, and in his presence there was only one way to do that: Hammett's way. I was so fascinated by their relationship that, in order to get it straight in my mind, I put them into a novel. In *The Sound of Bow Bells* I arranged what I knew from my own observation with what I guessed could be the only plausible reasons for the gaps that were otherwise inexplicable. I know life is not neat, but I can't help being annoyed that it is not. When I stumble into a chance to tidy it up a bit, I never walk away from the lucky opportunity. It is one of the rewards of living a life of the mind.

One weekend at Hardscrabble, when Lillian was working on the script of a movie for Goldwyn that was released as *North Star*, I came down early on Sunday morning. It was not early for me. I always get out of bed at five. But there had been a party the night before and it did not break up until late. It was after midnight when Dash and I were emptying ashtrays and carrying glasses out to the kitchen and Lillian was saying good night to her guests out on the driveway. Leaving Peggy asleep in the guest room, I was pretty sure, as I tiptoed down the stairs to the kitchen to make coffee, that I was the only one in the house who was awake. Halfway down the stairs I heard voices. I stopped and listened. Lillian and Dash were talking in the living room. Wondering whether I should continue on down to the kitchen or turn and go back up to the guest room, I became aware of something in their voices that sounded familiar. I pushed things around in my head and remembered.

Lillian and Dash were talking to each other in a way that reminded me of the time in Hollywood when Sidney Skolsky brought me into Jack Warner's office. I had never heard businessmen, not even in my days with Mr. Geschwind on Seventh Avenue, sound the way Sidney and Jack Warner sounded when they were discussing Bette Davis's contract demands. Not even at a creditors' committee meeting. In the cold, hard, impersonal tones of a couple of workmen calling off measurements to each other as they prepared to cover a basement floor with linoleum. A few moments went by before I realized Lillian and Dash were discussing a snag in the *North Star* screenplay.

He had apparently made a suggestion for solving the problem. She did not like the suggestion. Why not? She told him. She was disliking it for the wrong reasons, he said, now listen again. He laid it out once more: a, b, c, d. Like a hammer tapping in the tacks to hold down the linoleum. Pause. No, Lillian said. Without impatience. Without irritation. But with unmistakable firmness. Exactly like his. Both voices hard, clear, and impersonal. Both starting again from the beginning.

It was not like any story conference I had attended in Jerry Wald's office. Neither of the two people in the living room below me was trying to make a score. It was clear that it mattered to neither who came up the winner. What mattered was breaking the snag.

I thought of afternoons in Arthur Kober's apartment, trying to help him with a plot. I thought of my own grim periods of marking time, waiting for the festering block to erupt. I envied the two workmen downstairs. They had obviously devised a better method than Arthur's or mine.

When we gathered for lunch I had a feeling that they had licked the problem. They were both telling funny stories about working in Hollywood. While I was out in the kitchen getting more ice Lillian came in to check on whatever it was she had going in the oven.

"Was that story true?" I said. "About Herman Mankiewicz and the *Citizen Kane* script?"

Lillian giggled.

"Dash never lies about Orson Welles," she said.

"You sound as though you enjoy working on screenplays," I said.

"I hate it," she said. "The only way I can get through the damn things is pretend I'm working on something that really matters. I do the scene the way I hear the people talking in my head. Then Dash puts in the dissolves and the fades and the jump cuts and all the rest of that Hollywood shit."

When it came to social life at Hardscrabble he put in more than that. I remember one weekend when the four of us were lying around on the porch in a pleasant torpor, not talking much, content to allow our digestive juices to work without interruption on one of Lillian's superb lunches, when suddenly we were in the middle of a cops-and-robbers break-in scene from a Mack Sennett comedy.

Accompanied by the nasty bark of a horn that Hammett, who knew everything, later identified as a Klaxon, a long, black Cadillac limousine came roaring up the driveway. It stopped so suddenly, like a racing greyhound pulled up in full flight by a choke chain, that what Hammett later called the tonneau rocked as though on the verge of a somersault. The front doors slammed open. From behind the wheel and out of the other front seat leaped two big, heavyset, scowling men. They wore double-breasted black suits and black snap-brim felt hats. In my aston-ishment there was room for a moment of special surprise: the men were not holding guns. With swift glances they raked the shrubbery on both sides, glowered at the screened porch door, then moved back to the car and opened both rear doors.

From one side stepped a short dumpling of a man, also dressed in black, but his hat was a Homburg. From the other, in a sort of shambling, sidestepping slithery motion that did not seem to involve the use of feet, as though she was rolling herself out of the vehicle, came a fat woman so totally shapeless that I wondered how I had identified her as a woman until I saw her smile. It was captivating in an old-fashioned Pola Negri sort of way, except that she was a faded blonde and there was nothing of the vamp about her. She looked like the middle-aged barmaid in the local pub at Bletchley who had been the wife of the owner. By the time I had this all sorted out, Lillian had stepped down from the porch and greeted the fat couple with cheek kisses. The two men wearing black snap-brim felt hats got back into the car and sat impassively on the front seat, arms folded across their chests, glaring straight ahead while Lillian introduced Peggy and Dash and me to Maxim Litvinov, the then Soviet ambassador in Washington, and his wife Ivy.

He spoke no English. Not during his stay on Lillian's porch, anyway. His wife babbled English almost without pause in a Cockney singsong. I remembered from the newspaper accounts published at the time Litvinov was appointed ambassador that he had met his wife in England, where he lived in exile for many years after he fled from Russia following the revolution of 1905. Mrs. Litvinov explained that they had been up in Tanglewood at the music festival, and the ambassador, to whom she referred as Himself, had expressed a desire to pause on the drive back to Washington for a visit with Lillian. It lasted seventy-two minutes. I timed it.

It puzzles me now that I did. The only sensible explanation is that forty years ago I was a different person. This was a time in my life when I was very self-conscious about how I had chosen to spend it, and my East Fourth Street training kept cautioning me not to spend it wastefully. The world around me, I had read somewhere, was the writer's oyster. There were obviously a lot of writers around but, apparently, only one oyster. I kept worrying about missing out on my share. Over and over again, no matter where I was or what I was doing, that sharp East Fourth Street poke in the ribs would catch me up and start hissing in my ear.

"Stop daydreaming. Pay attention. This is something important. Try to remember everything you see and hear. There could be a story in this."

I tried hard that day at Hardscrabble, and I remember all

of it, but the story escaped me. The difficulty, I think, was not the language barrier so much as the way we were distributed on the porch. In making room for the ambassador and his wife we found ourselves broken up into three couples on three couches. It was as though a director had distributed us on a stage for a scene in a drawing-room comedy. Lillian and I were side by side on a couch at the left. Peggy and Hammett were side by side on a couch at the right. In between, the ambassador and his wife also sat side by side, on a third couch that faced what in a theatre would have been the audience but, at Hardscrabble, was Lillian's huge blue spruce. As soon as the dialogue started it was plain who was going to control it.

Lillian said, "Was it a good program?"

Ivy Litvinoff said, "I didn't think it was much, a bit heavy on the Mozart for my taste, but let's find out what Himself has to say."

She then directed a stream of Russian at her husband that I found it difficult to believe was not more than a translation of Lillian's five-word question. Litvinov listened with a patient, faintly amused fat man's smile, looking not unlike the man in the Admiration cigar ads. When his wife finished he hosed her down with a stream of Russian more enveloping and much longer than hers. When he finished Ivy Litvinov turned to us.

"No," she said.

"No what?" Lillian said.

"No, Himself doesn't think it was a very satisfying program," Ivy Litvinov said. "Himself is not particularly fond of music. Himself would like to know what Mr. Hammett does."

"You know what Mr. Hammett does," Lillian said. "Tell him."

Mrs. Litvinov did, in Russian. Again the explanation seemed much too long. When she finished the ambassador embarked on another long speech, again delivered through the amused fat man's smile.

"What did he say?" Lillian said.

"Himself wants to know what the young man does," Ivy Litvinov said.

Lillian started to answer but I stopped her. I remembered

386

that the newspaper stories had reported Litvinov was a Jew named Wallach who had changed his name after he joined the Social Democratic Party.

"Let me try it," I said.

"I didn't know you speak his language," Lillian said.

"I don't," I said. "But he may speak mine."

I told the ambassador in Yiddish what I did for a living. As he listened Litvinov smiled and nodded, as though he was reading a favorable report card that a young member of the family had just brought home from school. When I finished he replied in Yiddish.

Sharply, Ivy Litvinov said, "What did Himself say?"

"He said I don't look like a writer," I said.

Ivy Litvinov giggled.

"That's because Himself thinks writers have to be good-looking," she said. "Himself believes that anybody seeing Turgenev or Pushkin for the first time would know at once they were good writers because they were such handsome men."

Lillian laughed and said, "As handsome as Dash?"

Ivy Litvinov looked at Hammett with suddenly narrowed eyes, as though she was trying to guess his weight. Dash squirmed on the couch, crossed and recrossed his long legs with obvious embarrassment, and the blush that worked its way out of his open collar and across his face made it clear he was not happy. Peggy laughed and gave him a reassuring pat.

"Go ahead," Lillian said to the ambassador's wife. "Ask him."

Mrs. Litvinov went at it again. Her husband listened, chuckling slightly, as though he was pleased with the situation he had created. When his wife finished he launched into his reply, chuckling all through it. By the time he finished, his wife seemed to be in a state of shocked disbelief. She muttered something irritably. Litvinov shrugged and laughed softly. He replied with a touch of emphasis that seemed to indicate he was disagreeing with something she had said. When he finished, Ivy Litvinov rolled her eyes to the heavens and shrugged with a gesture of helplessness.

"What did he say?" Lillian said.

"Himself says he means no offense," Ivy Litvinov said.

"Himself agrees Mr. Hammett is not an unattractive man, but Himself believes there is only one truly handsome man among us."

"Who?" Peggy said quickly.

Ivy Litvinov nodded toward Peggy's husband. Clearly astonished—but no more astonished than I was—Lillian gave me a look. I knew that look. She was checking to make sure everybody in the cast was talking about the same character. Then she turned to Hammett.

"Did you hear that?" she said.

"Yes, but it loses something in the translation," Hammett said.

On another occasion Lillian and Peggy drove to the village for some spices Lillian wanted for preparing the turtle Dash had caught in one of his traps. He and I were left alone on the porch. We were talking about James Gould Cozzens, to whose work I had introduced Hammett. Dash said he didn't care for Cozzens' politics but he admired his technique.

"He has an instinct that's always the tip-off when you're in the hands of a good writer," Hammett said.

"What's that?" I said.

"He knows when to stop," Hammett said.

I'm not quite sure why this gave me the courage to raise a subject that had been on my mind for a long time. Hammett was not a man you praised to his face. I never did, even though I managed to restrain myself on a number of occasions only by mentally clapping both hands over my big mouth. Neither was Hammett a man to whom you talked about his work. Nobody had to tell me about the first. I knew it the moment I met him. The second I arrived at more slowly, when the meaning of a few dates began to come together in my mind.

In 1937, when I met him, the publication of Hammett's last book was only three years behind him. The public, however, had apparently become accustomed to shorter intervals between his appearances in the bookstores. The columns were full of jokes about his laziness, tales of his drinking bouts, and quotations from Bennett Cerf—he had given Hammett a $15,000 advance on a new novel, to be called *There Was a Young Man*—

about novelists who made a career out of writer's block. My own experience with the problem, while not extensive and never yet even close to being serious, had made me sensitive to the time lapse since Hammett's last performance. I sensed that the question I was so anxious to ask would not be well received, and I managed to keep my mouth shut. Until the day I found myself alone with him on the porch at Hardscrabble. He was in a good mood and, in discussing James Gould Cozzens, we had just been talking about something in which he was interested and knew a good deal about: technique. Before I could get my hands across my mouth I heard my voice.

"You mind if I ask you a question?"

"Why should I?" Hammett said.

"It's about one of your books," I said.

There was no discernible change in his manner as Hammett said, "Which one?"

The Thin Man," I said.

The smile with which he surrounded the word "Shoot!" should have warned me. I think perhaps it did, but I'd been sitting on this question for a long time. Like the occasional snag in a story that I chose to treat by disregarding it until it was ready to emerge under its own power, so did this question.

"Around about page fifty in *The Thin Man,*" I said, "Nick Charles comes back to his hotel and finds that kid there, Gilbert Wynant. You know where I mean?"

"It's the place where they've just learned the kid's father tried to commit suicide in Allentown, Pennsylvania."

"That's right," I said, assuming from his effort to help me locate the exact place in the story that he was glad I'd raised the subject. "The kid's been a pain in the ass, wasting Nick Charles's time by asking a lot of silly questions about all kinds of things, and at this point he comes up with a question about cannibalism. Remember?"

"Of course, yes," Hammett said.

"Well, in order to get rid of the kid," I said, "anyway that's what it looks like to me, in order to get him out of the way, Nick Charles takes a book down from the shelf—"

"Duke's *Celebrated Criminal Cases of America,*" Hammett said.

"That's right," I said. "And he turns to one of the cases—"

"Alfred G. Packer, the Maneater," Hammett said. "Who Murdered His Five Companions in the Mountains of Colorado, Ate Their Bodies and Stole Their Money."

"That's right," I said, delighted with the way he was responding to what I had been assuming for so long he would find annoying. "Nick Charles gives the book to the boy and puts him in the corner of the room to read it, so he, Nick Charles, can talk without interruption to the boy's sister, Dorothy Wynant. While the reader is involved with the scene between Dorothy Wynant and Nick Charles, the boy sits there in the corner of the room reading. What puzzles me is this. I can understand the device of giving him the book, because it shuts the boy up so Nick Charles can be free to have the scene with the sister, but what I don't understand, and I've read this part of the book several times, what I can't figure out is why you quote the whole Alfred G. Packer story in full?"

The sudden silence on the porch was my first hint that perhaps I had made a mistake after all.

"What I mean is," I said, talking faster, "I don't understand why we, the reader, I mean, why we have to know the entire Alfred G. Packer story. It has absolutely nothing to do with *The Thin Man* story which we, the reader, I mean, which we're following."

Silence. I could hear my heart making noises. I became aware of the breeze rustling through the enormous beautiful blue spruce that faced the porch. I wished I was dead.

"What I mean is," I said, not quite desperately, but aware that I was beginning to sweat, "I mean the author must have had some purpose, you must have wanted to convey something to us, the reader, I mean, but I can't figure it out. After all," I said with relief, as though I had reached the conclusion of a brilliantly conceived and beautifully delivered argument, "it runs to over two thousand words, the Alfred G. Packer story, I mean, and that's a lot of words, isn't it? If it has no purpose in *The Thin Man* story, I mean? I mean I'm sure it has a purpose, but I can't figure it out, so I was wondering if you . . ."

My wondering ground to a halt. The faint breeze moving

390

through the blue spruce was beginning to sound like a police whistle. Hammett laughed and shrugged.

"Oh, hell," he said, waving his hand in a gesture of dismissal. "I had a word count on the book, and when I finished the damn thing I found myself twenty-two hundred words short, so I took down the first thing I could find on the shelf, which happened to be the Duke book, and I flipped it open, and the Alfred G. Packer section seemed just the right length, so I put it in. Ah, here come the ladies with their spices. Let's go see if our turtle will like what they've brought."

He stood up and went down to the car. I did not follow. I have never felt like cutting my throat. Even in my worst moments of depression, when things have looked so black that thoughts of self-destruction may have crossed my mind as a possible solution, they have never lingered long, and the idea of doing it by cutting my throat never even got a chance to linger. It is too untidy. My ingenuity, I felt sure, would be equal to coming up with a method less painful and more neat. Nevertheless, if there ever was such a moment in my life it was on the porch at Hardscrabble on that day when I was left alone with my thoughts and that Goddamned blue spruce.

I knew I had done something stupid. I had invaded the fiercely guarded privacy of a sensitive man. All at once I could see what his life had been like during all those years since 1934 when *The Thin Man*, his last book, had been published. The first four books had been written in San Francisco when he was young and unknown and still sharpening the tools of his craft. Then he had exploded out of obscurity onto the New York literary scene. When I met him he showed no signs of not enjoying every moment of it. No signs, at any rate, that I was aware of. I was myself so dazzled to be in his presence that I never gave him a thought that was more complicated than admiration, which, of all the emotions, must surely be the most irritatingly simpleminded to anybody but a simpleton.

Looking back on it, I see that, during my early contacts with Hammett, I was no different from the autograph hounds who hang around stage doors. That moment on the porch at Hardscrabble was a watershed. Thinking about it later I saw a stricken man, an artist whose talent had not played fair with him. It must have been a horror to discover that his gift had abandoned him when he was just beginning to feel its full power. The autograph seekers clamoring at the stage door did not, of course, even suspect the existence of the horror. The idol they were showering with adulation was a man who had come to the end of the road, a man who was never going to write another book, and the ironic twist was that he was the only one in the whole world who knew it. He was a star who could not sneak offstage to lick his wounds or take up some new identity and bury himself in an obscure career elsewhere, the way I suddenly remembered several of the characters in his stories had solved their not dissimilar problems. He could not escape. He could not, as he once expressed it, open his fingers wide and see his fist vanish. It was not his style to turn and run. He was caught and frozen into immobility by the spotlight at stage center. He had to go on living the role of the admired and envied, one of what Noël Coward in a sliver of autobiography had christened destiny's tots.

Lillian must have known all along, or certainly for a long time, what I grasped later, like a comic strip character over whose head a balloon erupts with the word "Boing!" It seemed to me this was the explanation for the seriousness with which she treated Hammett's insatiable lust for knowledge. She never stopped talking, always with admiration, about his endless, totally unchanneled reading. As though this was the explanation for his failure to continue producing books, she made a virtue of the indiscriminate reading, using his hunger to acquire the knowledge of everything—from archery and how to build a swimming pool to the life of insects and higher mathematics—to prove the point she made over and over again: he was an intellectual, better than the common run of men, absorbed in the pursuit of something far more important than the fabrication of stories: the meaning of life itself.

Lillian may have believed what she was saying, but I doubt it. She was too smart. I think she knew he was finished, but she loved him too much to let anybody know she knew it, above all Hammett himself. I liked him enormously and, as a writer aware of the disease that hangs as a threat over all writers and by which he had been struck down while he was still in his green years, I felt deeply for him. I was, however, a boy from East Fourth Street. I knew that the lust for acquiring all the world's knowledge was neither unique with intellectuals nor the explanation for withdrawing from the world's work. It is a universal desire, a natural instinct, like the creativity of children, which exudes charm but only rarely has anything to do with genuine talent, and it comes early, arriving simultaneously with the child's desire to make pictures with finger paints.

I could see Hammett at seven or eight, clutching his first borrower's card, standing in the Saturday-morning line on the front steps of the Hamilton Fish Park Branch of the New York Public Library, waiting for the doors to open, poised for the race against the other kids to the shelf through which he was working his way alphabetically in his hunger to absorb it all. I could see the young Hammett on that line, but only in my mind. In actual fact, of course, he had not been there. Maybe, if he'd been born on East Fourth Street, he might have been. But Dashiell Hammett was born in St. Mary's County, Maryland. Eventually, of course, he got to the equivalent of that line but, as somebody has observed in another connection, that was in another country, and besides the wench was dead. Hammett should have met her when the kids of East Fourth Street met her. He would have got her out of his system before, in his desperation, he turned to her as a sick man, hoping to ease his pain in the frantic acquisition of perhaps worthy but in the end useless knowledge. As Casey Stengel used to say about the frustration of trying to produce a viable batting order by juggling hitters who could not hit because you did not have enough men on the team who could: "You can't hide them!" Not from another good player, anyway. And Dashiell Hammett, in his short prime, was one of the best.

On the porch at Hardscrabble I felt so sorry for him that some time went by before I realized the person for whom I was really feeling sorry was me. I knew damn well I couldn't repair the damage I had done Hammett, so I turned my attention to figuring out how I could repair the damage I had done myself.

I stood up and went out to the kitchen. Lillian was dicing something on a chopping board. She always looked reassuring in a kitchen. It was like stumbling on Genghis Khan trying to zip a baby into its jammies. Some of my courage came back.

"Where's everybody?" I said.

"Dash took Peggy down to the lake for another look at that fucking turtle," Lillian said. "We have to use this marvelous sauce on a stupid chicken."

"I just did something dumb," I said.

She gave me a quick look, knife poised over the chopping board.

"You want to talk about it?" she said.

I told her what had happened on the porch. She listened with a deep frown. The intensity of her absorption did nothing to raise my spirits. I could see from her face that my analysis of what I had done was not too far off the mark. When I finished she looked down at the mess on the chopping board and pushed the stuff around with her hand for a few moments, still scowling. Then, unexpectedly, she burst into a giggle.

"He really said that?" she said.

I stared at her in astonishment. I'm still not sure why. It was certainly not the reaction I had expected. She must have understood my confusion. Her grin disappeared.

"I mean about the word count?" she said.

"That's exactly what he said," I said with a touch of irritation. "You don't think I'd make up a thing like that?"

"No, of course not," Lillian said. "It just seems too silly."

"Of course it's silly," I said. "I never heard of anybody getting a word count from his publisher on the number of words he expects him to put into a novel."

"Neither have I," Lillian said.

It was my first hint that perhaps Hammett had invented the explanation on the spot, to get out of the awkward moment in which a passing dumbbell had trapped him.

"You were with him when he was writing *The Thin Man*," I said. "Did you ever hear him say anything about a word count?"

Lillian did not answer my question. She may not have heard it. I could see from her face, from the way she was pushing the mess on the chopping board into a central mound with the flat of the knife, that she was rethinking her thoughts. I'd seen her do that before. She seemed to find it helpful. Then she broke the silence with another giggle.

"You know, that's very naughty of Dash," she said. She sounded as though she was excusing a child for an attempt to escape punishment for an indiscretion by inventing a lie so outrageous that he knew no adult would believe him. "He really shouldn't say things like that," Lillian said.

It was all she did say. By the time Peggy and Dash got back from the lake with the news that the turtle—which Dash had hacked out of its shell—was crawling with some kind of revolting parasite and we'd better begin planning to have something less exotic for dinner, Hammett seemed to have forgotten the incident on the porch. I knew, of course, that he had not, and I knew Lillian had not. A window had been blown open inadvertently on something neither of them wanted to see. Of the three people involved, Hammett, of course, handled it best. Why not? He knew more about it. With luck the other two would never have to know more than they already did.

twenty-eight

When I was in my last year at De Witt Clinton High School the autobiography of Rudyard Kipling was running serially in the *New York Times*. It was called *Something of Myself for Friends Known and Unknown*. From this absorbing story this unknown friend remembers only one line:

"Always flee from a success."

The reason these five words stick in my memory is that, while I thought then and still think now the advice is sound, I felt then and have more reason to feel now it is incomplete. Flee where? From *"Gunga Din"* to *Captains Courageous?* Try telling that to Emily Brontë when *Wuthering Heights* hit the best-seller lists, and she was trying desperately to think of an idea for her next book.

In 1958 I published *The Enemy Camp*, my eleventh novel. It was a Book-of-the-Month Club selection, a best seller, and—counting three volumes of short stories and two collections of travel essays—my sixteenth published book. Wondering what I was going to do next, I remembered Kipling's advice. Before I could reach a decision I had a phone call from Hal Prince. He and his friend Bobbie Griffith were then (as Robert L. Griffith and Harold S. Prince) the most successful new production team that had surfaced on the Broadway scene since the end of the war. They had produced, in what is known on Times Square as rapid succession, *The Pajama Game*, *Damn Yankees*, and *West Side Story*. Hal told me on the phone that he and Bobbie had just obtained rights to do a musical play about the life of Fiorello La Guardia. Would I be interested in writing the book?

I had never, of course, written the book for a musical. It occurred to me, however, that I had never written a short story before I sent "Anything for a Laugh" to George Jean Nathan's *American Spectator*, nor had I ever written a novel before I sent *I Can Get It for You Wholesale* to Dick Simon's Simon & Schuster. As I held the phone to my ear with Hal Prince at the other end, into my mind came the page from Kipling's *Something of Myself for Friends Known and Unknown* in which, when I was still in high school, had appeared the five words of advice that had stuck in my mind.

The opportunity Hal Prince had just offered was not "*Gunga Din*" to *Captains Courageous*, but it was *The Enemy Camp* to another area of New York life that I knew the way Emily Brontë knew the Yorkshire moors.

"Drop a hat," I said to Hal Prince on the phone.

While the contracts were being put together I started hunting for a story among my recollections of growing up in New York during the years when Fiorello La Guardia was the dominant figure on the political scene. I found that my memories kept going back to the years long before he became mayor, the days when Fiorello was a congressman from Greenwich Village before we entered World War I, and I was a four-year-old in kindergarten at P.S. 188 on East Fourth Street. My memories of those early years were limited to the pictures of Fiorello that appeared regularly on the front pages of the *Jewish Daily Forward* and the comments I heard at home. These comments, which passed over my head at the supper table between my father and mother, were highly favorable. I did not realize until years later that this was extraordinary. My father and mother were socialists. Fiorello La Guardia was a Republican. Republicans were to our family what the Hatfields were to the McCoys. Fiorello La Guardia, however, was the great exception. New York at that time was so tightly controlled by Tammany Hall, the Democratic seat of local power, that the only way La Guardia could fight them was by running on the Republican ticket. Years later, even though the legislation he introduced in Congress as a Republican proved to be the blueprint for Franklin Delano Roosevelt's New Deal, La Guardia the Republican was driven out of office by FDR's 1932 Democratic landslide sweep of the country. When La Guardia decided in 1933 to run for mayor, therefore, he had to do it on a Fusion ticket. For the next twelve years, during his three terms in office, he dominated the New York political scene the way the New York Yankees dominated the sports scene. In my mind he remains as inseparable from the days of my nonage as Clara Bow and Jack Dempsey. And yet, when I tried to dig out of my recollections the ingredients for my story, only two things loomed up as inescapably characteristic.

One, Fiorello La Guardia had been incapable of staying away from a fire, so that almost every day the front pages showed a new picture of the familiar squat, rotund figure encased in a floor-length black fireman's raincoat, surmounted by a fire chief's white helmet, standing in the middle of a four-alarmer shouting directions to the men manning the hoses and the policeman directing traffic. And, two, during one of the city's crippling newspaper-delivery strikes he had kept the kids of New York in touch with what was happening to Harold Teen, Dick Tracy, Winnie Winkle, and Andy Gump by reading the comic strips aloud to them on radio station WNYC every Sunday morning, thus creating an indelible image that penetrated to the far corners of the world. I remember being asked about Fiorello La Guardia in London, Paris, Bombay, Kuala Lumpur, Singapore, and Australia.

By conducting a Gallup poll of my own I made the astonishing discovery that these were the two things most of my contemporaries remembered about this compelling figure out of my youth. How to make a play of them?

I turned, as any citizen who claimed East Fourth Street as his own his native land would have turned, to the New York Public Library. I discovered that, just before his death, La Guardia had published the first volume of what he had planned as a three-volume autobiography. An hour after I took the book down from the shelf I found my story. The first volume dealt with the period of Fiorello's life that, except for a few of his intimates, was almost totally unknown to the public at large: his youth.

I met him only once, early in the war, before I went overseas, when I was a member of a Writers War Board committee. I don't remember what the committee was organized to do but I remember that, like so many committees, the first meeting of this one began when somebody asked, "Does anybody here know the mayor?" Beatrice Kaufman, wife of George S. Kaufman and chairman of our committee, did. The committee's next meeting was at City Hall. When we were led into the mayor's office, the familiar figure looked up from his desk and—in the familiar, squeaky, nasal voice—bellowed, "Bea, did you and George ever get that Mary Astor thing straightened out?"

I seem to recall that they did, but I saw no place for the incident in the play Hal Prince and Bobbie Griffith were looking for. We found it because I was lucky in my collaborators. Jerry Bock and Sheldon Harnick—who went on to write the score for, among many others, *Fiddler on the Roof*—took to the Fiorello legend the way all the participants did as soon as they made contact with the project. This included George Abbott, who, when he started putting the cast through its paces, was either seventy-three or seventy-four. Nobody seemed to be sure of the number, and nobody had the temerity to ask.

Watching George Abbott work was, I found, like watching Jack Dempsey go after the other man in the ring. He never hesitated. He always knew what he wanted, said so clearly, and kept the performer at it until he got it right. I watched him from the place where, before rehearsals got under way, he told me he always wanted me to be when he was working: in the row behind him, two seats to his left.

"I don't like anybody on top of me," he said. "But when I want you for something I want you to be there."

It was, of course, an order. Which I, of course, obeyed. I had only recently learned that it was part of the loosely defined—but in the theatre clearly understood—process of collaboration. Until I started to publish stories in *The New Yorker* the word "collaboration" had been for me no more than a word in the dictionary. When I received my first set of galleys from the magazine, and I realized that my editor had felt he had the right in the name of the publication for which he worked to ask me to make corrections in my story, my reaction included a not imperceptible amount of resentment at what struck me as an intrusion on my rights. This feeling of resentment vanished, of course, with the realization that, if I refused to help the editors fashion my story more closely to the sort of product they wanted to see in their magazine, they could refuse to purchase my story. By the time I moved on to writing novels my reaction to editorial suggestions changed in degree but not in kind: they still felt somewhat like intrusions on my rights as an artist, and I use the word "artist" as advisedly as I use the word "somewhat." My differences with the editors of my novels, however, were in the main matters of opinion, and I was fortunate in the people with whom I had these differences. Harsh words never intruded, tempers never flared. Almost immediately after I started to work in the theatre I realized that the word "collaboration" had emerged from the dictionary and taken its place at my worktable. I was not the only one who had to shove over to make room for the intruder. In the case of *Fiorello!* there were, to begin with, three of us: Jerry Bock the composer, Sheldon Harnick the lyricist, and me.

As soon as we reached agreement on the general story line we separated to work on our contributions to the telling of our story, and met at regular intervals to see how our story was coming along. These sessions were usually held in Hal Prince's apartment on East Sixty-ninth Street. The meetings were pleasantly informal but rigidly held on course by the agreed-upon story line. My first major lesson in this for me new form of collaboration came at the first joint session. I handed out copies of the first scene to everybody in the room and then read it aloud. The last line I uttered was: "Fiorello now sings a song about the way he feels."

Dead silence. I looked at the faces by which I was surrounded. None reflected what I sensed was a major flaw in what I had written. None but Jerry Bock, who smiled gently and said quietly, "What we'd like to know before we write the song, Jerry, is exactly how at this point in the story Fiorello feels."

What I had left out was what I never would have left out in

400

a short story or a novel: the character's reaction to the scene the author had just put him through. I explained to my collaborators that I had left it out in the scene I had just read aloud because I did not want the lyricist and composer to feel I was impinging on their terrain.

"Unless you impinge in your way," Sheldon Harnick said, "we can't stay on course with you as you tell the story in your way."

"Boing!" I said, and told them what I'd had in mind when I ended the scene with "Fiorello now sings a song about the way he feels."

At our next meeting, and all the meetings that followed, when my scene came to the "Fiorello now sings" point, included between the parentheses that followed was a detailed description of the emotions flowing from the scene that caused him to break into song. By the time we had on paper a finished script, with score and libretto completely integrated, I felt I had learned my job as a collaborator in the musical theatre. Then George Abbott joined the project as director, and my comprehension of the meaning of the word "collaboration" in the theatre expanded with dramatic abruptness.

"It's always a moment that has a certain amount of sadness in it," Jerry Bock told me, undoubtedly sensing the feelings I was trying to conceal. "Up to now the thing has belonged to us, we created it. Now it's almost as though it's being taken away from us, turned over to those who must get it in front of an audience."

It was the difference between putting something down on paper and setting it up on stage. After that initial moment of sadness I sensed soon enough what I could see Jerry Bock and Sheldon Harnick from previous experience already understood. The collaboration process did not stop with the beginning of rehearsals. Things the collaborators had set down on paper to their complete satisfaction did not always satisfy the director. I had never before given much if any thought to the director's task. During the time I watched George Abbott mount *Fiorello!* and tried to carry out his editorial orders, I thought of little else.

I remembered what, years before *Fiorello!*, Somerset Maugham told me about directors. He distrusted them. In the English theatre of his day they were known as producers. He did not mind their suggestions. Or so he said after his day in the theatre was done. What he minded, Maugham said, was the director's insistence that his suggestion was an order he would not have had to issue if the author had been skillful enough to write the scene the way the director, if he had been a writer, would have written it in the first place.

"Like most people who have very few ideas," said Maugham, whose work indicates clearly that he was not one of these people, "the director tends to put great store by the one or two ideas that do on occasion come to his mind."

I don't think Maugham would have had this feeling if he had worked with George Abbott. What Abbott set great store by, I soon saw, was only the idea that worked on stage. He didn't care where it came from. It came from him often enough to blunt the edge of any discomfort that might be felt by the collaborators who have worked with him to produce the script he had signed on to direct. Caught up totally in doing his job, Abbott had very little time to waste on social niceties. He reminded me of an artist in front of a canvas he had contracted to complete before a difficult, often impossible, deadline. His tools were a palette and a brush. On the palette he placed an assortment of blobs of paint. To the world at large these blobs were known as a composer, a lyricist, a librettist, a costume designer, a set designer, a choreographer, an orchestra, a conductor, a musical arranger, as well as the performers. Getting all these complex elements up on that canvas, always with the sound of the inexorable beating of that clock in his ears, using nothing but that single brush—the concept inside his head—it is no wonder that, when he felt the need for a new blob of paint on his palette, he had no time to go seek it out himself or, on occasion, to remember to ask for it the way a guardsman in a Lehár operetta asks the countess for a dance.

"When I want you for something," he had told me during the first day of rehearsal in the banquet room of Al & Dick's Steak House on West Fifty-fourth Street, "I want you to be there."

402

The situation was not quite the same, of course, as fetching a Lou G. Siegel Special for Monroe Geschwind, but my role as a collaborator was identical. On the first day of rehearsals in New Haven, I was intensely aware of this. The set had arrived the day before. When the company got to New Haven the carpenters had just started setting it up. They worked all night. The next morning, when Abbott started putting the performers through their paces, they were working in something as new to them as it was to the collaborator who was watching them from two seats to Abbott's left in the row behind him. It was vastly different from working within chalk marks on the floor of the banquet room in Al & Dick's Steak House. The difference became bluntly clear to me during the rehearsal of a small scene near the end of Act I that I must have seen dozens of times at other rehearsals.

It involved moving a chorus boy offstage. He was a dancer who, for this scene, was doubling as a messenger who comes into Fiorello's office with a telegram. The scene consisted of three simple moves. The boy enters, he hands the telegram to Fiorello, and he exits. No dialogue. It was so simple that I could not understand why Abbott made the boy repeat it several times. Finally he swung his head to the left and spoke across his shoulder.

"What's he doing wrong?"

I didn't know and I was puzzled by my ignorance. The scene looked to me as it always had. I didn't think the actor was doing anything wrong. I suspected the problem was his lack of familiarity with the brand-new set. I had not, however, been asked for that kind of opinion.

"I don't know," I said.

"Neither do I," Abbott said with a scowl. "Let's try giving him a few words."

I thought for a moment.

" 'Telegram, sir, from Ben Marino,' " I said.

Abbott snapped his fingers.

"That'll do it," he said. He turned back to the stage. "Ron?"

"Yes, sir?" Ron Hussman said.

"Try this," Abbott said. "When you come in you say to Tom, 'Telegram, sir, from Ben Marino.' Tom, you take the telegram without a word and, while you're tearing it open, you, Ron, you make your exit without a word. Okay?"

"Yes, sir," Ron said.

"Tom?" Abbott said.

"Got it," Tom Bosley said.

"Try it," Abbott said.

They did. Abbott spoke across his shoulder.

"That better?"

I had been asked for an opinion.

"It doesn't seem so," I said.

Abbott didn't answer. He turned back to the stage.

"Let's try it again," he said.

It was tried three times.

"Ron?" Abbott said.

"Yes, sir?"

"Why do you keep rubbing your nose?" Abbott said.

"It's the coatrack," Ron said.

"What coatrack?" Abbott said.

"It's nailed to the wall just outside the door," Ron said. He pointed to the scenery door through which he had been making his exit. "It's dark out there, and I can't get around it, so I have to put my hand up over my face to keep from bumping into it, sir."

"Ruth!" Abbott bellowed.

Ruth Mitchell, the stage manager, erupted from the wings.

"Yes, Mr. Abbott?"

"What's that coatrack doing out there?"

"It's part of the previous set," Ruth said. "At the change, when the flat turns, everything on the wall turns with it including the coatrack."

"You mean it can't be moved?" Abbott said.

"Not without changing that part of the previous set, Mr. Abbott."

Abbott scowled down at the floor. He tugged his long chin. Everybody on stage, it seemed to me, was holding his or her breath, so I held mine. Abbott looked up and snapped his fingers.

"Let's get that line out of there," he said. "Ron?"

404

"Yes, sir?"

"Don't say anything," Abbott said. "Come in without a word, hand the telegram to Tom without a word, turn and make your exit without a word. Got it?"

"Yes, sir," Ron said.

"Tom?" Abbott said.

"Got it," Tom Bosley said.

"Okay, Ruth, thank you," Abbott said. "Let's go, everybody."

The rehearsal resumed. When we broke for lunch Abbott asked me to eat with him. We went across the street to Kaysey's. He studied the menu for a while then ordered the pancakes and sour cream with blueberries on the side.

"Do you like blueberries?" he said.

"Yes," I said.

"Good," Abbott said. "You can have mine."

"Don't you like blueberries?" I said.

"Can't stand them," Abbott said.

"Then why did you order them?" I said.

"They come with the pancakes," Abbott said. "I can't resist ordering everything that comes with what I'm paying for." He grinned impishly. "Neither can I see food I'm paying for go to waste. I've eaten here many times. The pancakes are wonderful, and you'll like the blueberries, so you won't have to order dessert."

When the blueberries arrived, and he shifted them to my plate, I had my courage up.

"You mind if I ask you something?" I said.

"Of course not," Abbott said.

"That scene when Ron Hussman brings in the telegram," I said. "The one that was giving you all that trouble?"

"What about it?" Abbott said.

"What made you do what you did?" I said.

"Indecision," he said.

I gave him a look of my own.

"You certainly didn't sound indecisive," I said.

"That was the point," Abbott said.

"What point?" I said.

405

"A director in the theatre is like a general in a battle," Abbott said. "He can afford to make every mistake in the book, he can even afford to make mistakes that haven't yet gotten into the book, but the one thing he can't afford to do under any circumstances is let his actors or his troops know he doesn't know what he's doing during every moment the battle is going on. In the theatre, as on the battlefield, being decisive is more important than being right. Ron Hussman had no idea that for some reason all of a sudden I didn't know how the dickens to get him offstage. I could have called Ruth earlier, of course, and asked what was wrong out there."

"Why didn't you?" I said.

"It would have damaged my reputation for infallibility," Abbott said with a grin. "This way I got my answer with no loss of face."

"What about Ron Hussman's nose?" I said.

Abbott forked up a piece of pancake, dipped it into the sour cream, gave the combination a short critical examination and, with the precision of a jeweler setting a gem into place on a diadem, he eased the loaded fork into his mouth.

"The inconvenience to Ron Hussman's nose is part of his training," Abbott said, chewing contentedly. "He'll get over it, and if he's got the makings of an actor he'll be a better actor for the experience."

Cushioning my impertinence with what I hoped was a disarming smile, I said, "Suppose Ron catches on how he gained this piece of experience?"

Abbott's right eye flicked in what could or could not have been a wink.

"Then some day when his acting days are over," Abbott said, "he may turn out to be a director."

I wondered if it was as simple as that. I've come to know quite a few directors. Some, naturally, are better than others. I became aware slowly that the good ones have more than talent. They have whatever it is people mean by the word "character." I know what I mean by it: a combination of traits, some not immediately discernible, all firmly embedded, that add up to making a person unique. Somebody who in many ways may

406

not be unlike many other people but who, in enough recogniz-
able ways, is clearly different from all other people. So that
whatever he or she does, especially in their work, bears his or
her signature as unmistakably as their fingerprints. I have had
this feeling about a number of people—Somerset Maugham, Miss
Merle S. Marine, Bennett Cerf, Fred Schwed, Jr., John O'Hara,
Elizabeth Ann (a.k.a. Peggy) Weidman, Richard Rodgers, Carl
Brandt, Harold Freedman, Major John Hackett—but I've never
felt it so strongly as I did with George Abbott.

The first rehearsals of *Fiorello!* were held in a banquet room
over a steak house on West Fifty-fourth Street called Al & Dick's.
The Weidman family was then living at One Gracie Terrace,
the last apartment house on the cul-de-sac in which East Eighty-
second Street ends before it plunges into the East River. Abbott was living in a co-op at Seventy-seventh Street and Fifth
Avenue. At the end of the first day of rehearsals, which was a
long one, I decided to treat myself to a taxi ride home. As I
stepped into a cab George Abbott came out of Al & Dick's.

"Going my way?" I called.

"Which is your way?" he said. I told him. He said, "You
could coast right past my door."

"Let's do that," I said.

It was a pleasant ride. I thought he'd want to talk about the
play but he surprised me by asking if I knew anything about
Ulysses S. Grant. I told him I had read Woodward's biography
called *Meet General Grant*. Abbott told me that, for his birthday,
his daughter Judy had given him a subscription to the Book-of-
the-Month Club, and the current selection was a new biography of General Grant.

"Is it good?" I said.

"I didn't know he drank," Abbott said.

It was the first hint I had about something of which I learned
later almost everybody in the English-speaking theatre was apparently aware: the director of *Fiorello!* was a teetotaler. The
way the hint was conveyed in the taxicab indicated that perhaps the director of *Fiorello!* was a teetotaler the way Tommy
Manville was a blonde fancier: both seemed to have a tendency
to overshoot the mark. Some time later, when I'd had more

407

experience with performers as well as blondes, I discovered that, while some were both, with none was it possible to overshoot the mark so far as teetotalism is concerned. It is better to spot a drunk before he or she signs for the part. So far as I know, George Abbott always did.

After a week of rehearsals above Al & Dick's the Broadway Theatre became available. The *Fiorello!* company moved into it. The stage door of the Broadway abutted on an attractive little Italian restaurant. On our first day at the Broadway Abbott called a staff luncheon conference. Eleven of us gathered around the largest round table the restaurant had available. While the waiter was distributing menus Abbott raised a forefinger in a gesture so commanding that all conversation ceased abruptly.

"Separate checks," he said to the waiter.

After lunch, when the waiter started to distribute the checks, Abbott's imperious forefinger again silenced the chattering table.

"I'll take my check and Mr. Weidman's," he said to the waiter.

The stares this brought my way called for immediate attention.

"Thanks, George," I said, "but you don't have to buy my lunch."

"Yes, I do," Abbott said firmly. "For a week you've been giving me free taxi rides home every day after rehearsal. I owe you something in exchange."

My taxi fares for the preceding seven days from Al & Dick's to Gracie Terrace by way of Seventy-seventh and Fifth had averaged $3.50 each. Seven times $3.50 comes to $24.50. Half of $24.50 is $12.25. My lunch check, including tip, which Abbott insisted on paying, came to $3.75. I applauded the touch of noblesse oblige. I raised an eyebrow at the arithmetic.

About people, however, I learned not to question Abbott's opinions. Not to his face, anyway. One day, when he was feeling energetic, he asked if I'd care to walk home with him. There were a few points about the script he wanted to discuss. One of them dealt with the end of the scene in which Fiorello learns his wife has died. Did I think it was too gloomy? I did not. To bolster my opinion I drew a parallel with a scene from *The*

Royal Family by Edna Ferber and George S. Kaufman. Abbott's response took me by surprise.

"Do you know Kaufman?" he said.

"Yes," I said.

"Do you like him?" Abbott said.

"Very much," I said.

"Why?" Abbott said.

The question was so obviously serious that I felt I had to treat it seriously. Saying George Kaufman was a nice guy or a very funny fellow would not, I felt, strike George Abbott as an adequate answer to his question. I forced myself into a few moments of silence as I considered why, aside from his being a nice guy and a very funny fellow, I liked George Kaufman.

"I like his attitude toward his work," I said finally.

"How do you mean?" Abbott said.

I told him about the time, when I was working for Max Schuster, Simon & Schuster was about to publish the autobiography of Dorothy Rice Sims, wife of P. Hal Sims, the famous bridge player. It was a very funny book called *Curiouser and Curiouser*. At a Simon & Schuster sales conference one of the salesmen pointed out that, while P. Hal Sims was a public figure, only a small circle of her friends knew Dorothy Rice. Dick Simon thought if we could get a famous person to write an introduction to the book, it would have a better chance. Max Schuster suggested George Kaufman because Dorothy Sims and Kaufman were regulars at the Knickerbocker Club bridge games, and Max asked me to approach Kaufman because he was aware that I knew the playwright. I called Kaufman. He said he'd be delighted to do it. I sent him a set of galleys. Three days later, without advance notice, he walked into the Simon & Schuster office, asked to see me, and handed me three double-spaced typewritten pages.

"Thanks," I said. "I'll read it tonight."

"It's a thousand words," Kaufman said. "Read it now."

"I can't read with somebody watching me," I said.

"What do you do in the subway?" Kaufman said.

"I don't read manuscripts in the subway," I said. "I can't form an opinion if I'm being watched while I read."

"Your men's room free to all comers?" Kaufman said. "Or do I need a key?"

I gave him my key. I read the three pages. They were delightful. When Kaufman came back I told him so.

"Delightful," he said sourly. "There were cocksuckers who said that about what the Nazis did to the Reichstag."

"You want me to get another opinion?" I said.

"Get several," Kaufman said.

"All right, but I can't do it now," I said. "People have appointments. Some are out of the office. I may not get anybody today. I'll have to call you tomorrow."

When I did I had the opinions of Max Schuster, Dick Simon, Jack Goodman, Albert Leventhal, Maria Leiper, Lee Wright, and Quincy Howe. They all thought the introduction was delightful.

"I know Dick and Jack and Albert and Lee," Kaufman said. "I play bridge with them. How about the others?"

"Max and Maria and Quincy?" I said.

"What do they play?"

"So far as I know, nothing," I said. "You want me to ask them?"

"No, it's too late," Kaufman said. "Will you do me a favor?"

"Of course," I said.

"Will you see I get galleys on this thing?" Kaufman said.

"You'll get them," I said.

The day I sent them up to his house Kaufman walked into my office, again unannounced.

"I made a couple of changes," he said, handing me the galleys.

I scanned the sheets. In red ink he had crossed out the word "very" in the opening paragraph and, near the end of the last galley, he had inserted a serial comma.

"That okay?" he said when I looked up.

"Fine, yes," I said. "If that's the way you want it."

"What do you mean if that's the way I want it?" Kaufman said. "You guys are the publishers. I want it to be the way you want it."

"You've got it the way we want it," I said.

"You sure?" Kaufman said.

"Yes," I said.

"Honest?" Kaufman said.

"Honest," I said.

"When does the book go to press?" Kaufman said.

"Tomorrow," I said.

"So this is the last shot at making corrections?" Kaufman said.

"That's right," I said.

But it wasn't. At five o'clock he came into the office again. Could he have another look? I called Philip Van Doren Stern in the Production Department.

"Sure, yes," Phil said. "But it was just going to the printer. I'd better bring this to your office myself and wait."

He did. We both waited while Kaufman read the galleys again. When he finished he looked out the window for a few moments, then put the galleys down on his thigh, pulled out a fountain pen, unscrewed the cap, and made a small mark. When he handed the galleys back, Phil Stern and I both examined them. Kaufman had removed the serial comma.

"Is that all right?" he said.

"What about it, Phil?" I said.

He was the office authority on matters of style.

"Some people like the serial comma," he said. "Some people don't."

"I'm not some people," Kaufman said. "I'm one person who wants to get it right."

"We could call F.P.A.?" I said.

The conductor of "The Conning Tower" had for years been conducting a campaign in his *Herald Tribune* column calling for the universal use of the serial comma. He and Kaufman were members of the Algonquin Round Table. "F.P.A. would know," I said.

"Fuck F.P.A.," Kaufman said. "Leave it out."

Years later, during rehearsals of *Fiorello!*, when George Abbott asked me why I liked George Kaufman, I related this anecdote.

"You mean that's why you like him?" Abbott said.

411

"Among other reasons," I said.

"What do you find likable in that incident?" Abbott said.

"It shows a man who takes his writing seriously," I said.

"He was doing a favor for a friend," George Abbott said. "He wasn't getting paid for it. Wasting your time and that other man's time about a comma. You see a man who takes his writing seriously. I see a damn fool."

Some time later, when I told this anecdote to Arthur Kober, who had known George Kaufman for years before I met him, Arthur laughed.

"Boy, you walked into that one," he said. "Didn't you know that for years Abbott and Kaufman were bitter rivals?"

I didn't know it but, in finding out as I did, I was able to sort out my feelings for this unique man, an amalgam of Broadway hip and Yankee shrewdness. As I write he is in his ninety-eighth year, and he still remains a refreshing mixture of Nathan Detroit and David Harum.

An illustration of what I mean occurred the day after *Fiorello!* opened in New Haven. The reviews were excellent. The public response was gratifying. The morning after the opening there was a line at the box office that kept getting longer all day. Everybody in the company was elated. Everybody, that is, except Abbott. At the morning meeting in the lobby of the Shubert Theatre, during which he gave the cast notes on the previous night's performance, even I, who was in a state of euphoria, was aware of the undercurrent of worry in his voice. At a later conference with the producers and the authors I was able to isolate the one point that was upsetting him most. It was a song called "Marie's Law."

Abbott had directed it to be sung after hours in Fiorello's Greenwich Village law office by his secretary Marie, who loves him but about whose existence—except as a devoted slavey— Fiorello remains almost totally unaware. Abbott felt the song had fallen flat on opening night. Stephen Sondheim, a close friend of Hal Prince who had come to New Haven for the opening, agreed. Steve suggested that the song would be more effective if it was sung later in the show, after Fiorello is elected to Congress, during a visit Marie pays to her boss in his Washington office. Almost everybody, including Jerry Bock and Sheldon Harnick, who had of course written the song, agreed with Steve. Responding to these strong urgings, Abbott redirected the song so that it was sung in the Washington office. It went into the show that night for the second performance. There seemed no doubt about the wisdom of the shift. This time "Marie's Law" stopped the show.

After the performance the staff was summoned to a meeting in the office of the manager of the Shubert Theatre. On my way to the meeting I stopped in the lobby to tell Peggy and Jeff and John I'd be tied up for a while and would meet them later at the hotel. As I turned to leave them Abbott came striding along, on his way to the manager's office. He stopped short and spoke to Peggy.

"May I talk to the boys for a moment?" he said.

They had been introduced to him the night before, in the lobby, as we were going in to the opening. So, of course, had scores of other people. I could tell Peggy was surprised, even a bit uneasy, as she turned to Jeff and John.

"You remember Mr. Abbott?" she said. Jeff and John nodded. "He wants to talk to you."

Abbott leaned down.

"You saw the show last night?" he said.

Two solemn nods.

"You remember the song 'Marie's Law'?" Abbott said.

Silence. Two absolutely expressionless faces stared up at him.

"It goes like this," Abbott said, and very softly he sang the first verse. "You remember that?"

Jeff and John nodded.

"Tonight it was sung in another place," Abbott said.

"Washington," Jeff said.

"That's right," Abbott said. "Tonight it was sung in Washington. Now, boys, tell me, where did you like the song best? Where it was sung yesterday? Or where it was sung tonight?"

Jeff and John looked at each other. They put their heads together and whispered. When they straightened up they looked tense. Jeff gave John a small shove. The shove released a single word.

"Tonight," John said.

Abbott straightened up.

"You liked it better tonight?" he said.

Both boys nodded. Formally, one at a time, Abbott shook their hands.

"Thank you," he said as he straightened up. "You have been a big help." With a courtly bow he added, "Thank you, Peggy."

Ten days later, when we opened in Philadelphia, "Marie's Law," sung in Fiorello's Washington office, was singled out for special mention in all the reviews, which were even better than the New Haven reviews. The next morning the line at the Erlanger Theatre box office stretched down the block and around the corner. The line grew longer with each day of the run. We were all interviewed by the local papers, and asked to lunch by local civic organizations, and assured by enthusiastic visitors from New York that we were about to bring to Broadway the hit of the season. With no previous experience to measure against, it did not occur to me to question what amounted to a ten-day avalanche of praise. Business at the box office confirmed it. I moved around in a pleasant glow, not really aware of how I spent my time. I knew I went to the theatre, lunched with Abbott and Jerry and Sheldon or all of them, returned to the theatre, went back to the hotel for dinner with Abbott or Jerry and Sheldon or all of them, then returned to the theatre and stood at the back and basked in the glow that seemed to rise like a vapor from the audience.

On Wednesday of our second week in Philadelphia, three days before the end of the run, with only three more evening performances and one matinee to go before we broke camp and headed for Broadway, I was standing at the back of the theatre, watching the curtain calls, listening to the applause, hearing something I had read about all my life but had never heard: members of an audience on their feet yelling "Bravo!" I felt a tap on my shoulder. I turned.

"You free?" George Abbott said.

"Sure," I said.

"Let's take a walk," he said.

We left the theatre ahead of the crowd and walked down

toward the lights of Market Street. For a while Abbott was silent. Then, as we turned into Walnut, which at that hour was deserted, he spoke quietly.

"You know we're in trouble, don't you?" he said.

I fished around quickly in my mind for one of the many traditional leg-pulling retorts, and came up with a serviceable one. Before I uttered it, however, I realized the man beside me was not a leg-pulling type. I took a quick glance at his face. I had never seen him look more serious.

"No, I'm afraid I don't," I said.

"None of the others do, either," Abbott said.

I didn't know what he meant by the others. In a swift montage the face of every member of the company ran through my head. I saw nothing but happy smiles. Mentally I replayed a bit of the sound track from the audience yelling "Bravo!" The sinking feeling in my stomach did not stop sinking. My eyes were still on Abbott's face.

"In trouble in what way?" I said.

"We don't have a showstopper in the second act," Abbott said.

I didn't want to say I don't know what you're talking about, even though I didn't. In my mind the show, which had a few rough spots in New Haven, and perhaps a touch of awkwardness that showed up in Philadelphia, had been polished to the point where for me it had been for more than a week what it obviously was for the audience and seemed to become more so with each passing performance: a smoothly flowing stream of delight.

"You don't know what I'm talking about," Abbott said.

I brought my mind up from the sinking feeling in my stomach and faced the semidarkness of the street along which we were walking.

"I thought everything is going so well," I said.

"It's going too well," Abbott said.

"I don't know what that means," I said.

"We're listening to the applause," Abbott said.

"Is that a wrong thing to do?" I said.

"Applause doesn't always travel," Abbott said. "All that

handclapping we're hearing here in Philadelphia won't be heard by the critics in New York. They'll be seeing what we should be seeing now, while the seeing can still do us some good."

"What's that?" I said.

"There's no emotional release in the second act," Abbott said. "There's no explosion."

Staring at him, I was aware I was making an effort not to add stupidity to my look of confusion.

"In a comedy the audience gets its emotional release at intervals all during the play, laughing at the jokes," Abbott said. "In a tragedy they don't get a chance to release any emotion until the final curtain. That's why when the curtain comes down they explode in wild applause with tears streaming down their faces. In a musical you must give them both. In our show they're laughing all the way through to the end which, judging by the applause, they seem to like."

"What's wrong with that?" I said.

"They don't know they've been cheated," Abbott said. "They don't realize they should have been given something in the middle of the second act to break the mood they've sustained from the beginning, something that would give them a chance to explode, which would provide us with a chance to start building to an even bigger climax, so that when we get to the final curtain we'll really earn those bravos we're now getting at the end almost automatically. Do I make myself clear?"

"No," I said.

"All right, then, let me try another way," Abbott said. "Once when we were having lunch you told me how you work with Herb Mayes at *Good Housekeeping* on short stories," Abbott said. "Assume for the moment that I'm Herb Mayes. You've just outlined to me a story about a man named Fiorello. As Herb Mayes I'm not sure the story would suit my magazine, but I'm not sure it won't, so I say to you please tell me the story as though it's a legend, a fairy tale. Can you do that?"

"I'll try," I said.

I forgot Walnut Street and put myself into the dining room attached to the *Good Housekeeping* testing kitchen. I summoned up the smell of the glop the motherly waitress in the gingham

416

apron had set before me and the delicious odor of the minute steak she had set before Herb.

"Well," I said, "in this story what we'd be doing is telling a version of the legend about Jack the Giant Killer. His neighbors, the poor people, the farmers, the peasants, who've all been oppressed and living in terror of the giant, they decide to forget their differences and squabbles, and they band together to save themselves from this son of a bitch who's been terrifying them, and by God they succeed. By working together they manage to destroy the giant. Then, as soon as they accomplish what they set out to do, as soon as they're successful, success goes to their heads. Again they start wrangling among themselves, fighting for credit, who did this and who did that, and they have a falling out, which is all the giant's successor is waiting for, so—"

Abbott's forefinger came up and stabbed at the night sky over Walnut Street.

"So we must bring those politicians together again!" he said in the loud, clear tones that I had come to recognize were as close as he ever allowed himself to come to a display of excitement. "The politicians are our peasants," he said. "They joined together to help Fiorello slay the giant called Tammany. Success went to their heads and they and Fiorello had their falling out. Without noticing it we let them disappear from the play. That's what's been bothering me. So now—"

"So now we have to bring the politicians back into the play," I said.

Abbott gave me a slanting look.

"If I bruise Ron Hussman's nose often enough I may end up turning him into a director," he said. "If I can teach you to stop listening to out-of-town bravos I may end up turning you into a playwright. Let's get back to the hotel."

We went to his suite. It was almost two o'clock in the morning. He gave me a yellow foolscap pad and a pencil, pushed me into a chair, and started pacing.

"Here's what we need," he said. "Just one scene. Not too long. Three or four pages, maybe less, but here's what the scene must have in it."

He listed seven plot points, ticking them off one by one on

those long fingers. The points were very small. Threads, he called them.

"If we get all those threads into that one small scene, we'll have a rope strong enough to hang a showstopper on," Abbott said. "Any questions?"

"When do you want this?" I said.

He looked at his wristwatch. I looked at mine. It was ten minutes after three in the morning.

"Bring it up at seven," he said. "Now clear out of here. I need some sleep."

At six o'clock I typed clean copies of the new scene, shaved, and took a shower. At seven sharp I pressed Abbott's door buzzer. He opened the door as though he had been waiting inside with his hand on the knob. He took the scene and pointed to a room-service table.

"Have some coffee," he said.

He dropped into a chair. I poured a cup of coffee. He read the scene, flipped back to the first page, and read it again. When he looked up he poured a cup of coffee for himself.

"Let's get the musickers up here," he said.

It was his word for the composer and lyricist. I had typed copies for Jerry Bock and Sheldon Harnick. Abbott and I sipped coffee while they read. The way I felt reminded me of the day following my graduation from De Witt Clinton High School when I had answered Mr. Geschwind's *New York Times* want ad and, after he dictated a letter and I typed it, I had to wait while he read it before I would know if I had a job. I tried to keep calm by counting my heartbeats. Sheldon looked up first.

"What's this about a little tin box?" he said.

Sheldon was born in Chicago. It occurred to me for the first time there were areas about the life of Fiorello La Guardia that Sheldon had not lived through in person.

"I wrote that in the middle of the night from memory," I said. I glanced at my watch. "Later, when the public library opens, I'll go over and see if I can find some stuff on the Seabury investigation that might help."

"What's the Seabury investigation?" Jerry Bock said.

I started to explain the commission that FDR, then gover-

418

nor of New York, had set up to investigate corruption in the Jimmy Walker administration.

"No, no," Sheldon said. "Not all that. Just this part about a little tin box. What's that?"

I explained about the series of corrupt policemen who had been asked by Judge Samuel Seabury to explain under oath the source of the money that had found its way into their subpoenaed bank accounts.

"The newspapers had a field day with the answers," I said. "One cop, for instance, whose salary was somewhere around fifty or sixty dollars a week, had a two-hundred-thousand-dollar brokerage account with Bache and Company. When Judge Seabury asked where he got the money he said he didn't know. Every week, he said, when he received his salary, he turned it over to his wife. She gave him some spending money, then took care of the rent and the other bills, and if there was anything left over, she put it in this little tin box she kept on the shelf over the stove in the kitchen."

Sheldon Harnick stood up and tapped Jerry Bock's shoulder.

"Let's go," he said.

Jerry Bock followed him out of the room.

"Why don't you get some sleep?" George Abbott said.

I went down to my room. The telephone woke me. As I reached for it I glanced at my watch. Nine-thirty.

"Can you come down to my room?" Jerry Bock said.

When I came in he was at the piano. Sheldon was standing beside him with a sheet of yellow foolscap.

"Listen to this," he said.

Jerry played and Sheldon sang a new song called "Little Tin Box." When they finished they turned and looked at me expectantly.

"I'm not talking till you tell me something," I said.

"What?" Jerry Bock said.

"You walked out of Abbott's suite at a quarter to eight," I said. "It is now—" I looked at my watch—"twenty minutes to ten. You wrote that song in one hour and fifty-five minutes?"

"Only the lyric," Sheldon said.

419

"What about the music?" I said.

"Listen," Jerry Bock said.

He started to play the tune again but, this time, instead of the words of "Little Tin Box," Sheldon sang an entirely different set of lyrics. My research, I remembered, had turned up the fact that, after voting for the draft in 1917, Fiorello had resigned his seat in Congress and enlisted in the U.S. Army Air Force, which was then being organized, and he served overseas until the end of the war. In our early conferences Jerry Bock, Sheldon Harnick, and I agreed it would make a dramatic episode in the story. It did, especially after they came up with a rollicking song called "Take a Flier!" Everybody connected with the show, including the producers, was crazy about the song until George Abbott appeared on the scene as director. He felt it was a good song but the air force material slowed down the movement of the story. He cut the scene and the song. I forgot all about it, but not Jerry and Sheldon. They put the song aside and waited.

"For what?" I asked.

"We didn't know," Jerry Bock said. "We just felt the melody was so good that its time was bound to come."

The morning after my midnight walk with George Abbott, it did. The three of us went over to the theatre and, during a break in rehearsal, Jerry and Sheldon played the song. Abbott was delighted with it. So was the cast. Abbott started rehearsing the song at once. That night it went into the show. During the second act, when the music started, I could feel the small hairs on the side of my jaw begin to prickle. When the words "Little Tin Box" rose on the melody the audience roared with the delighted shock of recognition. They began to sway with the rhythm. When the song ended I understood for the first time in my life what people mean when they say something brought down the house. I was standing beside George Abbott at the back of the theatre. He leaned toward me and said, "That was a productive walk we took last night."

It was better than that. The New York critics were as enthusiastic as the first-night audience. A week after the reviews my agent Harold Freedman reported that "*Fiorello!* is now the hottest ticket in town." Five months later, when we were nominated for ten Tony Awards, none of us was surprised. Starting with that first phone call from Hal Prince, the whole experience had been for me what Major John Hackett at Bletchley used to call a piece of cake. It seemed only appropriate that we should pick up the icing as well.

The Tony Awards dinner was a black-tie affair at the Hotel Astor. The distribution of awards in multiple categories to a not inconsiderable number of enterprises, whether on stage or screen, is a complex business. It requires the advance planning of an assault on the beaches of a fortified enemy. No matter how careful the plan, however, once set in motion an inner motor begins to take over. Strange reactions erupt. It is not unexpected for a winner to be overcome, even more understandable for a loser to be furious. Sometimes these get out of hand, more often not. Actors are trained to conceal as well as project. Not all participants in a Tony Award dinner, however, are actors. Keeping an eye on the participant I understood best—me—I was able to chart my emotions from a pleasant feeling of anticipation at the beginning of the evening to an almost uncontrollable euphoria toward the end. The anticipation had not been bold enough to guess at the reality: in the musical category *Fiorello!* won everything in sight. Best play, best production, best direction, best score, best lyrics, best book, best—it seemed to me—run of luck since Christopher Columbus did not reach the place for which he set out.

A week later we were advised that *Fiorello!* had been chosen by the New York Drama Critics' Circle as the best musical of the year. The presentation ceremony was not public. It was held in the Lexington Avenue apartment of John McLain, drama critic for the New York *Journal-American.* The only people present were all the New York critics and all the authors of the winning plays. George Abbott, Jerry Bock, Sheldon Harnick, and I went in a group.

Ten days later, on May 2, 1960, at two-thirty in the afternoon, the secretary to Dr. Grayson Kirk, president of Columbia University, came out of his office on Morningside Heights and distributed to the waiting press the list of 1960 Pulitzer Prizes. The award for drama went to *Fiorello!*

My mother's call reached me first.

"Mr. Mawg-ham was right," she said. "That a college like Columbia University, when they decided to give you a prize like this, they should go and pick a day to do it that it's the twelfth anniversary of the founding of the State of Israel, if you listened to me and became a lawyer a wonderful thing like this it never could have happened!"

The second voice I heard came not over the phone but from the opening page of *David Copperfield*: "Whether I shall turn out to be the hero of my own life, or whether that station will be held by anybody else, these pages must show."

Jullyiss Widdermeunzer feels they do. Me, I'm not so sure. I can suddenly hear more than the words of David Copperfield. I can hear the anxiety in the voice of his creator. Working his way through an exercise not unlike the one I have just completed, Dickens must have grasped what I can now see clearly: there are no pages that can say it with finality. No matter how skillful the presentation of the case, there can never be a final verdict. In the end the jury is always still out. Like Dickens and David, Jullyiss and I will just have to wait and see. Fortunately, it's something we're both good at. We've been doing it all our lives.